PAINTING IN TEXAS

The Nineteenth Century

c-1. Theodore Gentilz: *Shooting of the Seventeen Decimated Texians* or *Drawing of the Black Beans*
Oil, 1885, 13⅝″ x 17½″ (Courtesy of Mr. Larry Sheerin, San Antonio, Texas)

PAINTING IN TEXAS

THE NINETEENTH CENTURY

By Pauline A. Pinckney

Introduction by Jerry Bywaters

PUBLISHED FOR THE AMON CARTER MUSEUM OF WESTERN ART, FORT WORTH, BY THE UNIVERSITY OF TEXAS PRESS, AUSTIN AND LONDON

Library of Congress Catalog Card No. 67–28794
Copyright © 1967 by Pauline A. Pinckney
All Rights Reserved

Type set by Service Typographers, Inc., Indianapolis
Printed by the Steck Company, Austin
Bound by Universal Bookbindery, Inc., San Antonio

To my beloved family

PREFACE

THE WESTWARD MOVEMENT of the frontier in America was accompanied by tragedy, excitement, and humor. Artists pictured the Texas frontier with unadorned reality, while generations struggled for freedom and progress. The newcomers did not lack interest in what was about them—their discomforts and their extreme hardships did not seem to blunt their appreciation of their surroundings nor hinder their effort to succeed. In a society where political life was rough, financial depressions frequent, communications slow, hazardous ague with its devastating effect always threatening, and trouble with the Indian ever-present, men and women developed great determination and self-reliance. In one sense, then, they could not be called poor, but particularly rich.

No chronicler or traveler of the early nineteenth century failed to dwell on the beauty and plenty of the land —the abundance of game, the luxurious grasses and wild flowers—and at the same time the loneliness and fascination of its broad plains. Although great adjustment had to be made both physically and psychologically by the forest-adjusted peoples of the Eastern coast, yet the untamed and the unspoiled appealed to the newcomer— the emigrant artist. Nor did he overlook the crop of potential sitters among the politicians, cattlemen, and dashing Mexican leaders. Limners came as early as the 1820's with canvas and paints, going from place to place seeking subjects. Often in the early part of the century their portraits served a useful purpose in the family with no larger audience than its own members or the neighbors.

The artists put on canvas the strange scenes around them: the Indian, wild beasts, hills, and prairies. These artists belong to a class we may refer to as average American citizens who contributed to some degree in conquering the wilderness, in winning the Texas Revolution, and in establishing the infant republic.

Sometimes the lack of technical proficiency of an artist limited his ability to express himself, sometimes the lack of proper tools; yet these artists (often unschooled) arrived eventually with something of intrinsic and lasting value. Artists who came to Texas very often had developed, before coming, a simple style or manner of working, of painting in an individual fashion, and we find therefore a great variety in their paintings. Whenever similarity is found it is from the influence of environment rather than any common study or the following of idioms in painting. The wonder is that these men progressed in their art with only an occasional glimpse of what was going on elsewhere—we wonder how they learned, with so little means of communication with other parts of the United States, of the progress in luminosity or the discovery of new pigments.

It was the eagerness of the artist to record the strange and exciting scenes and events that kept his work from becoming monotonous. Many of the portrait painters (untrained professionals) did not have the finish of a Sully or an Allston or even of artists of lesser skills; nevertheless, many presented work with a perception of character. They came from England, from Germany, from the Southern states, and from the Northeast—often stopping in New Orleans, as if to get reassurance before entering a pioneer country. The newcomers were eager for the excitement of the frontier—for greener fields in which to practice their art. With a modest degree of skill, they made portraits of political figures and professional men and their wives; they sought new fields in which their commissions might bring a modest living. Had they not heard of the genuine individualist Sam Houston and his weakness for having his portrait painted! Houston attracted young men. He was an actor and had a number of equally talented supports, but in his audience were many rascals and second-rate men—a state of affairs which comes with every new territory. Perhaps the artists were told of opportunities in Texas by such cultivated men as Stephen F. Austin, Ashbel Smith, Mirabeau B. Lamar, and Samuel May Williams, among a score of others. Perhaps they came for less plausible reasons—Texas was perhaps on the path of the Yankee itinerant limner; perhaps some answered the call for volunteers to defend the land and then remained to paint.

It is a strange phenomenon that the early part of the century brought a number of well-equipped artists from Europe to this country seeking a land of peace in which to practice their art, while in the latter half of the century the American thought that to prepare himself as an artist he must make every effort to reach Europe, leaving the peace of his country for the turbulent countries across the ocean. The idea of foreign study grew even more important in the minds of American teachers as they experienced European study. In the latter days of the 1870's and 1880's, therefore, many Americans sought training in Dusseldorf, Dresden, Paris, and London. In some cases, these artists became so imbued with the European life and practices that they cannot be identified to any great extent with Texas and its people. These are treated only briefly.

In this study less importance has been placed on evaluation of their work than on facts about the artists and what they accomplished and the circumstances under which they worked. Because of the great diversity of their paintings, a general chronological order is followed rather than any semblance of style.

Of these men and women in Texas, little has been known. In fact, few have been mentioned in exhibitions or in writings on American painting. It is the aim of this study, through biographical notes and illustrations, to acquaint the reader with some of these artists whose work has merit. We not only gain knowledge of the artists, but also to some extent recognize the overemphasis on other less-important personages and events— thus bringing into better balance facets of our social history. Even more important is the fact that in rediscovering our own roots we will come to a better understanding and, therefore, a better grasp for shaping our future.

This book is an endeavor to tell the story of the noteworthy frontier artists, many of whom came even before Texas was a republic, when colonization was in progress. They came across its borders to take up the business of painting. Their portrait, genre, and historical paintings and prints have kept visible the men and events associated with early Texas and the Southwest. They expressed themselves in many different media and, like artists everywhere at the time, were realists.

These artists have provided us with an important part of the content of our knowledge of our state through their accurate observations and their graphic recordings. To this group belong the soldier-artist, the explorer-artist, the surveyor-artist, and the plain citizen-artist, and it is this group of recorders of events and people from approximately the 1820's to the 1880's who have so richly deserved our attention. While there appears to be great inequality in the accounts of the artists, it should be stated that some were elusive characters about whom little has been recorded. It is hoped that readers will find in this record some clues that will help in identifying other artists and in discovering additional facts concerning them.

It was through the help of the Amon Carter Museum of Western Art, and particularly the kind assistance of Mr. Mitchell A. Wilder, that this publication was made possible.

To a large degree, information on the artists has necessarily been obtained from their descendants and has been substantiated by documentary material. To these who have helped me in this task grateful acknowledgment is extended. Many individuals in small towns— from Dickinson, to Abernathy, to Jefferson—have shown a nostalgic desire to make known these artists before their work is entirely forgotten. It was through the appreciation of our state history that I found, with the help of the custodians in the various University of Texas libraries, the information needed for the background material; I thank the personnel of the Barker Texas History Center, the University Archives, and the University Newspaper Collection. Other libraries and art museums which came to my aid were the Newberry Library, Chicago; Frick Reference Library, New York City; Yale University History Division; the John Carter Brown Library, Brown University; and the San Jacinto Museum, San Jacinto Monument, Texas. It would be a decided omission if I did not mention especially those who took time to confer with me on different phases of my work: Mr. Bertrand Baker, of the Texana Library at The University of Texas; Mr. Wilson Duprey, of the Print Department of the New York Public Library; Mr. A. Hyatt Nayor, curator of prints, Metropolitan Museum of Art; Mr. Paul Rossi, of the Thomas Gilcrease Institute of American History and Art, Tulsa; Miss Josephine Cobb, of the National Archives; Mr. John Ewers, of the Smithsonian Institution; Mr. William Campbell, of the National Gallery; Dr. Forrest Muir, of Rice University; Mr. James Day, of the Texas State Archives; and Mrs. Virginia Taylor, of the General Land Office, Austin. Others who have given so freely of their time and advice are Mr. R. Henderson Shuffler, of the Texana Library; Mr. Kim Taylor, of The University of Texas Art Department; Dr. Schultz-Behren, Miss Kathleen Blow, and Dr. Nettie Lee Benson, of The University of Texas; Mrs. Mary L. Ulmer, Houston City Library; Miss Mildred Stephenson, of the Rosenberg Library, Galveston; Miss Martha Utterback, of the Witte Museum, San Antonio; Miss Carmen Perry and Miss Catherine McDowell, of the Daughters of the Republic of Texas Library, San Antonio; Mrs. Lena Kolb, of Austin College, Sherman, Texas; Mrs. Carl Swanson, of the Austin City Library; Mr. John Mumford, of the Dallas Museum of Art; Mr. J. P. Bryan, of Lake Jackson, Texas; Mrs. Katherine Stout, of Fort Wayne, Indiana; Mrs. Vivian Moore, of Harrodsburg, Kentucky; Mr. Oscar Haas, of New Braunfels; Mrs. Malcolm McLean, of the Amon Carter Museum of Western Art, Fort Worth, Texas; Mrs. F. T. Baldwin, of Houston, Texas; Mr. Richard Norton, of the R. W. Norton Museum, Shreveport, Louisiana; Miss Marcella L. Hamer, of the El Paso Public Library; Mr. Carl Hertzog, Dr. W. H. Timmons, and Dr. Rex Strickland, from the Texas Western College of El Paso; Mr. George Bland, Jr., of Weston, West Virginia; Mrs. Frank Adams, of Springfield, Missouri; and Mr. Austin D. Kilham, Charlottesville, Virginia.

P. A. P.

Austin, Texas

CONTENTS

Preface vii
Introduction by Jerry Bywaters xvii

1. *Provincial Texas* 3
    An Unknown Artist of the Austin Colony, *p. 4*
    Lino Sánchez y Tapia, Jean Louis Berlandier,
        and José María Sánchez y Tapia, *p. 6*
    James Strange, *p. 9*
    Ambrose Louis Garneray, *p. 10*

2. *Gentlemen of the Brush* 14
    Thomas Jefferson Wright, *p. 15*
    George R. Allen, *p. 23*
    Ambrose Andrews, *p. 27*

3. *Image of the West* 30
    William M. G. Samuel, *p. 30*
    George Catlin, *p. 31*
    William Tylee Ranney, *p. 39*
    John James Audubon, *p. 43*
    Seth Eastman, *p. 49*

4. *Artists on the Go and the Panorama Decades* . 56
    J. E. Churchill, *p. 56*
    Thomas Flintoff, *p. 57*
    James G. Benton and Charles L. Smith, *p. 68*
    Peter A. Moelling, *p. 73*

5. *European Influx: A Medley of Styles* . . . 74
    Richard Petri, *p. 74*
    Hermann Lungkwitz, *p. 86*
    Eugenie Aubanel Lavender, *p. 97*
    Theodore Gentilz, *p. 99*
    Louisa Heuser Wueste, *p. 118*
    Carl G. von Iwonski, *p. 122*

6. *Politics and Portraits—beyond Our Borders* . . 138
    Martin Johnson Heade, *p. 139*
    Augustus Behné, *p. 141*
    L. M. D. Guillaume, *p. 145*

7. *Artist-Reporters on Excursions into Texas* . . 147

PRINTS OF TEXAS SCENES
    William Sandusky, *p. 148*
    Erhard Pentenrieder, *p. 151*
    Daniel P. Whiting, *p. 151*
    Helmuth Holtz, *p. 152*
    Eigenthum d. Verleger, Gezeicht von C. O. Bahr,
        William C. A. Theillepape, and Louis Hoppe, *p. 153*
    Agustus Koch, H. Brossius, and T. M. Fowler, *p. 154*

THE BARTLETT SURVEY
    John Russell Bartlett, *p. 155*
    Henry Cleves Pratt, *p. 155*
    Agustus Hoppin, *p. 158*

THE EMORY SURVEY
    Arthur Schott, *p. 163*
    A. de Vaudricourt, *p. 163*
    John E. Weyss, *p. 163*
    Paulus Roetter, *p. 164*
    John H. Richards and William H. Dougal, *p. 165*

THE GRAY SURVEY
    Carl Schuchard, *p. 167*

8. *Native Artists and Late-Comers* 168
    Stephen Seymour Thomas, *p. 168*
    Ella Moss Duval, *p. 172*
    Edward Louis Grenet, *p. 174*
    Ida Weisselberg Hadra, *p. 177*
    Thomas Allen, *p. 179*

9. *With New Vision—the State as a Patron
    of the Arts* 186
    Louis Eyth, *p. 188*
    Henry McArdle, *p. 190*
    William H. Huddle, *p. 196*
    Robert Jenkins Onderdonk, *p. 203*

Appendix. *Little-Known Artists* 211
Sources Consulted 215
Index 225

ILLUSTRATIONS

Color Plates   *Facing Page*

Theodore Gentilz
   c-1. *Shooting of the Seventeen Decimated*
        Texians or *Drawing of the Black Beans* .   iii
   c-8. *Surveying in Texas before Annexation*
        to U.S.   100

Lino Sánchez y Tapia apres José María Sánchez y
   Tapia
   c-2. *Yguanés*   12

William M. G. Samuel
   c-3. *West Side Main Plaza*   28

George Catlin
   c-4. *A Commanche War Party on the March Fully*
        Equipped for War, Texas   36

James G. Benton and Charles L. Smith
   c-5. *"Independence Hall," Washington-on-*
        the-Brazos Panorama   68

Richard Petri
   c-6. *Going Visiting* ["Austin, Texas" and
        "1849" were added by an unknown
        person]   84

Hermann Lungkwitz
   c-7. *Hill Country*   92

Henry McArdle
   c-9. *Battle of San Jacinto*   188

William H. Huddle
   c-10. *Still Life with Fruit*   196
   c-11. *The Surrender of Santa Anna* . . .   204

Julius Stockfleth
   c-12. *The Home Stretch of the* Volunteer *on the*
        27th of September 1887   212

Black-and-White Plates   *Page*

Unknown Artist of the Austin Colony
   1. *Stephen F. Austin*   5

Lino Sánchez y Tapia apres José María Sánchez y
   Tapia
   2. *Cheraquís*   8

Louis Garneray
   3. 1ère *Vue d' Aigleville Colonie du Texas*
        ou Champ d'Asile   12

Thomas Jefferson Wright
   4. *J. Lyle Smith*   16
   5. *Juan N. Seguin*   19
   6. *Self-Portrait*   20
   7. *Lydia Ann Mason*   22

George R. Allen
   8. *Henderson Yoakum*   24
   9. *Temple Lea*   25
   10. *Mrs. Nancy Lea*   26

William M. G. Samuel
   11. *East Side Plaza at San Antonio*   31

George Catlin
   12. *Stephen F. Austin*   33
   13. *Joseph Chadwick*   37
   14. *Elks and Buffalo Making Acquaintance*
        on the Texas Prairie on the Brazos . .   38

William Tylee Ranney
   15. *Preliminary Sketch for* Hunting Wild
        Horses   40
   16. *Hunting Wild Horses*   41
   17. *The Lasso*   42

John James Audubon
   18. *Least Tern*   45
   19. *Spotted Sandpiper, Buffalo Bayou, Texas* .   46

Seth Eastman
   20. *Plaza at San Antonio, Texas*   51
   21. *Live Oaks Two Miles from Fredericks-*
        burg, Texas—Encampment of
        Caddo Indians   52

Thomas Flintoff
   22. *Pryor M. Bryan*   58
   23. *Mary Angelica Bryan*   59
   24. *Thomas Jefferson Chambers*   60
   25. *Abbie Chambers*   61
   26. *Guy Morrison Bryan*   62
   27. *Stephen F. Austin*   64

28. *George W. Smyth* 66
29. *The Jones Children* 67

Richard Petri
    30. *Music Festival Poster* 76
    31. *Elise Lungkwitz* 78
    32. *Self-Portrait* 79
    33. *Profile of Man with Glasses* 80
    34. *Lipan Indian* 81
    35. *Indian Maid* 82
    36. *The Pioneer Cowpen* ["Austin, Texas" and "1849" were added by an unknown person] 84
    37. *Fort Martin Scott* [unfinished] . . . 85

Hermann Lungkwitz
    38. *San Antonio de Béxar* 87
    39. *View of Fredericksburg, Texas* . . . 90
    40. *The Alameda, San Antonio* 92
    41. *Old Mill Bridge* 93
    42. *Military Institute, Austin* 94
    43. *Deer in the Pedernales* 95

Eugenie Aubanel Lavender
    44. *Father Frank* 96

Theodore Gentilz
    45. *The Oxcart* 100
    46. *The Fandango* 101
    47. *The Funeral of an Angel* 102
    48. *The Camel Ride* 104
    49. *Mexican Oxcart and Jacal* 106
    50. *San José Mission* 107
    51. *San José Mission Window* 108
    52. *The Watermelon Race* 109
    53. *List of Paintings* 110
    54. *Barilleros, San Felipe* 111
    55. *Gathering Juice from the Maguey Plant for Pulque* 112
    56. *Selling of Cardinals on the Plaza* . . 113
    57. *Comanche Chief* 114
    58. *Fishing with Bow and Arrow* . . . 115
    59. *Comanches on the March* 116
    60. *Otter Belt, Quahadi* 117
    61. *Business Card* 117

Louisa Heuser Wueste
    62. *Adelina Wueste Staffel* 119
    63. *Sarah Riddle* 120
    64. *Emmy, Mary, Bertha* 121

Carl G. von Iwonski
    65. *Theatre at the Old Casino Club, San Antonio, Texas* 123
    66. *The Schenck Sisters* 124
    67. *Johanna Steves* 126

68. *Edward Steves* 127
69. *Still Life: Bottle, Gun, Powderhorn Pipe* . 128
70. *Marie Oekers* 130
71. *Lily Carolon* 131
72. *Sam Maverick and the Terry Rangers* . . 132
73. *Bivouac of Confederate Troops on the Las Moras, Texas* 133
74. *Lipan Indian* 134
75. *Lipan Indian* 135

Martin Johnson Heade
    76. *Sam Houston* 140

Augustus Behné
    77. *Sam Houston* 143

L. M. D. Guillaume
    78. *The Battle of San Jacinto* 144

Unknown Artist
    79. *San Antonio* 148

William Sandusky
    80. *View of Austin* 149

Erhard Pentenrieder
    81. *Main Plaza, San Antonio, Texas* . . . 150

Daniel P. Whiting
    82. *Birds-eye View of the Camp of the Army of Occupation* 152

Eigenthum d. Verleger
    83. *View of Galveston* 153

Louis Hoppe
    84. *Julius Meyenberg's Farm* 154

Henry Cleves Pratt
    85. *Portrait of John R. Bartlett* 156
    86. *View of Smith's West Texas Ranch* . . . 157
    87. *Church at El Paso del Norte* 158

Agustus Hoppin
    88. *Prairie-Dog Town* 160

Arthur Schott
    89. *Military Plaza—San Antonio, Texas* . . 161

A. de Vaudricourt
    90. *Río San Pedro—above Second Crossing* . 162
    91. *The Plaza and Church of El Paso* . . . 164

John E. Weyss
    92. *Brownsville, Texas* 165

Paulus Roetter
    93. *Cactus* 166

Stephen Seymour Thomas
    94. *Weighing the Puppy* 170
    95. *San José Mission* 171

Ella Moss Duval
    96. *Dr. Ferdinand Herff* 173

Edward Louis Grenet
    97. *The Mexican Candy Seller* 175
    98. *Lily Carolon* 176

Ida Weisselberg Hadra
    99. *Dr. Weisselberg* 178
    100. *View of the Military Academy*
        from East Austin 179
    101. *Tenth Street, Austin, Looking West* . . 180
    102. *Bridge over the San Antonio River* . . . 181

Thomas Allen
    103. *The Market Place, San Antonio* 182
    104. *Mexican Women Washing at*
        San Pedro Spring 183
    105. *The Portal of San José Mission* . . . 184

Louis Eyth
    106. *Stephen F. Austin* 187

107. *The Speech of Travis to His Men*
    at the Alamo 189
108. *Death of Bowie: A Command from*
    the Mexicans that He Be Killed . . . 189

Henry McArdle
    109. *Moses Austin Bryan* 191
    110. *Dawn at the Alamo* 192
    111. *Settlement of Austin's Colony* or
        The Log Cabin 194

William H. Huddle
    112. *The Slave* 197
    113. *Self-Portrait* 198
    114. *Sam Houston* 200

Robert Jenkins Onderdonk
    115. *The Twohig House* 205
    116. *View of the Old Ursuline Academy* . . 206
    117. *Mrs. Floyd McGown* 208

INTRODUCTION

DURING THE middle fifty years of the nineteenth century territory destined to be Texas was the location of an unusual number of events which influenced American history, politics, geography, and folklore.

The territory was like the hub of a giant gambling wheel, radiating its magnetic attraction into the Old South, into the states of Virginia, Tennessee, and Kentucky, deep into Mexico, and across the ocean to England, Germany, and France. With each turning year fortunes and lives were staked, and great areas of land changed hands through the gambling instincts of a few men who chanced their way into history.

In this center of activity, the southwestern push of American settlers and armies met the Plains Indians and the soldiers of Spain and Mexico. It was a time and place of challenges, nationalistic and ethnic, of stirring events taking place against a landscape which itself was an extreme of forests and treeless prairies, of mountains and deserts.

Such a mélange of historic and romantic affairs should have generated a great mass of graphic records in words and pictures. Countless regional and some national newspapers, journals, and books did chronicle most aspects of Texas history in fact, fiction, and folklore, but until now the known and published paintings, drawings, and prints providing this same service have been relatively few in number compared to the plethora of events. Even these examples have more often than not been poorly preserved, have been casually documented, and when reproduced have shown up only as faint replicas of usually strong originals.

This book contributes much toward mitigating many of these documentary shortcomings concerning the art and artists of the period to which this study limits itself. The personal diligence and "searching" instincts of the author have brought to attention obscure pictorial examples which have remained unknown or little noted over these many years. Many "new" and interesting art-

ists are brought to light and life, filling out the art roster to a very respectable number with a surprising range of accomplishments. Many of the works by these artists, and even the already better-known examples of our art history, are here given reproduction of such fidelity as to make it seem they are seen accurately for the first time.

In addition to providing a wealth of pictorial material in convenient form, this book at the same time illuminates some social and political history of the region, which until now had only verbal images.

If, because of little previous evidence, it has been thought that few artists and graphic reporters lived in Texas during the nineteenth century or that few traveling artists paused long enough to sketch and paint, we must gratefully adjust these notions because of the collected facts and illustrations in this volume.

Not only were many artists and near-artists painting in Texas, but they were also representative of the varying styles in art found elsewhere in the United States; their number included types corresponding to other artists of the time or of an earlier period in the East and Middle West—unknowns and primitives; explorer-soldier-surveyor-artists; limners; genre painters; painters of landscapes, portraits, and historical events; women painters; painters of Indians and, finally, of "cowboys."

Some Texas artists were "ordinary" citizens who also painted; others were European born, trained in Düsseldorf or Munich or Paris, who brought their cultivated talents to the wilds of German or French colonies near San Antonio and Austin; yet others were native or adopted Texans who sought, for short periods, technical skills in European studios so they could paint their home landscapes and political friends with greater fidelity and assurance.

As elsewhere, the earliest pictorial records of this area were practical efforts of cartography or settlement plan. A map of the coast was dated 1551 and a woodcut of a buffalo a few years later. Father Morfi drew his plan of

San Antonio in 1780. A likeness of Stephen F. Austin was made in oil on ivory in 1824 by an unknown artist and later paintings and engravings used this as a reliable source. But the earliest on-the-spot paintings made by a known eyewitness were the 38 small paintings by José María Sánchez y Tapia, Lino Sánchez y Tapia, and Dr. Jean Louis Berlandier, which tell much about the Indians, Mexicans, and Anglo colonists of the time.

Perhaps the first citizen-painter of consequence was Major James Strange, constable, farmer, and stock raiser in Austin's colony, who foresightedly painted General Santa Anna and Colonel Almonte. The earliest example of an "imaginary" rendering of a factual spot was the print of Champ d'Asile by Garneray. Such fanciful re-creations of historic fact have always had special interest and sometime even replace facts (witness such classic renderings as *Washington Crossing the Delaware* or *Custer's Last Stand*).

The limner, unsophisticated "taker of likenesses," was in Texas early also. Although working almost a century later than their counterparts in New England, and in competition with the popular daguerrotype, T. J. Wright, in portraits of Sam Houston and Juan Sequin, and George R. Allen, with stern renderings of Mrs. Nancy Lea (Houston's mother-in-law) and Temple Lea, compare favorably with Smibert, Feke, and Blackburn. In the art of miniature portraits, Ambrose Andrews was a well-trained academician who worked in Texas some five years and produced portraits, including those of Sam Houston and Governor Henry Smith.

In the years shortly before and after Texas won independence, years of surveying, soldiering, and settlements, a special kind of artist appeared in Texas, as in other areas of the expanding American frontier—and often it was the same artist. George Catlin, William Ranney, and Seth Eastman were all artist-explorers or artist-soldiers.

During the year 1834, when Catlin was in northwest Texas recording the life and customs of the Comanches, he wrote of his Indian friends and models, "Art may mourn when these peoples are swept from the earth, and the artists of future ages may look in vain for another race so picturesque in their costumes, their weapons, their colours, their manly games and their chase." Though pre-occupied with Indian portraits and studies, Catlin took time to do a "life" portrait of his scout friend Joe Chadwick, and an earlier study of Stephen F. Austin.

Ranney fought as a soldier at San Jacinto and thereby

received land on which he lived in the 1830's. But, no farmer, he spent the majority of his time in Texas recording the life of the pioneer settlers in much the same style as Mount, Bingham, and Wimar. Some of his most effective later works painted in his New Jersey studio, of wild horses and "incidents" on the prairie, were developed from studies made during his stay in Texas.

The number of Audubon's paintings of birds and animals directly attributable to notes made in Texas are few, but his diaries indicate he spent some productive times on Buffalo Bayou.

Seth Eastman was among the best known of the soldier-artists recording frontier and Indian life in the Southwest. His Texas sketches numbered some seventy drawings, and many paintings were derived from them. His on-the-spot drawings made in Texas in 1848 and 1849 are accurate and valuable records of time and place in the environs of Matagorda Bay, Seguin, San Antonio, and Fredericksburg, and in Comanche country along the Frio and Leona Rivers. In his capacity as soldier-topographer-artist and later illustrator for the Bureau of Indian Affairs, Eastman was one of the more important illustrators who worked for the government.

Between 1845 and 1857 there were many surveys for boundaries, railroads, and wagon roads. Such surveys usually included artists as well as soldiers, surveyors, and scientists. The first surveys after Texas annexation were concerned with the western boundary of the state. The Bartlett survey, published in 1854, its successor the Emory survey, and the A. B. Gray report remain among the most interesting sources for study of the visual recordings of history and geography of that time.

H. C. Pratt, Augustus Hoppin, Arthur Schott, A. de Vaudricourt, John Weyss, Paulus Roetter, and Carl Schuchard were among the well-trained artists who served on these surveys and produced the illustrative material to give the published reports such importance in recalling the look of forts, townships, life of the settlers and Indians, as well as the character of specific landscapes, rivers, and even plants, animals, birds, reptiles, and fishes.

These more authentic recordings were supplemented by "views," made by such "limners" of towns as Agustus Koch, H. Brossius, and T. M. Fowler. Many of these views were engraved in Europe and served as the first pictorial reports from Texas settlers to their European kinfolk.

Among the nonartists were some of the most refreshing and fanciful recorders of the time. Drawings by the San Antonio merchant Erhardt Pentenrieder delineated the various missions, Indians, and animals and reptiles. Mayor Theillepape of San Antonio in 1856 drew a letterhead overflowing with picturesque symbols of the region. The gay and naïve rendering of Julius Meyerberg's farm by Louis Hoppe harks back to the spirit of Edward Hicks. And who but Sheriff William M. G. Samuel could paint on the courthouse walls better views of San Antonio from the courthouse windows?

Perhaps the most valuable pictorial records, artistic as well as historical, were made by some remarkably talented German and French artist-settlers who came to Central Texas in the 1840's and 1850's.

Richard Petri and his brother-in-law Hermann Lungkwitz were among the Germans to settle New Braunfels and Fredericksburg. Petri's drawings and paintings of the daily life in these settlements are wonderfully perceptive examples of genre painting. He would often paint the "people" in Lungkwitz's landscapes of the small German communities, the countryside, or city views of San Antonio. Petri's death at age thirty-three by drowning in the Pedernales deprived Texas history and Texas art of much unrealized and invaluable material; yet he accomplished enough to prove his ability as a fine draughtsman.

Lungkwitz made the first solid contributions to landscape painting in Texas. The hill country was his most favored subject but he also produced many paintings of the missions and streets and plazas of San Antonio. Lungkwitz joined a fellow countryman artist, Carl G. von Iwonski, in establishing a photographic studio in San Antonio in the 1860's. This partnership was an important combined operation, enabling the two artists to record the early citizens in both photographic portraits and painted portraits.

Iwonski came with his parents to settle in New Braunfels. His view of this townsite, published as a print in 1855 in Leipzig, was one of the "views" which aroused European interest in Texas. His portraits of the Guenthers, the Steves, the Mavericks, and many other families were among the best figure paintings produced by any artist in Texas.

With the second group of colonizers sponsored by Count de Castro came the young French artist Theodore Gentilz. His many small paintings, filled with people, were to become the most important series of genre works in the compressed art history of early years in Texas. His

duties as surveyor for Castroville, Quihi, d'Hanis, and some areas of northern Mexico made him an expert observer of the daily life of Indians, Mexicans, and Anglos. He crammed his small-scale pictures with these pictorial observations which are among the most complete sources for historical specialists in early colonial and frontier life.

Several women artists applied their talents to the Texas landscape and people. German-born Louisa H. Wueste and French-born Eugenie Lavender were among the first of the formally trained, both coming to Texas from Europe in the 1850's and both living out their lives in the state. Ella Moss Duval was born in Louisiana, received careful art training in Germany, and had a studio in New York before coming to San Antonio where she painted many portraits, among them the fine likeness of Dr. Herff. A student of Mrs. Duval and Lungkwitz, Eda Weiselberg Hadra was born in Castroville and lived and painted in Austin and San Antonio.

Toward the end of the century the painters of the people and landscape of Texas were to be natives—Americans and even Texans—although some were European trained. Edward L. Grenet, the son of a Frenchman in San Antonio, was given opportunity to study art in New York and Paris before returning to Texas to work on portraits and genre subjects.

S. Seymour Thomas was a precocious youngster, born in San Augustine, who at fifteen painted missions and figures with remarkable skill. Much like that of Copley or Sargent, his work changed when he went to Europe for extended study, and his later style lost a convincing literalism inherent in his early Texas paintings. A large equestrian portrait of Sam Houston by Thomas is in the San Jacinto Museum. Thomas Allen was a Düsseldorf-trained artist from St. Louis who worked in San Antonio in 1878, leaving some picturesque versions of the "Mexican town."

The most important artists in Texas by the turn of the century were three painters whose artistic mission was almost the same: to give Texas history and its protagonists authentic visual form on a large scale. Between the three of them, all of the military struggles attending Texas independence would be re-created on canvas with accuracy and drama.

H. A. McArdle had been a map maker for Robert E. Lee and was the painter of *Lee at the Wilderness*. When he came to Texas in 1867 to settle at Independence and teach at Baylor Female College, McArdle's ambition was to do justice in paint to Texas military events; from James DeShields, Dallas historian and collector, he received encouragement and commissions, as did other Texas artists. *Dawn at the Alamo* and *Battle of San Jacinto*, both heroic in size, now hang in the Texas Senate, finally having been purchased for $25,000 in 1927.

William H. Huddle, who was born in Virginia and studied painting in Munich, was perhaps the most capable of all these painters both in historical compositions of many figures and in the execution of individual portraits. His paintings of Davy Crockett and the surrender of Santa Anna, both in the foyer of the State Capitol, are among the important historical paintings of America. His "Gallery of Governors" added much of interest to the new Capitol, which was dedicated in 1888. Portraits of Madam Candelaria, and Governor and Mrs. Roberts, as well as his self-portraits were further proof of Huddle's ability as a figure painter, ranking him with the best of his time in other states.

Robert Jenkins Onderdonk represented the coming of another and final period in this study of art in Texas. Onderdonk was an American-born and New York-trained artist who, after becoming a resident, was painter and influential teacher, head of a distinguished family of artists, and "professor" who aided the community growth of the arts, especially in San Antonio and Dallas. In addition to landscapes and portraits of political and professional celebrities, Onderdonk also created his versions of history (as did Huddle and McArdle), the most notable being the large painting, *Davy Crockett's Last Stand.*

With the introduction of the Onderdonk family and the end of the century, this chronicle of art in early Texas fulfills the ambition set for itself. The result is an excellent reference work on our art to help fill out a scanty section in the library of Texas history. The biographical sketches of the major artists are carefully researched and informative, attesting to the author's energy and tenacity toward a difficult task. Enough historical material is employed to place each artist in his environment and to demonstrate how the daily life of the pioneering painter was most certainly an integral part of his art—whether in such outpost villages as New Braunfels, Castroville, and Fredericksburg or in the "civilized" towns of San Antonio and Austin.

The artists working in Texas before 1890 lacked the acceptance and patronage of their Eastern counterparts, but the painters in Texas had the good fortune to be living with bold, courageous, and ingenious people in the process of taming a new and wild country. Such people and such landscapes made compelling subjects for a number of artists of diverse backgrounds and varying talents. Each of these artists has received careful and devoted attention in this valuable book by an author who demonstrates an unflagging respect for her estimable project.

JERRY BYWATERS

Southern Methodist University
Dallas, Texas

PAINTING IN TEXAS

The Nineteenth Century

But art means more than the resuscitation of the past: it means the free and unconfined search for new ways of expressing the experience of the present and the vision of the future. When the creative impulse cannot flourish freely, when it cannot freely select its methods and objects, when it is deprived of spontaneity, then society severs the root of art.

John Fitzgerald Kennedy, *Creative America,*
"The Arts in America," p. 6

. . . the history of art will become sterile unless it is constantly enriched by a close contact with the study of man.

E. H. Gombrich, *Art and Illustration,*
Preface, p. x

CHAPTER 1

PROVINCIAL TEXAS

ART OF TEXAS during the frontier period was varied, individual, and lively, and for these qualities, if no others, it may well claim our attention. In paintings, sketches, and prints the early settlers pictured in esthetic terms the countryside and its people. Glancing back briefly into the period before the American settlement, when the three-cornered explorations were going on for the benefit of the Mexican and European crowns, one sees that the leaders were obligated to make reports on the strange land, and this required an artist-cartographer. Therefore, we find a few pictorial representations of the primitive country made at a very early date. A woodcut, appropriately of a buffalo, was drawn for Francisco López de Gómara's *La Historia General de las Indias*, published at Antwerp in 1554. This illustration is in the account of the expedition of Francisco Vásquez de Coronado, whose explorations (c. 1540) were in search of the fabled Seven Cities of Cíbola.[1] Even before this time Álvar Núñez Cabeza de Vaca set out from Spain in 1527 on his ill-fated expedition. A planisphere was painted in 1551 by Sancho Gutiérrez commemorating this expedition to the coast

of Texas, in cartographic splendor, showing birds, animals, and Indians.[2] In 1780 Father Juan Agustín Morfi included in his manuscript "Memorias para la historia de Texas," a colored plan of San Antonio.[3] In each case these recordings added bits of pictorial material to our historical heritage.

When the colonists came in the early nineteenth century they found little to encourage them in any artistic endeavor. They found few traces of previous culture—only fragments of history in Indian mounds and pictographs, waiting to be interpreted. Only the missions built by the Spanish were to be found on the vast uninhabited areas, with a handful of Mexicans around them. Each mission—San Juan Capistrano with its three bells in the façade, San José with its heavily carved entrance, and Espíritu Santo de Zuñiga, known as La Bahía, with its

[1] Francisco López de Gómara, *La Historia General de las Indias*, p. 276.

[2] Thomas T. McGann, "The Ordeal of Cabeza de Vaca," *American Heritage*, XII (1960), 32–35.

[3] Father Juan Agustín Morfi, "Memorias para la historia de Texas" (MS in Library of Congress).

heavy ramparts and bastions—reflected in a different way the iconography of its founders.[4] Another fine example of Spanish architecture was the governor's palace, built in 1849, with its paneled red cedar doors four inches thick.

Painting was sometimes indulged in by the mission fathers, and brightly colored frescoes decorated the walls painted by the *Indios reducidos* in a mingling of Indian and Spanish, pagan and Christian, and even expressions of Aztec tradition. But hardly a trace of these paintings remained after a century of filibustering Americans, Indian uprisings, and the ravages of time and neglect. The cultural past was found by the emigrant chiefly in the written word and the remains of richly carved time-worn architecture.

By 1825 the Spanish had come and gone. The Mexicans had taken over from the Río Bravo del Norte (Río Grande) to the Sabine. The first organized American community was the Austin colony, founded by Stephen F. Austin and developed through the plans envisioned by his father, Moses Austin. With great difficulty young Austin had negotiated with the Mexican government for a legalized grant for American settlers. The colony consisted of about two thousand souls.[5]

An Unknown Artist of the Austin Colony

It was in the 1820's, at the time of the American settlements, that artists first painted Texas scenes and portraits of Texans. One of the first known colonial paintings was a full-length water-color portrait of Stephen F. Austin, impresario of Texas' first colony. It was in the fall of 1824 that young Austin, then thirty-one years old, walked briskly with his artist companion toward the mouth of the Brazos de Dios to a beautiful spot on the curving river. Here the artist painted Austin standing against the trunk of an old tree with his dog at his side, a gun beside him, and a hatchet in his belt.[6]

Guy Morrison Bryan wrote August 20, 1891, to Mrs. S. M. W. Compton, granddaughter of S. M. Williams:

My dear Madam:

If you could take the trouble to get one of your kinsman to go with you to my dollar point place, six miles from Highland and ten across the Bay from Galveston you will find suspended in the parlor of my residence there the original painting (from which the enclosed engraving was taken) of Stephen F. Austin, the best likeness of him extant.[7]

Bryan makes a statement about the picture of Austin as a frontiersman: "The picture you refer to with dog,

gun and hunting suit is from an engraving I had taken from a watercolor painting and presented to my grandfather; the scene represents the appearance of a spot on the Brazos a short distance above the mouth in 1824. If you prefer the hunting scene I will give you its history."

This small water-color painting is by an unidentified artist. Since this appears to have been the favorite mode of representing a frontiersman, the artist used the customary background and familiar accessories in his portrait of Austin. When the painting was sent to the engraver years later, he added to the setting some details making the portrait more individual in character, for example, the volumes of laws of Mexico and of the colony placed at Austin's feet; he also put in an obscure place the word *Cano*, possibly a bit of hidden humor or possibly the name of the original artist (Plate 1).

This engraver was Charles K. Burt (1823–1892), from Edinburgh, Scotland, "Portrait, Historical, and Landscape engraver" of New York, who had received the original water color from Guy Morrison Bryan. Throughout his life Bryan took a decided interest in artists and their work, often speaking in their behalf.[8]

A bust portrait of Stephen Austin was painted in 1835 by a German of New Orleans, and a full-length portrait given to the state by Guy Bryan was described in 1856 by the *Texas State Gazette*:

We have been shown by the Secretary of the Senate a full length portrait of Stephen F. Austin. It is a present to the state from Guy M. Bryan and is indeed one that we'll long commemorate the liberal hearted donor—the portrait represents Col. Austin in Mexico in the year 1853 [1835]. One hand holds the "Constitution del Estado of Texas," while the other directs our attention to it. On the table are two volumes entitled "Ley de Colonization" and "Constitution U. S. M." The subject of the historical sketch is in the prime of life and his eagle eye seems to shine with peculiar bright-

[4] Charles Mattoon Brooks, Jr., *Texas Missions—Their Romance and Architecture*, pp. 91, 103.

[5] L. G. Bugbee, "The Old Three Hundred," *Quarterly of the Texas Historical Association*, I (1897–1898), 109.

[6] J. C. Clopper, "Journal and Book of Memoranda for 1828, Province of Texas," *Quarterly of the Texas Historical Association.* XIII (1909–1910), 62.

[7] Letter, Guy M. Bryan, Quintana, Texas, to Mrs. S. M. W. Compton, San Antonio, Texas, August 20, 1891. The University of Texas Archives, Austin.

[8] George C. Groce and David H. Wallace, *New York Historical Society's Dictionary of Artists in America 1564–1860*, see Charles K. Burt, p. 98.

1. Unknown Artist, Charles K. Burt, Engraver: *Stephen F. Austin*
   Engraving, c. 1824, 5½″ x 4½″ (Courtesy of the Texas Memorial Museum, Austin, Texas)

ness as it gazes upon the sacred instrument in his hands. We feel at once apprised that he, at this early day, is realizing visions of a glorious future for Texas. We may well say that though Texas has had her dark days she is now upon the sure path to prosperity, and her sons will ever look upon this picture with feelings of love and reverence for one of the earliest founders of the country. Mr. Johnson intends putting a suitable frame around it and when it is hung in the Representative Hall it will greatly adorn the Chamber.[9]

These two portraits were probably destroyed when the State Capitol burned in 1881.

Bryan's letter to Mrs. Compton gives us information that supplies a sort of hallmark of individuality to the painting when he wrote that the painting of Austin showed him in his fringed buckskin suit, which was dyed a dusky black from the bark of a tree and tailored by two sisters of the Old Three Hundred, Mrs. Jane Long and Mrs. Alexander Cavit. These ladies no doubt concluded that Austin's broadcloth frock coat, which he was accustomed to wearing at the various reconnaissance meetings with dignitaries in Mexico City, was not suitable to wear as a frontiersman. A somewhat less interesting painting was made in oil on ivory from the original. This painting is now in the collection at The University of Texas.

It is interesting to note that in 1820 the adventurous, tough-minded artist Chester Harding (1792–1866) painted Daniel Boone in a similar setting in Tennessee. This curious penniless limner painted the portrait on a fragment of tablecloth in place of a canvas and took the painting back to St. Louis, where he engaged James Otto Lewis (1799–1858), later the famous Indian portraitist, to engrave his painting on copper.[10] Another artist who followed much the same design was Ralph E. W. Earle (c. 1785–1838) in his portrayal of Andrew Jackson, engraved by J. H. Bufford (c. 1805–?).[11]

Americans had long been leaving the states east of the Mississippi. They moved from the forested areas westward to the plains country in a wave of frontier movement—one of the most important periods of America's history in molding its democratic ideology. The colonists now coming to Texas had watched the wave of migration to the Ohio Valley and the successive political and economic changes and developments that had gone into the pattern of democracy in empire building. These settlers now coming farther west, into Texas, were imbued with the idea of freedom: the freedom of the individual, a disavowal of the old social order, and, for

many, a longing for the fulfillment of their own lives—some as artists. Each day these newcomers faced new horizons, challenging their utmost energy and spirit.

By the middle of the 1820's Austin's colony was a thriving community, where the pioneers were busy planting crops, building log cabins, and warding off the Indians. The story of the difficulties of colonization and, later, gaining independence from Mexico is not unlike the story of the struggle of the pioneer in making a home and gaining independence on the Eastern seaboard a few decades earlier. There was, however, one important difference with the early Texans: they were confronted with a different ideology—that of the Mexicans, unknown to them and difficult to understand. They were soon to be faced with the imposition of the Mexican way of life—and in time an army to carry out its will!

Lino Sánchez y Tapia, Jean Louis Berlandier, and José María Sánchez y Tapia

In 1827 there was a busy period of political uncertainty concerning Texas on the part of Mexico. She was already suspicious of what might happen to her provinces across the Río Bravo del Norte, and especially was she concerned about what might be brewing in the Austin colony and on the eastern boundary along the Sabine. These strong suspicions led the Mexicans to acts of surveillance.[12] Consequently, strange developments and political events in Mexico brought a boundary commission to Texas, and with it the first artists of this continent to make on-the-spot drawings of the early inhabitants of Texas.[13]

This reconnaissance was authorized in 1825 by Lucas Alamán, minister of foreign affairs. Landing at Vera Cruz, the commission started from Mexico City the tenth of November, 1827, and moved leisurely along the Camino Real to Monterrey (January 7, 1828), where they were guests of Bustamante for twenty days; then the caravan moved on to Laredo.

The commission was under the leadership of General Don Manuel Mier y Terán, who was to look into the

[9] *Texas State Gazette*, Austin, May 17, 1856.

[10] Letter, Mrs. Ruth F. Field, Missouri Historical Society, St. Louis, to author, March 5, 1964.

[11] Groce and Wallace, *Dictionary*, see Ralph E. Earle, p. 203, and J. H. Bufford, p. 94.

[12] Paul Horgan, *Great River: The Rio Grande in North American History*, Vol. 2, "Mexico and the United States," pp. 491–494.

[13] José María Sánchez y Tapia, "A Trip to Texas in 1828," translated by Carlos E. Castañeda, *Southwestern Historical Quarterly*, XXIX (April, 1926), 249–250.

matter, principally, of marking the eastern boundary between the provinces and the United States. The members of the commission were competent men: the head of the group, the studious and patriotic scientist Don Manuel Mier y Terán; Ralph Chovell, minerologist, and assistant and companion to Mier y Terán; and the noted Swiss explorer and scientist Dr. Jean Louis Berlandier, who had studied with the famous botanist Augustin Pyrame de Candolle at the Geneva Academy. In De Candolle's laboratory Berlandier also learned the sketching, drawing, and painting of objects of natural history. His instructor was Jean Christophe Heyland, botanical artist and illustrator for De Candolle.[14] José María Sánchez y Tapia, a young lieutenant, had been chosen by Terán to accompany the commission as cartographer. Though no mention is made that Lino Sánchez y Tapia accompanied the commission, the sketches attributed to him are strong evidence that he did. There is a certain uniformity to the work that makes us suspect Lino Sánchez had more to do with finishing and assembling the sketches than either of the other two—José María Sánchez or Dr. Berlandier. Each illustration has a notation "d'apres José María Sánchez y Tapia," "d'apres Lino Sánchez y Tapia," or "d'apres Louis Berlandier," thus giving us the information that each had assisted in some way in the original work.[15]

The instructions to the commission were that all points between the two countries (comprising what is now Texas and the United States) were to be marked as agreed upon in the treaty made with Spain in 1819, and that an estimate was to be made of the cost and the number of troops needed for maintenance of a watchful garrison on the eastern boundary. The commission started from Mexico City. The route chosen was through the southern part of what is now Texas, from the west to the east, where there was some habitation for protection. This route (through sparsely settled country) also furnished the artists an excellent opportunity to depict the inhabitants of the various scattered settlements, as well as members of Indian tribes.

The pageantry of the train was colorful; both Indians and drovers joined the caravan, adding to the already long line of cavalry remounts and wagons of instruments and supplies. But what seemed most unusual was the carriage which transported Don Manuel, with its huge wheels in the rear and, in front, wheels "little superior to that of a wheelbarrow."[16] The carriage described in diaries of both General Mier y Terán and José María

Sánchez was picturesquely painted and carved, "a specimen of the ingenuity and cunning workmanship of man."

The trek across the state required several months, and as the party passed Parrita (uninhabited), José Sánchez described the evergreen oaks and other trees "which make Parrita beautiful":

Its beauty was intensified by the green of the fields, bright with rain. The night was serene and peaceful; during the watch we kept as a precaution against surprise by the Indians, the silence was broken only by the wailing of the screech owl (a small owl different from those found in Mexico), the call of the wolves and coyotes, the croaking of the water-frogs, and the gentle murmur of the breeze as it glided through the leaves, all blending [in] a surprising harmony that filled the soul with a strange melancholy known and felt only by sensitive hearts.[17]

When the commission reached San Antonio, José Sánchez remarked on the crooked streets and the architecture, which was of "no notice."[18]

José Sánchez's youthful exuberance in his writings and his keen observations give us a clue to his success as an artist. He remarked on the colorful landscape "dressed in the most vivid colors of smiling and budding spring." He clearly discloses his sensibility to his surroundings and gives us a sample of his romantic literary efforts; evidently, writing was not a skill he lacked. He described an evening "on the desert":

The night was so peaceful and the atmosphere so clear and transparent that in the bright blue of the sky not even the smallest star that adorns the immense dome was hidden from the eye. The vast grandeur disclosed in the myriad of stars kindled the imagination and led me to reflect upon the great mystery of the unknown and the boundless power of the Supreme Being that brought everything out of chaos by his infinite power.[19]

It was a spring morning in April, 1828, after several months of travel, when the expedition arrived at San Felipe de Austin, on the Río de los Brazos de Dios. Stephen Austin was in his log cabin (serving as both

---

[14] Ohland Morton, "Life of General Don Manuel de Mier y Terán as It Affected Texas-Mexican Relations," *Southwestern Historical Quarterly*, XLVII (1943–1944), 37–38.

[15] José María Sánchez y Tapia and others, Sketch Book, Nos. VI, VII, VIII, XI, Thomas Gilcrease Institute of American History and Art, Tulsa, Oklahoma.

[16] Clopper, "Journal and Book of Memoranda for 1828."

[17] Sánchez y Tapia, "A Trip to Texas in 1828," p. 255.

[18] *Ibid.*, p. 257.   [19] *Ibid.*, p. 253.

Cheraquís.

Cherokees : Indigènes des E.U. du N. Amérique emigrés aux environs de Nacogdoches.

2. Lino Sánchez y Tapia apres José María Sánchez y Tapia: *Cheraquís*
    Water color, 1827–1828, 10″ x 8″ (Courtesy of the Thomas Gilcrease Institute of American History and Art, Tulsa, Oklahoma)

home and office), studying his maps, when he was interrupted by his confidential secretary, Samuel May Williams, who had been acting in Austin's temporary absence as host to the boundary commission. Austin slipped from his stool, drew back his narrow shoulders, and straightened his spare body. Presently, before him stood youthful, alert Lieutenant José Sánchez.

That morning Mier y Terán had left the business of talking with Austin to José Sánchez. They discussed the temperament of the colonists and their wants. José had noticed on approaching the village some forty or fifty small houses, some of one room, scattered over the rolling land; beyond the village was the main settlement, where there were perhaps two thousand thriving colonists, and beyond that were enormous regions scarcely inhabited at all. After leaving Austin he expressed in his diary the same sentiments that Mier y Terán expressed later in his report:

The diplomatic policy of this empresario, evident in all his actions, has, as one may say, lulled the authorities into a sense of security while he works diligently for his own ends. In my judgment the spark that will start the conflagration that will deprive us of Texas will start from this colony. All because the government does not take vigorous measures to protect it. Perhaps it does not realize the value of what it is about to lose.[20]

José Sánchez, a quiet observer, wrote vividly of many of the tribes he visited as he crossed the provinces—the "Comanches," "Taucahues," "Tahuacanos." The artists on the commission depicted some of the peaceful tribes —the "Tejas," "Nadacos," "Yguanés" (Plate c-2), "Cados," "Cheraquís" (Plate 2), "Kickapoos," and "Quichas," "who continually visited at Nacogdoches."[21] Perhaps they are unusually quiet because the unfortunate adventurer Ellis Peter Bean, acting as Indian agent at Nacogdoches, was selected by Mier y Terán as an intermediary so that the best results might terminate their visit.[22]

Probably having been directed to record the people and their occupations, the artists as "eye witnesses" included drawing of Indians, calling attention to varied types. They include details of costume and an instrument or tool which would indicate the subject's occupation: a crudely made hoe in the hand of one Indian, a basket of vegetables in the hands of an Indian woman, or a catch of fish in another picture. There is an apparently related pair of drawings of the Comanches showing symbols of occupation (during war and peace) on which

the artist—in this case José Sánchez—had made notations. On one is written, "Comanche en vetement l'orsq: vont a la guerre," and on the other, "Comanche en vetement l'orsqsont paix."[23] The artists did not attempt any elaborate backgrounds for their sketches; backgrounds are indicated occasionally with a small faint line of trees on the horizon, minutely painted.

As the caravan passed from one plantation or hacienda to another, they sketched Mexicans, Indians, and rancheros. A few of the subjects are mounted, in a static pose, representing, in one case, the rider on the legendary great white prairie stallion, in another on a prancing brown stallion. It is interesting to note that they did not include the wild horse or the buffalo; their mission, diplomatic in nature, took them into settled areas. Their subjects for the most part are industrious quiet citizens, as one would find in any of the old communities of docile Indians. Although organized in the name of science and motivated by Mexican national interests, the commission turned out to be of historic importance, politically, scientifically, and culturally.

James Strange

While Mier y Terán and his commission were observing what might happen to the Mexican provinces in East Texas, an artist about whom there are many unanswered questions was getting settled in the Austin colony.[24] This was James Strange (c. 1786–?), who we know painted the portraits of the Mexican General Antonio López de Santa Anna and Colonel Juan N. Almonte.[25]

After Strange came to Texas he was made constable of the San Jacinto District, served on the jury at Harrisburg in March, 1838, was known as a farmer and stock raiser, and eventually earned the title of major.[26] Our first real knowledge of him comes from a report given

[20] *Ibid.*, pp. 270–271; Morton, "Life of General Don Manuel de Mier y Terán," pp. 121–122.

[21] Sánchez y Tapia and others, Sketch Book, Nos. XIII, XIV, XV, XVI.

[22] *Ibid.*, Nos. XIII and XIV; Morton, "Life of General Don Manuel de Mier y Terán," pp. 127–129.

[23] Sánchez y Tapia and others, Sketch Book, Nos. II and III.

[24] Marian Day Mullins, *The First Census of Texas, 1829–1836*, Special Publication of the National Geneological Society No. 22 and *Texas Citizenship Lists 1821–1845* and other Records of the Republic of Texas. Bugbee, "Old Three Hundred," p. 116.

[25] *Telegraph and Texas Register*, Columbia, August 2, 1836; William Ransom Hogan, *The Texas Republic*, p. 179.

[26] *Telegraph and Texas Register*, Houston, March 31, 1838; April 14, 1838.

at the time of the grounding of the schooner *Mary* on Red Fish Bar, when he spoke of "taulking of running hir aground," and he thus gives a dialectic clue to a possible Scotch background. One surmises that he was possibly a descendant of Sir Richard Strange of South Carolina, an artist-engraver from Scotland.[27]

As a first settler and a single man, Strange was entitled to a labor of land (under the Spanish and Mexican title), which he chose in what is now Harris County. He served as constable for the Austin colony, district of San Jacinto, recorded April 3, 1825. Later, having served at least three months in the Texas Revolution of 1836, he received a bounty of 320 acres.[28] The census record of 1826 adds the information that he was born in South Carolina and that he had come to Texas by way of the Isle of Cuba!

Strange, having served in the army, recognized the interest there might be in portraits of the Mexican leaders, and he conceived the idea of painting portraits of General Santa Anna and Colonel Almonte in what he termed "a historical painting against a background of Longwood of Texas and adjacent scenery." When the auspicious time came to paint these gentlemen, Cos was in prison in Galveston.[29]

History records that after the Battle of San Jacinto, Santa Anna and his colleagues, Almonte and his secretary Don Ramos Caro, were taken first to Quintana, near Columbia, Texas, on the Brazos. While the Texans were at their wits' end to know what to do with their prisoners—for there were threats against their safety from revengeful Texans—they decided to take the prisoners by a circuitous journey to the plantation home, "Orozimbo," of Dr. James A. E. Phelps, about twelve miles from Columbia, where they were to be guarded

by thirty or more soldiers.[30] It is evident that Major Strange was able to paint the officers' portraits here, although Dr. Phelps did not think it important to mention the presence of the artist nor did he record the cost of boarding Strange in his list of expenses, as he did in the case of his prisoners. Could it be that Major Strange was one of the guarding soldiers?

A contemporary description in the newspaper states that the portrait of Santa Anna shows him in his uniform as major general (General de Division), the highest Mexican military grade, so indicated by the light-blue sash and the three different crosses of furbished metal representing three separate orders instituted by his government to commemorate Santa Anna's notable successes.

. . . notable Epochas called 1st, 2nd, and 3rd: the first, white ribbon, and cross of four points being that of "Independence" and granted in 1821 for the military of 1810 and 1811 when Mexico first raised the cry of emancipation from the Spanish yoke. The second, indented tri-color, red, white and green with cross of six points suspended from a Liberty cap for the battle of Cordova, 1821, and the treaty of that name made by Iturbide with O'Donosjo [sic] which fixed the independence of Mexico; and the third cross of four points, ribbon, green for the victory of "Tempico" in 1829, when the Spaniards under Barradas invaded Mexico.[31]

Colonel Almonte's portrait bears one cross, that of the first epoch, "Independence," with the uniform of colonel of the Cavalry. The news reporter comments that Santa Anna's likeness is remarkably striking and correct but that the painter has not been so successful in delineating Almonte. The account notes that Santa Anna gave Strange a note "manifesting his approval of his likeness" and stating that "no other of the same description has ever been taken to the United States." One may interpret the report to mean that the artist followed his plan of painting both officers on the same canvas, which furnishes a clue in locating the painting. We are quite certain that Strange was able to make the portraits between May and November of 1836, while both prisoners were at "Orozimbo" and before Santa Anna was removed to Washington, D.C.

Just how much painting was done by the Major is not known, but his portrait of Santa Anna may have provided a basis for the many engravings which were made in the East. Strange remained in Texas (Brazos County) at least until 1845, for it was then he adver-

[27] Eugene C. Barker (ed.), "Report of James Strange, Austin Colony, on Schooner *Mary*," *The Austin Papers*, Vol. II, April 3, 1825; Alexander Strange, *The Strange Family, 1911*, pp. 11–19, 32–33.

[28] General Land Office Records, Captain Duncan Co., Muster Roll Book I, p. 66; Mexican and Texas Titles, Harris County, August (1. 661.) The Muster Roll Index, Companies engaged in Texas Revolution 1835–1836, shows J. Strange drafted, Lynchburg, March 8, 1826. The census record of 1826 lists persons between 25 and 45 years of age, and his name appears, still single as a "farmer and stock raiser."

[29] *Telegraph and Texas Register*, Columbia, August 2, 1836.

[30] Antonio López de Santa Anna, *The Mexican Side of the Texas Revolution by the Chief Mexican Participants*, translated by Carlos E. Castañeda, p. 137.

[31] *Telegraph and Texas Register*, Columbia, August 2, 1836.

tised for his missing bounty claim of 320 acres—the grant he had won for his service in fighting these same Mexican leaders at the Battle of San Jacinto.[32]

Ambrose Louis Garneray

Among the earliest and most significant prints depicting Texas in the very early years of its settlement were those engraved in 1830 by Ambrose Louis Garneray (1783–1857) of Champ d'Asile, the French colony on the Trinity River.[33] With the opening of the nineteenth century the French Revolution and the Napoleonic wars sent many enthusiasts for liberty and many political refugees—terrified and destitute—fleeing to America. A colony of some four hundred French and "San Domingoans," with soldiers of fortune joining them in Philadelphia, and all under the leadership of Charles François Antoine Lallemand and General Antoine Rigaud (both conspirators against the French government), settled on the Trinity as "Champ d'Asile" [Field of Asylum] or the "Society for the Cultivation of the Vine and Olive." Thus designating themselves by name as an agricultural community, they disavowed any aggressive intent.[34]

The whole episode concerning this settlement, the false motives of which were laid bare by the French novelist Balzac, brought the highest officers of France, the United States, and Mexico into an argumentative huddle. Many French citizens contributed heavily to the enterprise (including Joseph Bonaparte) believing they were aiding victims of the Bourbon restoration, but in time it became evident that the movement was not wholly of charitable instincts but planned chiefly to remove the regimented imperial officers from the Paris scene and restore the Bourbons to the throne.[35]

We find the enthusiastic Lallemand in Texas on the Trinity in May of 1818. He describes in his manifesto their territory on the Trinity as

. . . a vast extent of territory at present uninhabited by civilized mankind, and the extreme limits of which are in possession of Indian tribes who caring for nothing but the chase, leave the broad acres uncultivated. Strong in adversity we claim the first right given by God to man, that of settling in this country, clearing it and using the produce which nature never refuses to the patient laborer—we ask peace and friendship from all those who surround us and we shall be grateful for the slightest token of their good will.[36]

Many authors have written of the storm they encoun-

tered at the time of their landing, the unpleasant weeks on Galveston Island, their aid from Lafitte, their illness and being lost in the forest, and finally their arrival on the Trinity.[37] In spite of the difficulties of settlement, enthusiasm for their new home was unbounded. They made the old Trinity fairly ring with their Song of Texas:

> Only honor lies behind us
> Peace within our hearts we feel;
> Happiness has come to find us.—
> The laurel grows in Champ d'Asile.[38]

Neither was it their hardships or fears of the Indians that compelled them to abandon their colony. When they heard through friendly Indians that Spanish provincial troops from San Antonio, aided by some Indian tribes, were marching against them, their first thought was to resist, but realizing the disadvantages of their shortage of food and their small number, they packed up and took "French leave."[39]

Some years later, when Champ d'Asile was described in song and story, it was envisioned by the artist and engraver Ambrose Louis Garneray. Born in Paris, he was the son of the famous Jean François Garneray "French portraitist and painter of architectural and faithful subjects," and his father furnished him every opportunity to learn the art of engraving in the best French tradition. But young Garneray was off to sea at the age of thirteen, visiting the many seaports around the world. When he returned he was patronized by Louis XVII for

[32] *Telegraph and Texas Register*, Houston, May 21, 1845; 1850 Harris County Census, Texas State Archives, Austin.

[33] Felix Allgemeines, *Lexikon der Bildenden Kunsler*, pp. 202–203; Engraving *1ère Vue d'Aigleville, Colonie du Texas ou Champ d'Asile*, Print Division, Library of Congress; I. N. Stokes and Daniel C. Haskell, *American Historical Prints: Early Views of American Cities from the Phelps Stokes and Other Collections*, p. 78 B-35, E 38.

[34] Harris G. Warren, *The Sword Was Their Passport: A History of American Filibustering in the Mexican Revolution*, p. 212.

[35] Jack Dabbs (Trans. and Ed.), "Additional Notes on Champ d'Asile," *Southwestern Historical Quarterly*, LIV (April–July, 1951) 347–358; Charles A. Gulick, Jr. (ed.), *Papers of Mirabeau B. Lamar*; "Champ d'Asile in Texas," by Louis Pierre Anquetal (1827), V., 47–48; Jesse Siddall Reeves, *The Napoleonic Exiles in America: A Study in American Diplomatic History, 1815–1819*, pp. 10–11, 103; Thomas W. Martin, *French Military Adventures in Alabama, 1818–1828*, pp. 9–14.

[36] Just Girard, *Adventures of a French Captain*, translated by Lady Blanche Murphy, p. 64.

[37] *Ibid.*, pp. 21–23.

[38] *Ibid.*, p. 103.

[39] Reeves, *Napoleonic Exiles in America*, pp. 90–102.

3. Louis Garneray: *1ère Vue d'Aigleville Colonie du Texas ou Champ d'Asile*
Engraving, 1830, 22.8cm. x 33.3cm. (Courtesy of the Print Division, Library of Congress, Washington, D. C.)

his marine paintings.[40] One of his marine scenes depicting a whale hunt—judged by Herman Melville as one of the finest ever painted—is in the Melbourne Museum, Vermont.[41]

Just when he made the engravings of views of foreign ports is not clear, but included are views of London, Havana, and Rio de Janeiro. In 1834 and 1835, according to Stokes and Haskell in *Early Views of American Cities*, Garneray drew scenes of New York, Baltimore, Philadelphia, Boston, and New Orleans for engravings, and executed an oil painting, *The Battle of Lake Erie* (1822).[42]

Although he was in New Orleans—which is not a great distance from the site of Champ d'Asile—and could have visited East Texas, it is the general opinion that he may never have set foot on Texas soil, and until additional facts are known, we may only conjecture about the accuracy of his Texas engravings and treat

them as imaginary concepts. The glorification of events as the artist conceived them and the numerous details foreign to the locale persuade us to treat them as contrary to historic truth, yet the inference of reality stirs the imagination and makes us value them almost as much or more than realistic scenes.

In a view of "Aigleville," part of the colony of Champ d'Asile whose name alludes to one of Napoleon's victories, Garneray shows fine costumes and carefully built defenses (Plate 3). His representations of the defenses "built as if by magic" and carried to completion rather

[40] M. Bryan, *Bryan's Dictionary of Artists and Engravers, 1785–1824*, edited by G. C. Williamson Bell, II, 216; Ulrich Thieme and Felix Becker, *Allgemeines Lexikon der bildenden Künstler*, pp. 202–203; Groce and Wallace, *Dictionary*, see Garneray, p. 250.

[41] Ivan T. Sanderson, "A-h-h B-l-o-o-w-s," *American Heritage*, XII, No. 1 (1960), 48–49.

[42] Thieme and Becker, *Allgemeines*, pp. 202–203.

Yguanés.

Iguanees ou Yuganis: Indigènes des E: U: du N: A: emigrés sur les rives de l'Atoyac, du Neches et de l'Angelina.

c-2. Lino Sánchez y Tapia apres José María Sánchez y Tapia: *Yguanés*
Water color, 1827–1828, 8″ x 10″ (Courtesy of the Thomas Gilcrease Institute of American History and Art, Tulsa, Oklahoma)

contradicts conditions as they must have existed on the frontier. Against the stone barricades in the background are shown French soldiers in complete French military uniforms (including cockaded hats), pushing wheelbarrows and sawing wood. Ladies and children dressed in the latest French regency modes are enjoying bananas. The rich presentation of costume embellishments and the carefully designed street sign, "Aigleville," all make us doubt the pictorial truth of his prints. Garneray, "designer and engraver," makes his prints more enigmatical by signing his name in reverse (an oddity not resulting from the printing of the plate), seemingly deliberately making the print more puzzling to the viewer.[43]

The "Champ d'Asile" prints represent examples of Garneray's precise and masterly designing, as well as examples of some of the best craftsmanship of the high period in French engraving. They suggest all the romance, the excitement, and the dauntless spirit of the French temperament, but on retrospection they reveal the tragedy and shortsightedness of those who prompted the settlement. Although we accept Garneray's Texas prints as imaginary concepts, they symbolize the adventures of the brave French who attempted to settle in a free country—a theme with which we must be wholeheartedly sympathetic.

[43] *1ère Vue d'Aigleville Colonie du Texas ou Champ d'Asile, Dessiné et gravé par Yerenrag,* Print Division, Library of Congress.

CHAPTER 2

GENTLEMEN OF THE BRUSH

IN THE FIRST DECADES of the nineteenth century, when well-established American artists Charles Wilson Peale, Thomas Sully, John Trumbull, and Gilbert Stuart were busying themselves with bewigged and embroidered waistcoated Americans, many young artists on the Eastern seaboard were looking with questioning eyes toward the alluring yet forbidding frontier. Here, they thought, might be room for a young artist in the less populated South, where patrons would not be so demanding, where there would be land to settle and where they could experience the excitement that all knew the West could provide. But those artists who came found the going hard. In addition to painting, and taking part in the defense of their adopted country, they were compelled in almost every case to turn their hands to whatever tasks the undeveloped country might demand.

In 1836, when Texas was able to throw off the Mexican yoke and turn to establishing the infant republic, her future looked bright, but the Indian was still to be dealt with, and frontier life was a vexing problem. Yet while the years of the Republic were some of the most difficult, they were also some of the most important to her social and cultural history.

With characteristic American enthusiasm for the new West, immigrants once more began to flow across Texas' borders. The more experienced advised that immigrants bring coffee, rice, flour, a good rifle or musket, and at least one hundred rounds of ammunition.[1] They further admonished:

Those who wish to enjoy the advantages of this country should come prepared to defend it, though there is scarcely a probability that the dastard hordes of Mexico can ever pollute the soil of Texas, *the War is not yet closed*; we want no cowards, therefore, let only those who are willing to encounter dangers come at the twilight hour to share the dear bought purchase of heroes.[2]

One of the principal roads for immigrants from the Southern states entered Texas at Gaines Crossing over the Sabine River, and just west of this point was San Augustine. The press announced that this road from

[1] *Telegraph and Texas Register*, Houston, May 2, 1837.
[2] *Ibid.*, May 2, 1837.

San Augustine west to Nacogdoches and south to Washington-on-the-Brazos had become so crowded that immigrant families were advised to provide themselves with adequate provisions before leaving San Augustine. They were also warned of raids by the marauding Comanches.[3] Of the large number of new settlers from the Southern states between 1836 and 1845, Kentucky seemed to provide the largest number.

Thomas Jefferson Wright

Beginning his twelve years of life in Texas in the spring of 1837, was the artist Thomas Jefferson Wright (1798–1846), from Mount Sterling, Kentucky (earlier known as "Little Mountain Town"). In making a decision to come to Texas, Wright no doubt, as many American artists of the East, had a sensitive feeling concerning the status of the artist and preferred a new location. On his arrival he announced in the Houston paper his intention of painting portraits for the citizens of that city. At once he became one of the founders of the local Masonic Order (Holland Lodge No. 36),[4] along with Sam Houston, Thomas Weston, and Anson Jones; a few years later he was elected major in the Texas militia.[5] Wright was a man of distinctive appearance, and like his father, a Welsh tailor, he dressed neatly. He was a man of great stature and, when required, could swing a strong fist. Through his knowledge of the Indian and his sympathetic attitude, which was attuned to that of Sam Houston, he won a place as Indian agent during the days of the Republic. But the most important fact about Jefferson Wright was that he was a successful "gentleman of the brush."

Thomas Jefferson Wright and his brother Benjamin Wright (names showing the patriotic overtones of the Welsh parents) probably came to Texas about the same time. Benjamin bought cheap land, eventually totalling eighty thousand acres, at one dollar per acre along the upper Trinity. He helped found the little town of Cincinnati in Walker County, which during the 1830's was the terminus for steamboats bringing supplies and passengers up the river, one hundred miles from the Gulf. On Benjamin's becoming a man of means, Jeff Wright painted his portrait in a yellow brocade waistcoat, silk stock held with a jeweled pin, and a watch band of woven Indian beadwork. Although Jeff went about his portrait painting in Houston, Huntsville, and Nacogdoches, he often found a home in Cincinnati, where the two brothers sometimes worked as cabinet makers.[6]

Before coming to Texas, Jefferson Wright painted a number of the Wright family and citizens of Culpeper, Virginia. Many of these paintings are signed and dated from 1831 to 1833.[7] One of these made while he was still in Mt. Sterling is the portrait of J. Lyle Smith, born in 1828, who as a young man left Kentucky (1857) to make a home in Huntsville, Texas. His three-quarter-length portrait (Plate 4) shows the boy at the age of six, dressed in Lord Fauntleroy style—dark coat, large white collar, and red vest—his dog beside him, in a painting of simplicity and charm.

In many of Wright's early paintings he uses the age-old device of indicating in the background the interest or the profession of the sitter. In the portrait of his sister, Harriet Wright Smith, he shows from a window in the background a view of her home. In the portrait of his brother-in-law, Robert Thompson Smith, he painted behind the sitter his wool carding factory, said to have been the first west of the Alleghenies. In the latter portrait he shows a level of skill—a certain draftsmanship—which he does not always maintain during his years in Texas.

We get our first substantial information about Jefferson Wright as an artist from the Houston paper of May, 1837: "We have recently visited a small gallery of paintings in this city from the palette of Mr. Wright and we are highly pleased with their appearance. The portraits of this gentleman bear evidence of much genius and application. We recommend him to the notice of the amateurs of the Fine Arts."[8]

---

[3] *Ibid.*, March 3, 1838.

[4] *Ibid.*, March 17, 1838. Thomas Jefferson Wright presented a resolution for the appointment of a committee to draft the Constitution of the Grand Lodge of Texas at a meeting held at the Capitol at Houston, December 20, 1837. *A. S. Ruthven, Grand Master, Proceedings of the Grand Lodge, 1837–1856*, I, 10–11.

[5] *Telegraph and Texas Register*, Houston, March 17, 1838; June 15, 1842.

[6] Letters to the author from the following: Mrs. Gay Thompson Clarke, New Orleans, May 5, 8, 27, 1959, August 20, 1959; Mrs. Bruce Stout, Fort Wayne, May 15, 1960, Franklin, Indiana, April 10, 1963; Mrs. Vivian Moore, Harrodsburg, Kentucky, November 20, 1959, February 22, 1960; Dr. Hubbard W. Smith, Greely, Colorado, March 6, 1960; Lucy C. Smith, Huntsville, Texas, manuscript notes in possession of Mr. Robert Hanman, Austin, Texas; *Telegraph and Texas Register*, Houston, August 4, 1838.

[7] Letter, Mrs. Henry W. Howell, Jr., Frick Reference Library, October 17, 1959, to author.

[8] *Telegraph and Texas Register*, Houston, May 9, 1837; June 3, 1837; October 7, 1837; October 11, 1837; December 16, 1837; February 17, 1838.

4. Thomas Jefferson Wright: *J. Lyle Smith*
   Oil, c. 1836, 29½″ x 21½″ (Courtesy of Mr. Robert S. Hamner, Austin, Texas)

Again in the following month the press called attention to his "professional services" to the people of Houston and spoke of his "Gallery of National portraits." According to visitors the exhibition contained some eighteen pictures. A diarist throws some light on the reference to "National" portraits by stating that: "Right [sic] had an exhibition of paintings [;] among them was one of General George Washington." This full-length portrait was placed on the platform by Sam Houston when he made political speeches, and no doubt reached an unrepairable state.

When the well-traveled Mary Austin Holley wrote her daughter on December 30, 1837, while her boat was at anchor in Red Fish Bar at the mouth of the Trinity, she stated that the President (Sam Houston) had dined with them and had "gallanted them to the capitol where in one wing there was a gallery of distinguished characters of the last campaign" (probably portraits of Houston and Deaf Smith, the famous fearless scout). There was also a room used by a portrait and miniature painter, A. Andrews, who was exhibiting portraits of General Houston and Governor Henry Smith. "You see," she wrote, "the arts flourish in this new land already."[9] This statement and others of 1837 indicate that the city of Houston was early a center of cultural activities.

To catch the support of a wider circle of patrons, Wright advertised in October of that same year that he was including "Fancy Lettering" among his accomplishments.[10] Few artists of this time lived entirely by portraiture. They also painted decorations on walls, and did house painting, sign painting, or carpentering. Indeed, it did not enter their heads that the artisan's work was not as profitable or honorable as portraiture.

As to the training Jefferson Wright had for his career, there is little that can be vouched for. When he was twenty-four (1822), however, he was introduced to the great American portraitist of Philadelphia, Thomas Sully (1783-1872), by his friend Matthew H. Jouett (1782-1827), a portrait painter of Fayetteville, Kentucky, and a distinguished pupil of Gilbert Stuart (1755-1828). The early historian Henry T. Tuckerman speaks of

Jouett as being "humerous, a tasteful man and was the best portrait painter west of the mountains." But on November 12, 1822, Jouett wrote to Sully that he felt the smothering effect of isolation: "I share no competition of any sort here, I see no good pictures to compare my daubs with, consequently am getting deeper and deeper into the mire of mannerism and that of the worst kind." So far there is no information of Wright's having received any real training from Jouett; this fact is indicated in Jouett's remarks to Sully when he states that he could not "speak decisively" of young Wright's abilities. Had Wright had any training under Jouett, he would have, no doubt, remarked on it. It was, however, the custom for the older and more prosperous artists such as Sully and Jouett to allow neophytes to visit their studios, watch them paint, and even be permitted to copy a painting. Thus the young artists of talent could visit the well-established artists and learn whatever they were capable of absorbing or imitating. No information is available to assure us that Jefferson Wright made a journey to visit Sully, but he very likely did so.

The first half of Jouett's ebullient letter introduces one of the "young gentlemen of the brush" and gives us an insight into the character and capabilities of Wright. Jouett wrote from Fayette County, November 12, 1822:

Dear Friend

The kindness with which you have heretofore honored my letters and commissions of every sort leaves but little ground to distrust the entire success of this application in favor of my young friend Jefferson Wright to whose acquaintance I hereby entreat you to be introduced. You will find Mr. W. amiable, modest and entirely upon the reserve. He visits Phila. with the view to avail himself of the helps of the academy and the artists in portrait painting. Of his abilities I cannot speak decisively—they are reputed promising in this country and I believe them to be so. By his enthusiasm and industry he has become enabled to visit your city and with prospects of a tolerably longer stay—Altho entirely devoid of the graces of early learning—you will find him by no means destitute of those lights characteristic of a good mind attentive to the object of its pursuit. He earnestly solicited to be made acquainted [with] you. Indeed all the young gentlemen of the brush in this country look upon you as the Elijah in the arts, and push forward with hopes of immortality if they can but touch the hem of your cloak—and so you see if you are annoyed by we poor provincial children of the brush, you must attribute it mainly to that good report that accompanies your name. Be assured of one thing, the

---

[9] Mary Austin Holley to Mrs. William Brand, December 30, 1837, Mary Austin Holley Papers, Vol. 11, December, 1832–July, 1846, pp. 99–100, The University of Texas Archives. Mary Austin Holley illustrates her diary with sketches of the Capitol at Houston and old plantations such as The Wharton Place and Peach Point. She demonstrates here her skill in quick sketching.

[10] *Telegraph and Texas Register*, Houston, October 7, 1837.

amiable subject of this letter will never obtrude upon one busy moment of your time whilst in the city—; you will only have to say to him go and he goeth, do and he doeth. "Your advice will be law and your council, will be as strength unto Weakness."

For an introductory I think I have said enough. You will please let me hear from you, often. If I cannot see you I love to hear what you are engaged about. Your sincere friend

Matt H. Jouett[11]

After painting the family portraits in the early 1830's, Jefferson Wright then came to Texas, where he found a friend in Sam Houston. Advertising and this influential friendship brought him commissions from prominent political figures. Among the portraits painted during 1838 was one of Juan Nepomucena Seguin (Plate 5), of French descent, born in San Fernando de Béxar (San Antonio) in 1806, son of Erasmo Seguin, formerly of Mexico. In 1838 Seguin, then a colonel, was honorably discharged from the Texas army to take a seat in the state Senate. Jefferson Wright has painted him in his army uniform, austere but pleasant. As in Wright's self-portraits (Plate 6), he painted the face large, against a plain background. Inscribed on the reverse side by an unknown hand are these words: "Artist Jeff Wright."

When he painted this portrait of Seguin, Wright was evidently sojourning in Nacogdoches, where he was serving as Indian agent for the Texas government. Various accounts give us clues to the activities and whereabout of the artist as an Indian agent. From May 10 to August 18, 1838, Sam Houston approved, "101 days at five dollars per diem, $505.00 out of the Indian Fund for Jeff Wright's services." An account of June, 1838, shows that Jeff Wright provided Chief Fox Field, the Indian interpreter, with "pants, shirt, vest, hat, blanket, and silk handkerchief" at a total of $20.50. Attached to the account is a bill for the Chief's stay at Hydes Tavern in Nacogdoches, affirmed by Fox Field's "mark."[12]

Jeff Wright did not serve long in the capacity of Indian agent. For one reason, his portrait work seemed to be absorbing all of his time. Information concerning his resignation is found in a letter addressed to Henry Raguet from J. Reily, Nacogdoches, Texas, who related an incident of diatribe which occurred between the artist and the Indian fighter, George Bonnell, when the latter accused Wright of resigning as Indian Agent because of fear. Two fistfights resulted, and their dispute was not finally settled until the enraged artist in very strong words challenged the accuser (a privilege of the frontiersman) to a third contest.[13]

Soon after Jeff Wright served as Indian agent, he painted a banner, or flag, that was ordered by the Republic's commissioners, requested through Sam Houston, as a gift to the Comanche Indians. Ten dollars was paid the artist, from the Indian fund of 1843, with the receipt signed by Sam Houston.[14]

Without doubt the widening of the circle of Jeff Wright's patronage may be attributed to Sam Houston's interest in portraiture. When Houston was courting Anna Raguet he wrote her February 1, 1838: "My friend Jeff Wright has completed my portrait for your father's parlor, until I have as good a mansion. It will be taken to you because it is said to be the best likeness taken of me and withal an elegant painting. I am sure you will fault it but I will not tell you why or wherefore."[15] Because of Houston's frequent references to his portraits, one may surmise that Jeff Wright probably painted Houston more than once.

Houston wrote to Ashbel Smith to take his portrait to Memphis with him, "if there is no other place to leave it," adding, "I think more of it than any other likeness." Later (1850) in a letter to Houston, Ashbel Smith mentions the fact that one of Houston's portraits could not be taken to Washington by a Mr. Ashe, as he was traveling with only a carpet bag.[16] The interest in this particular portrait may indicate that there was sentiment attached to it, and, in addition, that there was more than a passing friendship between Houston

[11] Letter, Matthew H. Jouett, Fayette County, Kentucky, to Thomas Sully, Philadelphia, Pennsylvania Historical Society; November 12, 1822, Henry T. Tuckerman, *Book of Artists: American Artist's Life*, p. 68.

[12] Indian Papers, Nacogdoches, June 17, 1838; August 10, 1838; September 11, 1838, Texas State Archives, Austin.

[13] William Ransom Hogan, "Rampart Individualism in the Republic of Texas" *Southwestern Historical Quarterly*, XLIV (1940–1941), 459; letter, J. Reily, Nacogdoches, to Col. Raguet, November 20, 1838, The University of Texas Archives, Austin.

[14] Dorman Winfrey (ed.) *Texas Indian Papers, 1825–1843*, I, 201–202, 279.

[15] Sam Houston, *Writings of Sam Houston, 1813–1865*, II, 190; III, 236. Anna Raguet married Dr. Robert Irion (March 20, 1838). This portrait, owned by one of the descendants, was burned in recent years in Marshall, Texas.

[16] Houston, *Writings*, V, 94. It is a tradition in the Wright family descendants that Jeff Wright and Houston were related through a Virginia branch of the Wrights; at Houston's marriage to Miss Allen some of the Wright boys were present. It was probably Houston who influenced them to come to Texas.

5. Thomas Jefferson Wright: *Juan N. Seguin*
   Oil, 1838, 26½″ x 24¼″ (Courtesy of the Texas State Archives, Austin)

6. Thomas Jefferson Wright: *Self-Portrait*
    Oil, c. 1837, approx. 33″ x 30″ (Courtesy of Mrs. Katherine S. Stout, Fort Wayne, Indiana)

and the artist. When Houston's residence in the city of Houston was not occupied and he was afraid it would not get proper care, he wrote Thomas M. Bagby in his accustomed rough manner: "That fellow Kelly has lied to you out and out. There is not one word of truth in his statement. If you can't rent it . . . Let my friend Jeff Wright have it."[17]

In July, 1842, William Bollaert, a traveler in Texas, made note in his diary that he had seen Wright's portraits in the city of Houston and not heretofore mentioned: ". . . Bowles, the Cherokee chief—and an unfinished one of Gen. Houston."[18] The whereabouts of these are unknown, but it is feared that they may have been destroyed in a fire at Louisville, Kentucky, where the artist sent some of his work to be framed. These were said to represent some of his best Texas paintings.

Houston wrote to Thomas M. Bagby at Huntsville (three years after the artist's death) that he was uneasy about the location of some of his portraits: ". . . the one in green military dress and one in citizen's dress also, green."[19] He also inquired about his portrait of Deaf Smith. These portraits of Houston, if existing, have not been located and may have met the same fate as those in Louisville. With the rich dark blue-green used also in Wright's portrait of Dr. Thomas Chalkley, the artist gives an air of elegance and suggests a knowledge and an appreciation of work of a much earlier period than his own.

As time passed, Wright became well known and was considered the leading portraitist of Texas. In the year 1841 the *Telegraph and Texas Register* of Houston carried the following, perhaps slightly overstated, announcement concerning Wright's work:

We lately visited the room of Mr. Jefferson Wright in this city, and were agreeably surprised to notice the remarkable accuracy which characterizes the portraits he has finished. We have never seen the distinctive features of the human countenance delineated with more accuracy by any artist. A person after examining these portraits can readily comprehend the remark "the canvas breathes," for life itself seems infused into his figures. We have often heard of "natural bonesetters," natural poets, etc., but this is the first time we have met with a natural painter. It is worth a journey from the remotest extremity to the Republic to secure a portrait from this excellent artist.[20]

When the artist was at the height of his popularity he made the mistake of sketching some politicians, rep-resenting them as being on both sides of an issue. This cartoon (location unknown) was said to have pictured some of his compatriots in the awkward position of straddling the roof of the state capitol in an uncouth and uncomplimentary position. It was frowned upon and put the artist in the situation of having to regain friendships and his former position in the community.

In late 1842 Wright's portrait work was interrupted by a period of active military duty. The Mexican army in 1842 had entered San Antonio with the idea of an attack, but, while they were repulsed, it was feared by many sources that it would be only a matter of time until Texas would be harassed again by the Mexicans. In November, orders were sent out by Brigadier General Edwin Morehouse for the assembling of the Texas Militia, those who "can mount themselves and are willing to cross the Rio Grande." Jeff Wright, major, put aside his brush and palette and shouldered his gun. His orders, published in Houston, stated that his regiment, "the Milam Guards," would review, be inspected, drill, and parade on November 12 at Houston on the Court House grounds. The Texas army left Houston under the command of General Alexander Somervell shortly thereafter.[21] The upshot of the affair was that Somervell's army crossed the Río Grande, after capturing Laredo, and then Guerrero. It was on the concluding expedition that a segment of the army remained in Mexico, resulting in the disaster of the Mier Expedition. Wright and his regiment returned before the start of the Mier affair; he came away the wiser and unscathed, and was soon back in East Texas painting portraits.

One of the best known of Wright's portraits and one of his most skillfully executed is of his niece, Lydia Ann Smith Mason (Plate 7), who after her marriage to James Mason came to live in Huntsville, Texas. Wright was not skilled in painting hands, and in some instances he conveniently tucked them out of sight. It was customary in colonial times to charge more when hands were painted. John W. Jarvis (1780–1840) advertised, "Portraits with hands $60, portraits without hands $40. Sketches on paper with hands $15 and $20; without

---

[17] Houston, *Writings*, III, 236.

[18] William Bollaert, *William Bollaert's Texas*, edited by W. Eugene Hollon and Ruth L. Butler, entry for July 19, 1842, p. 119.

[19] Houston, *Writings*, V, 92.

[20] *Telegraph and Texas Register*, Houston, June 2, 1841.

[21] *Morning Star*, Houston, November 8, 1842; November 10, 1842.

7. Thomas Jefferson Wright: *Lydia Ann Mason*
   Oil, c. 1838, approx. 33″ x 30″ (Courtesy of Mrs. Katherine S. Stout, Fort Wayne, Indiana)

hands $10."[22] Painting hands may have been a special problem to Wright; yet the portrait of his niece Lydia Ann Mason shows the hands very carefully executed. Care was given to the smallest details of costume— jewelry, lace, and a tortoise-shell comb (probably Mexican). Wright was a timid man and painted few women other than relatives, as far as it is known. A sketchy portrait of a young woman whom he admired was carefully concealed on the reverse side of one of his self-portraits now in possession of the descendants of the Wright family.

Wright's work reflects that of an artist of considerable talent, but often betrays a lack of training. This shortcoming appears chiefly in his portraits when he uses definite edges blocked in, as in his self-portrait, in his face paintings—an indication of the artisan's method of work. Occasionally, his emphasis is chiefly on the head of his sitter, sometimes with only a slight indication of the body and an unrepresentational background.

When Jefferson Wright returned to Kentucky on a visit to his home in May of 1846, he became ill and died. It was thought that he actually contracted yellow fever before leaving Texas. In his twelve years in Texas, he contributed greatly to the Republic by painting portraits of its heroes in a simple, vigorous manner. As time passes more of his work may come to light.

George R. Allen

When George R. Allen (1830–?), a modest self-disciplined itinerant painter, completed a portrait of Henderson K. Yoakum (Plate 8), of the law firm of Yoakum and Taylor, in Huntsville, Texas, he announced in the *Texas Banner* his intentions of remaining a short time there as a portraitist. Yoakum's portrait was referred to in complimentary terms in the daily paper, but only meager biographical information was given of the artist: "We have examined with much pleasure a piece of his work executed in this place, which as a specimen of art displays talent of superior order; he was born in Connecticut, is possessed of a large share of enterprise and love of adventure, which is characteristic of all sons of New England."[23]

Allen was a typical limner of his day. Arriving in Huntsville from Washington-on-the-Brazos, he took rooms "adjoining Keenan's Hotel,"[24] advertised that he would make a short stay, and invited the ladies and gentlemen of Huntsville and Walker County to take advantage of the opportunity offered them. The editor

of the *Texas Banner*, no doubt coached by the young artist, explained the lasting qualities of an oil portrait in contrast to the daguerreotype, and then added, ". . . to say nothing of their value as parlor ornaments." As a final word in behalf of the limner, the *Texas Banner* also stated, ". . . he made his way out to the West for the purpose of following his noble profession—a profession of which he promises to become a distinguished ornament."[25]

Perhaps Allen felt at this time that the daguerreotype might replace the oil portrait, as in fact history shows us that it did replace, to a degree, the miniature. As early as the 1850's the daguerreotypist from the East with his unwieldy machine had reached Houston and some of the larger communities. In the progress of his art Allen came to the conclusion that he had better make the best of a bad bargain and use the machine to his advantage, but he was aware of the failure of the camera to replace the artist's work. It had been demonstrated to him through experience that the camera caught the features at one summarizing moment, but the portraitist work must rest on many moments of impressions which make up the artist's image. When Allen reached Richmond, Texas, in 1856, he had taken rooms in the Masonic building and advertised that he painted portraits "from life or copies from daguerreotypes."[26] Years later, after Sam Houston's death, William Huddle used the daguerreotype as an aid in his portraits, with the result of a much more lifelike portrayal than Matthew Brady's fine daguerreotype, which many thought surpassed an oil portrait.

At the time Allen was painting Yoakum's portrait, the lawyer was living in Huntsville, afterward moving to his country home in the community called "Shepherd's Valley." Here he prepared a history of Texas, published in 1856 in two volumes, from documentary material, much of which was furnished by Sam Houston. The bust portrait of Yoakum rescued a decade ago from the crumbling walls of his home in Shep-

[22] *Long Island Star*, Brooklyn, New York, August 24, 1809.

[23] *The Texas Banner*, Huntsville, October 20, 1849.

[24] *Lone Star and Southern Watchtower*, Washington, Texas, May 10, 1851.

[25] *The Texas Banner*, Huntsville, October 20, 1849; letter, Mrs. Sam Houston, Huntsville, Texas, to her husband in Washington, D. C., January 28, 1850, The University of Texas Archives, Austin.

[26] *Richmond Reporter*, Richmond, Texas, July 12, 1856.

8. George R. Allen: *Henderson Yoakum*
   Oil, 27″ x 22″ (Courtesy of Mrs. W. T. Robinson, Huntsville, Texas)

9. George R. Allen: *Temple Lea*
   Oil, c. 1849, 29″ x 24″ (Courtesy of Mrs. Ben Calhoun, Houston, Texas)

10. George R. Allen: *Mrs. Nancy Lea*
Oil, c. 1849, 33″ x 27½″ (Courtesy of Mr. and Mrs. Ben Calhoun, Houston, Texas)

herd's Valley represents the Texan in a simple yet dignified manner. There is little color except for the flesh tones; the background is without design. Written on the reverse side in large bold letters are these words: "George R. Allen, age 19, Huntsville, Texas, 1849."[27]

The artist, having limned with some success, was in a favorable position to interest members of the Houston family at nearby "Raven Hill" with his portrait work. The next portraits therefore were of Temple Lea (Plate 9) and of Mrs. Houston's mother, Mrs. Nancy Lea (Plate 10). She had taken up her residence in 1847 at "Raven Hill" while Houston was in the United States Senate. Mrs. Lea had in mind, through her daughter (a very seriously religious person), to influence or convert her son-in-law to a concept of life more in keeping with her own. Mrs. Lea had the artist paint her portrait in a pose which revealed that her religious ideas lay in strict adherence to and reverence for the sacred book. To make this conviction firm the artist shows her patiently pointing to a verse in the open Bible before her. She is shown in a dark costume with a white lace collar and is wearing a lace cap or bonnet tied under her chin. Allen has painted the portrait in solid Dutch style with severe simplicity but warmth. The earnestness and honesty of his sitter cannot be questioned.

There were evidently other portraits by Allen painted in the Houston household, for Mrs. Houston wrote concerning the portraits to her husband in Washington, D. C. (January, 1850), ". . . very few persons consider mine a good likeness," and she continues her comments, "Mother's is thought by some persons to resemble her very much, but I do not think it is a perfect likeness."[28]

After his stay in Huntsville, Allen seemed to have made Galveston the center of his travel to the various towns—traipsing the distances from Washington in 1851, Galveston in 1852 and again in late 1856, to Richmond in 1856, and to San Antonio in 1858.[29]

Ambrose Andrews

In a heterogenous society such as existed in Texas during the early settlements, we find individuals of contrasting experiences and training working side by side. Ambrose Andrews (c. 1805–?), another "gentleman of the brush," came from a sophisticated area and had had the advantage of some art training.[30] Associated with him was Jefferson Wright, who had talent and the experience of earlier pioneer life in the Kentucky hills. One congenial fact emerged concerning the two artists —both came to Texas with the idea that they might carry their talents to fruition in a land of promise.

Andrews, however, did not have the stamina required for pioneer life. After almost four years in and around Houston, he reported gloomily that he had not found the new country "a promising field for an artist of any kind."

It will be seen by a card in our advertising columns that Mr. Andrews the artist is about leaving us for the United States. A new country is certainly not a field promising great success to artists of any kind and more particularly is such a country illy qualified to induce the early immigration of those devoted to the profession of portrait painting;—We are pleased to learn that it is the intention of that gentleman to return to Texas after an absence of a few months and to bring his family for the purpose of establishing here his permanent residence.—Among his paintings will be found some of the most admirable miniature likenesses of distinguished characters in Texas; with those of General Houston and Governor Smith, none who know these gentlemen can fail to be pleased. His room will be arranged for the reception of visitors until his departure.[31]

As Andrews was expressing this idea, however, the energetic Jefferson Wright, of tougher fibre, was being fairly successful making likenesses in Houston. Andrews was the son of Elijah and Mary Ann Stone Andrus of West Stockbridge, Massachusetts. His boyhood training was at nearby Troy, New York, and later, in the fall of 1824, with the financial help of Philip Schuyler, son of the famous Revolutionary War patriot, he was able to attend the National Academy of Design in New York City.

He won this assistance, we think, by painting the young Schuyler family group in water color, 1824, an early attempt at group portraiture. This naïve painting (now in the New-York Historical Society) of the father,

[27] Evelyn M. Carrington, "Yoakum, Fiery Historian of Shepherd's Valley," *Dallas Morning News*, August 21, 1932.

[28] Letter, Mrs. Sam Houston, Huntsville, to General Houston, Washington, D. C., January 28, 1850, The University of Texas Archives, Austin.

[29] *Galveston News*, August 16, 1856; *Richmond Reporter*, July 12, 1856; *San Antonio Herald*, July, 1858 (date incomplete).

[30] George C. Groce and David H. Wallace, *New-York Historical Society's Dictionary of Artists in America, 1564–1860*, see A. Andrews, p. 10; A. Andrews, Frick Reference Library, New York City; Asbury Papers, Texas State Archives, Austin; *Telegraph and Texas Register*, Houston, October 18, 1837.

[31] *Morning Star*, Houston, April 29, 1841. *Telegraph and Texas Register*, Houston, April 29, 1837; June 11, 1838; April 28, 1841. Andrew F. Muir, "Intellectual Climate of Houston," *Southwestern Historical Quarterly*, LXII (January, 1959), 318.

mother, and five children in the parlor of their Schuyler-ville home, near Albany, was painted with a certain attentiveness and perception which Philip Schuyler thought gave promise of an artist. So it was that young Andrews had the opportunity of attending the National Academy, the best school that the East provided at that time.

When December came, the artist was out of money, and for this reason a few months later, April 8, 1825, he addressed a letter to "My Worthy Patron," explaining his penniless condition and reporting how he had spent the first months of 1825: "I therefore took advice of Mr. [William] Dunlap as to the best way of spending my time while in the country, and went to my father's where I spent the winter calmly pursuing such of my studies as could be attended to, without an assistance of an instructor."

He further explains that Colonel John Trumbull was not to return from Washington until spring and that he had borrowed from Mr. Renegale a book on anatomy and a statue of Hercules, which might help him in his drawing.

Andrews' wordy letter[32] to his patron tells of his ardor for his chosen profession and is full of long discourses, one on the importance of learning to draw:

Excellence in drawing is the foundation of excellence in every department of the arts. Drawing constitutes the basis of the art of painting and those will be most sure of success in the art who have perseverance to lay this foundation permanently in the beginning and he who by an industrious application acquires excellence in drawing lays a foundation capable of supporting any superstructure which his subsequent research may enable him to erect.

He explains how he attempted to improve his mind by reading. This portion of his letter gives us not only a knowledge of the artist's character but also an insight into the life of an art student of that era:

The great deficiency of my early education renders it doubly necessary for me to appropriate a portion of my time to the cultivation of my mind; this, I consider, and even have done since my first serious commencement in the art as an art as among the primary objects of my attention. This winter my principle reading has been Allison, on *Taste*, Stuart's *Philosophy of the Human Mind* and Greek mythology. But Spring returns with all quickening powers, and I feel its influence in an increasing ardor for the studies of my art. There are pleasures in the practice of this art of the most refined nature and which none but artists and those who love the art can know. But, to come to the point, I am in want of another

hundred and from what passed at our last interview I believe I may expect the loan of it from now on.

The next few years of Ambrose Andrews' life are rather sketchy, but as an itinerant painter he probably went from place to place in New England painting miniatures. In the fall of 1837 he took the big jump to Texas, seeking a broader field for his creativity. We know he arrived from New Haven, heading the list of arrivals in Galveston, October 18, 1837, on the New York packet, *Holycon*, D. V. Soullard, master, for with other passengers he thanked the captain for a good trip and announced that "A. Andrews and Lady would take up residence in Houston."

The following month information appeared in the Houston press informing ". . . the ladies and gentlemen of the city and vicinity that he had taken the house formerly occupied by President Houston where specimens of his paintings may be seen." At the same time Mrs. Andrews announced that she was opening a school where "the various branches of English education will be taught."[33]

An exhibition of paintings by the artist was probably the one referred to by Mary Austin Holley on December 30, 1837, when she wrote her daughter that she had accompanied President Houston to the Capitol to view the work of a portrait painter (probably paintings by Jefferson Wright), and had then gone down the hall to view the work of a portrait and miniature painter. We may assume from this information that Wright and Andrews were known to each other. In Wright's studio there was on exhibition a portrait of Sam Houston and one of Deaf Smith.[34] A miniature by Andrews of Sam Houston was made and exhibited in 1849 at the National Academy of Design in New York City.[35] In the *Morning Star*, April 29, 1841, he announced sadly that he was contemplating leaving for the United States, and that he had in his studio a miniature of General

[32] Letter, Ambrose Andrews, Great Barrington, Massachusetts, to a member of the Schuyler [Philip Schuyler] family, April 8, 1825, "My Worthy Patron" (Holograph), New-York Historical Society, New York City.

[33] *Telegraph and Texas Register*, Houston, October 18, 1837.

[34] Letter, Mary Austin Holley to Mrs. William Brand, December 30, 1837, Mary Austin Holley Papers, The University of Texas Archives, Austin, II, 99–100.

[35] Mary Bartlett Cowdrey, *National Academy of Design Exhibition Record, 1826–1860*, I, 10; letters, Mrs. Henry W. Howell, Frick Reference Library, New York City, to author, October 17, 1957; March 11, 1960.

c-3. William M. G. Samuel: *West Side Main Plaza*

Oil, 1849, 21½″ x 35¾″ (Courtesy of Bexar County [at the Witte Museum, San Antonio, Texas])

Houston and one of Governor Smith, and that "those who know the gentlemen cannot fail to be pleased."[36]

When he left Texas in April, the press had this to say about the artist's stay in Texas:

Mr. Andrews (portrait and miniature painter) being about to leave Texas for a few months, desires to express to his fellow-citizens his grateful acknowledgement for their liberal patronage since his arrival in this country. He has recently moved to apartments over Andrew's and Swains' office formerly the President's house and having collected a considerable number of pictures that he has painted during the three years residence in the city he respectfully invites the ladies and gentlemen of Houston and vicinity to call and view them before they are returned to their respective owners which will be in a few days. All persons indebted to Mr. Andrews are requested to make payment as soon as convenient to Andrews and Swain who will act as their [his] agent during his temporary absence.[37]

But Andrews, as far as we know, did not return to Texas; in fact, in June, 1841, he established a studio in New Orleans at 8 Charles Street (upstairs),[38] where he worked for two years. In June, 1844, Andrews exhibited in St. Louis, and among his pictures was a miniature of Sam Houston. In 1848 at the Pennsylvania Academy of Arts he displayed *Sunlight, Moonlight,* and *Fishing in the Lower Adirondacks.* In 1849 at the American Art Union he exhibited four landscapes of Canadian scenes. Also in 1849 at the Academy of Design, New York City, he exhibited his miniature of Sam Houston, giving his New York address, and in 1856 he exhibited his portrait of Henry Clay at the American Institute. He also exhibited in London at the Royal Academy in 1859.[39]

36 *Morning Star*, Houston, April 29, 1841.

37 *Telegraph and Texas Register*, Houston, April 8, 1841.

38 *New Orleans Daily Picayune*, June 24, 1841; August 17, 1841; August 12, 1842; November 3, 1842; December 25, 1842.

39 Mary Bartlett Cowdrey, *American Academy of Fine Arts and American Art Union Exhibition Record, 1845–1857*, I, 10, #227; Academy of Design Exhibition, New York City, 1849, miniature of Sam Houston; Groce and Wallace, *Dictionary*, p. 10; American Institute Exhibition, portrait of Henry Clay, 1856.

CHAPTER 3

IMAGE OF THE WEST

William M. G. Samuel

ONE OF THE early arrivals in San Antonio, probably in the late 1830's, was William M. G. Samuel (1815–1902), an immigrant soldier from Missouri.[1] He became a stalwart officer of the law and was accredited with having rid San Antonio of some of its worst characters. Our only claim to his attainment as an artist is that he recorded, with affection, people and scenes from the courthouse windows, with an unpretentiousness and a naïveté that only an untrained hand and a Philistine mind could produce. As far as one is able to discover, in 1849 he began painting pictures he thought appropriate decorations for the bare walls of the old Bexar County Courthouse—undertaking his task quietly and as unobserved as the pigeons cooing under the eaves of the roof. For almost a century his paintings, assuming the color of the darkened, smoky walls, hung unnoticed. Finally they were "discovered" in the 1930's.[2]

During the days of the Revolution and the Republic, every male was made to feel that if he had a skill he was under obligation to put it to use. In Samuel's case, his marksman's skill was noted by Big Foot Wallace during the Indian Wars, a skill known on the frontier as a dead shot. Samuel served in General John E. Wool's Army of Chihuahua in the Mexican War.

One of his means of livelihood on reaching San Antonio was making cement in a lime kiln. We find that during the Civil War he was at the old Spanish powder house east of the city, making inspections, timely dressed in officer's uniform with bright red sash.[3]

A man of fearless character, his skill with a gun soon put him into a saddle as justice of the peace of Medina County. In 1877–1878 Samuel served as county court commissioner, and in 1878 and 1880 he was peace officer and a notary public.[4] In 1881 and 1882 he was elected deputy sheriff and helped to put under arrest some persons who were terrorizing the town.[5]

It was back in 1849 that he signed and dated the real-

[1] *San Antonio Express*, November 8, 1902.
[2] Frederick C. Chabot, *With the Makers of San Antonio*, p. 142.
[3] *San Antonio Express*, November 8, 1902.
[4] *San Antonio Express* (Magazine Section), September 5, 1948, p. 94.
[5] *San Antonio City Directory*, 1877–1878; 1881–1882; *San Antonio Campaign News*, September 22, 1888; *San Antonio Express*, November 8, 1902.

11. William M. G. Samuel: *East Side Plaza at San Antonio*
Oil, 1849, 21½″ x 35¾″ (Courtesy of Bexar County [at the Witte Museum, San Antonio, Texas])

istic paintings of views from the windows of the court-house, facing the four cardinal points of the compass. From one window, facing west on the main plaza (Plate c-3), Samuel pictures the primitive Casas Reales, with the old residences (including what was said to be the first two-story dwelling in San Antonio) of some of the most important families of the Canary Islanders from Galicia. On the suggestion of the Marquis de Aguayo they had come to San Antonio in March of 1731, under the leadership of Juan Goras, and formed the nucleus of the villa of San Fernando de Béxar, the first regularly organized civil government in Texas.[6]

[6] Mattie Alice Austin, "The Municipal Government of San Fernando Béxar, 1730, 1800," *Quarterly of the Texas Historical Association*, VIII, No. 4 (1904–1905), 293–294, 301.

* The presence of Catlin in Texas at any time is open to question. Although he painted a number of pictures bearing Texas place names, Dr. John C. Ewers has suggested that they may have been painted in England for use in connection with a proposed colony on the upper Brazos.

Looking from the courthouse, on another side of the main plaza (Plate 11), Samuel shows the Granado-Bethencourt home, the Cabildo or Municipal Hall, and the Padron-Chaves home. In front of these homes he shows merchants and other people coming and going, intent upon business, and the familiar chickens and dogs.

During quiet periods of Samuel's long service in the local government, he made portraits of some of his associates and friends. Among those identified as Samuel's work on the walls of the courthouse were primitive paintings of Sam Houston, Big Foot Wallace, Deaf Smith, José Antonio Menchaca, and a self-portrait.

George Catlin*

George Catlin (1796–1872), the well-known artist-ethnologist particularly associated with the American Indian, contributed to organized information about the West in both his writing and art—presenting new data and new experiences. Furthermore, he was a successful portraitist of civilized man. By 1834 he had recorded in portraits many Indians west of the Mississippi. He was the first artist to attempt, through his exhibitions of drawings and paintings, an interpretation of these nations in their uncivilized state. He was now to record the wild Comanches, the least known of all tribes (Plate c-4). They had yet to make their first treaty with the United States government. Ten years later George Deas, assistant adjutant general and brother of the artist Charles Deas, described the Comanches to Lieutenant W. A. C. Whiting. The proposed army camp, he said, "should hold in check the fierce bands of the Northern Comanches, the destroyers of Bent's fort, and pest of the Western routes and the fiercest and most intractable plunderers of Mexico known."[7]

To explore Indian life and make recordings, Catlin realized that he must make great sacrifices and undergo extreme hardships, encountering death and the unknown West in as uncertain an enterprise as an astronaut who ventures into the modern unknown. We are therefore prompted to ask what inspired Catlin to make hazardous explorations among these primitive people and what preparation did he have for such an undertaking. We find this question partly answered in his fascination for the subject:

Man in the simplicity and loftiness of his nature and unfettered by the disguises of art, is surely the most beautiful model for the painter; and the country from which he hails is unquestionably the best school of the arts in the world. . . . And the history and customs of such a people preserved by illustrations, are themes worthy [of] the life time of one man, and nothing short of my life shall prevent me from visiting their country and becoming their historian. . . . I set out on my arduous and perilous undertaking with the determination of reaching, ultimately, every tribe of Indians on the Continent of North America, and bringing home faithful portraits of their principal personages and full notes of their character and history. I designed also to procure their costumes and a complete collection of their manufacturers and weapons and to perpetuate them in a "gallery unique" for the use and instruction of future ages.[8]

Perhaps sounder grounds for his interest are found in his boyhood experiences in Broome County, New York, or the incidents and Indian legends told to him by his parents about the neighborhood of Wilkes-Barre, Pennsylvania, where he was born.[9]

His deep-seated curiosity about Indians furnished a stimulus for work throughout his life. In addition, Catlin, like many young contemporaries, possessed driving energy and a strong heart. One realizes in studying his writings and paintings that he went about his work with a grave sense of importance.

While reading law in Litchfield, Connecticut, young Catlin had been painting miniatures on ivory which passed the critical eyes of fellow citizens, and he earned the approval of Anson Dickinson (1779–1852), the celebrated miniaturist of Litchfield.[10] Catlin's early success was demonstrated in a miniature of his wife, Clara, and one of his mother.

His parents, Putman and Polly Sutton Catlin, were sympathetic when he decided to leave a newly started law practice in Lucerne, Pennsylvania, to become an artist. His father in particular was a man of some culture; he was interested in the art of the past and appreciated the role of the artist in society. Recognizing his son's ability and earnestness, Putman Catlin favored the new venture.

Selling his law books, the neophyte left Litchfield for Philadelphia and soon found the company of Thomas Sully, John Neagle, Charles Wilson Peale, and Rembrandt Peale.[11] In 1824 Catlin completed the much admired, well-executed self-portrait. In the same year he was selected a member of the Pennsylvania Academy of Arts.

The time generally given for his portrait from life of Stephen F. Austin is between 1832–1835. Austin traveled in and out of St. Louis and New Orleans on diplomatic and personal matters, and it was probably on one of these occasions that he met the artist and sat for his portrait (Plate 12). On the reverse side of the canvas is written "Steph Austin/G Catlin Pinx." This portrait shows a professional skill and is one of the few remaining life portraits of the famous colonizer.[12] Catlin's work in portraiture of civilized man was never of his choosing. He painted many of these portraits chiefly through neces-

[7] Letter, George Deas, San Antonio, to W. A. C. Whiting and Governor Hansborough Bell, January 14, 1850, Governor's Letters, Texas State Archives, Austin.

[8] George Catlin, *Letters and Notes on the Manners, Customs, and Condition of the North American Indian*, I, 2–3.

[9] Harold McCracken, *George Catlin and the Old Frontier*, p. 22.

[10] George C. Groce and David H. Wallace, *New-York Historical Society's Dictionary of Artists in America, 1564–1860*, see Anson Dickinson, p. 179.

[11] John C. Ewers, *George Catlin, Painter of Indians and the West*, Smithsonian Report No. 4251 (1955), p. 484.

[12] Interview, Mrs. Raymond Cook, Houston, information on portrait inscribed "Steph Austin/G Catlin Pinx."

12. George Catlin: *Stephen F. Austin*
Oil, c. 1832–1835 (Courtesy of Mrs. Raymond Cook, Houston, Texas)

sity—to earn enough money to continue his travels. Later in his career he wrote from Paris to a friend that he had seventy water-color portraits of distinguished Indians—". . . every one painted from life, fully colored, with trinkets, weapons, costumes, etc., complete . . ."— that he had incurred a small bill at his hotel and "some other trifling items that must be paid." In 1860, when he was in South America gathering topaz and amethyst, he asked Sir Thomas Phillips for help. He had painted a portrait of Baron Alexander von Humboldt, he needed money (words flowed from his pen), the occasion demanded a gift, and he would part with the portrait only to Sir Thomas Phillips![13]

Starting back in 1826, when he successfully made a portrait of Red Jacket, the Seneca chief, and other portraits in Western New York, he continually had in mind his plan for recording the aboriginal Indians and their activities before they had vanished. When Indians came into the Eastern cities to make treaties, "in silent and stoic dignity," he would see them as they strutted about the city dressed in all their Indian finery and would resolve anew each time to go into the land of the wild tribes to record their activities.

In 1828 twelve paintings were exhibited by the American Academy of Art, including *Red Jacket*, a full-length figure of Governor DeWitt Clinton, and one of Secretary of the Treasury Oliver Wolcott (c. 1825). Much later in his career he went to South Carolina to paint the portrait of Osceola, completing it in his studio in New York. This is one of Catlin's most admired portraits of Indians.

It was while in Albany that he met and married Clara Bartlett Gregory.[14] Soon after their marriage they spent a short time in Richmond, Virginia, "restoring my lost energy," he wrote, and completing a commission to paint in water color a group picture of the entire Constitutional Convention of Virginia (1829–1830). This picture included the 115 members which Catlin did individually in miniature.[15] While Catlin and his wife were in Richmond, Dolly Madison came to see Clara Catlin, then ill, and Catlin painted a miniature of the First Lady. As Loyd Haberly, Catlin's biographer, put it, ". . . he painted the great Lady in miniature—lovably, lively and droll in her quaint turban."[16]

As soon as he recovered his strength from a siege of weariness, Catlin put his wife in safe hands and set out for St. Louis—this time determined to realize his chosen work. At St. Louis, while he was painting the portraits

of General William Clark (of the Lewis and Clark Expedition) and General Winfield Scott, the first real opportunity came to reach his objective. General Clark recognized his ability and the advantage of having an artist go into the field with him with pencil and brush. A friendship developed, and as a result Catlin accompanied General Clark to the tribes of the Iowas, Sioux, Omahas, and Fox. As he sketched and painted, he took copious notes. In 1832 another opportunity came to visit the wild tribes as a guest of the American Fur Company. His adventures took him eventually into the valleys of the Missouri, the Kansas, and the Platte Rivers, to a large area east of the Rockies, and to the Indian country of the Great Lakes, giving him opportunity to make a large number of paintings.[17]

In 1833 he exhibited in Pittsburgh, Pennsylvania, his interpretation of the life of the Indian—uncertain as to the reception his work would receive in the more sophisticated centers. After a visit to the Southern Plains, however, he exhibited in New York, Pittsburgh, Cincinnati, Philadelphia, and Boston. His Indian exhibitions no doubt stimulated interest among American artists in the picturesque West. Having had success in this country, Catlin packed up his pictures in the fall of 1839 and took them to Paris and London, where he exhibited with great success—the English especially enjoyed the primitive and exotic. There he wrote and published his classic two-volume work (1841), *Letters and Notes on the Manners, Customs, and Condition of the North American Indian.*[18]

But before the event of his foreign stay he made a trip to the Comanche country. In 1834 the United States government ordered an expedition of mounted dragoons, stationed at Fort Gibson on the Arkansas River (near the present city of Tulsa, Oklahoma), to establish better relations between the Comanches and Pawnee Picts and the few settlers in the area between Fort Gibson and the Rockies. Catlin asked to accompany the dragoons, and received permission from Secretary of War Louis Cass. The regiment was led by General Henry Leavenworth

[13] Letter, George Catlin, Paris, France, to Sir Thomas Phillips, Original Letters, 1840–1860, Thomas Gilcrease Institution of American History and Art, Tulsa, Oklahoma.
[14] McCracken, *George Catlin*, p. 26.
[15] *Ibid.*, p. 27.
[16] Loyd Haberly, *Pursuit of the Horizon: A Life of George Catlin, Painter and Recorder of the American Indian*, p. 34.
[17] Ewers, *George Catlin*, pp. 485, 490–491.
[18] Catlin, *Letters and Notes*, II, 37.

and Colonel Henry Dodge. Delighted at the opportunity to visit and sketch the Indians in this section of the Southern Plains,[19] Catlin again expressed his earnest desire to record the Indian in his primitive state:

You will agree with me that I am going farther to get sitters than any of my fellow artists ever did but I take an incredible pleasure in roaming through Nature's trackless wilds and selecting my models where I am free and unshackled by the killing restraints of society . . . though the toil and expense of travelling to these remote parts of the world to get subjects for my pencil, place almost unsurmountable and sometimes painful obstacles before me, yet I am encouraged by the continual conviction that I am practicing in the true school of Art and though I should get as poor as Lazarus, I should deem myself rich in models and studies for the future occupation of my life.[20]

During preparations at Fort Gibson, Catlin met an old acquaintance, the gay, fiddle-playing Joe Chadwick, who was to accompany the expedition. Joe was to prove a great aid to Catlin in his sketching, and helped nurse the artist when fever struck. In the meantime, Catlin enthusiastically obtained supplies and a good cream-colored Texas mustang. The mounts for each company had been selected entirely of one color: one company of bays, one of blacks, one of whites, one of sorrels, and one cream-colored—forming a mile-long train.

On June 19, 1834, the regiment was about to leave Fort Gibson. In a letter to his father-in-law, Catlin explained that he had no time to write at length "for already the hills are echoing back the notes of the spirit-stirring trumpets."[21]

After traveling two hundred miles with the "noble dragoons," they arrived at the Red River near the mouth of the False Wichita. This was probably the most satisfying and beautiful time of the year to visit the area:

I am already in the land of the buffalo and the fleet-bounding antelopes. We are at this place on the Red River having Texas under our eyes on the opposite bank . . . and the country about us is a panorama too beautiful to be painted with a pen; it is like most of the country in these regions composed of prairie and timber alternating in the most beautiful shape and proportions that the eye of the connoisseur could desire, and the plains about us literally speckled with buffalo.[22]

Colonel Dodge ordered the dragoons to move forward, although sickness (which finally overtook the artist himself) had befallen many of his men. Catlin entered a

part of the country almost uninhabited by white man. The objective was the Comanche and Pawnee Pict country, and Catlin expected that while peace talks were going on between Colonel Dodge and the chiefs an opportunity he had long anticipated would arise for him to paint. This opportunity did come and his notes supply on-the-spot information about the countryside, wild life, buffalo hunting, and lassoing of wild horses. His pencil sketches of the Comanches, their spectacular horsemanship, and their villages, and of the dragoons meeting with the Comanche war party all make a significant contribution to the early history of this area.

As they proceeded on their mission of making peace with the Comanche, there was concern about contacts of the dragoons and the Indians. It was a serious matter with the dragoons, for their number had been greatly reduced by sickness.

After peace talks with the Comanches, Colonel Dodge moved further west to the leaders of the Pawnee Picts (later known as the Wichitas), a tribe friendly to the Comanches. These Indians had built a village on the North Fork of the Red River. Catlin was forced to remain at the Comanche village because fever had overtaken him. He instructed his companion Joe Chadwick to make notes and sketches of the Pawnee Picts. On assigning Chadwick the task of making notes and sketches, Catlin remarked that Chadwick was "a gentleman of fine tastes." It was these sketches that Joe was able to make at the Pawnee Pict village that were later put on canvas by Catlin.

Joe wrote October 23, 1834, from New Orleans:

. . . my last was dated at Fort Gibson giving you a sketch of our summer campaign. I remained at Ft. Gibson until the 18th of September. From the time of our arrival until the Dragoons separated—you can hardly conceive how the poor soldiers suffered from sickness—the change of diet—the intense heat—the thermometer standing from 110 to 118 degrees in the shade.[23]

[19] Ewers, *George Catlin*, p. 488.
[20] Catlin, *Letters and Notes*, II, 37.
[21] *Ibid.*, II, 38, 52–61; Thomas Donaldson, *The George Catlin Indian Gallery in the U.S. National Museum, the Smithsonian Institution*, p. 479.
[22] Catlin, *Letters and Notes*, II, 45.
[23] Letters of Alfred, Joseph, and Edward Chadwick to members of the family, Nos. 35, 36, and 38, collection of Austin D. Kilham, Charlottesville, Virginia; letters, Austin D. Kilham to author, giving information from Mrs. Frank E. Adams, Springfield, Missouri,

Edward Chadwick wrote from Exeter, March 3, 1833, that Joe was going out on "that expedition"; and on September 31, 1834, he wrote that he wished he were with him, a sentiment he expressed often. Joe's letters to his family also mentioned Catlin's having asked him to make sketches for him.

After nearly two years Joe Chadwick returned to St. Louis, where he met with Catlin and they reviewed their experiences of "the numerous rambles in their former campaigns." Catlin had Joe to sit for his portrait (Plate 13), while he "related two incidents which had happened to him," which pleased Joe exceedingly. Catlin wrote later in his *Notes* (1841) "I rejoiced to find that I had given to it [the portrait] all the fire and all the game look that had become so familiar and pleasing to me in our numerous rambles in the far distant wilds of our former campaigns." Catlin added in a note: "Poor Chadwick! a few days after the above occasion he sent his portrait to his mother, and started for Texas, where he joined the Texas army with a commission from General Houston, was taken prisoner in the first battle he fought and was among the four hundred prisoners who were shot down in cold blood by the order of Santa Anna."[24]

Joe Chadwick's study at West Point had included engineering, and a span of time as a draftsman in the Surveyor General's office (Salary: $500 per annum), where he was "busy engaged in drawing." When he reached Texas in 1835 he was put to work immediately in restoring part of the old La Bahía presidio and making a working drawing of the whole plan. Chadwick's drawing of the presidio has been the basis for its restoration in the past few years. He had joined the Georgia volunteers under Colonel James Fannin, becoming his adjutant, and was with Fannin at the capture of Goliad.

June 29, 1966, August 11, 1966; Lois Burkhalter, "My Real Friend Joe," *American Heritage*, XVI, No. 3 (April, 1965), 44–45. Chadwick also stated that Lieutenant Eastman was at Fort Gibson and that he, Eastman, had at one time attempted suicide. (If this reference is to Seth Eastman it has not been stated elsewhere in the knowledge of the author.)

[24] Catlin, *Letters and Notes*, II, 155; Ewers, *George Catlin*, p. 509.

[25] George Catlin, Drawings [originals in ink] of Indian Portraits, Nos. 138, 144, 146, Ayer Collection, Chicago Historical Society, Chicago, Illinois; *Catlin's North American Indian Portfolio: Hunting Scenes and Amusements, Rocky Mountains and Prairies of America from Drawings and Notes of the Author George Catlin*, pp. 1–32.

[26] Catlin, *Letters and Notes*, p. 156.

Catlin's fine crayon portrait of Joe has been preserved with many of Chadwick's amusing letters written while at West Point. It reflects Catlin's tenderness and the admiration he had for his friend.

Some of Catlin's scenes, showing the excitement he felt and the pressure of time in getting the action he desired in his sketches, give us typical examples of his field work in their rendering by his characteristic quick brush stroke. On the other hand some of his delicately painted scenes on the plains—Indians in action, and the elks and buffalo (Plate 14)—are delightful in a sense of semi-expressionism, and in their delicacy appear similar to a Japanese print. These in oil were done perhaps in the quiet of his studio with a steadier hand.

Catlin at one period of his life made a large number of portraits of individual Indians with pen and ink. Among these the artist designated as Texas Indians are Shee-de-a (Wild Sage), a Pawnee Pict maid; Ha-nee (the Beaver), a Comanche whom Catlin described as "one of the most terrible warriors on the American Continent, seated on the ground with implements of war, a handsome pipe, and a tobacco pouch"; and a Pawnee Pict, Wee-Tar-ro-Shar-no, whom Catlin described as a Texas Indian, "an aged and venerable head chief of the tribe with a beautiful pipe in his hand and the battles of his life painted on his robe [belonging to] one of the smaller tribes living in one of the villages on the Red River near the eastern base of the Rocky Mountains, latitude 32°."[25]

His ethnological philosophy appears frequently, expressed in romantic terms. He wrote:

I sat down and wrote in my note book: "The West, not the Far West" for that is a phantom traveling on its tireless wing; but the West, the simple West—the vast and vacant Wilds which lie between the trodden haunts of present savage and civil life—The great and almost boundless garden-spot of earth! This is the theme at present. The "antres vast and deserts idle" where the tomahawk sleeps with the bones of the savage, as yet untouched by the trespassing plowshare—The pictured land of silence, which in its melancholy alternating echoes backward and forward the plaintive yells of vanished red men, and the busy chaunts of the approaching pioneers.[26]

In 1872 the Smithsonian Institution, Washington, D. C., received several hundred pieces of Catlin's work, comprising three fourths of this entire collection. Mr. Joseph Henry, secretary of the Smithsonian Institution,

c-4. George Catlin: *A Comanche War Party on the March Fully Equipped for War. Texas*
Oil, 1834, 19½″ x 27⅝″ (Courtesy of the Smithsonian Institution, Washington, D. C.)

13. George Catlin: *Joseph Chadwick*
Crayon, 1836–1837, 11″ x 8″ (Courtesy of Mrs. Frank E. Adams, Springfield, Missouri)

14. George Catlin: *Elks and Buffalo Making Acquaintance on the Texas Prairie on the Brazos* Oil, 1834, 19½″ x 27⅝″ (Courtesy of the Smithsonian Institution, Washington, D. C.)

summed up Catlin's work shortly after the artist's death when he wrote on December 13, 1873: "They [his paintings] will grow in importance with advancing years and when the race [of] which they are the representation shall have entirely disappeared, their value will be inestimable."[27]

William Tylee Ranney

Artist William Tylee Ranney (1813–1857) spent enough time soldiering in Texas in the 1830's that many of his genre paintings are flavored with the rough life of the Texas frontier. Surprisingly, he avoids any actual war scenes, but instead, recognizing human uniqueness, he portrays the activities peculiar to the pioneers.

When the call was made in the Eastern states in early 1836 for volunteers to help free Texas from the grasp of Mexico, Ranney, a Connecticut youth, left his New York art studies for New Orleans, where he enlisted with Captain Hubbel. The massacre of the Texans at the Alamo had just occurred, but he arrived in time to join, on March 12, Captain C. A. W. Fowler's outfit and to fight in the battle of San Jacinto (not in the Mexican War as has been reported). On completion of his service, partly in Columbia, Texas, he received, as an unmarried man, a bounty warrant of 320 acres in the central-eastern part of the state.[28] During this period in Texas he recorded in pencil sketches the hunter, trapper, and horseman—all adventurous and picturesque Southwestern types.

The artist's father, Captain William Ranney, of Scotch-Irish descent, was master of many famous clipper ships; his mother was the former Clarissa Gaylord. Although both parents were from Middletown, Connecticut, a coast town, apparently no attempt was made to influence the son toward a seafaring life.

When the boy was only thirteen he lost his father at sea. Young Ranney had been apprenticed to an uncle, William Nott, proprietor of a tin shop in Fayette, North Carolina. During his seven years in the artisan's shop the youth made sketches. A self-portrait at the age of eighteen (c. 1831) showed talent. Ranney also absorbed the idea of studying drawing in New York—a wish that was fulfilled in his entering the Institute of Mechanical Arts in Brooklyn. However it was here that he interrupted his studies for the Texas adventure.

After returning to his studies at the Institute in 1838, Ranney exhibited a portrait of "Mr. Thompson," at the National Academy. In the same year *A Courting Scene* was shown at the Mechanics Institute Fair, New York City, enabling him to win his diploma.[29] This painting (location unknown) was his first genre subject—the form in which he realized his most successful expression.

Information on the activities of Ranney between the years 1839 and 1843 is limited. We know, however, that he was in New York, and that in 1843 he advertised as a portraitist, feeling perhaps that this was the more lucrative way to paint.[30] In 1848 he married Margaret O'Sullivan of Cork, Ireland. Among the portraits he painted during this period, and that are today available to measure his success, are one of his mother, Clarissa Ranney, two of his wife, Margaret Ranney, one of his son, a second self-portrait, and one of an artist friend, Edwin White (1817–1877), who was a genre, historical, and portrait painter.[31]

About this time there was a growing interest in America in genre painting, and Ranney was soon exhibiting scenes of hunting and fishing around New York. In 1846 he exhibited, at the American Union, *Marine View, Coast Scene with Figures*, and *Shad Fishing on the Hudson*. In 1847 he completed and exhibited several historic-genre canvases, *First News of the Battle of Lexington, Veterans of 1776 Returning from War*, and *Washington's Mission to the Indians*. In 1850 he was elected a member of the National Academy of Design and afterwards exhibited there regularly.[32]

But a new phase of genre painting showing the Western scene was gaining the attention of the American public. In this theme the work of Charles Deas, Seth Eastman, and Alfred Jacob Miller, among others, apparently was finding ready purchasers. The movement was enhanced by the success of William Sidney Mount (1807–1868) in carefully executed genre pictures of

27 McCracken, *George Catlin*, p. 16.

28 Bounty Warrants, Nos. 425, 237, 1535, Military Service Records, Book I, p. 104; Land Office Muster Rolls, p. 85 (1836), General Land Office, Austin, Texas.

29 Francis S. Gruber, *William T. Ranney, Painter of the Early West*, pp. 5, 7, 25; Dumas Malone (ed.), *Dictionary of American Biography*, XV, 377–378.

30 Business Card, "Portrait Painter, No. 30 University, New York," owned by nephew, Claude J. M. Ranney, Malvern, Pennsylvania.

31 Letters, Claude J. Ranney, Malvern, Pennsylvania to author, April 21, 1960, September 22, 1960, July 29, 1961.

32 Mary Bartlett Cowdrey, *American Art Union Transactions, 1844–1849*, p. 31; *American Academy of Fine Arts and American Art Union Exhibition Record, 1845–1857*, see "Ranney."

15. William Tylee Ranney: *Preliminary Sketch for* Hunting Wild Horses
Black crayon heightened with white, c. 1836–1838, 6⅞″ x 10″ (Courtesy of The Corcoran
Gallery of Art, Washington, D. C. [collection of Mr. Claude J. Ranney])

incidents in daily life. Ranney's brush was led to improvise on sketches from his adventures in the Southwest. Having known the frontier, he had only to relive his experiences in imagination to produce realistic paintings. Studies of frontier characters he had known and scenes of his short, romantic life on the plains revealed the direction of his best achievement.

Some of the New York City artists were discovering that Hoboken, New Jersey, was a suitable place to paint. It was close enough to Manhattan for practical purposes; yet it was away from the freneticism and distraction of the city. Robert Weir (1803–1889), professor of art at West Point, William Mason Brown (1828–1898), Charles Loring Elliott (1812–1868), and others were finding desirable isolation in New Jersey. Ranney, an outdoor man by nature and having had a taste of the wide-open spaces in Texas, moved to the thinly populated section of West Hoboken. He fenced the spacious grounds of his home so that he might own horses and other animals, thus having an opportunity once more of

observing animals in motion. He built a large home that included a studio two stories high, and for the first time since leaving Texas he was able to install his many relics of that region. Henry T. Tuckerman, the early art historian, visited Ranney's studio, and gives in his *Book of Artists* (1867) a description of the interior:

. . . so constructed as to receive animals, guns, pistols, and cutlasses hung on the walls, and these with curious saddles and primitive riding gear might lead a visitor to imagine he had entered a pioneer's cabin or border chieftain's hut. Such an idea would, however, have been at once dispelled by a glance at many sketches and studies which proclaimed that an artist and not a bushranger had found a home.[33]

Many of these same pen-and-ink, pencil, and crayon drawings of animals, of trapping, of lassoing wild horses, and of views of the emigrant trains have recently been exhibited with the large genre paintings. They have

[33] Henry T. Tuckerman, *Book of Artists: American Artist's Life*, pp. 431, 432.

16. William Tylee Ranney: *Hunting Wild Horses*
   Oil, 1846, 36″ x 54½″ (Courtesy of M. Knoedler & Co., New York City)

greater charm in many cases than the larger paintings, for they have a likeliness and an intimacy to the rough-and-tumble life that makes them appealing. Several dozen small humorous pencil sketches tell of incidents during his soldier-life experience. The spontaneity and the haste of the artist to capture action make these drawings more interesting to us than the larger oils done under the pressure of making a finished painting. Often the latter appear merely picturesque, lacking sometimes complete modeling. On the other hand, smaller preliminary sketches, many originating in Texas, show

such bits of action, as the wild horse with its flying mane and tail in a study preceding *Hunting Wild Horses* (Plates 15 and 16), or the tautness and restrained, tense energy shown in the study of the hunter in *On the Wing*.[34]

No other artist of the Western scene, even Alfred Jacob Miller or Catlin—Ranney's better-known contemporaries—was able to depict the wild horse with such

34 William T. Ranney, Collection of Original Sketches (approx. 50), Corcoran Art Gallery, Washington, D. C. (1961).

17. William Tylee Ranney: *The Lasso*
Oil, 1846, 31" x 42" (Courtesy of Mr. Claude J. Ranney, Malvern, Pennsylvania)

accuracy and beauty. Catlin's description of the wild horse has been quoted many times by authors, and Ranney has painted them with the same appreciation. In *The Retreat* and other pictures, the artist has used a background of the prairie, an unbroken vista giving a sense of vastness and loneliness. Ranney has placed his initials as a brand on one of the horses.

Ranney's paintings from 1846 to 1849, signed and dated and exhibited in New York, show an absorption with the Western scene. These large oils suggest in their titles what he actually encountered: *The Trapper's Last Shot, Stampede* (1848), *Scouting Party* (1851, two copies), *Advice on the Prairie* (1853, 2 copies), and *Encampment of Covered Wagons*. Others which have the flavor of the pioneer country are *Mexican War Drummer* and a *Study of Oak Trees*. In *The Trapper's Last Shot* and *The Lasso* (Plate 17) the rider's identity has been suggested by an authority, Frances F. Victor, in her *River of the West*, as Joe Meek, a six footer, big, sturdy, and wearing a black beard and sideburns. If not the man himself, it is the apotheosis of the fast-riding, tough, lighthearted Joe Meek.[35]

By the 1850's Ranney's paintings had grown to a large collection, many of which had been exhibited at the National Academy. In 1853 he became ill, and from that time to the end of his life in 1857 he produced little. His many friends, and he had many for he was particularly popular among the artists, realized at the time of his death that, after a long illness, he was leaving his wife and sons in dire circumstances. They made up an exhibition of his work, some hundred examples from his studio and various galleries, with almost as many works painted and donated by other contemporary artists. A special sale that was held at the National Academy of Design on December 20 and 21 of the year

following his death realized over $7,000 for his family. An inventory of Ranney's work (108 separate pieces) at this sale makes it possible to estimate to some degree the range and extent of his genre and portrait paintings.[36]

Ranney seemed not to have any interest in the Indian, or in landscape in particular, but in the local, chance events of life in the Southwest. In recent years Ranney has taken a place of equal importance with such artists as William Sidney Mount, George Caleb Bingham, and Albert Bierstadt.

John James Audubon

"But different travelers have different eyes" commented the artist and ornithologist John James Audubon (1785–1851), as he made an appraisal of George Catlin's work on the upper Missouri River.[37] While Catlin's eager eyes were seeing and recording the Indian in his natural habitat, Audubon, with the same priceless, eager enthusiasm, was seeing and recording the birds of America. A trip to Texas was part of what he termed his "third American Tour," when he experienced life on the frontier and saw a great deal of bird life that was to help him in his writings and enable him to make some of his remarkable drawings. He was aware that he was entering a bird kingdom—the whirling flocks with the varied strains of their songs in the tree tops gave him inspiration. He stated that his trip to Texas was short but rewarding.[38] "In the course of my last journey in search of information respecting the birds which at one season or other are found within the limits of the United States, I observed so vast a number of them in Texas that probably more than two-thirds of our species occur here in Texas."[39]

Audubon's great interest in birds began when he used to wander as a boy through the open spaces in Nantes, France, and it probably was later under the tutorage of the noted artist Jacques Louis David (1748–1825) that Audubon's remarkable aptitude in drawing and his ambition to make a study of birds was molded. When he came to America, Dunlap states, Audubon studied with Sully in the spring of 1824.[40] Audubon's disputed place of birth (which researchers now agree was San Domingo in 1785), his adventures as a youth after his father brought him to America (1803), and the attempt to make a merchant of him—all these facts have been treated vividly and precisely by his recent excellent biographers. They have told of his failures in business in Ohio and Kentucky, his hardships and privations during his explorations up and down the Ohio Valley and

[35] Francis Fuller Victor, *River of the West*, pp. 41–56, 229; Stanley Vestal, *Joe Meek, the Merry Mountain Man*, pp. 5, 173, 219.

[36] *New York Times*, November 21, 1857; Gruber, *William T. Ranney*, p. 11.

[37] John James Audubon, *Audubon and His Journals*, edited by Maria R. Audubon, II, 10.

[38] Francis Hobart Herrick, *Audubon, the Naturalist: A History of His Life and Time*, II, 166; Samuel W. Geiser, "Audubon's Visit to Texas," *Southwest Review*, XVI (Autumn, 1930), 108–121.

[39] John James Audubon, *The Birds of America from Drawings Made in the United States and Territories*, p. 25.

[40] Audubon, *Audubon and His Journals*, I, 105; William Dunlap, *History of the Rise and Progress of the Arts of Design in the United States*, edited by Frank W. Bagley and Charles Goodspeed, III, 205; John James Audubon, *Bird Biographies*, edited by Alice Ford, p. 46.

the lower Mississippi, his marriage to Lucy Bakewell (1808), and the long separation from his wife and boys. All this has been brought to the attention of readers, but the importance of his trip to Texas has had little notice.

Earlier, in 1826, Audubon thought he had collected enough material to consider publication of his work, but his idea now included other areas, requiring additional travels. He planned to traverse "the swamps of Florida, the wilds of Missouri, and the Rocky mountains and on to the Pacific." In 1836 he wrote his friend Edward Harris of New Jersey, whom he referred to as "a gentleman farmer, quiet, prosperous and sedate," that he was eager to have him make a trip South with him:

You well know how anxious I am to make my works on the birds of this country as compleat [sic] as possible within my power; you know that to reach this end I have spared neither time, labours or money. You are also aware that although this undertaking may never remunerate me, I am so enthusiastic as to indulge in the hope that God will grant me life to effect all this; but I am becoming old and though very willing, doubt whether I could support the fatigue connected with a journey of several years, and separated from my dear family.[41]

Audubon planned to go first to Florida, but the Reverend John Bachman—renowned scientist of Charleston, South Carolina, and a lifelong friend—wrote that it was most unwise to go there at that time, as the Indians were on the war path; he explained that they would "make no bones of scalping an ornithologist 'secundum mortem'." Dr. Bachman recommended a different area: "Of Texas I think better, and thither or along its borders, you may I think venture—for the Texans are our friends. I suppose the Gen'l [General John Coffee Hays] will keep the Comanches quiet."[42]

Audubon, perhaps a bit discouraged, postponed his journey South. Besides he needed money to finance such a trip. Accompanied by his son John Woodhouse Audubon (1812–1862), then fifteen, the artist sojourned a few weeks in New York, Boston, and Philadelphia. When they turned homeward, Audubon had gained considerable information on the birds of that region and had obtained some fine specimens. He also had added some thirty subscribers to the list for his publication on birds, and he had letters of introduction from Daniel Webster and Washington Irving in his pocket.[43]

When father and son reached Washington, they were entertained by President Andrew Jackson. Just at this time, 1837, Texas was in the critical period following the revolution, and Audubon cryptically notes that he found the President "very adverse to the cause of Texas."[44] He laid before the President his plan to go South and his need of a United States cutter. Jackson gave his consent conditionally, explaining that the use of a ship for the excursion was hard to obtain, since the Indians were giving trouble in Florida and the ships were in use there. After a short time, however, the Honorable Levi Woodbury, secretary of the treasury, was able to arrange for the use of a cutter. In the meantime, Audubon had decided (spring of 1837) to venture the visit to Florida and Texas. With son John and Edward Harris, his assistant, he chose the overland route to Charleston, then proceeded to Pensacola. When they arrived in Pensacola they learned that the schooner *Campbell* awaited them at New Orleans. This was good news. The *Campbell* was a vessel of fifty tons, "four grunters" on her deck, provisioned for two months, with a crew of twenty-one, and accompanied by a small black cutter, the *Crusader*. The party left New Orleans for Galveston, exploring the coast line en route. They arrived, according to Audubon's notes, April 24. On the morning of the twenty-fifth they were greeted officially by the secretary of the Texas Navy, C. Rhodes Fisher. Audubon's arrival in Texas was announced in the *Telegraph and Texas Register*, Houston, May 2:

The U.S. Revenue Cutter [*Campbell*], Capt. Turner, arrived at Galveston on the Twenty-fifth [April] bearing the Celebrated ornithologist Audubon and son; Mr. Harris accompanies this gentleman and is associated with him in his scientific researches. Audubon is one of the few Americans whose fame has extended throughout the civilized world and whose services commanded a national tribute of respect from the United States.[45]

A short while after the arrival, the *Campbell* was crippled, and instead of going immediately up the Trinity, the party was forced to remain on Galveston Island for about three weeks. This delay gave Audubon an op-

[41] Herrick, *Audubon*, II, 147–148.

[42] *Ibid.*, II, 148; Walter Prescott Webb (ed.), *The Handbook of Texas*, see John Coffee Hays, I, 789.

[43] Herrick, *Audubon*, II, 152–153.

[44] *Ibid.*, II, 156, 165.

[45] *Telegraph and Texas Register*, Houston, May 2, 1837; Geiser, "Audubon's Visit to Texas in 1837"; Herrick, *Audubon*, II, 165; original drawings by John James Audubon, New York Historical Society, New York City.

18. John James Audubon: *Least Tern*
    Water color, hand lettered and signed, 1837, 21¼″ x 15″ (Courtesy of the New-York
    Historical Society, New York City)

Spotted Sandpiper

1. Male 2. Female

Drawn from Nature by J.J. Audubon, F.R.S. F.L.S.   Lith & Printed & Col & by J.T. Bowen, Phila.

19. John James Audubon: *Spotted Sandpiper, Buffalo Bayou, Texas*
Engraving and water color, 1837, 7¼" x 8½" (Courtesy of the Library of Congress, Washington, D. C.)

portunity to record at leisure the wild life on the Island —a veritable paradise for birds: wild turkeys, ibises, and many species of ducks. On May 5 he wrote: "Hunted birds over the interior of Galveston today, there were marsh hawk, skimmers and the spotted sandpiper or tatler, already well grown." A bit later he noted: "We reached a comfortable house where we spent the night after previously examining several miles of country around."[46] This place, we learn from his notes, was the home of Squire Isaac Batterson from Connecticut, justice of the peace of Harris County. The plantation was located at Clinton, on Buffalo Bayou.

At this time Audubon made a significant note, ". . . today I found the Ivory Billed Woodpecker (which is described by one naturalist as formerly from Texas, Illinois, and Indiana) in abundance and secured specimens."[47] Audubon explained on one occasion how he managed to draw, make notes, and secure specimens on the spot: he carried his drawing board strapped about his waist, notebooks in his pocket, and a gun on his shoulder. Thus equipped, he was able to move about freely and accom-

[46] John James Audubon, *Ornithological Biography*, pp. xii–xix.
[47] John James Audubon, *Birds of America*, III. No. 66.

46

plish his work on foot. He shot the bird if he needed a specimen and, placing it on the board, made a drawing at once. Later details were taken from the stuffed specimen.

While at Galveston he made note of the Bartramian sandpiper and the least tern (Plate 18), referred to by Audubon as the "lesser tern":

The Bartramian Sandpiper is the most truly terrestrial of its tribe with which I am acquainted. It is even more inclined to keep away from water than the killdeer plover. . . . The dry upland plains of those sections of Louisiana called Appellousas and Attacapas are amply peopled with this species in early Spring as well as in Autumn. They arrive from the vast prairies of Texas and Mexico where they spend the winter; in the beginning of March or about the period of the first appearance of the Martins (Herundo Purpurea) and return about the first of August. . . . I found it very abundant along the finely wooded margins of that singular stream Buffalo Bayou in Texas where we procured several specimens.

. . . hundreds of pairs of [least] tern were breeding on the islands of Galveston Bay. Also on one of the islands I found eight or ten nests belonging to herons of different species. . . . The common tern is strangely rare just now; only a few were arriving from the West. The Gadwell duck is quite abundant on all the island ponds and inlets of the islands and shores of Galveston Bay.[48]

The artist spoke of the abundance of the roseate spoonbill, ". . . more so, along the Galveston Bay." While here he found eight or ten nests of them and obtained specimens. The telltale godwit was found in considerable numbers along with the yellow-shank snipe. He stopped to make a sketch of the spotted sandpiper (Plate 19). These delicately drawn birds are shown against their natural habitat of the head waters of Buffalo Bayou.[49]

The journey on Buffalo Bayou was interrupted by several delays, which gave Aubudon an opportunity to observe and sketch. Reaching Red Fish Bar at the mouth of the Trinity, the party was detained by the grounding of their boat. It was just at the time of the year when the migration of birds was in full swing. Audubon wrote that the trip had been unusually fruitful although he found no new species. "But," he continued, "the mass of observations that we have gathered connected with the ornithology of our country has, I think, never been surpassed. . . . I feel myself tolerably competent to give an essay on the geographic distribution of the feathered tribes . . . with naught but facts and notes on the spot and at the fitting time."[50]

A week later (about May 15) the party reached Houston. Scarcely had the ink dried on the official papers establishing the independence of Texas. It was the day after the first celebration of the victory at San Jacinto, and Audubon was to have an interview with General Houston, whom he found dressed in his velvet ball suit of the night before. Audubon's comments characterize the General and add interesting footnotes to the history of the struggling years of the young Republic. Indeed, the reader may conclude that this visit was a part of the artist's observation of wild life, figuratively and literally. A victory pole bearing a silk flag with a single star was standing, though a bit awry. A melee of participants still remained—a large number of drunken Indians and dejected looking Mexican prisoners. After listening to a speech by General Houston and signing a peace treaty, the Indians (part of the Comanche tribe) turned to celebrating with a great deal of noise—a part of the day's council meeting. The numerous stumps of newly-cut trees and the boggy streets added to the general feeling of wild disorder.[51]

The artist recorded his impression of the scene; he spoke of General Houston's "block house" as "consisting of two rooms with a passage through, after the Southern fashion," and also referred to by him as the White House with "two pens and a passage."[52] Audubon's own description of the visit in a letter to a friend, William MacGillivary "of sturdy Irish fibre,"[53] is—coming from one who had not experienced one single iota of the struggle for independence—both amusing and revealing:

The moment we stepped over the threshold, on the right hand of the passage, we found ourselves ushered into what in other countries would be called the ante-chamber; the ground floor, however, was muddy and filthy; a large fire was burning; a small table covered with paper and writing materials was in the center; camp beds, trunks, and different materials were strewn around the room. We were at once presented to several of the cabinet, some of whom bore the

[48] Audubon, *The Birds of America from Drawings*, V, 248; IV, 118.

[49] Andrew Muir (ed.), *Texas in 1837*, pp. 108, III; original drawings by John James Audubon, New-York Historical Society, New York City.

[50] Herrick, *Audubon*, I, 147.

[51] Gieser, "Audubon's Visit to Texas in 1837."

[52] Henry McArdle, Notes on Sam Houston, Author's Collection.

[53] Audubon, *Audubon and His Journals*, I, 64.

stamp of intellectual ability, simple, though bold in their general appearance . . .

The President was engaged in the opposite room on national business and we could not see him for some time. Meanwhile we amused ourselves by walking to the capitol, which was yet without a roof, and the floors, benches, and tables of both houses of Congress were as well saturated with water as our clothes had been in the morning. Being invited by one of the great men of the place to enter a booth to take a drink of grog with him, we did so; but I was rather surprised that he offered his name instead of cash to the bar-keeper.

We first caught sight of President Houston as he walked from one of the grog-shops, where he had been to prevent the sale of ardent spirits (to the Indians). He was on his way to the house and wore a large coarse hat and the bulk of his figure reminded me of the appearance of General Hopkins of Virginia, for like him he is upwards of six feet high, and strong in proportion. But I observed a scowl in the expression of his eyes that was forbidding and disagreeable. We reached his abode before him, but he soon came and we were presented to his Excellency. He was dressed in a fancy velvet coat, and trousers trimmed with broad gold lace; around his neck was tied a cravat somewhat in the style of seventy-six. He received us kindly, was desirous of retaining us for a while and offered us every facility within his power. He at once removed us from the ante-room to his private chamber which by the way was not much cleaner than the former. We were severally introduced by him to the different members of his cabinet and staff, and at once asked to drink grog with him, which we did, wishing success to his new republic. Our talk was short, but the impression which was made on my mind at the time by himself, his officers and his place of abode, can never be forgotten.[54]

After thanking Houston for his offer of horses and for his hospitality, the party returned to the yawl, and, because of the swell in the Trinity, the swirling waters took them swiftly down to Buffalo Bayou. Houston's friendship, gained in the short interview, made it possible for the artist and particularly John, his son, to get information later on the location and habits of the cougar.

They reached Red Fish Bar on the fifteenth of May. At New Washington they stopped at "Orange Grove," the home of Colonel James Morgan. Here Audubon again had an opportunity to observe wild life and saw the climbing rattlesnake, "with recurved fangs." He was interested in this species because of a long controversy he had had with scientists on its habits. Audubon was impressed with this area and described it as "a fine

extent of woodland, surrounded by vast prairies, ornamented with numerous detached groves," which he said reminded him of "some of the beautiful parks of England."[55]

Ten days after Audubon's audience with Houston, Stephen M. Everett introduced a resolution in the Senate at Austin (May 25, 1837) recognizing the distinguished artist and scientist. Unfortunately, the resolution (given here in part) was not carried out, but was killed in the Committee on Foreign Affairs. It revealed, however, the interest shown in the work of a distinguished American artist when the Republic was yet in its youth:

As we have recently been honored by a visit from the celebrated and scientific Audubon whose fame, talents, and researches are known throughout the enlightened world I beg to offer the following resolution:—most sincerely hoping that through this honorable body Texas may evince to the world that she is, even now, while struggling for liberty, ready to foster genius and talent. . . . Resolved that fully impressed with the importance of promoting science and research and encouraging the notice and regards of gentlemen possessing these qualities and as a means of stimulating them to expose and investigate, this our Eden, Texas, that John James Audubon of the state of Louisiana, Esquire, Fellow of the Royal Society, etc., etc., etc., and the distinguished ornothologist and naturalist who has recently visited our shores, be and he is hereby vested with all the rights, priveledges and immunities of citizenship and that the President of the Republic be instructed to issue "Letters Patent" conformatory of the same with the great seal of the Republic affixed.[56]

Some years after his visit to Texas with his father, young John Woodhouse Audubon returned (1845) to gather information which was to be used in the publication of *Quadrupeds of North America*, published in 1852, a year after his father's death. In the fall of 1845 his father wrote to Spencer F. Baird, the scientist, that his son John "would leave for the West and South as far as the confines of Texas," and in the following December he wrote that John was "safe and sound I believe in Corpus Christi."[57] It was on this trip that John

[54] Lucy Audubon, *Life of John James Audubon, the Naturalist*, pp. 412–413.

[55] Herrick, *Audubon*, II, 79; Audubon, *Ornithological Biography*, IV, 61.

[56] *Telegraph and Texas Register*, Houston, May 9, 1837; May 25, 1837.

[57] Herrick, *Audubon*, II, 272–273.

met and talked with John Coffee Hays, Texas Ranger captain, and Sam Houston on the habits of the cougar. Hays advised him also concerning the choice of routes and the selection of Indian guides and hunters; he warned him to avoid certain camps and settlements where there was danger of being robbed, for this was the time when money, if one had any, was carried in coin.

Years later, when Maria Audubon wrote of her grandfather's work, she mentioned the delight he expressed when the picture of the cougar was received: "My grandfather's delight knew no bounds. He was beside himself with joy that his son, Johnny, could paint a picture he considered so fine; he looked at it from every point and could not keep quiet but walked up and down with delight."[58]

In 1849–1850 John made a trip from New York to Texas by boat and overland through Mexico to the goldfields of California. The journey through part of Texas proved difficult; nevertheless he was able to take notes and gather specimens of importance of both birds and quadrupeds; these he sent back to his father. When he traveled up the Río Grande in 1849 and reached Fort Ringgold, he described his stop there, telling of his enthusiasm and joy over the day's journey:

In the cool of the evening after I had done all I could for the comfort of those around me I stretched myself out with hat, coat, and boots off to look at the busy scene around me. Gaily and cheerfully everything went on under a clear sky like that of August at home with all the soft balmy summer-like feeling. About me, were the familiar notes of dozens of mocking birds and thrushes. I opened out the nucleus of my collections, a jay, a new cardinal were side by side with two new woodpeckers and a little dove all new to our fauna and I carefully spread them out to dry and admire them. The sun went down, our supper was ready and never did a company enjoy their meal more than we did the first two days we were ashore, when exercise and good health gave a relish to everything. Our guard was set and detailed for the night and I turned in on my blankets with a short prayer for health and continuance of blessings on my family.[59]

John James Audubon holds a unique position as an American artist through *The Birds of America*, a monumental work of 435 engravings from his original drawings. In 1845 he followed his *Birds* with the first volume of the *Quadrupeds*; in this he was assisted by his two sons, Victor and John Woodhouse. This publication, while it contains works of great power, does not equal his *Birds* in workmanship nor does it have the same esthetic appeal. Some half dozen or more of the illustrations of the *Quadrupeds* were animal drawings made with scientific accuracy from John Woodhouse's excursions into Texas. But the sensitive hand of John James Audubon shows the delight he had in painting birds in a manner closest to the wild splendor of nature.

Seth Eastman

About ten years after George Catlin and John James Audubon came to Texas, Seth Eastman (1808–1875), artist-soldier, who was to investigate the conditions of the Indians on the frontier, came and made sketches from another point of view. In his drawings he displays a greater skill than Catlin and certainly a broader interest than Audubon. Eastman's work shows an unusual ability to interpret the countryside. On his Texas travels he chose, because of the character of the government assignment and prevailing circumstances, to confine his sketches almost wholly to landscape, thus departing, temporarily, from an unshaken interest in the Indian. One is particularly drawn to his pencil sketches and water colors of pioneer "Dutch" homes, old live oaks with clinging Spanish moss, mesquite-covered hills, and glimpses of settlements and villages; only occasionally does he include a group of Indians, and then only as a minor interest.[60]

In 1848 he was ordered to the Río Grande, but when his company in the First Division of the United States Infantry reached New Orleans, his order was changed and, instead, he was sent to the west-central part of Texas to investigate frontier conditions. In this part of the state he remained nearly a year, completing a wealth of drawings full of interesting details. These were most often made from his saddle, and later, when he was in his studio or when conditions were more favorable, he put them into water color and oils.[61]

Eastman, born in Maine, was the son of Robert and Sarah Lee Eastman. His first training in art, as far as is known, was at West Point as a cadet in 1824 in a course in topographical drawing and landscape under the

[58] Audubon, *Audubon and His Journals*, I, 74.

[59] John Woodhouse Audubon, *Audubon's Western Journals: 1849–1850.*

[60] Robert A. Elder, Jr., "Seth Eastman," *Art Journal*, XXI, No. 4 (Summer, 1962); Seth Eastman, Diary (Holograph), August, 1846–August, 1849, Paul Adams, San Antonio, Texas.

[61] John Francis McDermott, *The Art of Seth Eastman*, p. 13.

French instructor Thomas Gilbrede (1781–1832).[62] The emphasis Gilbrede exerted in topography was in the presentation of a subject without exaggeration or dramatization, holding faithfully to the spirit and the aim of topography, but beyond this principle Eastman developed an eye for selection. He interpreted the landscape on the Hudson with as much individuality as he later showed in representing the image of the frontier landscape.

In 1833 Eastman was appointed an assistant drawing instructor at the Academy. In 1836 he rose to a lieutenancy. For a short period he took private lessons under his associate, Robert Leslie (1794–1859), and then spent a longer period of similar study with Robert W. Weir (1803–1889). The latter distinguished himself with his painting *Embarkation of the Pilgrims* for the National Capitol. Eastman at this time published his *Treatise on Topographical Drawing* (1837), used as a text at the Academy.[63]

During the period he was assistant instructor, Eastman married Mary Henderson, daughter of Dr. Thomas and Ana Marie Truxton Henderson. Mary Eastman became an author in her own right, and through the years did much to assist her husband in placing his pictures in exhibitions and in making sales.[64]

Eastman, with the additional instruction from Weir, was becoming quite successful in his landscape painting. Seventeen landscapes that drew much attention were painted in the vicinity of West Point. He had caught the spirit of those artists, whose painting of the scenic wonders expressed new interest in nature, inadvertently known as the "Hudson River School." His *View of the Highlands from West Point* was exhibited in 1836 at the National Academy of Design in New York. In 1838 eight of his paintings were accepted, and in the following year he was made Honorable Member (Amateur) of the National Academy. Between 1839 and 1848 he exhibited at the Western Art Union in Cincinnati, Ohio, and at the American Art Union in New York, and he was able to sell some of his paintings at the various exhibitions.[65]

In 1840 Eastman was given a government assignment which took him to Fort Crawford, Wisconsin—his first experience on the frontier. This duty did not prove altogether happy and must be charged off with some discredit to the artist.[66] It was his next assignments, during which he held the rank of captain—first to Florida to help end the Seminole wars and then to Fort Snelling,

Minnesota, for seven years—which were to mean a great deal to his career as a painter of Indian activities. When not on duty, Eastman was making sketches and painting scenes of savage life. His collection soon numbered several hundred.[67]

Shortly before Eastman's assignment to Texas, in 1847, the United States government authorized the Bureau of Indian Affairs to "collect and prepare for publication the history, condition and prospects of the Indian tribes of the United States," a report which was to be illustrated. Eastman had won approbation from the public, having made many sketches and paintings of everyday activities of the Indians during his assignments to various posts. Some of the titles are *Indian Women at Work, Sioux Indians Breaking Up Camp, A Dance of the Braves, Mourning for the Dead, Indian Hunters*, and *Indians Spearing Fish*. Eastman thought that he was particularly well suited to illustrate the publication that was to be sponsored by the Bureau of Indian Affairs.[68] He made a special effort to obtain an appointment, but the appointment was not made until later. He was disappointed when instead he received orders to go to the Río Grande.

In October, 1848, Eastman started down the Mississippi with Company D of the First Infantry Regiment. He used every possible moment to sketch, making numerous drawings of what he saw along the river banks, of the plantations, and of scenes in the towns wherever they anchored. In all of these, individuals appeared only as incidentals in the landscape. His long succession of sketches as he passed down the Mississippi suggest that the "three-mile panorama" exhibited by John Banvard, which was enjoying tremendous success in Eastern cities, may have prompted the execution of these realistic scenes. The artists of the panorama, John Rowson Smith

[62] David Bushnell, *Seth Eastman, Master Painter of the North American Indian*, pp. 1–18; Smithsonian Miscellaneous Collections. Vol. 87, No. 3, Smithsonian Institution, 1932.

[63] McDermott, *Art of Seth Eastman*, p. 2.

[64] *Ibid.*, pp. 1–5.

[65] John Francis McDermott, *Seth Eastman, Pictorial Historian of the Indian*, p. 24 and n. 16; McDermott, *Art of Seth Eastman*, p. 3; Mary Bartlett Cowdrey, *American Academy of Fine Arts and American Art Union*, see 1836, 1837, 1838, 1839, and 1840.

[66] McDermott, *Seth Eastman, Pictorial Historian*, pp. 17–18; B. B. McGinsey, "Seth Eastman," *Southwestern Historical Quarterly*, LI (1947–1948), 362.

[67] McDermott, *Seth Eastman, Pictorial Historian*, p. 51; Charles Lanman, *A Summer in the Wilderness*, p. 59.

[68] McDermott, *Seth Eastman, Pictorial Historian*, pp. 63–64, 78.

20. Seth Eastman: *Plaza at San Antonio, Texas*
Pencil, 1849, 6½″ x 9⅜″ (Courtesy of the Peabody Museum, Harvard University, Cambridge, Massachusetts)

21. Seth Eastman: *Live Oaks Two Miles from Fredericksburg, Texas—Encampment of Caddo Indians*
Pencil sketch, 1848, 6½″ x 9″ (Courtesy of the Peabody Museum, Harvard University, Cambridge, Massachusetts)

and Henry Lewis, both had visited Eastman at Fort Snelling in 1847 and urged him to join them in preparing a panorama, but Eastman wrote to Lanman that he disliked "to leave my Indian pictures." Later Lewis acknowledged his indebtedness for the use of two pictures in his book *Das illustrirte Mississippi*, which may have been used in Lewis' panorama.[69] When the Regiment reached New Orleans, General David E. Twiggs, United States Army, changed orders, and instead of going to the Río Grande the company proceeded to newly established Fort Martin Scott near Fredericksburg, Texas—a progressive German frontier settlement. From New Orleans they entered the Gulf and sailed to Matagorda Bay, landing at Indian Point (Indianola). Besides a map of the entrance to the bay, Eastman made four sketches, topographical in nature, of the coastline of Texas.[70]

From the coast they traveled up the valley between the Blanco and the Guadalupe Rivers to Seguin by way of San Antonio. They were now in Indian country, confronted with all the discomforts of the frontier. Eastman wrote that he "left San Antonio with forty-seven soldiers (seven sick), eight wagons, nine teamsters, one wagon master, twenty days' provisions, and ten days' forage." The bugle sounded at dawn each morning. They started on their trek with a canteen of water and rations for a day strapped to their saddles. In addition, the artist carried a drawing pad and pencil. While encamped near Seguin, he made six sketches of the terrain. A typical sketch shows old live oak trees shading a settler's log cabin enclosed by a log rail fence. In his sketches of oaks the artist gives a sense of their age and of their struggle to survive in an arid climate by depicting the gnarled, rugged branches, so characteristic of the live oaks.

Eastman stopped long enough at San Antonio, in November, 1848, to draw views of the missions and a view of the plaza from the old watchtower (Plate 20). Later he rendered these in water color and in oils.

Traveling north and west to the outskirts of Fredericksburg, the military train bivouacked at Fort Martin Scott. Taking up his sketching, Eastman drew views along the Sabinas Creek and in the vicinity of the settlement (Plate 21). From the post, on December 9, Eastman wrote his friend Henry S. Sibley, delegate to Congress from Minnesota, "I have at last arrived at my journey's end and landed I know not where." He gives in his letter to Sibley a further description of the fort and tells some interesting facts concerning the area:

> . . . but in a very fine country full of game and Indians . . . there [is] a trading post here [Fort Martin Scott]—Besides the Cumanches, we have the Delawares, Shawnees, Wakoos, and Lassan [Lipan] Indians—Santa Anna, the Cumanche chief, is to visit me in a few days when I am to hold my first talk with his honor—The country is full of game—small game—such as Buffalo, Bear, Deer, Catamounts, Tigers, Turkies in droves, a few quail and ducks—It would surprise you to see the herd of deer that we saw on our route—They are very tame and easily killed—Buffalo meat sells in town at three cents per pound, a deer at one dollar—Salt *eight cents per pound*. Flour twenty dollars per barrel, Vinegar one dollar per gallon, etc., etc. I wish you were here to go hunting with me; it is rather dangerous but very exciting.[71]

This same unexploited area, the beautiful valley of the Pedernales, furnished both Hermann Lungkwitz and Richard Petri (see Chapter Five) subjects for landscape and genre paintings.

Eastman lost no time in adding fifteen sketches of life around Fredericksburg and the fort to his collection. His delicate drawings display real skill and a passion for this type of work. Strange to say, in very few instances was he tempted to record the Indian. It was a country where the Indian was still in his wild state and to contact him unofficially was difficult. Instead, Eastman made delicate pencil drawings of the "Dutch" houses of Fredericksburg, various scenes of the military camp, and one of the old church (Vereins-Kirche) built by the first settlers. *Live Oaks with Two Small Figures* shows large trees with two small figures, one carrying a gun, with a dog following. This hunting scene (8¾" x 11¾") near Fredericksburg was painted in oil (1849).[72]

From Fredericksburg, Eastman and company went to Fort Inge on the Río Frío and the Leona River, where

[69] John Francis McDermott, *The Lost Panoramas of the Mississippi*, pp. 188 n. 16, 189 n. 33, 90; McDermott, *Art of Seth Eastman*, pp. 8, 14.

[70] Seth Eastman, *A Seth Eastman Sketch Book, 1848–1849*, p. xx.

[71] Seth Eastman, Diary, "Journal of the March from the Leona River Texas to San Antonio hence to Larado on the Rio Grande." August 1, 1848, August 14, 1849 (unfinished), Paul Adams, San Antonio, Texas; McDermott, *Art of Seth Eastman*, p. 14.

[72] Letters, Mrs. Katherine B. Edsall to author, October 3, 17, 27, 1960, enclosed list of fifteen sketches; Seth Eastman Sketches, Collection of Water Color Drawings, James Jerome Hill Reference Library, St. Paul, Minnesota.

the artist remained four months and made several studies of trees and boulders typical of that part of the state.

On August 1, 1848, Eastman began a diary or journal, which, with his sketches, describes for us a ten-day stay in San Antonio. The march of his company (First Infantry) was by way of the Seco River, the Medina River, and the settlement of Quihi. They arrived in San Antonio on the fifth and pitched camp at San Pedro Spring. The journalist made note that on that day he "dined with Genl. Brooks" (supposedly General W. T. H. Brooks). He also reports that he made several sketches, one of the San Juan Mission and another of San José (still other drawings of the missions were made in November, 1848). The journal describing San Antonio shows the artist's zeal as a traveler and his recognition of the unusual:

San Antonio is a Mexican town but rapidly becoming yankeerized–flat roofs are giving way to the old-fashioned shingled yankee roofs—Most of the houses—or rather many of them—are built of stone cemented with lime—others of Adobe, which are square or rectangular bricks of clay—baked by the sun—These make very handsome walls but cannot be very strong—If the outside be not coated with a thin coat of Lime—the Adobe will be liable to be washed to pieces by rain—The former class of Mexicans build their houses of posts stuck upright in the earth—having an opening for a door or window—A thatched roof is then put on and the crevices stopped with mud—and behold—a Mexican home. Sometimes a mud chimney is made—no floor excepting the hard clay—one room only—Generally cook out of doors— To bake they build a semidome of mud twenty to thirty feet from the house—when dry they build a fire inside until sufficiently heated—then put in the bread and stop up the door—San Antonio contains five or six thousand inhabitants —very narrow streets . . . cottages or retreats around it as is normally found around the towns and cities of the U.S. When you get to the end of the streets you are at the end of the town—nothing beyond it but a wild prairie over which the Indian roams as free and wild as the ground that he treads.[73]

The artist continues his description of the city, of the main and the military plazas. He relates, also, incidents of clashes which had occurred between the Mexicans and the Indians as a result of frequent stealing and of rough handling of the Mexican women by the Indians. He describes in detail the final settlement of an affair known as the Council House Fight, related evidently by an ob-server. Eastman intended going to the Río Grande but he went only as far as the San Miguel River. His diary ends on August 26, 1849.

Writing from San Antonio, Eastman described it as "full of desperate characters"—a report that brought great anxiety to his wife, who made every effort to bring him back to the East where she and the children were living. Eastman was called to Washington, where a special order of the War Department (dated February 27, 1850) awaited, requesting him to report for duty on March 1, 1850, at the Office of Indian Affairs to assist in the completion of the work of illustrating the six volumes of Henry Rowe Schoolcraft's notable publication, *Historical and Statistical Information Respecting the History, Condition and Prospects of the Indian Tribes of the United States*. This long-overdue assignment was important to Eastman; he would now be able to use his knowledge of Indians and his collection of paintings to best advantage. The assignment lasted through 1854.[74]

In May, 1855, five years after his first Texas trip, Eastman was sent to Fort Duncan on the western border of Texas, and the following August he was at Fort Chadborne.[75] Now he was in real Comanche country. A small water color, *Emigrants Attacked by Comanches* (6″ x 9½″), may have been sketched at this time; it depicts a scene that was actually experienced by many travelers. This threadbare subject among Western painters he probably later put in his oil for the *Indian Tribes of the United States*—portraying beleaguered emigrants, wagons placed in a circle for protection, while the men of the train deliver from the rear of the wagons a barrage of shots upon the mounted Indians. A few of the drawings may be identified as having been made at this time: *Crossing the Nueces River, Texas; Fort Brown, Texas; Mexican Jacal on the Río Grande above Brownsville;* and *Staked Plains*. Others on this West Texas trip may yet be identified.

There is no doubt that Eastman produced a larger number of valuable drawings, water colors, and oils than any other contemporary Western artist. Some five hundred items are accounted for, and, of these, some

[73] Seth Eastman, Diary, "Journal," August 1, 1840, Paul Adams, San Antonio, Texas.

[74] Henry Rowe Schoolcraft, *Historical and Statistical Information Respecting the History, Condition and Prospects of the Indian Tribes of the United States*, I and II.

[75] Webb (ed.), *Handbook of Texas*, see Seth Eastman, I, 539.

seventy drawings can be identified as associated with his trips to Texas. Only one other important assignment added materially to his achievements, and that was the work to be used at the National Capitol; as brevet brigadier general he was employed on this work from 1867 until the time of his death. Of these last paintings, Charles E. Fairman in his *Art and Artists of the Capitol of the United States* lists seventeen views of the forts for the House Committee on Military Affairs Room, and nine paintings in the House Committee on Insular Affairs Room.[76] Eastman's oil paintings, many of which were done in the latter part of his life, were executed with heavier brush force and with deeper color. These were in contrast to the sketches which accompanied his journal; the delicacy of the pencil sketches added to their charm. His sensitiveness as an observer of scenic images of the frontier makes him an important contributor to the story of the Southwest.

[76] Charles E. Fairman, *Art and Artists of the Capitol of the United States*, pp. 21–22.

CHAPTER 4

ARTISTS ON THE GO AND
THE PANORAMA DECADES

J. E. Churchill

ATTRACTED TO TEXAS, for the principal reason that it was a potential field for portraitists, many artists, hardy and enthusiastic, found their way from town to town. One limner, J. E. Churchill, about whom little biographical information is available, stated through the press at Washington-on-the-Brazos in May, 1851, that he was remaining a few months, taking rooms at the Temperance Hall. His habits referred to in this ascetical hint "to the citizens of Washington and surrounding country" concerning his location were perhaps, in part, a guarantee of his earnestness. He stated further that he "was prepared to take daguerreotypes, miniatures, and portraits in oil colors of various sizes, framed, cased in lockets plain or fancy in the latest and most approved style." He also was prepared to give lessons "in drawing and landscape painting."[1]

When next we hear of Mr. Churchill he was in Matagorda, and in addition to an advertisement, appearing at the same time was a comment by the editor of the *Colorado Tribune* that "Mr. C's productions are pronounced by conoisseurs to be excellent pictures as demonstrated by his portrait of Judge Meggison."[2] The Judge was then on his way to Austin to accept an appointment to the judicial bench. To add to the aesthetic atmosphere of Matagorda, Mr. Bennett, honorable secretary of the American Art Union (Texas) since 1837, announced from his Dry Goods Shop "to all patrons and lovers of the beautiful in art" that engravings could be obtained there by the Union's members.[3]

In October of 1852, still at Matagorda, the press stated that Mr. Churchill was "an artist of no ordinary merit and was offering his skillful pencil to those disposed to patronize his beautiful art and preserve their shadows as an heirloom beyond the reach of all devouring moth[s] of time!"[4] But he was evidently feeling the pinch of hard times, for he turned to bartering, as many artists of the frontier no doubt were forced to do. He

[1] *Lone Star and Southern Watchtower*, Washington, Texas, June 7, 1851.
[2] *Ibid.*, May 24, 1851; November 15, 1851.
[3] *Colorado Tribune*, Matagorda, Texas, September 4, 1853.
[4] *Ibid.*, October 25, 1852.

would take "cotton, sugar, horses, cattle, or land for his moderately priced portraits."[5] Some of "Mr. C's" Texas portraits may yet be located, but a few years later in 1861, he was advertising as a portraitist in Philadelphia.[6]

Thomas Flintoff

About the same time, at Matagorda, a more sophisticated artist, Thomas Flintoff (c. 1809–1892), arrived, having traveled through a large section of Texas with apparently more success. This sprightly Englishman of forty-one years, whose itching foot brought him to Texas, remained long enough to record, with liveliness and naturalness, likenesses of a score of citizens. His wandering life, characteristic of nineteenth-century portraitists, took him from town to town seeking commissions. He was born in Newcastle-upon-Tyne, England.[7] Though little is known of his early life, that he had received some training is evident in his work—his paintings show that he had at least been exposed to the elements of the English romantic style. Painting in the old tradition, that is, of working into the background the habitat of the sitter and indications of his profession. Flintoff displays a craftsman's skill and a discerning mind. Only occasionally does he revert to a quality of the primitive (thus revealing his lack of proficiency), as when he painted a group of children. Here, however, the result is a group portrait having a naïve childlike freshness and charm.

The exact time of Flintoff's arrival in Texas is not known. The first we hear of him is in May, 1851, when he was made known to Galveston folk through the press:

A crayon portrait of one of our old citizens . . . may be seen at the "Varanda" [the city of Houston's most luxurious tavern] it is a most admirable likeness . . . and is intended . . . to preserve more effectively a resemblance to the original while he sojourns in the North . . . as well as to form a criterion whereby to judge on his return what changes, a change of climate, scenery, and society, will cause on a thoroughly tried Texan.[8]

The news item refers, we believe, to Sam Houston, for he was then serving as United States senator and at the time was mentioned for the presidency of the United States.

On June 3 the *Galveston News* announced that Mr. Flintoff had ". . . likenesses more truthfully executed than had ever been shown to visitors . . . every person recognizes his acquaintances among the paintings quite

as readily as he would the original. . . . We understand that Mr. Flintoff proposes to leave the city."[9] The inference may be drawn here that since he had time to complete a group of paintings, the artist may have come to Texas some months before this first announcement of May, 1851.

It was in Galveston that Flintoff made the likenesses of Pryor M. Bryan and his wife, Mary Angelica Bryan, of Galveston and Liberty, Texas (Plates 22 and 23). The affluent gentleman dealt in land, cattle, and slaves. These much respected citizens were painted with warmth and dignity. The accurately painted hands of his subjects, and carefully painted lace of Mrs. Bryan's costume shows the attention Flintoff gave to details in his work. These portraits represent some of the artist's best work.[10]

Other well-executed portraits made while Flintoff was in Galveston were those of Thomas Jefferson Chambers and his wife (Plates 24 and 25). Mrs. Chambers, nee Abbie Chubb, thirty years her husband's junior, was a daughter of the harbor master of Galveston. Mrs. Chambers' thin lacy Mexican mantilla and jewelry gave the portraitist an opportunity to show again his skill in painting details. A contrast is obtained by the softness of her veil and the Robert Feke-ish stiffness of her bodice. A sheet of music, a polka, in her lap reflects interestingly the attempt of the artist to represent the lady in an appropriate and familiar setting. Thomas Chambers, a Virginian of considerable education, contributed a great deal to the welfare and progress of Texas through his knowledge of the Mexican language and laws. He attempted to run for governor in 1853, he was always a controversial figure on the frontier, and he died in his home at the hands of an assassin. Flintoff portrays him as being alert, his sharp eyes looking straight at the viewer. The books and sword in the painting identify him with

[5] *Telegraph and Texas Register*, Houston, February 24, 1841.

[6] *Philadelphia City Directory*, 1861, Portrait Painter; George C. Groce and David H. Wallace, *New-York Historical Society's Dictionary of Artists in America, 1564–1860*, p. 127.

[7] Letter, John A. Freely, Victoria Public Library, Melbourne, Australia, to author, February 16, 1959; E. Bénézit, *Dictionnaire— Critique et Documentaire des Peintres, Dessinateurs, Graveurs, et Sculpteurs*, Vol. II, see Flintoff.

[8] *The Weekly Journal*, Galveston, May 25, 1851; June 16, 1851.

[9] *Galveston News*, June 3, 1851.

[10] Letter, Samuel E. Asbury, Bryan, Texas, to E. Winkler, Austin, on portraits of Gen. Edward Burleson and Guy M. Bryan, Texas State Archives, Austin; Dallas Museum of Fine Arts file on Flintoff portraits, Pryor Bryan and Mrs. Bryan, owned by the late Watson Neyland, Liberty, Texas.

22. Thomas Flintoff: *Pryor M. Bryan*
    Oil, 1852, c. 32″ x 27″ (Courtesy of the late Watson Neyland, Liberty, Texas)

23. Thomas Flintoff: *Mary Angelica Bryan*
    Oil, 1852, c. 32″ x 27″ (Courtesy of the late Watson Neyland, Liberty, Texas)

24. Thomas Flintoff: *Thomas Jefferson Chambers*
Oil, 1851, 36¼″ x 28½″ (Courtesy of the San Jacinto Museum, San Jacinto, Texas)

25. Thomas Flintoff: *Abbie Chambers*
    Oil, 1851, 36¼″ x 28½″ (Courtesy of the San Jacinto Museum, San Jacinto, Texas)

26. Thomas Flintoff: *Guy Morrison Bryan*
Oil, 1851, 32″ x 22″ (Courtesy of the Barker Library, The University of Texas at Austin)

intellectual achievements and his service in the Texas Revolution. The portraits are signed and dated 1851.[11]

In the fall of 1851 Flintoff went to Austin, where he invited the members of the Legislature and the citizens of the city to inspect his work in his studio over the Post Office. Austin's *Gazette* stated: "He [Flintoff] trusts that his long experience in the business and specimens of his work to be seen at his rooms will be sufficient guaranty that satisfaction will be given to all who may favor him with their patronage."[12] The artist found a ready patron in the Legislature, for in December, 1851, Andrew J. Hamilton, member of the committee on contingent expenses of the House of Representatives, offered a resolution:

Resolved that the committee on Contingent expenses of the House of Representatives be authorized to make contact with Mr. Flintoff the portrait painter now in the city of Austin to repair the portrait of the Father of Texas, Stephen F. Austin, now suspended over the Speaker's chair and that they report thereon to the House at their earliest convenience.[13]

An amendment was offered and accepted to procure a new frame for the Austin portrait. Mr. Hamilton made the following remarks before the legislative body December 6, 1851:

Stephen F. Austin was emphatically the father of Texas; his name is associated inseparately with the first settlement and early struggles of her colonists. Pushing an enterprise from which an ordinary mind would have shrunk, dismayed, far beyond the limits of civilization, he planted in the remote wilderness a colony who bringing little else besides, brought with them the energy of their race and the spirit of Freedom which had been taught them at their father's fireside. They expanded into a nation who can proudly boast that they have enlarged the area of Freedom and redeemed an Empire to its faith and its hope.[14]

In spite of his announcement that he would refrain from further remarks on the subject, Mr. Hamilton addressed the chair:

I shall certainly, Sir, enter no encomium upon the original of that picture; his name is one of the household gods in every habitation in this country. . . . That there may be no fears of any sacrilegious alteration in these features I will state to the house that on the event of a passage of this resolution it is expected the gentleman from Brazoria [Guy Morrison Bryan] who has personal interest in everything pertaining to the illustrious name will superintend the contemplated repairs.[15]

In due time the likeness was repaired by Mr. Flintoff.

The name of the original portraitist was not recorded, but it is recognized as having been produced in the studio of a professional artist—perhaps at a time when Austin was in New Orleans on state business in the late 1820's or early 1830's.

Guy Morrison Bryan, who had helped to bring Flintoff's work to the notice of Austin citizens, employed the artist to paint a portrait of himself (Plate 26). This work, not perhaps on the same professional level as others, is signed and dated 1851, and is now the property of The University of Texas at Austin.

In 1855 Mr. Guy Bryan made a present of a portrait of Stephen F. Austin (Plate 27) to the Reverend Daniel Baker to be placed in Austin College at Sherman, Texas. This was painted by Flintoff in 1851 when he restored the painting of Austin now in the Senate Chamber. The Reverend Baker, on September 6, 1855, wrote to his son William M. Baker, Huntsville, Texas, the following information concerning the Austin portrait:

Mr. Guy Bryan has made the college a donation of a splendid painting, a fine likeness of Stephen F. Austin, large as life. It cost three hundred dollars. He had two painted by an English artist; one was designed for the senate chamber, the other for the House of Representatives at Austin but one has been given to our college. A fine present this. It will be a fine and very appropriate adornment to our college chapel.[16]

The artist here referred to is undoubtedly Thomas Flintoff from Newcastle-upon-Tyne, who had repaired the unidentified portrait of Austin which is in the Senate Chamber.

Working from a photograph in February, 1852, Flintoff finished a portrait of General Edward Burleson, a North Carolinian who came to Texas in 1830 and received a league of land in Austin's second colony. He served as a member of the Convention of 1833 at San Felipe and fought in defense of Texas at San Jacinto. His war service continued through the Cherokee war, when Texas' number-one enemy, Chief Bowles, was killed.[17]

---

[11] Walter Prescott Webb (ed.), *Handbook of Texas*, see Thomas Jefferson Chambers, I, 927.

[12] *Texas State Gazette*, Austin, October 29, 1851.

[13] *Ibid.*, November 1, 1851; *Journal of the House of Representatives* (Resolution) December 29, 1851, p. 401.

[14] *Texas State Gazette*, Austin, December 6, 1851.

[15] *Ibid.*

[16] William M. Baker, *Life and Labours of Reverend Daniel Baker, D.D.*, p. 530.

[17] Sion R. Bostick, "Reminiscences," *Quarterly of the Texas His-*

27. Thomas Flintoff: *Stephen F. Austin*
    Oil, 1851 (Courtesy of Austin College, Sherman, Texas)

A letter published February 14, 1852, in the *Texas State Gazette* signed "Texas" read:

But a short time has elapsed since the people of Texas had been released from the actual perils and exigencies of a long protracted war, the perils of which are yet sensitively felt by many of them. It is not therefore very strange that but little attention has been paid to the Fine Arts in Texas. In one branch of art, however, we have an artist now among us who is not surpassed by any man in the state and by few artists anywhere. The portraits of many ladies and gentlemen of the city of Austin and vicinity now seen in the studio of Mr. Flintoff would do credit to any artist. For accurate delineation of features and lifelike tone and expression they cannot be surpassed. . . . The first peculiarity which strikes you is that you not only look at the features but you see also imprinted upon them the trait which you know to be the prevailing feature of his character.[18]

When the portrait of General Burleson was exhibited, the press agreed that "the portrait from the hands of Mr. Flintoff adds a fresh laurel to his already high reputation as an artist." He was paid five hundred dollars by the state, a good sum in those days.[19]

The *Gazette* noted in the February 14, 1852, issue that although Mr. Flintoff had expected to leave for another state, he decided to go to Corpus Christi and Matagorda. But March found him still in Austin, for he had received a commission from the officers and clerks of the General Land Office to paint a portrait of George Washington Smyth of Jasper, Texas, who had served as commissioner the four preceding years (Plate 28). Mr. Smyth was requested to attend at such time "as his time would allow, the studio of Mr. Flintoff." Continuing, the *Gazette* declared that "the labours of Mr. Smyth had been of the most responsible and arduous character and he had discharged them with a fidelity and promptitude and an impartiality meriting the highest mode of praise from the state and the people of Texas."[20]

This fine portrait, signed by Flintoff, now hangs in

torical Association, V, No. 2 (1901–1902), 88, 95; Webb (ed.), *Handbook of Texas*, see Chief Bowles, I, 198.

[18] *Texas State Gazette*, Austin, February 14, 1852.

[19] *Journal of the House of Representatives*, December 29, 1851, pp. 401, 431–432.

[20] *Texas State Gazette*, Austin, February 14, 1852; March 6, 1852.

[21] Webb (ed.), *The Handbook of Texas*, see George W. Smyth, II, 629; *Texas State Gazette*, Austin, March 6, 1852.

[22] Letter, Mrs. Katherine Evans, granddaughter of the artist, concerning the portrait of the Jones children, to Miss Ima Hogg, Houston, Texas, April 6, 1961, copy to author; Webb (ed.), *Handbook of Texas*, see Thomas Jefferson Jones, I, 927.

the State Archives at Austin. The artist has chosen to paint the Texan seated, wearing a black suit, holding a quill pen high in his hand—the artist's means of signifying, no doubt, a professional man, as well as a signer of the Texas Declaration of Independence. But what warmed the hearts of his compatriots was the fact that in 1838, as commissioner in charge of determining the boundary between Texas and the United States along the Sabine River, Smyth was instrumental in bringing into Texas a strip of land 6 miles wide and 103 miles long. This beautifully timbered area, part of what was known later as "The Big Thicket," was a garden spot of the state and the home site of a number of the first settlers.[21]

The portrait of Smyth shows very clearly the artist's leaning toward the English romantic school. In the foreground of the portrait are carefully executed details, including a scroll in script bearing the legend "A Tribute of Respect to George Washington Smyth, Commissioner of the General Land Office, as a Tribute of High Regard for him by the officers and Clerks."

Flintoff did not confine his portraits to adults. One of his most valued paintings is that of the children of the William J. Jones family of Columbus, Texas (Plate 29). The father of the children, formerly from Caroline County, Virginia, and the mother, Elizabeth Giberson from Princeton, New Jersey, came to Texas in the same year, 1838; they met and were married in 1841. Jones served on the Supreme Court of the new Republic. Their estate of two thousand acres, "Virginia Point," near Columbus was a familiar spot to Texans. Here Judge Jones envisioned a seaport which would rival all ports on the Gulf. But destiny intervened, for yellow fever swept their way, causing the death of three of their oldest children within five days and forcing them to flee to Galveston. Flintoff, then in Galveston enjoying a certain amount of popularity as a portraitist, was asked to paint a group portrait of the four youngest children. Flintoff was living at the time next to young Jerry Hartley, from whom he borrowed a pet fawn which he included in the painting. The children are Lewellyn, the youngest, pictured in low-neck dress in the arms of Warrick, her six-year-old brother; Walter C. (who in 1899 became mayor of Galveston) is pictured holding a peach high in his hand; Ella, the oldest girl, in the front has her arm around the fawn. Each child's portrait is treated with individual care. A tree and drapery form a background for the group.[22]

This large (c. 4′ x 5′), ambitious painting shows the

28. Thomas Flintoff: *George W. Smyth*
   Oil, 1852, 35⅜″ x 27¼″ (Courtesy of the Texas State Archives, Austin)

29. Thomas Flintoff: *The Jones Children*
    Oil, c. 1851, 56¼″ x 42″ (Courtesy of Miss Ima Hogg, Houston, Texas)

faults as well as the virtues of the artist. His lack of complete three-dimensional skill is self-evident. The use of the fruit and the fawn reminds us of some of the early American primitives; their use adds greatly to the picturesque and decorative quality of the painting.

On arrival in May at Matagorda he took rooms at the Mansion House "for a short time." Of the time he spent here and at Corpus Christi, we know little. At Matagorda his work was praised in a reference to the "dilettanti of Austin" for his portrait of Burleson, and "the unsullied manner in which he renovated that of the venerated Stephen F. Austin."[23]

Thomas Flintoff disappeared from the scene in 1852 just as mysteriously as he had appeared a few years earlier. Some years later Mr. Rufus Burleson stated that when Flintoff left Texas he went to California, "where he flourished." It was thought by some of his acquaintances that he sought the gold fields of California. A few years after his Texas venture, we learn, he turned up in Ballarat, Australia. The fact that other Flintoffs migrated to Australia from England in 1842 is an indication that they may have been relatives of the portraitist and influenced his making his final home in Melbourne. Here he signed and dated, in 1859, a crayon portrait of John Basson Humfray. This portrait hangs in the public library at Victoria. Other portraits completed during the period from 1860 to 1880 (including a short period in the photographic business) are crayon portraits of G. A. Tomson (43" x 7") and of Sir William J. Clarke (6' 66" x 68"), who was created baronet in 1882. The artist died alone, or so the Melbourne newspapers reported in 1891.[24]

The portraits left by Flintoff in Texas show the influence of the English School. Though shortcomings in his painting appeared in his lack of flexibility, in many of his portraits he demonstrated his keen sense of perception and his understanding of human qualities.

James G. Benton and Charles L. Smith

Another interest developing in Southwest Texas in November, 1851, brings to mind Moelling's large painting of the Battle of Galveston (the painting was so large he had to to have a wagon carry it about). Lieutenant James G. Benton (1825–1861), a New Hampshire youth and a graduate of the United States Military Academy,[25] was making sketches for a "newsreel" of Texas events—"The Texas and California" panorama. He was in command of the San Antonio Ordnance Depot at the

time he made his drawings (1849–1852). Benton had entered the Ordnance Department of the United States Army as a specialist, designing and experimenting in gunnery. In the latter part of his life he published (1861) *A Course of Instruction in Ordnance and Gunnery for Use of Cadets of the United States Military Academy*, based on French sources. While at West Point he, like Seth Eastman, studied under Robert W. Weir, instructor in topographical drawing and free-hand drawing of the human figure.

To his own sketches he added those of one of the prisoners of the Mier Expedition (no doubt those made by Charles McLaughlin, included in General Thomas J. Green's account of the expedition in 1845), and a third group made by a Mr. Perrine of the gold fields of California.[26]

Messrs. Sala and Stearn, promoters of the idea, were to take the drawings to New Orleans, where a scenic artist Charles L. Smith, "well known in this city [New Orleans] for his long connection with the principal theatres of the city," was to paint the scenes on a canvas measuring nine feet wide and three hundred feet long.[27]

Following the general plan of many earlier panoramas, the scenes had been planned along a river, in this case the Brazos. Concurrent descriptions stated that the central scene was to be the old Independence Hall and "they contemplate taking a view of the Brazos River from Washington to San Felipe showing the crossing of the army." Furthermore, the *Lone Star and Southern Watchtower*, Washington-on-the-Brazos, reported that the intention was to make sketches of all the important

[23] *Colorado Tribune*, Matagorda, Texas, May 29, 1852.

[24] Letter, B. Collinwood Stevenson, Laing Art Museum, Newcastle-upon-Tyne, England, to author, June 17, 1960; letter, John A. Freely, Victoria Public Library, Melbourne, Australia, to author, February 16, 1959.

[25] *Lone Star and Southern Watchtower*, Washington, Texas, November 15, 1851; "Historical Sketch of Department of Drawing," *Centennial History of the United States Military Academy*, pp. 290–298; letter, Richard E. Kuehne. West Point Museum, to author, January 27, 1966; George W. Cullums, *Biographical Register of the Officers and Graduates of United States Military Academy of West Point, N.Y.*

[26] *Lone Star and Southern Watchtower*, Washington, Texas, November 15, 1851; November 17, 1851; Thomas J. Green, *Journal of the Texian Expedition against Mier*; *New Orleans Bee*, June 5, 1857; *New Orleans Daily Picayune*, April 30, 1852.

[27] *New Orleans Bee*, June 5, 1857. A George Augustus Sala is spoken of in connection with H. Alken in the preparation of the painting of the panorama *The Death of the Duke of Wellington* (Desmond Coke, *An Incurable Collector*, p. 49).

c-5. James G. Benton and Charles L. Smith: *"Independence Hall," Washington-on-the-Brazos Panorama*

Oil, 1852, 9' x 15' (Courtesy of the Republic National Bank, Dallas, Texas)

and thrilling incidents connected with the Texas Revolution." The plan included "views of the Missions of San Antonio, San José, Conception, and the Alamo—the battle and the fate of the Texans."[28]

The nine-by-fifteen-foot portion (Plate c-5) of the Texas panorama showing the historic building has been recovered and restored to its original freshness. The accuracy of Lieutenant Benton's sketches as a topographical student under Robert Weir can be accepted. Just what changes Charles Smith made in the panorama cannot be established, but it is a fact that panoramists attempted to identify the scenes to their audiences. Smith has done his work well, resulting in similitude and good craftsmanship.

While the sketching was in progress Messrs. Sala and Stearn, assisted by Mrs. Sala, felt obligated to entertain the citizens of Washington with the play *Loan of a Lover*, and later joined the "Thespians" in the play *Damon and Pythias*, a musical drama; between acts were "songs and Yankee stories."[29] Sala and Stearn reported later from New Orleans on the progress of the Texas panorama. From all indications, Messrs. Sala and Stearn had little to do with the actual art work, but appear to have been chiefly promoters and entertainers.

Sala was evidently a resident of Marshall, Texas, at one time, and had shown exhibitions of paintings; one in which he had a part was in Jefferson, Texas, an exhibition by "Sala and Witt." Mr. Sala painted a "banner for the Sons of Temperance who met at Rocksprings [Locksprings] Marshall." The banner was pronounced as showing "exquisite skill." He had also directed the "scenic views" decorating the walls of the Judge George Adkins Building, which had just been erected on the village square.[30]

When the preliminary sketches for the panorama were completed they were taken to New Orleans to the Smith studio. The plan was to have the opening night at the first State Fair at Corpus Christi, May, 1852, but plans were changed and the opening night was May 1, 1852, at the Dan Rice Pavilion in New Orleans. But on June 6, 1852, the *Texas Republican* had this to say concerning the painting:

Mr. Sala formerly of this place has sent us a large show bill of a moving panorama of the principal scenes in Texas and California containing about 10,000 feet of canvas . . . While at New Orleans we called at the room where the work was progressing . . . We regarded the painting as worthy of attention . . . a grand idea . . . a decided hit.[31]

Charles L. Smith, a New Yorker, had shown his ability in the theatre world as a scenic painter as early as 1840. We learn of this assignment when Noah M. Ludlow and Sol Smith called on him to assist in carrying out "the spectacular nature" of one of their productions. Further evidence of his success was in an ambitious undertaking in the fall of 1841 at the opening of a season at the auditorium in New York City. The *Republican* gives an account of the event, stating that the theatre opened with "a blaze of fresh paint by Mr. C. L. Smith."[32]

He aimed at once to be national and local. Likenesses of the various presidents of the union adorn the panel work of the first and second tiers, that of Washington occupying the centre place . . . the third decorated with old mythological devices expressive of the connection with the drama. The arms of the union form a beautiful centre from which nine richly executed panels diverge, each representing miniature national emblems borne aloft by flying Zephyrs and Cupids.[33]

A few years after his Texas painting Charles Smith became the artist of the panorama *Creation* and of *Perry's Expedition to Japan*, which was shown in many American cities.[34]

The history of the panorama began with the work of Robert Barker of Edinburgh, Scotland, in 1778. Barker may have gotten his inspiration from an embroidered panorama at Bayeux made shortly after the episode of the Battle of Hastings. This famous story of the eleventh century was made on linen in colored wool, seventy-seven yards of stitching showing William's victory. A border of mythological creatures and scenes from famous fables complete the rich panorama.[35]

As first conceived the panorama was simply a long painting showing continuous views of an area, or a succession of events—in a sense it was the predecessor of the modern travelogue or cinema. Barker was able to

[28] *New Orleans Daily Picayune*, April 30, 1852; *Lone Star and Southern Watchtower*, Washington, Texas, November 15, 1851.

[29] *Lone Star and Southern Watchtower*, November 22, 1851.

[30] *Texas Republican*, Marshall, October 11, 1849; January 3, 1850; March 7, 1850; May 17, 1851.

[31] *New Orleans Daily Picayune*, April 30, 1852; May 1, 1852; *Texas Republican*, Marshall, June 6, 1852.

[32] *Republican*, New York City, September 20, 1840.

[33] William G. B. Carson, *Managers in Distress: The St. Louis Stage (1840–1844)*, p. 157.

[34] *New Orleans Crescent*, June 5, 1857; *New Orleans Bee*, June 5, 1857.

[35] Kenneth M. Setton, "The Norman Conquest," *The National Geographic*, CXXX, No. 2 (August, 1966), 206–251.

display his first efforts—a series of views of the English fleet at anchor—at both Edinburgh and Glasgow. At least twenty panoramas were painted by Barker and his son Henry Aston Barker from 1788 to 1822, averaging from 10,000 to 27,000 square feet. Barker journeyed from London to Berlin where he displayed successfully his *Battle of Trafalgar* and *Views of Berlin*.[36] In the succeeding years a number of artists followed with similar plans, adding new ideas and inventions with each new painting. Panoramist Louis Mandé Daguerre with his advanced knowledge of photography made important innovations in the French panoramas, making the scenes more attractive to the viewer.[37]

An interesting difference in workmanship is reported in connection with the French and other panoramists' method of painting the scenes. While some artists chose to paint the canvas in an upright position, the French often used long brushes, walking directly on the canvas as it lay flat.

It was not long before the public was completely won over to the panoramic idea. Co-incidentally Frederick Catherwood's view of Jerusalem (1839–1840), shown at New York City in 1790, was thought to be the first panorama introduced to American audiences. Catherwood, of London, England, was a noted traveler, architect, and artist. He had been known particularly for his beautifully drawn and meticulously accurate sketches of Maya civilization. His panorama *Jerusalem* was described as "a vivid picture of the holy city" with "evidence of correctness of every detail."[38] The panorama struck the fancy of the public, hungry for any form of theatrical entertainment. Almost overnight artists of St. Louis and New Orleans were hard at work making a "newsreel," each claiming he would make one longer than any formerly displayed.

Handbills and notices appeared under a number of names other than panoramas, to wit, dioramas, cosmoramas, cycloramas, dionomoramas, and polopticomoramas. These were referred to as amusements for the millions, or the poor man's art gallery, depicting almost every important event in history.[39] Many were designed to follow the course of a river, as a river was the logical vehicle for a succession of scenes, and gave the pleasant illusion of travel. It was not difficult to interest Americans in the broad expanses of the new country. During the late 1840's and the '50's five panoramas were painted of the great Mississippi River alone.

By the middle of the 1850's, instead of being meas-

ured by feet, the paintings were claimed to be measured by miles. The customary way at this time of showing the panoramas was by means of vertical rollers—one roller from which the painting was released and another to receive it.[40] In this way the mile-long (more often less) succession of scenes passed before the viewers rapidly. This was a change from the earlier manner of showing when the long painting, made stationary, was placed in a circle with the audience in the center. By this earlier method of showing, the viewers did not get the illusion of traveling but were simply looking at a large painting. As time passed, additions were made to make the picture more realistic, such as having stationary figures placed in front of the passing scenes. This was called a diorama. The meaning of the scenes was made clearer by a lecture, even a pamphlet containing its history, and often the viewing was accompanied by music.[41] Thus the evening was reported to be both entertaining and "edifying." The usual charge for the showing was fifty cents. Ladies occupied the front seats.

On viewing one of these paintings of the Mississippi, John Banvard (c. 1819–?), an ambitious youth of simplicity and humor, declared that he would make a panorama of Old Man River, "longer than any in the world."[42] Banvard was a New Yorker, a self-made artist, with native skill and drive. After innumerable hardships he displayed his incomplete panorama in Louisville, Kentucky, in 1841; the complete version shown in 1846 included views from the Missouri River to New Orleans. After showing the panorama in the United States he took it to England and France where it was enthusias-

[36] *The Panorama with Memoirs of Its Inventor, Robert Barker and His Son, the Late Henry Aston Barker*, pp. 14–15; John Francis McDermott, *The Lost Panoramas of the Mississippi*, p. 5.

[37] Fondata Da Silvio D'Amico, *Encyclopedia Dello Spettacolo*, see Louis-Mandé Daguerre, pp. 1566–1567.

[38] McDermott, *The Lost Panoramas*, p. 8; Victor W. von Hagen, "Artist of the Buried World," *American Heritage*, XII, No. 4 (June, 1961), 8–18; George C. D. Odell, *Annals of the New York Stage*, I, 286; II, 143.

[39] *Daily Union*, St. Louis, September 23, 1850.

[40] Joseph E. Arrington, "Story of Stockwell's Panorama," *Minnesota History*, XXXIII, No. 7 (Autumn, 1953), 21, Daguerre 1822 picture and engraving from G. Tissander, *La Photographie*; McDermott, *The Lost Panoramas*, pp. 28–47, 157.

[41] Robert Reinders, *A Social History of New Orleans, 1850–1880*, II, 573–575.

[42] John Francis McDermott, "Barvard's Mississippi Pamphlets," *The Papers of the Biographical Society of America*, XLIII (1949), 48–62; McDermott, *The Lost Panoramas*, p. 20.

tically received. Needless to say, he had by this time accumulated a small fortune.

New Orleans, the mecca of American painters, became a center of activity along with St. Louis. The second panorama of the Mississippi was made by a French-born artist, Leon de la Pomarède (c. 1807–1892). The interest in the New Orleans paintings probably led to the painting of the Texas scenes. Pomarède, who came to New Orleans at the age of twenty-three, had had some training in Europe. He resumed his study in New Orleans with Modelli and Develle. His first success was winning the hand of Modelli's daughter. Modelli had made an impression on the public by painting a portrait of the city of New Orleans showing the busy port with ships and steamboats underweigh.[43] A clever pencil sketch of the harbor attributed to an unknown artist, now on view at the old Cabildo in New Orleans, may well prove to be the preliminary sketch of one of this group. Pomarède, impressed with the progress and success of paintings made in St. Louis, left for that city and was soon busying himself with the second panorama (that had been painted of the Mississippi), under the title *The Mississippi River and Indian Life*. He was assisted in this enterprise by T. E. Courtenay.[44] The notices of his work stated that the fine scenery of the upper river brought before the spectator the views "with all the vividness of reality, and the illusion—more nearly perfect by the appearance of the mimic steamboats which are seen transversing the river and blowing off steam in high-pressure style."[45] The comments continued with a description of beautiful Lake Pepin and the Falls of St. Anthony. Only a fragment of this panorama remains—significantly, an Indian signed by Pomarède—for it is recorded that the largest part of the work was destroyed in a fire in 1850 at Newark, New Jersey.[46]

A very different panorama was prepared in Egypt of the Nile River, and was advertised and displayed in the United States in 1852 as the *American Panorama of the Nile*. It drew crowds in American cities. A short description of this will give an idea of the elaborate undertaking and the task of selecting artists.

The lecturer "Mr. Glidden" took great pains in his elaborate explanation to arouse interest in his eight hundred-foot canvas when it was shown in New Orleans at the Old Commercial Exchange Building in 1852. He stated in his elaborate commentary that "it was a panorama that should interest everyone . . . the land" he told his audience, ". . . has been pressed with the footsteps of Abraham, Joseph, the

prophet Moses, Jeremiah, the Virgin Mary and the infant Savior. Every educated mind," he continued, "welcomes gladly any new source of information touching the spot where Sesostris conquered empires, and Alexander the Great founded cities, libraries and temples, where Solon, Pythagoras, Plato, Herodotus, Euclid, Lucian and Theocritus studied and wrote; where Julius Caesar and Mark Anthony led their mailed legions and laid them at the feet of Cleopatra, where fierce crusader and fiery Saracen fought for the Crescent and the Cross, where the young conqueror of Italy stood in the shadow of forty centuries of glory and as the veteran grenadiers moved down, the chivalry of Egypt already saw, perhaps, glittering before his mental vision the sword that was to lead him over prostrate Europe."[47]

The Daily Picayune tells us that besides the main geographical and architectural interests, the panorama showed something of the manners and customs of the people, "Turks, Nubians, Bedowins, dancing girls, tradesmen, boatmen, governors, and those governed."

The gathering of talent, a part of the elaborate preparation in making a panorama, was explained in the lecture by Mr. Glidden:

The painting was principally the work of Mr. Warren, president of the "New Society of painters in water-colors" in London, and to Mr. Fahey, secretary to the same institution. The celebrated Mr. Martin put in some magical effects in sun and moonlit scenes. Carbould filled in the Arabian horses, and Weigal the boats and similar objects that seem to spring forth from the canvas. The sketches from which every scene was drawn and painted are by the eminent Eastern traveler Joseph Bononi who took them with the camera lucida and by the most accurate measurements. Mr. Bononi is the very best of authorities in all matters connected with Egypt and its history, hence, the panorama may be confidently relied on for fidelity and comprehensiveness."[48]

Several American and foreign panoramas have been

[43] *New Orleans Daily Picayune*, November 27, 1849; November 28, 1849; McDermott, *The Lost Panoramas*, pp. 145–160; Groce and Wallace, *Dictionary*, see Pomarède, p. 510.

[44] *New Orleans Daily Picayune*, November 24, 1849; November 27, 1849; Groce and Wallace, *Dictionary*, see T. E. Courtenay, p. 150.

[45] *New Orleans Daily Picayune*, November 28, 1849.

[46] Interview, W. E. Groves, New Orleans, information on Pomarède by telephone; *New Orleans Daily Picayune*, November 24, 1849; November 27, 1849.

[47] *New Orleans Daily Picayune*, March 7, 1852. One of the pamphlets about this *American Panorama of the Nile* is part of a collection of early pamphlets in the New York City Public Library.

[48] *Ibid.*, March 6, 1852; March 7, 1852; March 10, 1852.

recovered. One of the Mississippi (1850) (probably not in its original length) by Dr. M. W. Dickeson and John J. Egan, is now at the City Art Museum of St. Louis, Missouri.[49] Several panoramas of the Sioux wars by John Stevens, a sign painter, were prepared in the 1860's. One is owned by the Minnesota Historical Society at St. Paul, and a second is owned by the Thomas Gilcrease Institute of American History and Art, at Tulsa, Oklahoma.[50] Only recently has Paul Philippoteaux's *Civil War* been added to the historic chronicles of Winston-Salem, North Carolina.[51] French panoramic views of the Palace and Gardens of Versailles by the noted American artist John Vanderlyn, whose original sketches were made on the spot, may be seen at the Metropolitan Museum, New York City.[52]

The great variety of subjects treated by the artists is illustrated by the following important panoramas that appeared in America, celebrating many events in history and literature: *The Battle of Waterloo, Battle of Genappe,* and *Mt. Vesuvius* (1830), *St. Helena and Funeral of Napoleon* (1838), *The Creation and Deluge* (1840's), *Grand Cosmorama of a Picturesque Voyage around the World* (1840), *Hudson River* (1848), *Voyage to California* (1840's), *The French Revolution* (1830, by Philippoteaux), *Pilgrim's Progress* (1860), *Skirving's Moving Panorama: Colonel Fremont's Western Expeditions,* and numerous others of equal interest.[53]

As to the quality of the painting in the panoramas, there is little basis for judgment; what little remains shows work in some cases done quickly and boldly for the fast-rolling views. It is a fact that the artists of several panoramas—John Stevens, T. E. Courtenay, Henry Lewis—were all scenic painters and no doubt followed the technique of quick broad strokes in stage-scenery style. This judgment is borne out by a comment from a citizen of New Orleans, Thomas K. Wharton, architect and artist, a man of sound judgment and an expert with the pencil, who, after viewing *The Bunyan Tableau* in 1855, commented that it "did not possess a single feature of artistic merit [but was] merely coarse 'scenic painting'."[54] On the other hand, such work as is shown in Paul Philippoteaux's representation of the Battle of Gettysburg is said to be superior painting. American views prepared for the panorama *A Whaling Voyage* by Benjamin Russell (now restored), which can be seen at the present time at the New Bedford Whaling Museum, refute Wharton's statement. Russell's interesting panorama, which required several years to paint, shows

the high moments of whaling life and the perils of a voyage in wind and wave.[55] If others were of equal skill a search for our American panoramas would be quite worth while.

Single sections of these paintings were never meant to be judged as paintings in the general sense—complete in themselves—for they were not conceived as such but as continuous scenes in chorographic order.

The educational impact of scores of these paintings as a source of communication in this era was no doubt great. The panorama was a popular form of entertainment, particularly in the East. George Odell in his *Annals of the New York Stage* says, at the time of a showing in the late 1850's of the *Mexican War, Napoleon's Wars, Perry's Expedition to Japan,* and *Battles of the Crimea:* "I am wearying of panoramas but I still view their wonders with sated eye."[56]

If the panorama had little influence on the art of the times, it called attention to the beauty of the land. On one occasion (1848) Dr. L. W. Baker, surgeon in the First Quartermaster's train, was traveling from San Antonio to New Mexico and was so impressed with the unspoiled beauty of the country he appealed to S. W. Swenson at Austin, and finally to Mr. P. T. Barnum in New York, to put money into the preparation of a panorama. The eight hundred miles presented were, he wrote, "a perfect epitome of all the interior of this great state." He mentioned in his descriptions "the majestic live oak . . . the beautiful Acacia . . . luxuriant grapes . . . a coun-

[49] McDermott, *The Lost Panoramas,* p. 173.
[50] Bertha L. Heilbron, "Documentary Panorama: John Stevens and His Sioux War Pictures," *Minnesota History,* XXX (March, 1949), 20.
[51] *This Week, Herald Tribune,* New York, Richard Harrety, "The World's Largest Painting," March 13, 1966, cover and p. 11; Paul Philippoteaux, *Battle of Gettysburg,* Century of Progress International Exposition (catalogue), Chicago, Illinois, 1933, pp. 5–56.
[52] Albert Ten Eyck Gardner, *Vanderlyn's Panorama of Versailles.*
[53] *New Orleans Daily Picayune,* March 24, 1857; April 29, 1857; June 6, 1857; McDermott, *The Lost Panoramas,* pp. 9, 10, 13, 68; Joseph E. Arrington, "Skirving's Moving Panorama: Colonel Fremont's Western Expeditions, Pictorialized," *Historical Society Quarterly* (June, 1964), 48–62.
[54] Thomas Wharton, Diary (Micro-film), April 19, 1854, Barker Library, The University of Texas, Austin; original in New York City Public Library.
[55] Ivan T. Sanderson, "A-h-h B-l-o-o-w-s," *American Heritage,* XII, No. 1 (1960), 59; Edgar P. Richardson, *Painting in America, the Story of 450 Years,* pp. 211–212; McDermott, *The Lost Panoramas,* pp. 15–16.
[56] Odell, *Annals of the New York Stage,* VI, 177; VII, 97, 540.

try that had never been trodden by the foot of white man."[57]

The panorama paintings in addition to their educational value created greater interest in the possibilities of landscape painting (if only in enlarging and intensifying the artist's canvas). It might be said that the era of the American panorama was a phenomenon of the times, adding a great chapter to the history of nineteenth-century painting.

Peter A. Moelling

The first we hear of the Reverend Peter A. Moelling, an emigrant from Neusdadt A. H. Rheinpfalz, Bavaria, is through the announcement that he was exhibiting his painting *The Battle of Galveston* in Houston during May of 1863. He was painting at that time another scene, *The Capture of the* Harriet Lane.[58] These paintings, now lost, depicted the events of January, 1863, when in Galveston Harbor the "Cotton Clad Squadron" went into action against the Federal Fleet.[59] Peter Moelling very likely witnessed the affair.

Moelling's announcement of May 25 stated that he needed a magnifying glass in order to point out to visitors the firing of the first gun by General J. Bankhead Magruder of the Confederate Army.[60] While this use of the magnifying glass indicates that the details were small, he may have been attempting in his painting something similar to a series for a panoramic view—he may have caught the fever of painting related successive scenes of a historic event. Furthermore, the painting was so large that he was unable to exhibit it further unless he could secure a wagon to transport it.[61] Having had success in exhibiting it at Houston, Chapel Hill, and Independence, he was now ready to take it to Washington-on-the-Brazos and Huntsville.

By July he had traveled to Hempstead.[62] Moelling's public exhibition, as far as we know, was a one-man affair—he did the painting, took it from place to place, gave his own lecture, and provided his own music. Both the words and music for songs have been attributed to him.

When he had reached Richmond (Texas), he exhibited under the auspices of the Ladies Aid Society (which was providing a refreshment table), and announced that he had with him *"The Battle of Galveston* and other paintings and prints."* This showing was for the benefit of the soldiers—"Open from morning 'til night at Herndon's Hall."[63]

Peter Moelling published a book in Galveston in 1857, *Reise-Skizzen in Poesie und Prosa,* a publication from the Apologetten printing office, where he served as editor of the *Christian Apologist,* and was known as "Reverend" Peter Moelling.[64] It is evident from his book that he had been traveling in the States before coming to Galveston. His book, in German, contains Longfellow's poem "Minnehaha" and a poem "The Falls of the Minnehaha" by Moelling himself. To make this fact clear he had enscribed on his own Byronic portrait the word "Minnehaha."[65]

This portrait and those of "our" ministers included in the book were lithographed by Orr of New York, but one is inclined to think that the preliminary sketches were made by Moelling.

[57] Letters, Dr. L. W. Baker to S. M. Swenson, Austin, March 9, 1852; S. M. Swenson to William S. Pierson, New York, March 13, 1854, The University of Texas Archives, Austin.

[58] *The Tri-Weekly Telegraph,* Houston, May 20, 1863.

[59] Charles C. Cumberland, "The Confederate Loss and Recapture of Galveston, 1862–1863," *Southwestern Historical Quarterly,* LI, No. 2 (October, 1947), 109–130.

[60] *The Tri-Weekly Telegraph,* Houston, May 20, 1863, pp. 145, 101, Rev. Peter Moelling, Description of Texas.

[61] *The Tri-Weekly Telegraph,* Houston, June 26, 1863, p. 205.

[62] *Ibid.,* July 13, 1963.

[63] *Ibid.,* July 24, 1863.

[64] Peter August Moelling, *Reise-Skizzen in Poesie und Prosa,* pp. 175, 176–177.

[65] *Ibid.,* "Reverend Moelling," title page.

CHAPTER 5

EUROPEAN INFLUX:
A MEDLEY OF STYLES

I N THE CLOSING YEARS of the eighteenth century and during the first years of the nineteenth century the painter in Europe was born to an era where changes already had come about and new concepts in art were in use. The coming of romanticism had begun its path —sensibility had replaced blind acceptance. Greater freedom had already encouraged the artist to identify himself with nature in a new romantic way. The artist's urge to express himself in a language of his own produced a great diversity of subjects and styles. When it came to genre painting the artist of this time had what was required. In addition to Gentilz' astute observation there were extraordinary and moving scenes, exotic characters. Picturesque life and unspoiled nature furnished material for subject matter. Particularly did Gentilz and Carl Iwonski recognize this, and they had the technical mastery to put it on canvas. The painter's own way of seeing the world and his own aspirations made the middle of the nineteenth century a greater period of individual work than ever before. Stimulated by new lands, away from academic restraint, his imagination enjoyed

free play. Representative artists were Wright, Allen, and Andrews in the United States, Flintoff from England, and others from France and Germany who joined the fantasia.

Richard Petri

In the paintings and sketches of two German immigrants, the story of pioneer life in Texas is told in lucid, realistic terms. Frederick Richard Petri (1824–1857) and Carl Hermann Frederick Lungkwitz (1813–1891), with five bewildered members of their two families, all natives of Saxony, landed at Indianola, Texas, in 1851; there was nothing more to view than a sparsely settled village, and, edging the water, a line of fishermen's huts. But looking overhead they saw dipping in all directions the sea gulls, sounding their melancholy plaint, and blue herons with silvery wings glistening in the sunshine: an omen of the wild beauty to be experienced.

Richard Petri, then twenty-six, was the youngest of the five children of Geb Weis and Heinrich Petri, burgher and well-to-do master shoemaker of Dresden.

Hermann Lungkwitz, thirty-seven, was the son of Freid-eriche Heckt and Johann Gottried Lungkwitz, a hose manufacturer of Halleander Saale. The two artists were among the many German emigrants who were to take up their painting in Texas.[1]

Four members of the families accompanying the artists appear frequently in Petri's pictures. Just before coming to America, Hermann Lungkwitz married Petri's sister Elise, who so often posed at the Akademie de Bildenden Künste for her brother's madonnas and other female figures. Elise and members of the Lungkwitz family—the seventy-eight-year-old mother (a brother Adolph, a silversmith, joined them later), a sister Teresa, and a sister Marie (who later married Jacob Kuechler)—made up the family group of six who were to become permanent colonists: a hearty group, with the exception of Petri, whose slight build, grave blue eyes, and slender expressive fingers bespoke the artist.

Both Lungkwitz and Petri had received their training at the Akademie de Bildenden Künste at Dresden. Petri entered in 1838 at the age of fourteen and emerged probably one of the best-trained talents of the Akademie —certainly among the most proficient to come to Texas. Both artists experienced disturbing events during the German revolution, and their last year of student life was anything but peaceful. Upon completing studies they went about their painting. Lungkwitz settled for a short time in Leipzig but returned to Dresden in 1849; becoming aroused by politics, he joined Petri with the "Freischerrer" in street riots.[2] No doubt both young men speculated on the strange, diverse, and puzzling conduct of man. When time permitted, they discussed ideas of freedom and self-determinism of the German people, and their own life fulfillment. In the spring of 1849 the political storm broke with all its force and the two artists found themselves armed against the oppressive yoke of Napoleon I. Behind street barricades they fought side by side with Wilhelm Richard Wagner, composer and poet, and associated with such other compatible and prominent young Germans as Franz Sigel, Friedrich Hecker, and Lorenz Brentano.[3] L. A. Franzl, a poet of the revolutionaries, glorified the student party in these lines:

> When Kaiser Joseph came in thunder
> To bind the Tongue's sweet liberty,
> Who dared to burst the bonds asunder?
> The University![4]

Upon finishing his work at the Akademie, Petri was offered the opportunity to travel to continue art study and to teach in the Akademie, but he did not accept because of his health. His success he attributed to his teachers Adrian Ludwig Richter (1803–1884) and Julius Hübner (1806–1882),[5] the latter noted for religious paintings. Hübner's influence would explain the large number of literary and religious subjects treated by the pupil.

Petri's work may be grouped in three parts: (1) mythological and Biblical scenes, (2) portraits, and (3) larger group scenes of activities of pioneer life. Many in the first group were made while Petri was still at the Akademie under the full influence of German romanticism. He made sketches of Prince Tancred and Clorinda for an oil painting illustrating the story of the pagan heroine Clorinda, from Torquato Tasso's *Jerusalem Delivered*. Another in this category, also painted while he was a student, is *Genoveva* (9″ x 10″), which received an award in 1844. His widely traveled teacher Ludwig Richter (son of Carl Richter, an engineer) was bemedaled in both Paris and Vienna and was known for his creation of the atmosphere of the fairy tale and the legend. When Richter exhibited *Genoveva* in 1844, Petri followed with a much smaller painting (c. 9″ x 9″), a conventionalized oil, showing Genoveva in the forest with the child, while a doe suckled the infant. An award by the Akademie for this painting is dated October 18, 1844. Petri received five other awards while at the Akademie. Other mythological drawings of his are *Beowulf Slaying the Dragon, The Myth of the Dragon's Teeth, St. Michael and Satan,* and *Dwarfs of the Nibelungen.*[6]

Another subject, drawn from the Bible and treated romantically, received an award in 1845—a silver medal for the oil *Die Versohnung und Essau darstellend—*

[1] Interviews, Mrs. Walter Wupperman and Ernest von Rosenberg, Austin; Samuel W. Geiser, *Naturalists of the Frontier,* p. 318; "Two Pioneer Texas Artists," University of Texas Exhibition List and Biographical Notes, Austin, April 13–15, 1934, author's collection.

[2] A. J. F. Zieglschmid, "Pioneer Artists of Texas," *American-German Review* (October, 1942), 4–6.

[3] Mae Estelle Meyers "Lives and Works of Hermann Lungkwitz and Richard Petri," M.A. Thesis, University of Texas, 1933, p. 46.

[4] Dr. Elfriede Underberg, "Herausgegeben Deutsche Literatur in Entwicklungsreihen, Reihen Politische Dichtung" *Die Dichtung der ersten deutschen, Revolution 1848–1849,* Vol. 5, p. 30.

[5] George C. Williamson (ed.) *Cyclopedia of Painters and Engravers,* see Adrian Ludwig Richter, IV, 41.

[6] Meyers. "Lives and Works," p. 33; original certificate of award in collection of Mrs. Henry Ulrich, Austin, Texas.

30. Richard Petri: *Music Festival Poster*
    Oil, c. 1851, 23½″ x 17¼″ (Courtesy of Mr. Max Bickler, Austin, Texas)

Eigene Erfindung (1845).[7] His religious pictures demonstrate not only skill and spiritual strength but also a remarkable intellectual grasp for one of his years. Notable works in water color and tempera are *Christ Entering Jerusalem, The Crucifixion, Madonna of the Roses* (6½" x 10"), *Adoration of the Kings and Shepherds* (7" x 5½"), *The Holy Family* (3" x 5"), *Madonna of the Cup* (c. 2" x 2½", made for a broach), *Mary Anoints the Feet of Jesus* (3½" x 5."), *Elijah Being Fed by the Raven, Elijah's Ascension into Heaven, Procession with the Holy Ark*, and an illustration, *Matthew 17:27*.[8] It is this group that best shows his sympathetic introspection and the real measure of his mind.

The failure of the liberal revolution of 1848 had already brought a number of cultured Germans to Texas, and the two artists—longing to pursue their art in peace—decided they, too, would come to America. Like many other political refugees, they accepted the advice and guidance of the German emigration society "Mainzer Adelsverein." From time to time books and leading newspapers had published favorable information on what they could expect to find in Texas.[9] Their first glimpse of America was from the deck of their ship at Hoboken, New Jersey, early in 1850. They went on to West Virginia, but thinking that Petri's health might be better in a milder climate, they shipped again to Indianola, Texas.

From Indianola they traveled north to New Braunfels in oxcarts. Progressing slowly, they tried to forget the difficulties of passage to America with little food and stormy weather in the "wooden box," as some called the crowded ill-smelling ship.[10] Now, on the unmarked frontier road, they felt little consolation when their eyes turned toward the wide prairies, where they suspected lurking Indians and howling coyotes, whose cries ripped the sky. But they were courageous. When evening came they felt a certain security within the circle of wagons and the bulwark of oxen and horses that guarded them from attack. With the glow of the campfire, the odors of cooking food and woodsmoke, and the fresh smell of cedars as the dampness of night came on, a feeling of warmth crept over the weary travelers. When all was quiet they could hear the stomping feet of oxen and horses, and the crunching of the corn as the animals were fed. They might even hear the plop of acorns or pecans falling from trees along the creek. It was fall in Texas and their new home was ahead!

Leaving the school of European romanticism and the bitterness of years of political strife, these young artists now entering the United States embraced its expansive mood. Breathing the very atmosphere of freedom, and stimulated by the wild surrounding beauty, they reached new dimensions in their art. Though they were pressed by material want, the work of each developed greater individuality and imaginative force.

While still on board ship Petri made delightful sketches of traveling companions: the captain at the wheel, an English lady passenger. Later, as the colonists journeyed from Indianola to New Braunfels, he sketched scenes along the way.[11]

At New Braunfels they found a progressive German settlement. Soon Petri made a poster in oil (possibly mixed with other media) to announce a music festival (Plate 30). The cleverly conceived poster has a medium-blue background, with small masks on the upper corners to indicate the tragic and comic themes in the music. One side of the face of the central male figure shows grief, the other joy. Petri's wording on the poster (in German) begins, "Please Gentlemen, Music for You! For the flute arranged by Apollo Sausel—Theme, Love, Hate . . ."

Pencil, crayon (Plate 31), water color, and tempera are his customary mediums. Only occasionally does Petri turn to oil. Among these few, examples are the fine portraits *Teresa Lungkwitz, Hermann Lungkwitz, Elise,* and *Shylock*, all student work.

In contrast, Lungkwitz worked chiefly in oils. Often the artists collaborated—advising now and then, or contributing a brush stroke. Probably an example of mutual effort is the drawing *San Antonio de Béxar*, made in 1851 and sent to Germany to be engraved. Tradition holds that the drawing in the central portion, namely the oxen and human figures, are Petri's hand, while the scenic work around the central portion is Lungkwitz'.[12]

[7] "Two Pioneer Texas Artists," p. 2.

[8] Meyers, "Lives and Works," pp. 36–37.

[9] Rudolph Leopold Biesele, *History of the German Settlements in Texas, 1831–1861*, pp. 226–227; J. V. Hecke, *Reife burch die Bereinigten Statten von Nord-America*, I, 195–203; II, 170–178.

[10] Adelina Wueste Staffel, San Antonio, letter to her mother, Mrs. Louise Wueste, Europe, quoted *American-German Review* (August, 1842), 20.

[11] Esther Mueller, "Hermann Lungkwitz and Richard Petri, Artists of Fredericksburg" (Newspaper clipping, no name or date).

[12] Ferdinand Roemer, *Texas, with Particular Reference to German Immigration and Physical Appearance of the Country*, translated by Oswald Mueller, p. 12; collection of Ernest von Rosenberg, Austin, preliminary sketch and completed oil.

31. Richard Petri: *Elise Lungkwitz*
Crayon, c. 1847, 7″ x 6″ (Courtesy of Mrs. Walter Wupperman, Austin, Texas)

Photographs being out of the question, Petri recorded the faces of members of the family with meticulous care, displaying an unusual perception of character. A second portrait of Elise, drawn with classical draftsmanship, as if by a fine steel point, is truly a work of art—with a blue ribbon in her hair, a coral necklace and broach in color, signed and dated 1847. A three-quarters self-portrait (c. 1852), drawn with frank realism, is done also with such precision that it has the appearance of an engraving (Plate 32). He used a light water color for the coat and the eyes. Similar portrait sketches with a fine pencil point are *Julia, Teresa* (a second one), *Robert Queisser* (a nephew), and *Adolph Lungkwitz*. Other sketches in a heavier crayon are *Profile of an Early Settler* and *Profile of Man with Glasses* (June 1852), the last is the only one with a humorous quality (Plate 33). A sketch of Lungkwitz in a heavier pencil shows his subject with liveliness and a sense of well-being.

Petri made a crayon portrait of scientist Ottomar von Behr, who came to New Braunfels about 1846. Later, in Sisterdale, Texas, he became postmaster and storekeeper, and maintained a lending library. He was a kinsman of the distinguished anthropologist and physician of California, Dr. Norman Behr, who worked in the field of meteorology and natural history. At the time Petri made the drawing, Dr. Ottomar von Behr was working at Sisterdale, experimenting with the improvement of wool.[13]

It was difficult for the colonists to establish a home and farm, for they were not accustomed to hard work. Pioneer life at times became almost unbearably hard, for the artists came from families of comfortable means and were unaccustomed to the hardships they were forced to undergo in Texas. Furthermore, their art found only small gain. After three years friends persuaded them that they would fare better on land near Fredericksburg, a thriving community founded by German emigrants in 1846. Here, six miles southwest of the town, near the Pedernales River, they built (1854) their log house. The Pedernales, a small but intermittently deep-flowing stream through huge rocks and tangled woods, was to provide them with exciting subject matter for their valuable paintings and sketches. Here were the Indians—Comanches, Caddos, and Lipan Apaches—troublesome and treacherous until the newcomers were able to make friends of them. This Petri did by opening doors to them and making presents of sketches of various members of the tribes.[14]

32. Richard Petri: *Self-Portrait*
Pencil and water color, c. 1852, 6¾″ x 4½″ (Courtesy of Mrs. Walter Wupperman, Austin, Texas)

Special mention should be made of Petri's drawings of Indian life; he gloried in their picturesque dress and exploits, making drawings of their activities and, what was even more venturesome, making portraits of individuals. The artist Seth Eastman had passed through this area, stopping at Ft. Martin Scott (1849) shortly before Petri was sketching Caddo, Lipan, and Comanche Indians, and enlarging our knowledge of the Indians of this area; but Eastman's chief interest, while there, was in the habitat of the Indian and the countryside of this area rather than portraits or drawings of their activities.

[13] Geiser, *Naturalists*, pp. 136, 318; Dumas Malone, *Dictionary of American Biography*, V, 148–150.
[14] Meyers, "Lives and Works," p. 67.

33. Richard Petri: *Profile of Man with Glasses*
Pencil, 1852, 8½″ x 7″ (Courtesy of Mrs. Walter Wupperman, Austin, Texas)

34. Richard Petri: *Lipan Indian*
Pencil and water color, 1852, 6½″ x 5½″ (Courtesy of Mr. Ernest von Rosenberg, Austin, Texas)

35. Richard Petri: *Indian Maid*
Water color and pencil, c. 1852, 8¼″ x 6¾″ (Courtesy of Mrs. Hunter P. Harris, Houston, Texas)

One fine portrait of Petri's is of a Lipan, showing his long black hair falling over his shoulders and around his neck (Plate 34). Added in fine detail is a gorget of three crescents, a type worn by his people and fashioned perhaps by Adolph Lungkwitz, the silversmith. It was said that the Indians were in the habit of bringing silver from the mines to his shop in New Braunfels for use in fashioning their ornaments and articles of various kinds.[15]

Another water color shows a Comanche chief on horseback, carrying a long lance. Behind him is his oval bullhide shield, and a red-and-blue blanket is draped about his body. Riding on a horse behind him is a squaw holding a child. This subject is extant both in pencil and water color. A small water-color portrait of a Lipan who wears a scarf of red polka-dotted material around his head is a striking example of Petri's Indian portraits. Another is a small water color (full length) of a child eating a slice of melon: the story told relating to this picture is that when Petri expressed a desire to paint the little Indian, the mother, like modern mothers, begged that Petri wait until she could make him a new suit.[16] In this fringed deerskin suit Petri finally painted him—plus the slice of melon. Among the water-color and pencil sketches of the Indians in various poses are *Indian Maid* (Plate 35), *Indians on Horses at a Stream, Four Indians on a Rock, Indian on a Horse*, and *Indian Mother and Child on a Donkey*.

A small sketch shows a group of gypsies or perhaps cartmen with their families around a camp fire, their wagons serving as shields against intruders. A man on horseback has just joined them.

As emigrants the artists were allowed to bring implements and materials of their trade or profession with them tax free, but although well supplied when leaving the homeland, these reserves became exhausted after a few months. Paper was so scarce that Petri used flyleaves from books, and even put to use the reverse side of his Academy awards. At such distances from sources of material, the artists often turned to supplementing their paints with those made from plants and soil.[17]

In this new environment, in spite of innumerable discomforts and scarcity of materials, the artists were able to turn their interests from Old World scenes and paint with remarkable appreciation and success. As a result, no richer pictorial record of early life in Texas exists than their paintings and drawings—an invaluable

contribution not only to our artistic heritage but also to the social history of the Southwest. Unfortunately some of Petri's work done on fragile material has been lost.

His drawings of everyday farm life are executed with the same warm domesticity and faithfulness found in old Dutch paintings. One almost can follow life on the frontier by examining his numerous paintings and drawings. With pencil and crayon he caught, as though by camera, the activities of tiny Martha and Max, the Lungkwitz children. He sketched them in every mood: at play, feeding the animals, reading by candlelight, riding the horses, crossing a stream.

The Pioneer Cowpen (Plate 36)—an amusing scene of life on a Texas farm—is a miniature painting rendered with painstaking realism. The artist's sister Marie, wearing a tight-fitting bodice and full skirt of the period, is milking "Butterfly," while Teresa milks the other cow. From the folds of Marie's skirt peeks the calculating household cat. Above the gate of the zigzag rail fence a rooster is crowing heartily. Beyond the fence, Hermann Lungkwitz, on horseback, is ready to tend the cattle. White curtains flutter from the window of a corner of the log house. This water color was sent to kinsmen in Germany to illustrate pioneer life, but strangely enough the picture found its way back to Texas.

A water-color and pencil drawing of similar size and workmanship, *Going Visiting* (Plate c-6), shows another frontier scene. It might be considered a companion piece to *The Pioneer Cowpen*. In this picture Petri shows the family in an oxcart driven by the artist himself, who walks beside the oxen with a long whip in his hands. He is wearing a red scarf and his "Garibaldi" (red) blouse with wide sleeves, which he wore when he joined the "Freischerer," the organization of students who helped to defend Dresden. Lungkwitz and his wife are on the front seat, and behind them are the "girls" dressed in all their finery, carrying ruffled parasols. They are about to cross Liveoak Creek, and in the distance can be seen the home of the well-to-do miller, Carl H. Guenther. This miniature painting, while it appears an anachronism—the details being too refined for pioneer life—

[15] Mueller, "Hermann Lungkwitz and Richard Petri, Artists of Fredericksburg."
[16] *Ibid.*
[17] Meyers, "Lives and Works," p. 63.

83

36. Richard Petri: *The Pioneer Cowpen* ["Austin, Texas" and "1849" were added by an unknown person]
Water color, 1843, 4″ x 6⅜″ (Courtesy of Mr. Walter Long, Austin, Texas)

c-6. Richard Petri: *Going Visiting* ["Austin, Texas" and "1849" were added by
an unknown person]
Water color, 4″ x 6⅜″ (Courtesy of Mr. Walter Long, Austin, Texas)

37. Richard Petri: *Fort Martin Scott* [unfinished]
Oil, 1857, 16½" x 23" (Courtesy of Mr. Ernest von Rosenberg, Austin, Texas)

reminds us in the same instant, through extreme contrasts of clothing and heavy muddy oxcart, of the' adjustments these pioneers were compelled to make in the undeveloped country. The inscription "Austin Texas" and the date "1849" were incorrectly added to *Going Visiting* and *The Pioneer Cowpen* years after the paintings were made.

An unfinished oil (1857) which Petri made of Fort Martin Scott (Plate 37) is one of his best genre paintings as well as one of the most important historically. This fort was established in 1848 by the United States Army to protect the steadily increasing number of pioneers from the Indians, and was named for Lieutenant Colonel Martin Scott, who distinguished himself at the battle of Monterrey, Mexico. The fort was abandoned in 1866. In 1850 Lieutenant William A. C. Whiting, army engineer and an artist of some note, wrote of Fort Martin Scott:

Placed in a section of country which is part of the rich valley of the Pedernales, clothed with a plentiful growth of postoak and cypress with abundance of building stone, lime and sand near by, and among the settlements rapidly increasing, it has almost all the requisites for the quarters and subsistence of troops. . . . The fine barracks of hewn logs already put up are ample for all present purposes and other than these no defensive works are necessary yet; for complete security against horse stealing by the Indians I would recommend that all public stables be enclosed by a strong picket fence.[18]

Although this painting of Fort Martin Scott is unfinished, Petri left in it a documentary record with many interesting details. One of the chief functions of a fort, in addition to defense, was to provide a trading place for both the Indian and the emigrant. In the 1840's and 1850's barter was the chief system of trade. The citizen traded cotton for sugar and coffee, bacon for boots, and corn for calomel, quinine, or whiskey. The Indian brought in buffalo skins, moccasins, and corn for which he received beads, hair-pipes, arms, cotton stuffs, and, if possible, whiskey.[19] Just such activities are shown by Petri at Fort Martin Scott. In the background are the log and rock buildings of the fort, and in the foreground an Indian wigwam; Indians and soldiers are standing or sitting around a campfire: Several squaws can be seen in the melee. At the center of the picture are a United States soldier and an Indian maid, who appear to be the chief attractions. It would seem that the soldier is

Captain George Thomas Howard, Indian fighter, who in 1850 was appointed Indian agent by the United States Department of the Interior.[20] The pencil drawing gives more details than the unfinished oil. In the foreground of it crawls a naked child, while an Indian can be seen stealing a drink from a flask in the pocket of one of the soldiers.

Other genre sketches pertaining to everyday activities help us envision frontier life, such as *Men Seated around a Table* (one plays a stringed instrument), *A Texas Bear Hunt*, and *Carrying Water from a Stream*.

In the seven years that Petri lived in New Braunfels and Fredericksburg, he did a surprising amount of painting and sketching. He died in 1857 from drowning. While swimming in the Pedernales River, his frail body (fever stricken from tuberculosis) succumbed to the rapid current—in view of the solitary hills and plains where he had spent so many contented hours with nature.

Many other European artists with an acquired technical skill migrated to this country in the middle of the century, and like Petri were able to take root and paint with enthusiasm. Such men as Karl Bodmer (1809–1893), Albert Bierstadt (1830–1902), and Karl F. Wimar (1828–1862) made brilliant contributions to our Western art annals. Although not as dramatic, Petri's small paintings and drawings of the Texas scene are of wider range and excel in draftsmanship the work of many transplanted European artists. He possessed a greater native skill than many frontier artists of the American scene, and had he lived into another decade he no doubt would have reached a place of eminence. So bound together were his talent, skill, and enthusiasm, that his work remains on the highest level.

Hermann Lungkwitz

March 14, 1813, was a day long to be remembered by the Germans of Halle an der Saale, for it was the day when Napoleon's army bombarded the city. It was also the day Hermann Lungkwitz was born, and it was in this same disquieted atmosphere that Lungkwitz spent

[18] William A. C. Whiting, *Reports of the Secretary of War, 31st Congress*, 1st Session Document, No. 64, p. 239.

[19] William Bollaert, *William Bollaert's Texas*; edited by W. Eugene Hollon and Ruth L. Butler, p. 190; interview, Ernest von Rosenberg, Austin, Texas.

[20] Register of old Nimitz Hotel, Fredericksburg: Major Howard, 1853; interview, Ernest von Rosenberg, Austin, Texas.

Main Plaza.

Alameda.

Alamo (1850.)

Mission de la Concepcion.

SAN ANTONIO DE BEXAR.

Mission San José

The New Bridge

San Pedro Spring

Mission San Juan

38. Hermann Lungkwitz: *San Antonio de Béxar*
    Engraving, 1851, 16″ x 17¾″ (Courtesy of the Amon Carter Museum of Western Art, Fort Worth, Texas)

his childhood. While he was still a youth, his parents recognized his unusual drawing ability, and on the death of a bachelor uncle he received a legacy which made it possible for him to attend the Akademie de Bildenden Künste at Dresden.[21] He was twenty-five years old on en-

tering, and Richard Petri, a precocious youth just fourteen, was entering also. Despite the difference in age they became fast friends, and we find that in the following years their friendship grew and became important to both artists. They studied together, fought together, and came to Texas together. Their friendship meant even more when, just before leaving Germany, Lungkwitz married

21 Exhibition List "Two Pioneer Texas Artists," pp. 1–4.

Petri's older sister, Elise.[22] Although as a whole their work was in different mediums in their art, they shared experiences and experiments which brought each encouragement and satisfaction.

Lungkwitz had not proved himself a brilliant student, but he had imagination and drive. He did not shrink from attempting the difficult in landscape painting—putting the simple and rugged into a work of art.

As a youth, he went to Leipzig with his father, who was buying wool for manufacturing hose; Hermann was not interested in wool, but the city with its wonders and curiosities was a delight to him. On completing his study he knew he would be expected to go to Leipzig with his father, who had continuously tried to interest him in becoming an expert in selecting fine wool; in this way, his father thought, the boy would have more remunerative work and be ready some day to step into his shoes in the manufacture of hose.[23] But Lungkwitz' courageous mind was set; he wanted only to be an artist.

Both Petri and Lungkwitz studied under Ludwig Richter, and Lungkwitz had an admiration and attachment for his teacher which lasted throughout his life. When Richter was in his eighties he wrote these lines to Lungkwitz, recalling how his later years grew pleasanter after their uneasy days at Dresden:

> Der Morgen küehl,
> Der Mittag schwüel,
> Viel Unruh bei dem Feste,
> Der Abend ist das Beste.[24]

As Lungkwitz' chief interest was in landscape, he followed the prescribed course, which included a sketching tour in the Alps. From this tour (1843) he brought small dark paintings with him to this country, *Scene in Tyrolean Alps, Sunset in the Salzburg Alps, Scene in the Austrian Alps, Forest and River of Halle*, and *Ruins of the Monastery* (Germany). While studying at the Fine Arts Academy in Dresden, he received an award for a landscape in 1843.[25] These flat dark paintings are in sharp contrast to his later paintings done in Texas, when he used more light and stronger color. We shall see how realism fused with the romanticism in which he was trained, became less important, and was replaced by imagination and enthusiasm in a new environment, where he painted with greater freshness and understanding.

Lungkwitz' outlook was always bright on his venture in coming to America. He wrote his brother from Wheeling, West Virginia, on his way to Texas: "We are entirely at ease regarding our existence in the United States since we have learned that a person (so long as he remains in good health) can if necessary get by with his art—without humbug—and with reasonable success and patronage make a living." He asked that his brother bring him a supply of "retoucher varnish."[26] Although battling against every primitive element of the frontier and with the daily struggle to live in an undeveloped area, Lungkwitz did not give up his art for any great length of time. The sharp edge of the hardships of his daily living could be forgotten in the quiet freedom he was experiencing—a truth so precisely expressed by Aldous Huxley in *On Art and Artists*: "For the artist the material obstacles in the way of unrestricted self-expression are easier to surmount than the mental."[27] The dates of his paintings show that wherever he was, he painted, whether in New Braunfels, Fredericksburg, San Antonio, or Austin. As the extremes of weather in the Fredericksburg area were of short duration the two artists would, after the chores of the farm were done, ramble through the woods with pen and brush, along the Pedernales and in the adjoining counties, recording what they saw. Lungkwitz reveled in the wild prairies, streams unexplored by the white man, gnarled trees, jagged granite rock hillsides, Indians, and wild life. He studied every facet of nature, for the wild scene seemed to make the strongest appeal to him, as it did to many other Europeans. When his landscape was put on canvas, there might be an Indian at the spring or a fisherman in a canoe on the river. Some of the paintings made from pencil sketches done close to his home near Fredericksburg are *Flatrock Creek* (1854), *On the Pedernales, Palo Alto Crossing, Clift and Road, Guenther's Mill on Liveoak Creek*, and *Hill Country* (Plate c-7).

[22] *San Antonio Express*, April 15, 1934; August 5, 1951; *Southern Intelligencer*, Austin, October 21, 1857.

[23] Meyers, "Lives and Works," pp. 5–8.

[24] Original note from Ludwig Richter, Germany, to Hermann Lungkwitz, Austin, c. 1857, collection of Ernest von Rosenberg, Austin.

[25] Award for landscape (engraved) 1843; A. J. F. Zeiglschmidt, "Richter's Sketches in the United States," *American-German Review* (February, 1943), 18–21.

[26] Letter, Hermann Lungkwitz, Wheeling, West Virginia, to Adolph Lungkwitz, New York, March 8, 1851, collection of Ernest von Rosenberg, Austin.

[27] Aldous Huxley, *On Art and Artists*, p. 1.

When the dark clouds of pre-Civil War days were threatening, provisions and materials were hard to obtain. With a growing family Lungkwitz felt the pinch of hard times, for there were Max and Martha now, and the twins, Alice and Helene. The death of his companion and helper, Petri, in 1857, was a distressing blow. Because of greater responsibilities added to his already heavy burden, the artist was constantly faced with the problem of maintaining his home. As his pictures were finding no purchasers, he decided to take up photography, the new medium for taking likenesses, and went to San Antonio (1866) to investigate the matter.[28] His decision proved to be the turning point in his career, more important than the photographic business itself. We know that he did not close his eyes to the facts that the art of landscape was coming into its own in America, and that the development of new pigments would open up a whole new world to the craft of painting. The coal-tar industry brought to the artist's palette a series of brilliant new colors, from mauve (1856) through the spectrum to magenta and cobalt violet (1859) and cobalt yellow (1861).[29]

In the early 1860's Lungkwitz joined an astute young Hungarian, Carl G. von Iwonski (1830–1922), of San Antonio, in a venture into photography. They set up a studio over the Bell Silversmith Shop on Houston Street.[30] It was, no doubt, Iwonski, already a well-established artist, who helped to sustain Lungkwitz' interest in painting, even though there was little sale for their work at this time.

Just how financially successful they were in the photographic business is not known, but both artists, as did others, discovered through this experience the use of luminosity. Lungkwitz' problem was how to interpret nature with new pigments and increased knowledge of light and of brighter hues. Now he must lay aside the sober Dresden palette that had been so long a part of the craft of painting as he knew it.

Lungkwitz was already known in San Antonio, from a trip in 1851, when he made a drawing of Bonham and Crockett Streets back of the Alamo, "Taken from Nature" for an engraving, San Antonio de Béxar (Plate 38). A later study of this subject, made in oil, is in Germany. Similar drawings were made of New Braunfels and Fredericksburg (Plate 39).

In 1865 Lungkwitz finished Enchanted Rock (25″ x 37″), a scene near Fredericksburg, a view he painted several times. After the fall of 1841 this place became

noted because of a single-handed battle between Ranger John Coffee Hays and a Comanche in which the renowned Indian fighter was the victor. In 1842 General Burleson, while on a campaign into the Indian country, visited the Enchanted Rock situated on the "Sandy"— a branch of the Pedernales. The formation was described as "one solid rock of dark color rising to the height of about 400 feet and covering a space larger than a common race track or about 200 acres of ground."[31]

Enchanted Rock is actually one of the small mountains or hills whose summits contain some dark-colored mica. Because these broad mica plates reflected the moon's or sun's rays with peculiar brilliance, the Comanches revered the hill with strange fascination. Earlier, Seth Eastman, in his travels through this area, not realizing it was actually a hill, called the first large rock he saw the "Enchanted Rock." When Lungkwitz found no immediate sale for his Enchanted Rock, he took it to New Braunfels and raffled it off for one dollar per chance. Fortunately an appreciative friend won the painting and valued it through the years. A second painting of the Enchanted Rock, slightly smaller but rendered in much the same mood and time, is among the Texas collection at the Witte Museum, San Antonio.[32]

The first painting of the Enchanted Rock reflects the mood of the artist in his interpretation of nature—he depicts a lonely, quiet scene. Three Indians, indistinct in form, stand together on giant weather-stained boulders between towering cliffs. In portraying the scene, the artist reveals his sense of the infinite. The tonal quality of quietness and repose reminds one of the work of Thomas Cole (1801–1848) and Thomas Doughty (1793–1886).

The Alameda, San Antonio (Plate 40) is a view of one of the streets in Old San Antonio with a long avenue of poplars. The height of the trees subordinates the surrounding life, causing the viewer to be captivated by an illusion of infinitude. In the foreground, with practical realism, the artist shows the remains of the old

---

[28] San Antonio Express, advertisement of photographic business, May 24, 1866.

[29] Edgar P. Richardson, Painting in America, the Story of 450 Years, pp. 218–219.

[30] San Antonio Express, May 24, 1866.

[31] Telegraph and Texas Register, Houston, November 18, 1840; October 19, 1842.

[32] Mr. Ernst Schuchard, San Antonio, Texas, information on "Enchanted Rock."

39. Hermann Lungkwitz: *View of Fredericksburg, Texas*
Engraving, 12" x 18" (Courtesy of the Amon Carter Museum of Western Art, Fort Worth, Texas)

acequia, built a century before by Indians under Spanish supervision to serve the missions with water from the San Antonio River. This painting suggests the much later (1895) and better-known *The Harp of the Winds* by Homer Martin (1836–1897). Other views painted in San Antonio are *Crockett Street* (1852), *Old Mill Bridge,* Vallita Street (Plate 41), *San Juan Capistrano,* and *San José de Aguayo.*

In 1870 Jacob Kuechler (who married Lungkwitz' sister Marie) became commissioner of the General Land Office at Austin and offered Lungkwitz (1871) a position as official photographer for reproducing maps. In this much needed service his daughter Martha assisted. On moving his family to Austin, he found that in addition to his photographic work he was able to take pupils in drawing and painting, later accepting a position as teacher in Texas' English and German school.[33] During the latter part of his stay in the Land Office, he was assisted by a friend and kinsman William von Rosenberg, a draftsman and fine topographical artist from Germany. Lungkwitz soon took up his painting with renewed interest in and around Austin. His landscapes, painted out of doors, are in rich clear tones noticeably contrasting with his earlier, European work. On trips to his old stamping ground on the Pedernales River, he did paintings of greater finish and brilliance.

Some of the Austin scenes are *Barton's Creek* (1888), *Military Institute, Austin* (Plate 42), *Hamilton's Pool, Old Mill, Barton's Creek* (1885), *Scene Southwest of Austin* (1888), *Hill of Cedars near Austin, Frame House on Shoal Creek, Split Rock, Shoal Creek, Texas River,* and *Mt. Bonnell.*[34] The last named shows a high point northwest of Austin, named after General George Bonnell, a famed Indian fighter during the days of the Republic. It was a fine lookout for Indians, and we have a published poem of a folklorist who discovered the strange presence of oyster shells on the hill.

> Then I repete again,
> How come you here? I might have
> Tho't some love sick Abrogoin had
> Brung you here from the coste when you was
> Fresh and click and bright to hang you
> On the years of his young squaw; but
> That wont do because here bushels
> Of you scattered around, and some's as
> Big as my foot!
> Kin it be true
> That orl that I can see from his High

> Pint, the woods, the hills and dales
> In times gone by was kivered up
> By oshants angry waves and where
> The scary doe, and nine pint buck
> Now crap the juicy grass, the por-
> Pers and the shirk fout, bled and blowed
> My what a thort![35]

The local editor reminded his subscribers that the painting of Mount Bonnell was on display in the artist's studio, and that Austin had two artists:

> Our citizens have always manifested a liberal spirit towards art whenever the opportunity has been presented . . . If our people knew that we have artists of genuine merit with reputations wider than the limits of our state they would surely give them liberal patronage, but true merit is ever modest, and few know there are two [Lungkwitz and Huddle] modest, hard working, painstaking men of genius who receive patronage and encouragement mainly from people of other states and cities. In the department of landscape painting, Mr. Lungkwitz, engaged in delineating views of the beautiful scenery about Austin has few equals . . . a small landscape of his now in his studio, a view of Mt. Bonnell in the distance is a perfect gem that needs only to be seen to be appreciated.[36]

Deer in the Pedernales (Plate 43), an achievement in landscape, stirs our imagination. A deer stands in a flowing stream; the broad sandstone boulders peculiar to this area, and the rough hillside covered with scrubby liveoak show the artist's devotion to wild, unspoiled nature. His frequent use of mundane rocks is a vivid example of this.

Had Lungkwitz enjoyed the stimulation of a more highly developed society and of the ablest in his craft, he might have achieved a greater plastic quality in his work, but it is also true that the artists in the frontier states, cut off from cultural centers, escaped the artistic self-consciousness so prevalent in the 1870's. It is the frankness and the simplicity of expression in his paintings that make them interesting. Whatever quality Lungkwitz may have lacked he had the gift of conveying the quiet, rugged beauty of the countryside. As someone said, his landscapes comfort the spirit.

It is a fact that the frontier existence of the artist pro-

---

[33] Meyers, "Lives and Works," pp. 84–86.
[34] "Two Pioneer Artists," pp. 1–3.
[35] *Southern Intelligencer,* Austin, October 21, 1857.
[36] *Austin Statesman,* July 8, 1877.

40. Hermann Lungkwitz: *The Alameda, San Antonio*
Oil, c. 1851, 9" x 12" (Courtesy of the San Antonio Public Library)

c-7. Hermann Lungkwitz: *Hill Country*

Oil, 1875, 25¾" x 35¾" (Courtesy of the Witte Museum, San Antonio, Texas)

41. Hermann Lungkwitz: *Old Mill Bridge*

Oil, 1856, 25½" x 33¾" (Courtesy of Mr. Ernst Schuchard, San Antonio, Texas)

42. Hermann Lungkwitz: *Military Institute, Austin*
Oil, 13½" x 19¾" (Courtesy of Mrs. Heinz Ullrich, Austin, Texas)

43. Hermann Lungkwitz: *Deer in the Pedernales*
Oil, 1875, 15½" x 23⅜" (Courtesy of Mrs. Hunter P. Harris, Houston, Texas)

44. Eugenie Aubanel Lavender: *Father Frank*
    Oil, 1879, 32″ x 26″ (Courtesy of the Incarnate Word Academy, Corpus Christi, Texas)

vided small means of bringing him knowledge of other artists' practices in distant centers. He had little opportunity to improve his technique except through experimentation. Sometimes engravings of other artists' work came to hand; a limited circulation of prints often aided the amateur and the self-taught. As early as 1837 "a splendid variety of plain and colored engravings and lithographs —at low prices" could be purchased at K. Keslers in Houston. The American Art Union circulated engravings through the "Honorable Secretary James B. Shaw Esq."[37] If the artist was fortunate enough to have $5.00 he might purchase (1850) through the Art Union some very good engravings copied by James Smilie, perhaps from one of Cole's paintings. Any inspiration which he might have received through association with other artists, except a few local representatives, was not possible. Only a trickle of knowledge came from groups such as the Hudson River School (arbitrarily so-called), scarcely enough to quench the thirst for new ideas.

Almost without exception the frontier artists worked in studios of daguerreotypes in out-of-the-way places, and most often in their own homes. Infrequent exhibitions gave little encouragement. Reputations were local. Lacking avenues of patronage and a reservoir of knowledge, they were compelled to experiment alone. This isolation, however, resulted in highly individual work of new, fresh vision. Lungkwitz left for the viewer's enjoyment seventy-two known oil paintings and some forty pencil sketches.

Eugenie Aubanel Lavender

An exhibition in Houston, Texas, a decade ago brought together a variety of paintings by Eugenie Etienne Aubanel Lavender (1817–1896), a trained and talented French woman, whose work was molded by strange and unusual circumstances in her life.[38] The early years she spent in her native Paris were during one of the most productive periods in nineteenth-century France; the later years on the Texas frontier furnished little opportunity for advancement in the craft of painting but provided stimulating experiences. Transplanted to Texas soil in 1852, she brought from her classes at the École des Beaux-Arts canvases still wet with paint, reflecting images of romantic realism inspired by literature and history.

The French Academy was then under the influence of Horace Vernet (1789–1863), whom Charles Baude-

laire, French historian, poet, and chief art critic of nineteenth-century France, called one of the "literary journalists."[39] But Eugenie's two teachers, Ary Scheffer (1795–1858) and Paul Delaroche (1797–1867), whose work, like Vernet's, leaned heavily toward historical and literary subjects, determined the character of her work.

Eugenie was born in a time of war and intrigue—the French Revolution. She was the oldest daughter of Julienne Antoinette Fortin and Etienne Aubanel. The latter's brother, General Aubanel, had marched to Moscow with the French Army, and was, of course, an ardent supporter of Napoleon and a political enemy of the English. Eugenie grew up with a dislike for the English, and also grew to resent the whole political situation.[40]

When Eugenie was eighteen, her sister married Count Chambonde de la Rouviere, and Eugenie felt keenly the loss of her companionship. Her parents, having recognized her deftness in drawing and wishing to ease her loneliness, sent her to Paris to study. Attending the Academy at the time was Marie Rosalie Bonheur (1822–1899), with whom Eugenie found genial companionship. In 1838 both received medals for their work, Rosa Bonheur for *Plowing in the Nivernaise*, and Eugenie for *The Greek*. The Academy at the time was under the patronage of Marie Amelie, wife of Louis Philippe, but the King himself presented the medals. Eugenie's medal bore the inscription "Pientre au nom de la Reine—Mlle Aubanel—1ére mention 1838—École des Beaux-Arts—Louis Philippe Roi des François."[41] Unforeseen changes in Eugenie's life brought this painting, *The Greek*, to the Mifflin Kenedys' South Texas Ranch, "Laureles," in the 1870's.

Following the custom of the period, Eugenie's marriage to a French nobleman was planned by her elders, but she had a mind of her own. She made convenient excuses for declining—she was genuinely in love with a suitor of her own choice, Charles Lavender (unfortunately, she thought, an Englishman!), a non-Catholic, and a son of a London lithographer. He was a graduate

---

[37] *Telegraph and Texas Register*, Houston, November 25, 1837; *Texas State Gazette*, Austin, January 8, 1859.

[38] [Sister Borremeo], "Biography of Mrs. Charles Lavender," Barker Library, The University of Texas, Austin.

[39] Charles Baudelaire, *The Mirror of Art: Critical Studies*, translated by Jonathan Mayne, p. 100 n.

[40] [Borremeo], "Biography," pp. 3–4.

[41] *Ibid.*, p. 2.

of Oxford, and when she met him he was a professor at the University of Paris. They were married on February 14, 1846.[42]

Charles Lavender was a man of broad interests and a restless soul, eager for adventure. He did not countenance Napoleon's shenanigans. The Lavenders were attracted to publications and pictures concerning Texas. The upheaval in France, the Napoleonic wars, perhaps constituted the main reason for their turning toward America, but adventure was in their blood—a romantic desire to visit "the faraway land of prairies and moss-covered trees"—this was the stimulus that set their journey in motion.

The French were friendly toward Americans with a sentiment that had extended through the years of the colonial America of Washington and Franklin, and it did not exclude Texas. Then, too, a cousin of Eugenie's —the famous historian and politician, François Pierre Guizot, premier of France from 1840 to 1848—was active in the recognition of Texas as a republic and was well versed in Texas affairs. Monsieur Guizot had business connections in New Orleans and may well have encouraged the adventurous trip of the Lavenders.[43]

Six years after their marriage (1852), with their two young children, they ventured forth to explore a new world—the Texas frontier. They left Le Havre on the good ship *England* on June 14, and reached New Orleans on August 2, after almost three months of rough weather and hardships. This did not lessen their enthusiasm, for they set about fitting out a prairie schooner with what they considered necessities for comfort. They hired two men to help them on their journey into Texas, during which time they had planned to hunt, to paint, and to explore at leisure. Upon reaching Houston and realizing that they must lighten their load, they left books and paintings to be picked up later.

Mrs. Lavender now made deer-skin clothes for herself and her husband and learned to carry weapons for her own protection. Their route to Waco, where they settled for a time, presented every difficulty the frontier held—Comanche raids, prairie fires, snakes, scarcity of food, and the dread of yellow fever.[44]

There were only six families in the neighborhood of Waco, and the artist recounted how eagerly they accepted gifts of her small paintings. She had no opportunity to replenish the supply of paint except by means of her own manufacture from the juices of wild plants and from clays. Two of these paintings done with home-

made materials were on exhibition in recent years, one a landscape, and the other a portrait of a man, both about 8" x 11". They were still clear and rich in color, just as the artist had predicted when painting them in the 1850's.[45]

Their travels for the next years took them to Brownsville, Corpus Christi, and New Orleans, where Mr. Lavender became head of Audubon College or "Lavender Hall."[46] At Brownsville, pressed by economic hardships, Eugenie was compelled to sell her prize picture *The Greek* to Captain Mifflin Kenedy, and in addition she sold her copies of the *Virgin of the Ruins* by Bartolomé Murillo (1617–1682), and *Madonna and Child*, after Antonio Correggio (1494–1534).[47] These copies and the one of *Napoleon at St. Helena*, by Paul Delaroche, were made while Mrs. Lavender was still at the Academy, where Vernet saw to it that she had this opportunity of copying and, as well, restoring other pictures for the French government.[48]

Eugenie was steeped in history and, as her teacher Ary Scheffer, was an admirer of Dante and Goethe. Scheffer had painted no less than a half-dozen scenes from Goethe's *Faust*. Eugenie painted two scenes: a young woman at the spinning wheel, and a scene where the old woman drives the young lover away with her staff. These seem to fill in, or add to, Scheffer's group on this very popular subject of their time. When Eugenie was painting her pictures, Charles François Gounod was preparing on the same subject his opera based on a libretto by Michel Carré and Jules Barbier.[49]

A small painting of a French village, one of her early works, is now in the halls of the Incarnate Word Convent in Corpus Christi. Among the portraits done at a latter period were those of Gaston McManus, her grandson, Mrs. McManus with her two children, and one of the Kleberg daughters. Her religious paintings were large and great undertakings. Three of these were *The*

[42] *Ibid.*, pp. 6, 7.
[43] Julia Waugh, *Castro-ville and Henry Castro, Empresario*, pp. 4–5; [Borremeo], "Biography," p. 5.
[44] [Borremeo], "Biography," p. 8.
[45] *Ibid.*, pp. 8–9; *The Republic*, St. Louis, Missouri, February 28, 1897.
[46] [Borremeo], "Biography," pp. 10–12; James W. Mobley, "The Academy Movement in Louisiana," *Louisiana Historical Quarterly*, 30 (1947), 880; *New Orleans Bee*, August 24, 1858.
[47] "List of Paintings of Mrs. Eugenie Aubanel Lavender," La Retama Library, Corpus Christi, no date.
[48] [Borremeo], "Biography," pp. 5, 13.
[49] *Ibid.*, p. 5.

Crucifixion, Father Frank (Plate 44), *St. Patrick Preaching* (5' x 10', 1896), and a Madonna. The last two named hung for many years in St. Patrick's Cathedral, Corpus Christi.[50]

While Mrs. Lavender showed clearly her ability in the craft of painting, she lacked a sense of appropriateness; her last paintings were crowded with unnecessary details and sentimentality, in part, a fault of the work of the 1870's. It was only in her portraits of religious figures done while in Corpus Christi, where simplicity was required, that she reached success.

Theodore Gentilz

Artist Jean Louis Theodore Gentilz (1819–1906), known in Texas simply as Theodore Gentilz, left in his paintings a rich pictorial account of the people of San Antonio de Béxar and its environs. His genre paintings go beyond his visually convincing scenes in a strange, vigorous society, and reveal a sensitive perception and a compassionate understanding of his subjects.

Gentilz, an adventurous young Parisian "Peintre a deminataire," as he was designated by the Texas port authorities, sailed from Strasbourg and Kehle in November, 1843. His ship, the *Heinrich*, Captain Audion, destination Galveston, carried part of the second contingent of settlers being brought to Texas by the empresario, Count Henri Castro.[51]

Why, apart from a wholesome curiosity and a love of adventure, did Gentilz, a promising young artist, elect to come to Texas is uncertain. His Parisian father and uncle were prosperous manufacturers of fine coaches and carriages, "Pourvoyeurs to his Majesty the King of England, Gentilz Brothers, Paris, France."[52] Perhaps he was persuaded by Count Castro himself, who had negotiated from Paris with Texas authorities in 1841 for permission to bring emigrants from France and Alsace-Lorraine. After a long controversy with Minister of Foreign Affairs François Guizot, a final agreement was reached wherein Texas was to grant the emigrants a parcel of land on the Río Grande and another that lay in parts of eight present-day counties. On the latter tract, along the Medina River, twenty-five miles as the crow flies from San Antonio, a strip of land was set aside by Henri Castro for the town of Castroville. This was to be the first home of the French emigrants.[53]

Just thirty days before Gentilz arrived in late 1843, the first contingent had landed. Among them was another equally adventurous spirit, Auguste Fretelliere, whose father was a wealthy wine merchant of Montpellier, France. Auguste's parents had permitted their son, who was not of age, to come to the new land only if he was accompanied by his tutor or mentor, another gentleman of Montpellier named F. F. Micheaud.[54]

After many hardships and extreme discomforts, both contingents of emigrants arrived in San Antonio de Béxar by way of Victoria, Texas. It was here at San Antonio, while awaiting the arrival of Count Castro, that the two youths became acquainted. Fretelliere's friendship was to have a greater influence on Gentilz than that of any other person.

Count Castro, who was to guide them to their new home, arrived several months later than his colonists. With the aid of the intermediary of the French vice-consul at San Antonio, Monsieur Micheaud had shown foresight in renting for himself and Fretelliere a small jacal on the river for two piastres a month. Soon Gentilz joined them, and here the three made their home until the arrival of Count Castro. Monsieur Micheaud proved himself to be an excellent guardian, with a level head, a knowledge of cooking, and a mastery of languages. Fretelliere later in life wrote in his "Adventures of a Castro-villian" the following comment on their sojourn in San Antonio in 1844:

My mentor was a master-cook and as he was an epicure he often regaled me with little dishes which were very tasty. An abundance of meat was to be had for five cents and we could choose the most delicate cuts. Sweetbreads, calves flesh and head not being appreciated by the Mexicans, they gave them to us for nothing. Corn and beans were the only vegetables cultivated, for others were not as yet known in this charming country.[55]

Fretelliere also tells us how, when their money was exhausted, they were obliged to barter for the things they needed. In trade for a pair of pistols which cost

[50] Letter, Mother M. Benedict, Corpus Christi, to author, January 6, 1965; interview, Mrs. Emily G. Murray, San Antonio.

[51] George Cupples, Henry Castro Papers, 1836–1846, Texas State Archives, Austin; Gentilz is pronounced "Jhonti," interview, Olin Fretelliere, his nephew, San Antonio; Frederick Chabot, *With the Makers of San Antonio*, p. 262.

[52] Trade Card in possession of author, gift of Olin Fretelliere; "100 French Immigrants Arrive at Galveston," *Telegraph and Texas Register*, Houston, June 21, 1843, and "Agreement of Castro and Ashbel Smith," September 27, 1843; Castro Papers.

[53] Waugh, *Castro-ville*, p. 3.

[54] Auguste Fretelliere, "Adventures of a Castrovillian," *ibid.*, p. 80.

[55] *Ibid.*, p. 91; two piastres equal about two dollars.

45. Theodore Gentilz: *The Oxcart*
　　Water color, 5¾″ x 8¾″ (Courtesy of Mr. John Peace, San Antonio, Texas)

two piastres in Paris, he received a "magnificent mare, a milch cow and a calf, a sow with eight little pigs, in addition to a measure of corn and a bushel of frijoles." Fretelliere had brought with him a sack of salt, and for a small portion of it he could have in trade "two chickens, or three dozen eggs, or butter."[56]

Being stranded in the strange town of San Antonio was extremely difficult for most of the immigrant families, but the light-hearted young Frenchmen seemed to make the best of their stay. They investigated every niche and corner of the town. No doubt this experience was the lure that brought Gentilz back to San Antonio later and helped to enliven his interest in painting the scenes about him.

After a wait of nearly a year, Castro arrived, only to delay the immigrants still further. Being responsible for some two hundred disgruntled colonists at his heels, Castro dared not take them to the settlement until he was sure that the Indians were quiet and that his way was

clear. He started with an advance convoy of twenty-seven male settlers, which included Gentilz, Fretelliere, and Micheaud. Even though it was in a drenching rain, the group's departure provided the town with a spectacle. The streets were thronged with the immigrant families, who watched the richly clad Castro ride out of San Antonio at the head of the slowly moving procession, accompanied by twenty armed guards, eight Mexican footmen and twenty-two oxen.[57]

The convoy stopped in the open country on the Medina River, where there was less danger from Indians. Their camp was near the spot that was to become Castroville. One of Castro's first acts was to write (September 1, 1844) to the secretary of state of Texas, the Honorable Anson Jones, urging him to send a group of Texas Rangers under Colonel Jack Hays to protect them from

[56] *Ibid.*, p. 92.
[57] *Ibid.*, p. 19.

c-8. Theodore Gentilz: *Surveying in Texas before Annexation to U. S.*
Oil, 1845, 7″ x 9½″ (Courtesy of Mr. Larry Sheerin, San Antonio, Texas)

46. Theodore Gentilz: *The Fandango*

    Oil, 1848, 9⅛″ x 12¼″ (Courtesy of the Daughters of the Republic of Texas Library,
San Antonio, Texas)

the Indians.[58] Hays had given them protection on leaving San Antonio and was well regarded. In the meantime, the men were being taught to protect themselves in case of attack. In actuality, Castro's fears were exaggerated. Although there were threats of Indian raids and incidents for which the Indians were responsible, no serious attacks were actually made on Castroville during the first years of its settlement.

The friendship between Gentilz and Fretelliere grew as they worked to make the settlement of Castroville a success. They began frontier life by farming, for it was in their contract that the members of the group must produce some of their essential food. In addition to the stipulated land grant in the immigrants' contracts, each man was given land for farming or gardening and a town lot.[59]

Castro was not long in discovering that Gentilz was able to write well in both English and French. Since Count Castro's official papers and letters were time consuming, he expanded Gentilz' duties to include writing "articles" for him. For this service the Count built him a small house, and Fretelliere joined him in the new place.

The story of Castroville settlement, its difficulties, and its progress is interesting in itself, but peripheral to the

[58] Henry Castro, Castroville, to Secretary of State, Anson Jones, Austin, September 1, 1844.

[59] Waugh, *Castro-ville*, p. 27.

47. Theodore Gentilz: *The Funeral of an Angel*
    Oil, 9" x 12¼" (Courtesy of the Daughters of the Republic of Texas Library, San Antonio, Texas)

career of Gentilz. Of specific interest is the fact that Gentilz soon added to his duties for Castro that of assisting in surveying the towns of Castroville and of nearby Quihi, and in 1847 of helping to establish the town of D'Hanis. His education had supplied him with the essentials for the work.

It was after one of these surveying excursions that he made an oil painting showing a party of surveyors at work (Plate c-8). The artist notes that this was "before Texas became a state."[60] The chief surveyor sighting the line forms the central focus of the painting. Workmen are shown clearing the ground ahead of him, with others behind managing the chain. A party of mounted guards protects the surveying crew.

But the fascination of the city was stronger than that of colonization. The two young immigrants decided to settle in San Antonio. Before doing so, they returned to France to satisfy the entreaties of their families. While

[60] Painting in collection of Larry Sheerin, San Antonio. Painting inscribed by artist, "Before Texas was a state."

in France in 1846 they disposed of their property, with the intention of investing in the development of Texas. On their return they settled permanently in San Antonio. Gentilz made his home, which was later to serve as a studio also, next to the Buffalo Camp Yard (with its picturesquely painted entrance) on Flores Street. Fretelliere settled further down the same street. In 1849 Gentilz made a second trip to Paris and while there married Marie Fargeix, returning the same year with his bride and his sister Henrietta. In February of 1852 Henrietta and Auguste Fretelliere were married.[61]

How different their new home from their native France! San Antonio was predominantly Mexican. Oxcarts (Plate 45)—their drivers walking beside them, long stick in hand, calling in a soft voice, "¡Andele! ¡Andele! ¡Pronto cabeza de hierro!"—passed along streets lined with lime-washed adobe houses, in whose doorways hung Indian corn and red peppers. The Alamo lay in ruins, the massacre of the Texans at the hands of Santa Anna having taken place only eight years before. The peace treaty signed on the Trinity in 1843 and the watchfulness of Hays' Rangers had settled the Indians for the time being. The narrow river winding through the town seemed to add to the aura of calmness and quiet. Small groups of young Mexicans knelt on the ground in games of monte bank, interrupting their play only to make the holy sign as the Padre passed. If one ventured onto the side streets, the habitual cock fights were always to be seen, with the small crowd peering over the shoulders of those closest in to see a famous red cock in flashing, cruel, bloody combat. The market place was a medley of carts, chickens, pigs running about, and women making tortillas. Such a strange variety of life gave Gentilz an overwhelming desire to record what he saw.

The stimulating scenes of Mexican life around Gentilz in his first days in San Antonio resulted in his painting *The Fandango* (Plate 46). Fretelliere, in his "Adventures," gives a verbal description of their visit to the dance in these words:

We had often heard of the "Fandango"; we resolved, Theodore and I, to go to one, and towards ten o'clock of a certain evening we walked over to the Military Plaza [governor's palace]. The sound of the violin drew us to the spot where the fete was in full swing. It was in rather a large room of an adobe house, earthen floored, lighted by six tallow candles placed at equal distances from each other. At the back a great chimney in which a fire of dry wood served to reheat

the café, the tamales, and enchiladas; opposite, some planks resting on frames and covered with a cloth, formed a table on which cups and saucers were set out. A Mexican woman in the forties, with black hair dark even for her race, bright eyes, and extraordinary activity, above all with the most agile of tongues—such was Dona Andrea Candelaria, patroness of the Fandango. At the upper end of the room, seated in a chair which had been placed on an empty box, was the music, which was a violin. That violinist had not issued from a conservatory but on the whole he played in fairly good time. He was called Paulo, and being blind, played from memory. The airs, for the most part Mexican, were new to me. The women were seated on benches placed on each side of the room. The costumes were very simple dresses of light colored printed calico with some ribbons. All were brunettes with complexions more or less fair but generally they had magnificent black eyes which fascinated me. As for the men they wore usually short jackets, wide brimmed hats, and nearly all the Mexicans wore silk scarves, red, or blue, or green, around their waists. The dance I liked best was called a quadrille. It is a waltz in four-time with a step crossed on very slow measure. The Mexicans are admirably graceful and supple. When the Quadrille is finished the cavalier accompanies his partner to the buffet where they are served a cup of coffee and cakes.[62]

Gentilz has painted this folk dance of the Mexicans in a simple manner. A preliminary drawing of the picture shows the artist's approach to the problem of painting a group, demonstrating his careful attention to perspective and his belief that art should be created through definite planning of every particular with mathematical accuracy. This, like most of his early work, is painted in flat tones with little gradation. In his later, out-of-door subjects, Gentilz painted in bright sunlight with deep shadows and used a higher scale and hue. Either through choice or because of the scarcity of materials, his work on wood or canvas is rarely more than nine by twelve inches in size.

Gentilz' artistic preparation in Paris had included the disciplined draftsmanship of the French academic tradition. He had attended the National School of Mathematics and Drawing. While still a student under twenty-four years old, he compiled "A Method of Perspective for Artists, Dedicated to the Memory of Viollet-de-Duc, the Eminent Architect and Artist, My Teacher on Perspective and History of Ornament." This manuscript,

[61] Frederick Chabot, *San Antonio and Its Beginning*, p. 80.
[62] Fretelliere, "Adventures of a Castrovillian," Waugh, *Castroville*, p. 93.

48. Theodore Gentilz: *The Camel Ride*
Oil, 1856–1857, 9″ x 12″ (Courtesy of Mrs. Jack Beretta, Sr., San Antonio, Texas)

handwritten with meticulous care, consists of two parts: Linear Perspective (Part I, 93 pages, 335 figures) and Serial Perspective (Part II, 93 pages, 226 figures). Gentilz states as the purpose of his work: "To teach perspective, not only according to certain conventions as it is in the case with architects and engineers but especially under all requirements useful to artists." Among the profusion of ink drawings which it contains are scales to illustrate the sizes of figures on horizontal, ascending, and descending planes. In a single case, small figures are drawn to illustrate the proper size in each plane. One table illustration shows, for example, how he determined the perspective from a given point to *A, B, C, E, I,* and *J.* Included in other notes are anatomical drawings of ani-

mals and detail drawings of the muscles of animals and humans. This thorough, painstaking document on the anatomical structure of the body and on space relationships between objects shows in Gentilz an approach to his art that reminds one of the Renaissance masters who successfully combined science and art.[63]

In Texas such strict studies as perspective were remote, but the influence of the theoretical aspects of his training in art made a definite mark on his work. This same influence later proved an asset in his teaching. His paintings are well planned, and reflect economy of detail—

[63] Theodore Gentilz, "A Method of Perspective for Artists," collection of the late Olin Fretelliere, San Antonio.

almost to excess. It is the intensification of life in a single theme that makes his pictures exciting. He was also away from any contemptuous attitude toward genre painting which may have existed then in Paris. In his new life he was free to paint as he wished, and the scenes around him seemed to fulfill completely his desires for colorful and interesting subject matter.

The Funeral of an Angel (Plate 47) could have been painted either in Mexico or in San Antonio. In this portrayal of a small procession as it makes its way along the street, Gentilz attempts in a simple way to show the calmness which the Mexican displays toward death. The father carries the coffin on his shoulders, followed by the priests. A little boy walking beside the procession carries the cover of the coffin. The men in the procession have not put aside their guns; in fact, one is firing his.[64]

The Camel Ride (Plate 48) has an interesting historical implication in its connection with the famous camel experiment conceived and put into motion by the then United States secretary of war, Jefferson Davis. The year 1848 found the United States with a vast territory to the West which had no transportation system connecting it with the East. If one wished to reach California during the gold rush, the trip meant crossing the Rockies or going the very hazardous way by clipper ship around Cape Horn, requiring several months. The West was truly isolated. In 1850 there was no prospect that a railroad would connect California with the East for half a century. But the immediate purpose for which the camels were to be used was to locate proper supply routes for the outposts in the Davis Mountains and the Big Bend country, and to locate a site on the Río Grande near the Comanche raiding trail. Whether the idea of using camels for transportation of military units originated with Henry C. Wayne, as has been thought, or with Secretary of War Davis, is unimportant; but in March, 1855, Congress appropriated $30,000 to import camels to transport military materials. The project was to be under the supervision of Major Henry C. Wayne and Lieutenant D. D. Porter.

On May 14, 1856, the ship *Supply* landed at Indianola, Texas, with thirty-three camels from Egypt and Arabia. On February 10, 1857, forty-four more were brought from Asia Minor by the same ship. The camels were taken to San Antonio and then to Camp Verde (built just the year before), sixty miles northwest of San Antonio, where they were to remain long enough to become accustomed to the new environment. While they were in San Antonio they were a source of endless amusement and interest to its citizens. The unusual story of their purchase, their rough voyage, and the difficulty in handling animals so unused to sea travel created general excitement and provided a heyday for news reporters.

Texas newspapers gave daily space to the health of the solemn visitors. Engravers included them in sketches of the Main Plaza of San Antonio. Gentilz found time to go to their stamping grounds beyond the Alamo to make sketches, which resulted in an amusing painting in oil of Elias, the expert Turkish handler, taking one of his two-humped Bactrian charges for its morning exercise. Elias, dressed in his native costume, with a stick in hand, is shown riding the camel at full gallop. Elias, who is so interestingly pictured by Gentilz, later settled across the border in Sonora, married a Yaqui Indian girl, and raised a large family. One son, Plutarco Elías Calles, known as "El Turco" when a youth, became president of Mexico in 1924.[65]

Love of people was no doubt the wellspring of Gentilz' art. Among his many paintings depicting the life of the Mexican people in San Antonio and environs are *The Tamale Seller* (Laredo Street, San Antonio), *The Candle Seller, The Water Seller* (Bracket, Texas), *The Drayman* (Negro driver), *San Pedro Spring, The Market, The Wedding at the Cathedral, Going to the City, Returning from the City, The Rooster Race* (1848), and *Bridge over the San Antonio River* (April, 1878). His handling of the Mexican jacal, an important part of the San Antonio scene which appears in the background of many of Gentilz' paintings (Plate 49), reveals his appreciation of the picturesque and his keen powers of observation. A decade later another artist, Robert Onderdonk, painted the jacal with the same friendliness, but in decay and surrounded by extreme poverty. The jacal and the adobe houses built along the river, both described so vividly by Seth Eastman in his journal (1849), have almost entirely disappeared.

[64] Collection of paintings, Daughters of the Republic of Texas Library, San Antonio.

[65] John R. Bartlett, *Personal Narrative of Explorations and Incidents in Texas, New Mexico, California, Sonora and Chihuahua, Connected with the United States and Mexican Boundary Commission during the Years 1850, '51, '52, and '53*, pp. 576–584; "Camels in Texas," *San Antonio Herald*, January 1, 1857; Sept. 12, 1857, Oct. 16, 1857; William H. Goetzmann, *Army Exploration in the American West, 1803–1863*, pp. 363–365; Harlan D. Fowler, *Camels in California: A Chapter in Western Transportation*, p. 88.

49. Theodore Gentilz: *Mexican Oxcart and Jacal*
Oil, 9″ x 12¼″ (Courtesy of Mrs. Theodore Klecka, San Antonio, Texas)

50. Theodore Gentilz: *San José Mission*

Oil, 19½″ x 27½″ (Courtesy of St. Mary's University, San Antonio, Texas)

51. Theodore Gentilz: *San José Mission Window*
Water color, 1882 (Courtesy of the Dallas Museum
of Fine Arts)

At several periods Gentilz painted the Spanish missions: *The Alamo* (1844), and later *San Juan Capistrano, Concepción, San José* (Plates 50 and 51), and *San Francisco de la Espada*. In 1844 Gentilz made the painting *The Fall of the Alamo*, which exists now only in photographic reproductions. Done only a year after Gentilz' arrival in Texas, it is important documentary material, for the artist had access to eye witnesses of the fatal morning. The scene shows the Texans in the early hours as they approached the line of battle. The depiction of the old mission is an example of the artist's skill in architectural perspective and layout. Gentilz noted the fact that he consulted Francisco Antonio Ruíz as well as others in making this painting.[66]

Gentilz' only other venture into historical painting is the *Shooting of the Seventeen Decimated Texians*, or *Drawing of the Black Beans* (Plate c-1), represent-

ing an event which occurred at Salado, Mexico, in 1843. This work is painted in the dark tones typical of Gentilz' early style of working. Architectonic iconography forms the basic structure of the painting. The inspiration for this painting is no doubt the drawing by Charles McLaughlin made for General Thomas J. Green's *Journal of the Texian Expedition against Mier* (1845).[67] McLaughlin was a prisoner with Green and made his drawings from life. There is a row of spectators across the front, their backs to the viewer. Some of these are soldiers standing stiff and erect as their shakos. Careful attention is given to detail within the somewhat naïve overall concept: the blindfolded prisoners crouching on a log at the left and the firing squad (which has fired its volley from the right) releasing a cloud of plumed smoke that rises in the center. Behind the smoke column at the rear a drummer boy stands by the man whose raised sword has just given the signal for the ill-advised shots, while near the prisoners at the left stands a priest with acolytes bearing candles and a crucifix.

Through the years Gentilz continued his work as a surveyor, plotting many sections of land in the neighborhood of Castroville as well as in the western part of the state. In 1882 he crossed the Río Grande to lay out roads and to make a map of fantastic detail of northern Mexico. The map of the Republic of Mexico drawn by Gentilz (1882) includes capitals of states, important towns, interior towns, haciendas, ranches, watering places, mail stations, mines, bishoprics, archbishoprics, ports of entry, coasting harbors, wagon roads, horse roads, railroads, unfinished railroads, boundaries of states, rivers, and mountains. Texas is also included. Additional information, such as statistics, heights of principal mountains, and approximate length of the principal rivers, is also given.[68] While here he made drawings for his paintings of life in the Mexican towns. "La Corrida de la Sandia," *The Watermelon Race* (Plate 52), pictures an event traditional on St. John's Day (El Día de San Juan), June 2. Gentilz portrays the moment just before the race begins. A line of mounted men awaits tensely, while in

[66] Interview, Olin Fretelliere, information and list of paintings by the artist in 1888 (holograph).

[67] Thomas Jefferson Green, *Journal of the Texian Expedition against Mier*, p. 154.

[68] Theodore Gentilz, Map of Mexico, revised and corrected by Lorenzo Castro, Texas State Archives, Austin; James P. Bryan and Walter K. Hanak, *Texas in Maps*.

52. Theodore Gentilz: *The Watermelon Race*
Oil, 9″ x 12¼″ (Courtesy of the Daughters of the Republic of Texas Library, San Antonio, Texas)

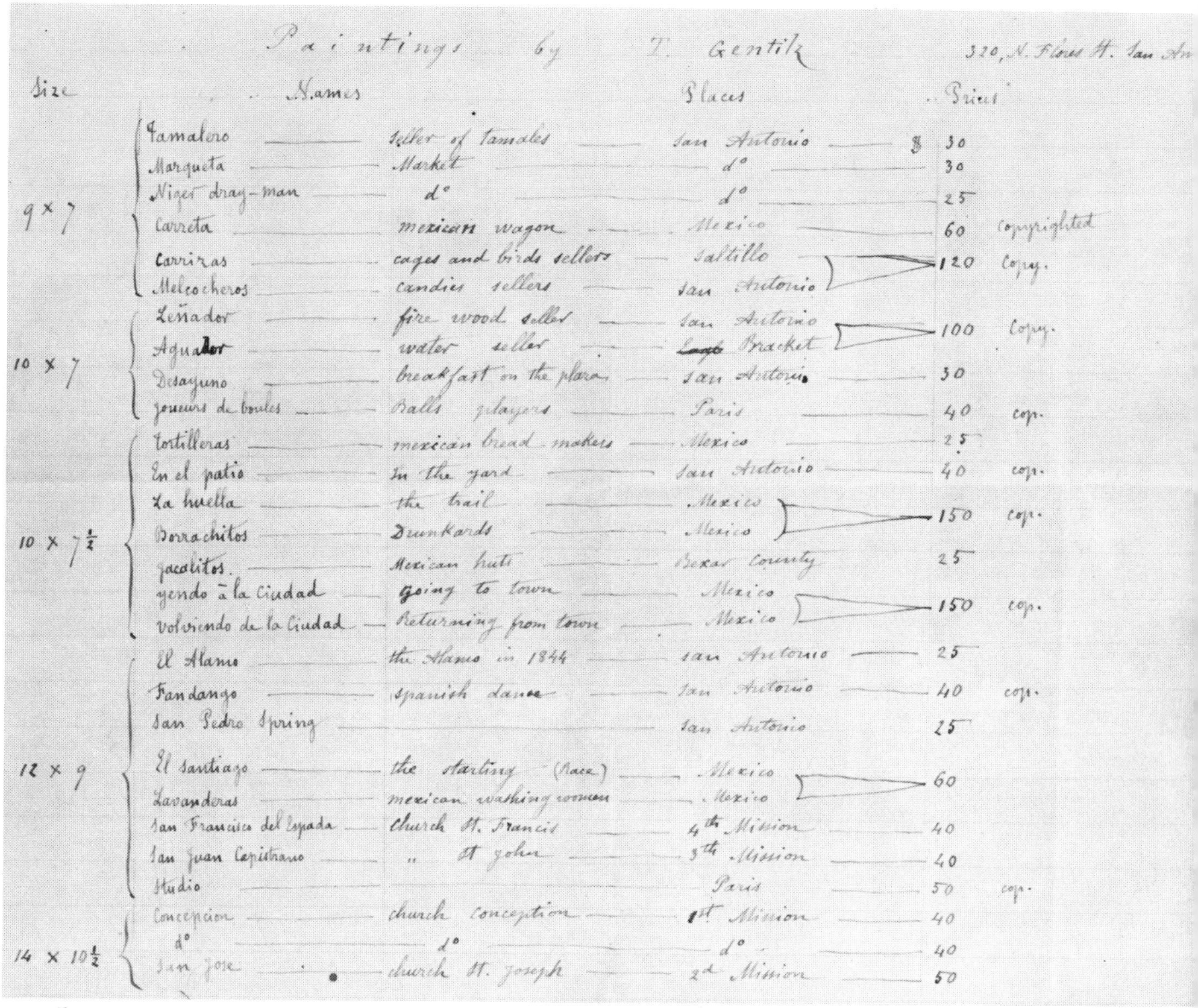

Handwritten list header: *Paintings by T. Gentilz* — 320, N. Flores St. San An...

Size	Names		Places	Prices	
	Tamalero	seller of tamales	San Antonio	$ 30	
	Marqueta	Market	d°	30	
9 × 7	Niger dray-man	d°	d°	25	
	Carreta	mexican wagon	Mexico	60	copyrighted
	Carrizas	cages and birds sellers	Saltillo	} 120	copy.
	Melcocheros	candies sellers	San Antonio		
	Leñador	fire wood seller	San Antonio	} 100	copy.
10 × 7	Aguador	water seller	Eagle Pass Bracket		
	Desayuno	breakfast on the plaza	San Antonio	30	
	joueurs de boules	Balls players	Paris	40	cop.
	Tortilleras	mexican bread makers	Mexico	25	
	En el patio	in the yard	San Antonio	40	cop.
	La huella	the trail	Mexico	} 150	cop.
10 × 7½	Borrachitos	Drunkards	Mexico		
	jacalitos	Mexican huts	Bexar County	25	
	yendo á la Ciudad	going to town	Mexico	} 150	cop.
	volviendo de la Ciudad	Returning from town	Mexico		
	El Alamo	the Alamo in 1844	San Antonio	25	
	Fandango	spanish dance	San Antonio	40	cop.
	San Pedro Spring		San Antonio	25	
12 × 9	El santiago	the starting (Race)	Mexico	} 60	
	Lavanderas	mexican washing women	Mexico		
	San Francisco del Espada	church St. Francis	4th Mission	40	
	San Juan Capistrano	" St John	3th Mission	40	
	Studio		Paris	50	cop.
	Concepcion	church conception	1st Mission	40	
14 × 10½	d°	d°	d°	40	
	San José	church St. Joseph	2d Mission	50	

53. Theodore Gentilz: *List of Paintings*
9″ x 7¼″ (Courtesy of the Daughters of the Republic of Texas Library, San Antonio, Texas)

the center of the line a man holds a watermelon in one hand. The point of the game is for the rest of the group to recover the melon from the man originally holding it. This painting and many others similar in subject matter to those of his San Antonio paintings were in a list which Gentilz compiled in 1888 (Plate 53) giving the location of the scene, the prices of the pictures, and the copyright date. Titles of a few will show the close similarity of subject to those treated in San Antonio: *Barilleros, San Felipe* (Plate 54), *Mexican Bread Makers, Metate Girl Grinding Corn, The Trail, The Drunkards,* and *Payday in the Market* (men from the mines of San Felipe, Coahuila, Mexico, being paid).[69]

Among the genre paintings completed in what might be called Gentilz' middle and late periods, there appears the use of more brilliant colors and greater contrast in hues. During this time he discarded his old supply of paint and secured fresher and more intense colors through the New Orleans market.[70] This change is quite

[69] Theodore Gentilz, List of His Paintings, 1888, owned by his descendants, San Antonio.
[70] Interview, Olin Fretelliere; notes of Louise Fretelliere concerning paintings of the "Fandango," 1848: ". . . both are finished copies of the original studies 1848, the paint used for the studies was inferior; for the copies, good quality from New Orleans," Castro Papers.

110

54. Theodore Gentilz: *Barilleros, San Felipe*
Oil, 9″ x 12″ (Courtesy of Mr. Larry Sheerin, San Antonio, Texas)

evident when one compares his *Fandango* of 1844 with his later painting *Gathering Juice from the Maguey Plant for Pulque* (Plate 55). In the latter he shows two Mexican men at work before the maguey plant (a species of agava) gathering the juice from which pulque is made. In large hats and clothes decorated in brilliant colors, they stand before the skillfully painted plants, beyond which are the mountains. The detailing of both the costumes and the long blades of the plant is done with delicate precision. Dark shadows and brilliant sunlight provide a strong contrast and involve the use of impasto which was used in some French paintings of the 1870's but was never a characteristic of Gentilz' work;

his paintings were done with a meagerly filled brush used to emphasize delicacy of detail. His work was never enigmatical, for realism required clarity and understanding in his genre paintings.

Selling of Cardinals on the Plaza (Plate 56) is one of the best of Gentilz' paintings of this period of more brilliant coloring, and it shows, as well, his appreciation of detail. The locale is determined by the inclusion of the old San Antonio cathedral in the background. In the foreground Gentilz has painted with minute brush strokes the bird cages and the imprisoned cardinals. The delicate rendering of the straw of the cages shows the skill of the artist and at the same time the precise craft

55. Theodore Gentilz: *Gathering Juice from the Maguey Plant for Pulque*
Oil, 9" x 12" (Courtesy of Mr. Larry Sheerin, San Antonio, Texas)

56. Theodore Gentilz: *Selling of Cardinals on the Plaza*
Oil, 8¾″ x 6¾″ (Courtesy of Mr. Larry Sheerin, San Antonio, Texas)

57. Theodore Gentilz: *Comanche Chief*
Oil, 11½ " x 8½ " (Courtesy of the Witte Museum, San Antonio, Texas)

58. Theodore Gentilz: *Fishing with Bow and Arrow*
   Oil, 8⅜″ x 11⅜″ (Courtesy of the Witte Museum, San Antonio, Texas)

of the Mexican women. A similar painting, *The Hour of Prayer* (painted in Mexico) shows the lumpy bodies of women half hidden under their varicolored shawls standing against the background of a church. At the sound of the angelus they have placed their net bags of pottery on the ground and bowed their heads. This painting also contains fine detail. In his late years delicate use of the brush is at its best when Gentilz made water colors of Texas wild flowers.

Among Gentilz' genre paintings is a small picture, *The Studio*, in which he shows a group of students in the Paris studio of Ramon Quesada Monvoisin (1794–1870), a classmate of his at the Academy in Paris. This painting is undated, and one may assume that it derives from a visit which Gentilz made to one of his friend's classes during a trip to Paris. Arranged across the small canvas are some fifteen students working from a nude model, while in the center may be seen the instructor giving criticism to a student. A clock on the wall—9:25 provides an interesting realistic detail.[71]

While the life of the Mexican provided Gentilz with his largest number of subjects, his paintings of the Indian are no less interesting. These depict scenes which he sketched while surveying, and then completed later

71 Letter from Paris concerning period of Roman Quesada Monvoisin, 1963, collection of Larry Sheerin, San Antonio.

59. Theodore Gentilz: *Comanches on the March*
    Oil, 11½" x 8½" (Courtesy of the Witte Museum, San Antonio, Texas)

in life. These are portraits in water color and pencil of the Comanche, Lipan Apache, and Kiowa. Late in the eighteenth century the Comanche had followed the buffalo or had been driven by enemy tribes down as far as Central Texas, while the Lipan, thought by some to be more docile, were to the west and southwest of Castroville and San Antonio. The Kiowa had been driven into the northern section of the Texas Panhandle and were therefore in the path of the surveying parties during the period of settlement. The Indian still enjoyed unrestrained freedom, for there were no fences and the land belonged to everybody.

Gentilz' first contact with the Indian occurred when, as a young man, he walked the twenty-five miles from Castroville to San Antonio with his companion Fretelliere. Later, when surveying with a group, all of whom were mounted and well armed, he carried his sketchbook in his saddle bag and was able to move about with greater security and ease. Gentilz met one of the Comanche chiefs (whom he recorded later in oil), and later told how he made friends with him by giving him a sketch and and a bit of tobacco. The chief posed for him dressed in a deer-skin suit, and he is shown riding a spirited horse (Plate 57). He holds a long spear and wears on his back an oval shield decorated with scalps, the trophies of success in battle.

116

The painting *Camp of the Lipans* (1845) shows the activities of the Indians in their camp on the Medina River. Unlike Seth Eastman in his Indian paintings, Gentilz most often makes the locale secondary and emphasizes details of the life of the Indians themselves. This is the case in his painting *Fishing with Bow and Arrow* (Plate 58), which shows the children being taught to ride, while some of the men are shooting fish with bow and arrow. *Indian Women Washing Clothes* and *Comanches on the March* (Plate 59) are other paintings by Gentilz which depict the life of the Indian. Important Indian portraits probably painted from photographs in his later years are *Big Tree* (Kiowa chief), *Otter Belt, Quahadi* (Plate 60), and *Squaw* (Wichita).[72]

From all available evidence, Gentilz was little concerned with the sale of his paintings, although some may have served as the basis for book illustrations. He wanted to paint, and his painting seems to have been so much a part of his very existence that he made little effort to dispose of finished works. As a large part of his time was spent in surveying and in teaching, the economic demands of everyday living were met in this way and the sale of his pictures was not a pressing matter, as it may have been with other pioneer artists. After his death in 1906, almost a hundred paintings were among the possessions bequeathed to his wife.

Following his mobile life as a surveyor, Gentilz settled down to teaching in San Antonio. A card announcing his studio was printed in 1879 (Plate 61). For a number of years he taught at St. Mary's College. His pupils even today speak of him with great admiration as a teacher. Two devoted pupils were his nieces, Louisa and Marie Fretelliere, who referred to him affectionately as "Tio Pelon."[73]

This man of small stature and quiet, industrious, and energetic ways did a remarkably large amount of painting, when one considers his other activities of surveying and teaching. While a few family portraits of his wife, Marie, his brother Jean Pierre (who visited Texas), and several self-portraits painted at different periods in

---

[72] Collection of Paintings at Witte Memorial Museum, San Antonio; interview, Olin Fretelliere; *Daily Mercury*, Houston, October 21, 1873; Gentilz' students, especially his nieces, followed his style so closely that collectors are often misled. However, Gentilz fortunately was explicit in signing his work with full name or overlaid initials.

[73] Interview, Olin Fretelliere.

60. Theodore Gentilz: *Otter Belt, Quahadi*
Crayon, 9″ x 7″ (Courtesy of the Witte Museum, San Antonio, Texas)

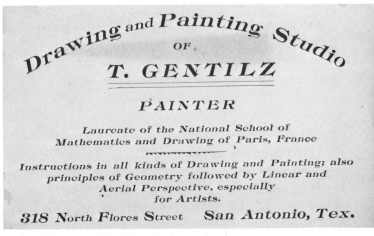

61. Theodore Gentilz: *Business Card*
3⅛″ x 5⅛″ (Author's collection)

his life add greatly to the interest of the work of this French-American artist, it is in the realistic portrayal of Mexican life in San Antonio and its environs that his greatest achievement lies.

Louisa Heuser Wueste

The strong internal pressures in Germany in the 1840's and 1850's brought another artist to Texas, Louisia Heuser Wueste (1803–1874). Her two daughters and one son had fled Gummersbach on the Rhine in 1852. Despite the daughters' report of a disagreeable voyage and undesirable conditions in Texas, Mrs. Wueste joined them in San Antonio in 1857. The prewar days in San Antonio were disturbing, and when the punishing years of the Civil War came, Louisa did not find a public interest in painting nor did she find the solitude she craved.[74]

Before coming to Texas, Louisa Wueste had lived among people interested in art and artistic activities. Her training in portraiture at the Düsseldorf School of Art was at a time when the school was at the height of its fame. Louisa had been brought up in some degree of luxury. Her mother was the daughter of Louisa Joegel Heuser, who before her marriage was the companion to Miss von Jendern, the lady in waiting to Queen Louise of Germany. Her father, Daniel Heuser, was an enterprising merchant and chemist dealing in indigo and paints. Both a manufacturer and an importer, Heuser was a shrewd businessman—in fact, at one time he was able to corner the indigo market.[75] Their daughter Louisa's portrayal of the astute old man in a small oil painting (10" x 12") shows him with his spectacles (Benjamin Franklin style) on the end of his nose, intently studying sheets of paper before him. A small cap on the top of his head and a kerchief around his neck add to the picturesqueness of the portrait and give an interesting insight into character.[76]

Besides Louisa's instinctive interest in her father's manufacture and importation of paints, she benefited from the constant discussion of techniques among the various artists in the family. In addition, Düsseldorf contained a wealth of art for her to see. Louisa's older sisters were married to artists—one to Conrad Lessing, a painter at the Court of William I—and her youngest sister, Alvina, was married to Adolph Schroedter (1805–1875). Both men had taught Louisa. One of the Lessing daughters married Anton von Werner, the court painter to Kaiser Friederick Wilhelm II. The teacher,

however, who had the most profound influence on Louisa's work was August Wilhelm Sohn (1829–1899), an eminent artist of genre and historical painting. Louisa's sister Adelina Heuser Jaeger was an artist of some ability.[77]

In 1821 Louisa married Dr. Peter William Leopold Wueste, a practicing physician in Gummersbach. The rearing of children interrupted her art career for a time. After Dr. Wueste's death, however, Louisa returned to her art work and decided to join her children Emma, Adelina, and Daniel in Texas.

In the spring of 1860, believing in her talent, she ventured to advertise in San Antonio that her studio at No. 18 French Building, "offers the services of her art training in taking likenesses in oil or drawing, as well as to give lessons in every branch of art."[78] A number of her portraits shown at that time may still be seen in the homes of her descendants: *Adelina Wueste Staffel* (Plate 62), *Dr. Daniel Heuser* (one in oil and one in crayon), *Old Gentleman Leaning on a Cane*, and several self-portraits (one in oil and two in crayon).

One of the first portraits that Mrs. Wueste painted after establishing her studio in 1861 is of the lovely Sarah Riddle at the age of nineteen (Plate 63). Sarah's romance stirred society in San Antonio. Robert Eager, a daring young Englishman, had come for a buffalo hunt and while in San Antonio he had seen Sarah, then quite young, and warned her parents that someday he would return to claim her. A few years passed, Sarah returned from a girls' school in Tennessee, and they were married. Louisa Wueste portrayed Sarah Riddle in an antebellum costume—a low-necked dress adorned with a red rose—with skill, charm, and sentiment.[79]

Mrs. Wueste was particularly interested in portraits of children. A horizontal painting of her three grandchildren, Emmy, Mary, and Bertha, with their dog, was a difficult undertaking (Plate 64). As she was not accustomed to painting animals, the dog does not enhance this work. Another painting, a vertical presentation of

[74] Mrs. Mary S. Elmendorf, "Our Ancestors," geneological notes on Wueste Family, in possession of Mrs. Stella Tylor, San Antonio, Texas, p. 11; Esse F. O'Brien, *Art and Artists in Texas*, pp. 19–20.

[75] Elmendorf, "Our Ancestors," pp. 2, 6–7.

[76] Collection of paintings of Mrs. Stella Tylor, San Antonio; collection of Mr. Armin Elmendorf, Portola Valley, California.

[77] *San Antonio Express*, February 20, 1849; Elmendorf, "Our Ancestors," pp. 7–9.

[78] *San Antonio Herald*, May 8, 1860.

[79] *San Antonio Light*, February 22, 1946.

62. Louisa Heuser Wueste: *Adelina Wueste Staffel*
   Crayon, 11½″ x 8½″ (Courtesy of Mr. and Mrs. Heino Staffel, San Antonio, Texas)

63. Louisa Heuser Wueste: *Sarah Riddle*
    Oil, 1861, 24″ x 18″ (Courtesy of Mr. Flo Eager Roberts, San Antonio, Texas)

64. Louisa Heuser Wueste: *Emmy, Mary, Bertha*
Oil, c. 1868, 19½" x 25¼" (Courtesy of Mr. and Mrs. Heino Staffel, San Antonio, Texas)

the three Bee children in the 1860's is similar. The ease and informality of both pictures reveal a certain folk quality which adds to their charm.

A portrait of a child, *Rowel Graebner*, at the age of three years, demonstrates Louisa's ability with the pencil, rivaling Richard Petri and Carl von Iwonski in this medium. It is a large portrait drawn with a steel-like point—a difficult task on so large a scale. A second portrait of this child was made in oil and is among work of Mrs. Wueste's at the Witte Museum in San Antonio.

Mrs. Wueste left San Antonio in the early seventies to live with her son, Daniel, in Eagle Pass, a border pioneer town. She found little encouragement of her art, but her interest was stimulated in the life of Mexican people along the Río Grande. In 1874 she wrote that the *Mexican Girl* (her last painting) would be on exhibition in August in San Antonio. The *Beggar Boy*, oil, and *Adelina Staffel*, a drawing, also were completed at Eagle Pass. Mrs. Wueste died in Eagle Pass in 1874.[80]

80 Elmendorf, "Our Ancestors," pp. 11–12.

Carl G. von Iwonski

Figuratively speaking, artist Carl G. von Iwonski (c. 1830–1922) was two separate individuals; at least that is how he was regarded and described by those who knew him. One man whom they knew was quiet and reflective, often deep in thought, his head bowed, elbows on his knees, and each finger on one hand touching the same finger on the other. This person, they thought, was apt to recognize tender human qualities in his chosen subjects. In the artist they observed also a gay, cynical young man who represented life in a light vein, displaying the grim, the grotesque, the coarse, the humorous—each painting carrying the conviction of something seen and experienced.

To call attention to Carl Iwonski's native skill would be recognizing only part of the reason for his success as an artist, for he showed in his portrait work a keen and sympathetic observation, while in other paintings he shows his rough antics and a quick and witty mind. During part of his twenty-seven years in Texas, he found himself in a hotbed of dissension. He and his fellow travelers were involved in many dramatic scenes as the years passed. While he affirmed his hatred of war, he did not, as some of his compatriots, flee to Mexico or elsewhere during the Civil War, but remained, and, with foresight, made use of passing events to his advantage as an artist. Even his entry into Texas took on an appearance of a tableau, thus sharpening early his interest in events of color and drama.

Iwonski joined the first group of immigrants to Texas

under the leadership of Carl of Solms-Braunfels of Germany in 1845.[81] On landing at Carlshafen (Indianola), the Prince brought all groups of the different contingents together at Agua Dulce, twelve miles from Indianola, before starting their hazardous and tedious march to New Braunfels. Prince Solms organized a company of twenty soldiers, and Iwonski was probably among this impressive group whose business it was to protect the immigrants on their way. They were, indeed, imposing in their gray flannel uniforms with black velvet collars and brass buttons, high riding boots, and cocked hats decorated with a slender black feather. Long lances swung at their sides and guns at their belts. They carried a flag bearing the words *Fuer die Auswander (er) in Texas.*[82]

Carl Iwonski left Ruchers Silesia, Germany, embarking at Bremen on the *Schiff, Johann Dethard*, Captain Otto, bound for Indianola. His father, Leopold von Iwonski, a disgruntled lieutenant in the Prussian army, his mother, Maria nee Kalinowsky-Tschirski, and a younger brother Adolph must have planned to come to the United States, for as soon as the father could sell the family estate "Hildersdorf," they followed close on the heels of Carl.[83] The period following their arrival in Texas was one of the most important in the state's cultural growth, and Carl Iwonski had a share in its advance.

The first training that Carl received in art had been in drawing and painting, when as a youth in Breslau he attended the local schools. On reaching New Braunfels he sought out an unidentified teacher for further instruction. These short periods comprise the artist's training, as far as we know. His success to a large degree must therefore be attributed to native skill and a deep desire to follow his ambition. Almost daily, objects of interest in a primitive environment challenged his skill and imagination in painting.

The Iwonskis first settled at New Braunfels on the Guadalupe River, where they built a blockhouse (which Carl made the subject of one of his early paintings), for the pioneer soon learned the importance of the blockhouse, as he had learned the practical value of the buckskin shirt and the Bowie knife. Then the family moved to Horton Town, a small village northeast of New Braunfels, where Carl busied himself for a time with the relocation of the family.[84]

We learn of the father's business acumen, when in 1846 and 1847 he was an agent for Acting-Governor

[81] Chabot, *With the Makers of San Antonio*, p. 174; Walter Prescott Webb (ed.), *The Handbook of Texas*, see Carl G. von Iwonski, I, 898.

[82] Biesele, *History of the German Settlement in Texas*, p. 38, quoted from "Meine Ankunft in Neu-Braunfels," in *Kalender der Neu-Braunfelser Zeitung fuer 1914*.

[83] The *Semiramis* ship list, fall of 1845, published by G. F. Oheim in Jahrbuch 1936—a supplement for *Neu-Braunfelser Zeitung*, p. 41; The Ship list, *Johann Dethard Neu-Braunfelser Zeitung* (Denknal Edition) August 18, 1938, gives the information that Leopold V. Iwonski, wife Marie nee Kalinawska, Carl von Iwonski and Adolph came at the same time, which does not agree with the above. The opinion of Oscar Haas, who made a special study of this, is that the above information is correct; Naturalization Papers District Court, Vol. B. New Braunfels, fall of 1854, gives Charles Iwonski as being already twenty-one years old. Carl Iwonski always used his European name, Carl G. von Iwonski (letter, Oscar Haas, New Braunfels, to author).

[84] Letter, Carlos Iwonski, El Paso, to Daughters of the Republic of Texas Library, San Antonio, October 12, 1940. Carlos is a grand-nephew of Carl G.

65. Carl G. von Iwonski: *Theatre at the Old Casino Club, San Antonio, Texas*
Oil, 9⅜″ x 14″ (Courtesy of Mr. H. Stirling Watlington, New York City)

Albert C. Horton, with power of attorney to sell land of the Horton league to settlers. In order to call attention to this beautiful area, Leopold Iwonski on one occasion, with the assistance of his son, gave a "public entertainment" on his farm at Horton Town in July, 1847. The entertainment included "a ball, general amusements, and refreshments of chocolate, coffee, cakes, tarts, general confectionary—also an elegant supper furnished with claret, white port, and Madeira wines—Gentlemen $5.00, Ladies free." He conducted a celebration which would vie with any modern real-estate promotion. The outcome on this occasion was the sale of 1,128 acres from the Horton tract to twelve settlers at three dollars per acre.[85] This real-estate bonanza put the Iwonskis on

their financial feet. It was not long before they moved to San Antonio, where Carl had better opportunities.

Their place of residence, near the landscape artist Hermann Lungkwitz, was at the southeast corner of Commerce and Rusk Streets. Later they occupied one of the Louis Gresser houses facing Garden Street (south of St. Mary's Street). Carl's association with Lungkwitz was no doubt a stimulating influence in his career, and their partnership some years later in a photographic ven-

[85] Letter of record, F. C. Humphrey, author, with information from the Controller's office, Austin, Texas; in Comal County Records Vol. A, pp. 52–64, December, 1846, and January–February, 1847; Comal County Records, 1849. Leopold Iwonski, "4th of July Public Intertainment, Horton's Settlement," 22nd June, 1847, *Neu-Braunfelser Zeitung* (no date).

66. Carl G. von Iwonski: *The Schenck Sisters*
Oil, 1870, 32″ x 31″ (Courtesy of Mrs. Louis Ramella, Austin, Texas)

ture strengthened this friendship.[86] Carl went about his art in earnest; he used to tell how he had received from an anonymous San Antonio patron two diamond shirt buttons in payment for his first commission.[87]

Iwonski's *View of New Braunfels* (1855), which is listed among the "Cityscapes and Prospects," deserves special mention. It is a panoramic view of the village from a nearby high point. In this he shows in the distance the octagonally shaped church, Vereins Kirche, and the neat little German emigrant houses; in the foreground, in addition to bovines and cacti, he shows Mr. Ernst Dosch, a hunter, mounted, while on the other side of the engraving is Dr. Ferdinand von Roemer, the naturalist, astride what he termed his "scientific mule." The doctor's own description on his return from a specimen-gathering trip, just as the artist records it in his sketch, is as follows:

For my collecting trips in the interest of natural history which were now to begin in real earnest, I bought a mule which in the course of time proved itself a useful servant, and which accompanied me on all my wanderings in Texas. He patiently allowed himself to be loaded with the manifold objects of natural history. Often he presented a grotesque appearance when I came home in the evening from a collecting trip, carrying in addition to myself a leather saddlebag full of stones, a bundle of plants, and a four- or five-foot chicken snake suspended from the pommel. . . . In gathering

objects of natural history I was assisted by practically the entire population of New Braunfels, especially the younger generation, since the peculiar types of animals, unknown in the native land, aroused their interest as much as mine. Nearly every day birds, snakes, lizards, turtles, fish, etc., were brought to me and by rewarding the finders with a small coin I was able to stimulate them to renew their search.[88]

A firm in Leipzig reproduced Iwonski's panoramic drawing of New Braunfels in an engraving, which was circulated in the United States. Another print from Iwonski's hand which has a great value, particularly to local historians, is a unique piece of work called *Germania Gesangverein*, which pictures the sponsors of the first song festival held in New Braunfels, October 16 and 17, 1853. In this, the artist is able to show fourteen members of the society in portraiture. They are seated informally around the table, their work spread before them—lighted by candles, stein in hand, each member appears in distinct character. In this drawing Iwonski records many of the early distinguished scholars and scientists of the settlement.[89]

The variety of subject matter in Iwonski's work shows the interest this pioneer had in painting the local scene and incidents—whatever the day might bring. A group painting in oil of the interior of the old Casino Club (which in time served as San Antonio's first theatre, opening January 17, 1858) at the time of a performance gives a view of the actors and part of the audience (Plate 65).[90] This painting shows Iwonski's ability to catch a group in action, which is remarkable in its naturalness and in the inclusion of simple details. In addition, during the Civil War, Iwonski made a drawing of a play, *The Unavoidable (Der Unvermeidliche)*, in which he took an acting part, as shown in the drawing, with four other citizens of New Braunfels and San Antonio. Iwonski had a definite interest in the progress of the theatre in San Antonio and often helped with the painting of the sets.[91]

Another historically interesting group portrait in oil showed the dictation of terms following the Franco-Prussian War. This hung for many years in the old Casino Club, and a second copy was said to have hung in one of Berlin's public buildings. From a photograph of the painting, the people depicted are, from left to right, "Crown Prince Frederick Wilhelm; German von Roon; Prince Frederick Carl, the Red Prince; Emperor Wilhelm I; General von Moltke; Chancellor von Bismark; Prince Carl; and General von Steinmetz." The

[86] *San Antonio Express*, May 24, 1866 (adv.), Photographic Gallery.

[87] Yanaguana Society, Catalogue, *Loan Exhibition of Old San Antonio Paintings*, December 3, 1933, p. 11.

[88] "Texas in Pictures," *Antiques Magazine* (June, 1948), 456; Roemer, *Texas*, plate 137; Malone, *Dictionary of American Biography*, VIII, 91–92; Roemer was collecting specimens in this area in the spring of 1845 with funds provided by the Society for the Protection of German Emigrants in Texas for the Berlin Academy of Science and with the approval of Alexander von Humboldt. His special mission was to study the conditions of the colonists in Texas and to report on the natural resources of the country.

[89] Carl von Iwonski, original sketch, 1857, *Germania Gerangverein, New Braunfels, Texas*, in possession of Mr. Walter Heidmeyer, New Braunfels; members represented: F. Movreau; H. Conring, C. Holtz, Jul Bremer, H. Seele, E. von Stein, G. Eisenlohr, A. Hartman, Ed Rische, A. Baier, Aug. Bechstadt, A. Schlameus, J. Rennert, and H. Schimmelprenning.

[90] Letter from H. Stirling Watlington, New York City, to author, June 21, 1964. Watlington is the grandson of Baron Carl Frederick von Griesenbeck, shown in the painting on the stage beside the actress to his right. In the audience on the front row (with her back to the viewer) in the spotted dress is Mrs. Mary Elmendorf.

[91] *San Antonio Express*, April 20, 1948; Oscar Haas, "Comal County's Part in the Civil War" (III), *New Braunfels Herald*, April 17, 1962.

67. Carl G. von Iwonski: *Johanna Steves*
   Oil, 1872, 33¾″ x 25½″ (Courtesy of Mrs. Edna Steves Vaughn, San Antonio, Texas)

68. Carl G. von Iwonski: *Edward Steves*
    Oil, 1873, 33¾″ x 25½″ (Courtesy of Mrs. Edna Steves Vaughn, San Antonio, Texas)

69. Carl G. von Iwonski: *Still Life: Bottle, Gun, Powderhorn, Pipe*
Oil, c. 1873, 12″ x 9″ (Courtesy of Mr. Ganahl Walker, Jr., San Antonio, Texas)

present location of the Casino copy is unknown and it is feared that it has been destroyed.[92]

Iwonski's paintings often picture one dramatic moment. This is true of a double-portrait in oil, *The Schenck Sisters* (Plate 66), which shows two young girls, Johanna and Caroline, dressed for a St. Valentine's Day party. One sister has received a valentine and the other sister is trying to see it; other valentines are on the table beside them.[93] While representing a true scene, the use of the letters also is significant in that, as in the old paintings, they indicate the social status of the girls; and including a letter in his painting was thought to display a certain technical skill of the artist. In spite of the action, the scene is presented with dignity and charm.

Numerous portraits of the conventional type rank in craftsmanship and interest with other Iwonski paintings. Mr. and Mrs. Carl H. Guenther, prosperous owners of the flour mill at New Braunfels, sat for individual portraits. Many families in San Antonio who could afford the luxury engaged Iwonski to paint family portraits, among them the Peter Gallaghers, the Edward Steves (Plates 67 and 68), the Sam Mavericks, and the Hardin B. Adamses.[94]

Probably no other artist who came to Texas showed such versatility and exact draftsmanship in his work as Iwonski. An oil painting, *trompe l'oeil* in character, displays against a white background a gun, a powder horn, a bottle of "fire-water" and a Dutch pipe (Plate 69). According to the owners of the painting, Carl Iwonski left it as a farewell gift to Edward and Johanna Steves to show his gratitude for hospitality while painting their portraits. Mr. Steves added to the illusion (as shown in sixteenth-century paintings) by enclosing the picture in a walnut cabinet-like frame.[95]

Though Iwonski was successful in the traditional oil portrait, one might well conclude that his real genius lay in sharp pencil portraits. In this extremely delicate work he found no rival except Richard Petri, the contemporary German artist, whose skill is exemplified in his portrait *Elise*. Iwonski traveled out of San Antonio from place to place to make drawings of children and grownups. When in Sisterdale (c. 1854), he made a remarkably fine portrait of fourteen-year-old Julia Kapp, daughter of Dr. Ernest Kapp. In Fredericksburg, Marie Oekers (Mrs. Ferdinand Simon), then sixteen, sat for a portrait drawn with the same steel-like point (Plate 70). Two similar signed sketches are those of Tabetha

Childress Grayson and Capt. Thomas W. Grayson, of the steamboat *Yellow Stone*, remembered particularly for protective custody of Santa Anna after his capture at the Battle of San Jacinto.[96]

One pencil portrait should be mentioned as a fine example of this type. It is of Lily Carolon (Plate 71), age three, daughter of the onetime mayor of San Antonio. A bust portrait shows the curly-haired girl wearing a low-necked dress, with a delicately designed Maltese cross suspended from her neck.[97]

Although during the fifties Iwonski soberly regarded the impending war, no doubt he appreciated another side of life in San Antonio, for often in his paintings the "other" Carl von Iwonski, with waggish humor, injects a note of gaiety and funmaking that throws light on tastes and interests of his time. *The Terry Rangers* (Eighth Cavalry), attributed to Iwonski (Plate 72), shows Sam Maverick, ranger, mounted, followed by companions, also mounted. Maverick in a gay mood is drinking from a canteen—the manner revealing a bit of the artist's rough humor.[98] This picture suggests the abundant humor, tragedy, and eccentricity of life in Texas at that time, and especially in thriving San Antonio.

This jesting characteristic of Iwonski's work appears in another painting he made, while visiting in Austin his friend Frederick Schenck, a great hunter. On Schenck's return from a trek he had given the German maid in the household a rabbit to prepare for cooking. In a short time he returned to find her picking the hairs from the rabbit. The incident so amused Iwonski that he put it into a picture: the hunter is standing in the doorway dressed in his hunting outfit, gun in hand, watching the process. There is a strong sense of rapid brush stroke—an exaggeration of his usual style—which suggests that

[92] Witte Museum, information on painting *Dictation of Terms of the Franco-German War*, photograph; *San Antonio Express*, April 20, 1948.

[93] Interview, Mrs. Louis Ramella, Austin, owner of the painting *The Schenck Sisters*, which is signed and dated.

[94] Chabot, *With the Makers of San Antonio*, Edward Steves, p. 406; Carl H. Guenther and wife, p. 398; and Manuel Yturri, p. 174.

[95] Interview, Mr. Ganahl Walker, Jr., San Antonio, owner of *Still Life*.

[96] Sophienburg Museum, New Braunfels, files; and files of the Daughters of the Republic of Texas Library, San Antonio.

[97] Interview, Mrs. Marion Jones, Austin, owner of the painting; interview, J. C. Butterfield, San Antonio, Texas, son of the sitter and original owner.

[98] Witte Museum, biographical file on Iwonski, San Antonio, Texas.

70. Carl G. von Iwonski: *Marie Oekers*
Pencil and crayon, 1864, 9¾ ″ x 8″ (Courtesy of the Sophienburg Museum, New Braunfels, Texas)

71. Carl G. von Iwonski: *Lily Carolon*
    Pencil, c. 1858, 8½″ x 6½″ (Courtesy of Mr. T. Griffith Jones, San Antonio, Texas)

72. Carl G. von Iwonski: *Sam Maverick and the Terry Rangers*
Oil, c. 1860, 11″ x 14½″ (Courtesy of the Witte Museum, San Antonio, Texas)

73. Carl G. von Iwonski: *Bivouac of Confederate Troops on the Las Moras, Texas*
Pencil sketch, 1861, 9½" x 13½" (Courtesy of the Library of Congress, Washington, D. C.)

74. Carl G. von Iwonski: *Lipan Indian*

Oil, 1849, 5½″ x 4½″ (Courtesy of Mrs. V. O. Westervelt, San Antonio, Texas)

75. Carl G. von Iwonski: *Lipan Indian*
   Oil, 1849, 5½″ x 4½″ (Courtesy of Mrs. V. O. Westervelt, San Antonio, Texas)

he did not intend this for the public eye or to represent a finished work. It remains as a reminder of the incident and a source of amusement among the Schenck descendants.[99]

Iwonski made several trips to his homeland. Like the majority of Germans—not in sympathy with the South, opposing both slavery and secession—he preferred to remain neutral. Texans generally understood little of European culture and were making life disagreeable for the German settlers. Iwonski made the best of the situation, and his realistic Civil War sketches contribute vividly to the history of the times.

In February, 1861, Texans sat in Convention Hall in Austin facing a decision as to secession from the Union. At that very moment General David E. Twiggs, of the United States Army, and his 160 men were drawn up in San Antonio on Main Plaza in front of Smith's Hotel, facing Colonel Ben McCulloch, Military Commander representing the Convention and demanding the surrender of Federal posts in Texas. General Twiggs was a Georgian and in sympathy with the Texans. He had asked for instructions from Washington, and when none were forthcoming he tendered his resignation, which was accepted. But time was running out and while awaiting his successor, McCulloch demanded that the Union force evacuate San Antonio and surrender to the Committee on Public Safety all Federal property except facilities for transportation to the coast. General Twiggs had no alternative but to surrender; consequently, property valued at three million dollars fell into the hands of the Texans.[100] Iwonski observed the proceedings and made a sketch of the surrender. This sketch and another, equally interesting, were sent to *Harper's Weekly* and are the basis of illustrations for the issues of March 23 and June 15, 1861.[101]

At this time, Iwonski and his partner in the photo-graphic business found a genial comrade in their landlord, old Samuel Bell, a flag-waving Unionist.[102] On the occasion of the surrender he followed the Union troops to the edge of town, but Iwonski had business in mind and accompanied the troops to the area near Fort Clark on the Las Moras Creek, where he made his second pencil sketch (Plate 73). This sketch, signed and dated 1861, we have in the original form as well as the copy in *Harper's*—to which was added by the publisher: "This was the first sketch received by *Harper's* following the surrender of General Twiggs."[103] In the two versions we can compare the artist's conception with the publisher's use of it.

"A Gentleman whose secessionist views are beyond question," commented the editor upon receiving Iwonski's note to the sketch:

After the surrender of San Antonio by General Twiggs, state troops were organized in order to take possession of the forts occupied by the U.S. Army. [Twiggs was occupying the Alamo at the time.] The above is a true picture of a portion of said state troops encamping on the Las Moras, near Ft. Clark, on their way to the upper posts, Hudson, Lancaster, and Davis. The picture ought to speak for itself. We need not remind you that the "U.Ss" and the "Q.M.Ds" imply their former owners; and add, furthermore, that no white man in these diggins will be astonished to see the poor Mexicans do all the "hauling of wood and drawing of water," the dons being engaged in smoking cigarrites [sic], eating sardines, drinking "Pat's favorite," superintending the killing of a stray pig, etc., etc. A lineal descendant of Montezuma stands sentinel by order No. I: "Put none but true Southerners on guard tonight!"[104]

The sketch is hastily but skillfully made. One sees the hauling of water, various members of the group drinking, preparation of the fire for roasting a pig, a man sharpening his knife on his boot, a don standing guard. In the background are wagons marked "U. S."

If one has the curiosity to look up *Harper's* version in the June 15, 1861, issue, he will find much the same details in both the print and the original drawings—the latter from the pencil of a skillful realist.[105]

On October 7, 1857, the New Braunfels *Zeitung* informed its readers that "the young artist, Mr. Iwonski," had made a "life-size" portrait of Sam Houston "from recollection."[106] In 1861 two well-executed sketches (6" x 9") were signed and dated, one of Sam Houston and the other of Houston's last home, "Cedar Point," in

[99] Interview, Mrs. Louis Ramella, Austin, Texas, granddaughter of hunter and owner of picture.

[100] Rupert N. Richardson, *Texas, the Lone Star State*, 2d ed., pp. 186–187; Jack W. Gunn, "Ben McCulloch: A Big Captain," *Southwestern Historical Quarterly*, LVIII, No. 58 (July, 1954), 17–18.

[101] *Harper's Weekly* (March 23, 1861), 182, 184; (June 15, 1861), 375, 381.

[102] *San Antonio Express*, March 3, 1882.

[103] Library of Congress, pencil sketch, *Las Moras*, by Iwonski.

[104] *Harper's Weekly* (June 15, 1861), 381.

[105] *Ibid.*, p. 375.

[106] *Neu Braunfelser Zeitung*, October 7, 1857.

Huntsville. The latter is inscribed by Houston, who states that the sketch was an "authentic view" of his home.[107]

Brief mention should be made of three important portraits of Indians. These small oils (5" x 7") have recently come to light and were supposedly painted in 1856: an Indian chief, a squaw, and an Indian child. If this date is correct, they were probably painted sometime after Iwonski left Horton Town. The subjects are probably Lipans. They are painted in the same pose and with the exact detail of three painted by Richard Petri about the same time in water color. Could it be that the two artists were acquainted? That possibility remains a pleasant speculation.[108] Other Lipan Indians are shown in Plates 74 and 75.

Carl Iwonski, a single-minded bachelor, traveled widely in Central Texas and was thought by some to be a humorous individual, but others recognized in the artist a quiet, reflective person. After twenty-seven years of painting in Texas, upon the death of his father in the 1870's, he and his mother returned to Germany. Iwonski's activities in Texas contribute much to understanding the era and the art of the period. At his native Ruchers, Germany, he continued his graphic comments upon people and events.

[107] Collection of former Governor Price Daniel, Liberty, Texas.
[108] Interview, Mrs. V. O. Westervelt, San Antonio, owner of the portraits.

CHAPTER 6

POLITICS AND PORTRAITS—
BEYOND OUR BORDERS

T HE PICTORIAL RECORDING of dramatic political and civic events of Texas, as well as the recording of likenesses of its actors, was not confined to its borders. Portraits of Sam Houston painted in Washington, D. C., and elsewhere (probably a greater number than of any other public figure of his time), may be accounted for after the passing of a century. His proclivity to have his likeness made can, no doubt, be laid to vanity. Houston, when quite young, had a taste of elegance in this respect when J. Ford of Philadelphia painted his portrait on ivory.[1] Guy Bryan and Robert Handy (close friends of Houston) became patrons of the arts when Bryan employed Flintoff to paint his portrait and others in the state government, Handy had a portrait painted of himself by a professional artist of Philadelphia.[2] While a senator, Houston sat for artists John Plumbe, daguerreotypist, and Martin Heade, portraitist, both living in New York City.[3]

Houston had a very definite interest in portraiture; he urged his friends to have their likenesses made and wrote often concerning the whereabouts of his own.

An early example, which has been copied by artists most frequently, is a portrait in which he wears a panther-skin vest. Here is a description of Senator Houston in the odd vest by a Washington correspondent:

In black pantaloons, a single vested blue military coat with bright buttons, and a vest made out of the skin of a panther with the hair outside. He always comes in in some singular dress half savage, half character, which, however, he soon lays aside and puts on what used to be called in Kentucky "his store clothes."[4]

Houston was a man of tangled paradoxes—at one

[1] Interview, Mrs. F. T. Baldwin, Houston, granddaughter of Sam Houston and owner of painting by J. Ford.
[2] Charles H. Hart (ed.), *Register of Portraits Painted by Thomas Sully, 1801–1811*; William Dunlap, *History of the Rise and Progress of the Arts of Design in the United States*, II, 279.
[3] Letter, Charles Bingham, of the American Antiquarian Society, Boston, to Taylor, of the Metropolitan Museum, September 22, 1932, New York Public Library; Dumas Malone, *Dictionary of American Biography*, see John Plumbe (1809–1857).
[4] *The Texas Republican*, Marshall, Texas, quoted from Sam Houston's unpublished correspondence, January 24, 1852.

time he might be compelled to pay for drinking glasses broken at a tavern and at another he might make the main speech at a temperance celebration or "blow out," as he termed such a meeting.[5] On one occasion he might be seen riding a mule to keep an appointment, bragging that he had passed every rider on the road, and at another time he might be seen riding in a carriage, dressed in a velvet suit, with all the graces of a gentleman, which certainly distinguished him at times.

In spite of Houston's paradoxical appearance and manners he was steadfast and sincere in his political theories—he felt strongly his obligations to his fellowman. But in the drama of political and civic events concerning Texas he did not always come out unscathed. Professor John Plumbe, Jr., of Philadelphia and New York, called "The Daguerre of America," a publisher, and a railroad financier, whose firm made a portrait of Houston, had something to say about Houston and his politics. In April, 1846, the *New York Sun* published the following unequivocal opinion of Houston's tactics:

We have been favored with a view of an excellent daguerreotype portrait of Sam Houston, the self-styled "political coquette" taken by Plumbe, corner of Broadway and Warren Streets. Nature and art could not do more to produce a faithful representation of that singular man now a member of the United States Senate. If our readers have any curiosity to see a man who was compelled to be the hero of one or two remarkable battles but a willing instrument on England's side in the annexation of Texas, they should go see Plumbe's daguerreotype of Sam Houston.[6]

The year preceding this announcement (1845), General Houston was accused by Willard Richardson, of the *Galveston News,* and Dr. Francis Moore, of the Houston *Telegraph and Texas Register,* of tergiversation in connection with the annexation. They stated that he had reversed his thinking in the matter of annexation of Texas to the United States, terming this reversal "coquetry."[7] In answer to these gentlemen, General Houston stated that he had directed the minister in Washington to withdraw the application of Texas for annexation and had furthermore courted the favor of both England and France. "But," he stated, "if ladies are justified in making use of coquetry in securing their annexation to good husbands, you must excuse me for making use of the same means to annex Texas to Uncle Sam." Up to this time, Houston felt that "for reasons of public policy the situation in regard to annexation forbid any explanation."[8]

Martin Johnson Heade

At this time Martin Johnson Heade (1819–1904), a young man of 27, painted a portrait of Sam Houston, signed and dated 1846. As Houston was in the United States Congress at the time, the portrait was most likely painted in Washington, D.C. Heade was little known until Robert G. McIntire called attention to him in his *Martin Johnson Heade,* published in 1948. Now examples of his work are found in many American art collections, in which he is represented chiefly by his extraordinary paintings of flowers and hummingbirds.[9] Time will tell, however, whether his early period of portraiture turns out to be a greater contribution to art in its substance than either his landscape work or his meticulously executed examples from nature. Heade's uncurbed, persistent restlessness, which took him to many parts of the world, may have cost him his full aesthetic realization.

Heade's parents, Joseph Crowell and Sarah John Heed, preferred the simple spelling of their name, but when Martin returned from a trip to England he used the earlier English spelling, "Heade." Their home at Lumberville, Pennsylvania, with the Delaware River at their back and the old canal and a long narrow road which followed it in front, was overhung with wild azaleas and mountain laurel. Thus Martin's boyhood was spent in a setting which brought with freshness nature's abundance and beauty. The old field-stone house, built at the turn of the century, which was the artist's birthplace, may still be pointed out. When Martin was a youth, the only school Lumberville could boast was a one-room octagon or "eight-square."[10] The pupils of all ages were seated in circles around the pot-bellied stove, and though he hardly had elbowroom, Martin

---

[5] Sam Houston, *Writings of Sam Houston, 1813–1865,* edited by Amelia W. Williams and Eugene C. Barker, V, 94; *Texas State Gazette,* Austin, August 30, 1851.

[6] *New York Sun,* April 2, 1846.

[7] *Telegraph and Texas Register,* Houston, April 6, 1845; June 4, 1845 (copied from *New Orleans Bulletin* of May 29, 1845); letter, Andrew J. Donelson to Miller, July 27, 1845, Miller Papers, Texas State Archives, Austin.

[8] Sam Houston, *Autobiography,* edited by Donald Day and Harry H. Ullom, p. 211.

[9] Robert G. McIntire, *Martin Johnson Heade,* Exhibition, Pennsylvania Academy of Fine Arts, 1847, pp. 55–58; Clara Clements and Lawrence Hulton, *Artists of the Nineteenth Century,* I, 340; Henry Tuckerman, *Book of Artists: American Artist's Life,* p. 542; Edgar P. Richardson *Painting in America, the Story of 450 Years,* p. 226.

[10] McIntire, *Martin Johnson Heade,* pp. 5–6.

76. Martin Johnson Heade: *Sam Houston*
Oil, 1847, 29½″ x 24½″ (The Governor's Mansion, Austin, Texas)

probably managed to spend his time sketching his favorite subjects, while hiding behind his largest book.

Martin's prosperous and observant parents were able to send him to take drawing lessons at nearby Newtown, Pennsylvania, from Thomas Hicks, nephew of the folk artist Edward Hicks of *Peaceable Kingdom* fame. Thomas, four years Martin's junior, was able to communicate his knowledge of painting to Martin, and, furthermore, in 1841 made an exemplary portrait (23" x 18") of his pupil, which now belongs to the Bucks County Historical Society in Doylestown, Pennsylvania.[11] Martin's father, an indulgent parent, allowed his son to study in Rome and to travel extensively in Europe. Thomas Hicks may have used his influence in this direction, as Hicks also spent several months in Rome at the same time.

When Martin Heade returned to the United States at the age of twenty-one, he settled down for a time in New York on Dey Street. Soon he exhibited portraits at the National Academy—one of his sister, *Portrait of a Young Lady* (1843) *Portrait of a Gentleman* (1852),[12] and in 1859 *A Gentleman*.

It was during this period of interest in portraiture that he painted the well-executed portrait of Sam Houston, which shows in the General's face the lines of success and struggle (Plate 76). It is a bust portrait of the firm-minded Senator—part of a red cape around his shoulders, a jaunty white tie, and a vest exemplify his transition from pioneer to statesman. The portrait was exhibited at the Pennsylvania Academy of Fine Arts in 1847 and later at the Yale School of Fine Arts in 1871. It now belongs to the state of Texas and is in the Governor's Mansion in Austin.

In 1864 Heade's love of travel took him to South America, where he was captivated by the beauty of the hummingbird and the tropical flowers. His ability to paint with great delicacy and brilliance (sometimes sensuous and unrestrained) the beauty of the native birds and the orchids of Brazil drew much attention. Publication of his work was recommended by our American envoy extraordinary and minister plenipotentiary, Honorable J. Watson Webb, to the Emperor of Brazil,[13] but Heade in 1865 went to London, taking his paintings with him. He found that difficulties in the proper reproduction of his paintings forced him to give up his project. The original designs were purchased in London when he decided that publication was impractical.[14] For his "significant achievement" in Brazil, he was made

"Knight of the Order of the Rose" by Don Pedro II, on March 30, 1864.[15]

Augustus Behné

During Sam Houston's second gubernatorial term, in 1859, some of his friends wanted to express their appreciation for his services by placing the General's full-length portrait in the State Capitol. But before the plan progressed very far, the question of secession became a real issue. During the pre-Civil War period the solidarity of Texas's citizens had been notable and had brought the state a long way. Now, progress lagged. As days passed, the fateful question became the most important and argumentative subject. It set friend against friend, and many of Houston's former supporters heartily disapproved of his stand as a Unionist.

The first official step concerning a portrait was taken in 1861, when the state legislature appointed Representative Robert Townes to find an artist.[16] Whether an invitation was extended to portraitist Gustavus Augustus Behné (1828–1895), from Pennsylvania, before or after he came to Texas is not clear, but in 1861 he was in Galveston with a studio at a Mr. Wedge's daguerreotype gallery at the corner of Tremont and Market Streets. The issue of the *Galveston News* which announced his presence stated that "one sees a fine portrait just completed of Judge Burnet, ex-president of the Republic—a full-size portrait by Mr. Behné, an artist of superior talent."[17]

Several legislators accompanied Mr. Townes to the home of Mr. Robert Robson, a wealthy cattleman from Scotland, where Mr. Behné was a guest. Here, near Richmond, Texas, at "Robson's Castle" they came to

---

[11] Letter, Mrs. J. Paul Sias, Bucks County Historical Society, Doyleston, Pennsylvania, to author, January 8, 1964; McIntire, *Martin Johnson Heade*, Plate XIX, pp. 7–8.

[12] McIntire, *Martin Johnson Heade*, p. 9; *Art Digest* (March 1, 1947).

[13] Letter, Honorable J. Watson Webb, Envoy Extraordinary and Minister Plenipotentiary, Petrópolis Legation of the United States, to the Emperor of Brazil Don Pedro II, February 20, 1884, collection of Mrs. Howard Houseley, Lumberville, Pennsylvania; signed letter in McIntire, *Martin Johnson Heade*, Plate XIX.

[14] Tuckerman, *Book of Artists*, p. 542.

[15] Citation by Don Pedro II to Heade, the Knight of the Order of the Rose, Bucks County Historical Society, Doylestown, Pennsylvania.

[16] Letter, Mrs. Charles Lungren, Lancaster County Historical Society, Lancaster, Pennsylvania, February 16, 1962, to author.

[17] *Galveston News*, April 6, 1861.

some agreement on the price and other details of the proposed portrait. As a consequence of this meeting, Behné went to Austin, and in spite of the difficulties in getting Houston for sittings he succeeded in making a number of preliminary sketches in pencil.[18]

While there was great respect for Houston in some circles, bitterness grew stronger in the days of 1861. Interest in the proposed project lessened, and when war began, it was forgotten. Houston was now sixty-nine, distraught and discouraged, and his anxiety for his state and country was expressed publicly:

I am now an aged man. My locks have become white in toiling, as I believe, for the liberties of mankind. Were I young, that I might look forward to the future, feeling that whatever danger might come, my strong arm would be at hand to defend my family, I would feel less anxiety than I do at present. The years that I have to endure the misfortunes of Civil War will be but few. If I could feel that with the close of my career would end the miseries of my race, I could share its misfortunes with patience, but to feel that the perils of revolution must continue, that its attendant horrors of bloodshed, rapine and devastation must still be visited upon it, would embitter my last moments, and after living to witness dissolution of the best government that ever existed I would sink into the grave without hope that freedom would be generated or our posterity ever enjoy again the blessing with which we are parted. Let us pause and ponder well before we take any action outside the constitution.[19]

Mr. Behné completed the portrait, but he had no taste for war, and with his wife departed Texas for Havana, Cuba.

Behné was well equipped to undertake the painting. He was a native of Nordhausen, Prussia, but in his youth, his parents, the John Henry Behnés, decided to leave Prussia. We learn from the artist that after his father's graduation in medicine (homeopathy) from the University of Wurtz he was questioned concerning his methods of practicing. But before leaving for America he provided for his son's education in art—Gustavus Augustus Behné studied for a period of time at the Düsseldorf School of Art and then at the Munich Galleries. After completing his studies in Europe young Behné joined his parents, who had settled in Reading, Pennsylvania. In order to become acquainted with methods of American art he studied for a short time with Thomas Sully (1783–1872) in Philadelphia.

Behné was said to have been a fine-looking youth, a linguist, and a musician. Before coming to Texas he exhibited in Philadelphia between 1855 and 1857 his *Holy Family* (after Van Dyck), *The Carousel*, and *Hay Making*. The last, a genre scene in rural Berks County, drew a great deal of attention. In 1856 the artist married Julia Meyer Keim, a native of Reading and a daughter of General George May and Julia Meyer Keim May. A few years afterwards he came to Galveston, where he made portraits of some of its citizens. Disturbed by the war in 1861, he spent several years in Cuba, as mentioned earlier.[20] When he returned, the war was over and General Houston had died.

When the constitutional convention of 1866 was held in Austin, the desire for a full-length portrait of Houston was discussed without thought of the earlier attempt. Representative Norton presented the resolution to procure the portrait:

Resolved by the people of the State of Texas by Delegates in Convention assembled, that the death of General Sam Houston, late Governor of the State of Texas is a national calamity, and that in consideration of his pre-eminent abilities, great experience and exalted patriotism, his high character and enthusiastic devotion to the interests and the cause of Texas, from the beginning of the struggle for independence, throughout our revolutionary war, our existence as a Republic, and our life as a state, and in appreciation of the faithful discharge of his duties as Commander-in-chief of the Army, as President of the Republic, as United States Senator and as Governor of the State, His Excellency the Governor is hereby authorized and empowered to procure, and place in the Representative Hall, his full length portrait, to commemorate his distinguished services and perpetuate his memory. Adopted unanimously.[21]

Apparently no reference was made to the Behné portrait, and the matter was put in the hands of Provisional Governor A. J. Hamilton.

Governor Hamilton wrote to Mrs. Houston on April 16, 1866, that the General's salary of $1,924.00 would be paid to her in gold (for "shin plasters," as Confed-

[18] Original letter, Gustavus Augustus Behné, Galveston, to A. S. Hamilton, Austin, March 31, 1866, collection of Mrs. F. T. Baldwin, Houston; Augustus Behné pencil sketch in collection of Paul Adams, San Antonio, signed by artist.

[19] *Civilian and Gazette*, Galveston, July 8, 1865.

[20] Morton L. Montgomery (comp.) *Biographical Annals of Berks County, Pennsylvania*, I, 712; letter, Mrs. Charles Lungren, Lancaster County Historical Society, Lancaster, Pennsylvania, to author, February 16, 1962.

[21] A. B. Norton, *The Journal of the Texas State Convention, February 7, 1866–April 2, 1866*, p. 266.

77. Augustus Behné: *Sam Houston*

Oil, 1861, approx. 52″ x 40″ (Courtesy of the Alamo Library, Daughters of the Republic of Texas, San Antonio, Texas [Photograph; location of original unknown])

78. L. M. D. Guillaume: *The Battle of San Jacinto*
Oil, 1892, 24¼″ x 48″ (Courtesy of the R. W. Norton Art Gallery, Shreveport, Louisiana)

erate money was called, were low in value) and that he would soon take up the matter of a portrait. He added these words to his letter: "I cannot express to you how grateful it is to my heart that at last even General Houston's late enemies have been compelled, in deference to public opinion, to publicly acknowledge his eminent ability, patriotism, and public service."[22] Equally important was the fact that he enclosed in his letter to Mrs. Houston one from the artist Behné, who had seen in the Galveston paper the Convention's interest in a portrait of Houston. Behné wrote as follows:

I see by the papers that the Convention [Constitutional Convention] authorized you to have a full-length portrait of General Houston painted for the capitol. My large picture [102" x 63"] was not finished until after the troubles began and [Sam Houston] was shamefully forced out of office and then there was no chance of having an appropriation made for the picture, much less, during the war, even had I been here, but I returned only shortly ago from Havana.

I must declare in justice to myself that no such picture could now be painted—after his death—he himself said it was the only portrait—oil or photograph—with which he was completely satisfied. Of the hundreds of persons who saw it, not one did or could have suggested an improvement. I thought it improper to exhibit it and held the picture until November though I could have sold it in New York to advantage, because I had painted the picture for a particular place and object and would not break my part of the contract. Thinking you might be a stranger to these facts, you must excuse the length of this epistle.[23]

The end of the affair was that the state did not buy the portrait, but the artist's friend Colonel Robson, the prosperous cattleman, did; he paid twelve hundred dollars in gold for it, to hang in his "Castle." In 1873 the painting passed into the hands of the Charles McNeils and was finally given to the Rosenberg Library at Galveston.[24] This two-thirds-length portrait (which presently cannot be located) exists in photographic form and in preliminary pencil sketches. The oil portrait (Plate 77) shows the General dressed in a black suit, his right hand extended as if he were making a public address. It is a substantial, clear-cut, well-executed portrait of Houston.

L. M. D. Guillaume

In the last half of the nineteenth century, Louis Mathieu Didier Guillaume (1816–1892), of Nantes, France, revealed in paint the charm and character of no less

than one hundred portraits of men and women of Virginia.[25] Among these was a portrait of Dr. Robert Louis Dabney, who later in life was to fill a significant role in the field of education at The University of Texas.

It is thought that Guillaume came to America through the influence of William Cabel Rives, United States minister to France. Guillaume's work was first noticed in this country when he exhibited three paintings at the National Academy of Design in 1855.[26] But in France he exhibited as early as 1837, at the Salon in Paris, an allegorical figure representing the French Republic—the climax of his instruction under Paul Delaroche (1797–1867) and Pierre Lacour (1778–1859). Guillaume's work in landscape and portraiture in Paris naturally sharpened and developed his insight for the genre-historical scenes which became important later in his career.[27]

The first of the genre-historical paintings came at the end of his service in the Civil War, when he followed General Robert E. Lee to witness the surrender. He made sketches of the participants, and because of his habit of working in detail, he made drawings of articles in the room; these studies were later incorporated in an impressive painting, which was purchased by the University of Michigan in 1895.[28]

Guillaume traveled from one place to another—Richmond, Norfolk, Lexington, Lynchburg, and Baltimore—before going finally to Washington, D.C., where he found sitters for his portraits in oils and pastels. It was probably in Virginia that he made the portrait of Dr. Robert Louis Dabney, who served as chaplain in the Southern army, and was to become professor of philoso-

[22] Letter, A. J. Hamilton, Austin, to Mrs. Sam Houston, Independence, Texas, April 16, 1866; letter, A. J. Hamilton to Mrs. Sam Houston (no date), Texas State Archives, Austin.

[23] Letter, Augustus Behné to Governor A. J. Hamilton, Austin; enclosed in Hamilton's letter to Mrs. Houston, Independence, Texas, original in possession of Mrs. F. T. Baldwin, Houston; letter, Mrs. F. T. Baldwin to author, March 31, 1866.

[24] Mrs. Fred Scott, *Austin American*, March 7, 1915, ". . . only authentic portrait of General Sam Houston to be taken."

[25] "Exhibition of 18th and 19th Century American Paintings from Lynchburg Homes," Randolph-Macon Woman's College, Lynchburg, Virginia, 1954.

[26] Mary Bartlett Cowdrey, *National Academy of Design*, p. 200.

[27] George C. Groce and David H. Wallace, *New-York Historical Society's Dictionary of Artists in America, 1564–1860*, p. 279; *Richmond Standard*, Virginia, March 27, 1880; *Washington Post*, April 17, 1892.

[28] Letter, Mrs. Ralph Catterall, Valentine Museum, Richmond, Virginia, to author, October 4, 1962.

phy from 1883 to 1894 at The University of Texas. The large portrait (24½" x 48") shows a three-quarters seated figure of the dignified professor, facing the artist. It is signed, in a fancy Spencerian hand, "L. M. D. Guillaume."[29]

Guillaume obtained great skill in fine details—particularly noteworthy in his portraits of women, where he had an opportunity to depict fabrics and delicate laces. An excellent example is the portrait of Mrs. Charles Worthington Ross (Cornelia Ringgold Potts) of Baltimore.[30]

While in Washington, Guillaume was tempted again to enter the field of historic painting. His *Battle of San Jacinto* (Plate 78) shows the routing of the Mexican army in April, 1836, by the victorious leader Sam Houston. This picture was evidently painted late in life when he was still under the patronage of W. W. Corcoran, for at the time of the artist's death in 1892 the battle scene was still on his easel. The participants are painted necessarily small and the leader is not easily recognizable. Guillaume did not exaggerate or overdramatize the action.[31]

[29] Collection of The University of Texas, Austin.

[30] "Exhibition of 18th and 19th Century American Paintings from Lynchburg Homes."

[31] *Washington Post*, April 17, 1892; letters, R. W. Norton, Norton Museum of Art, Shreveport, Louisiana, to Author.

CHAPTER 7

ARTIST-REPORTERS ON

EXCURSIONS INTO TEXAS

THE GRAPHIC ARTS were important mediums of communication in frontier Texas. The sketching for prints and sometimes the engraving of plates were skills the emigrant had acquired before coming to Texas and employed as an expedient to increase his income. The German emigrant often used the print to show his European friends and family what Texas was actually like. Illustrations were important to the many government survey reports made in Texas. An example of these early prints is shown in Plate 79.

Engravings on wood, copper, and steel were employed for illustrations, but the invention of lithography (c. 1819) gave more freedom in the preparation of the plate, in this case, a plate of stone. The artist found this medium more adaptable to his drawing when depicting action; consequently, the lithograph was widely used during the Civil War period. Engraving on metal, however, was a favorite means of reproduction and its traditions and techniques reach far back in history. The artist of the frontier seldom engraved his own work (chiefly because of the inconvenience in carrying materials); con-

sequently, the production of the print involved the work of two artists, one who made the original sketch and an artist-craftsman who put the drawing on the plate. The original was often sent either to one of the eastern cities in the United States or to Europe; thus the original often fell into the hands of someone unfamiliar with the locale. This problem led to many misinterpretations, but even with discrepancies and the transportation hazards of the times, the results were notable. In a few cases both the original drawing and the engraving are extant for comparison.[1]

Emigrant artists, such as German Hermann Lungkwitz and Polish Carl G. von Iwonski (whose prints have been mentioned in connection with their work), added to their income by drawing Texas scenes and sending them to Europe to be engraved, with fine results.

In Europe, engraving had reached a high standard by the nineteenth century, and the fine drawing required

[1] I. N. Stokes and Daniel C. Haskell, *American Historical Prints: Early Views of American Cities from the Phelps Stokes and other Collections*, pp. ix–xi.

79. Unknown Artist: *San Antonio*

Engraving, 5" x 7⅜" (Courtesy of the Witte Museum, San Antonio, Texas)

by the European schools became a tradition. During the middle years of the nineteenth century engraving in the United States was employed with most success: near perfection was reached by the engravers of bank notes, and the art spread chiefly through the many apprentices.

PRINTS OF TEXAS SCENES

William Sandusky

One non-professional artist who made successful prints was William H. Sandusky (1813–1846), a draftsman and surveyor of Austin. Hailing from Columbus, Ohio, he was the son of John and Elizabeth Clarno Sandusky, of French descent. Young Sandusky's grandfather, a Polish refugee, had settled in Virginia; a brother of his was sent from Virginia to the Lake Erie region to assist in dealing with the Indians, and was killed there. The town of Sandusky, Ohio, bears the family name.

The artist-draftsman Sandusky located advantageously near what served as a land office in Austin in 1838, a short time before the town was selected for the capital. J. H. Jewett, then secretary to President Mirabeau B. Lamar, wrote to Lamar from Houston stating that Sandusky had made several sketches from the public square in Austin and that these were being "copied and colored" by the artist.[2]

Taking up the duties of draftsman, young Sandusky assisted in the surveying for and the making of a map for Austin. He received $100 monthly while serving the state as a surveyor and later as registrar of the General Land Office. In 1840 he was appointed secretary to President Lamar. They became fast friends, and, in a letter to Lamar, Sandusky requests a copy of "The Parting Kiss" to add to the album of Lamar's poetry that

[2] Oliver W. Larkin, *Art and Life in America*, p. 253.

148

80. William Sandusky: *View of Austin*

Water color, 1839 (Pearl Cashell Jackson, *Austin, Yesterday and Today* [Austin: Steck Co. for the American National Bank, 1915] copy in Austin Public Library)

he was collecting. "I am not going to trouble you with one of those long letters you hate so much to read, but [am] just going to ask you the favor of a copy of 'The Parting Kiss' . . . I admire it so much that I wish to keep it among the collections of poetry you gave me which I am copying very neatly in an album for a keepsake."[3]

It is through information concerning Sandusky's work that we learn of the presence in Texas of the celebrated artist and traveler Heinrich Möllhausen, father of H. B. Möllhausen, who wrote President Lamar on February 8, 1840, regarding a commission to make three maps of Austin. Möllhausen had been in Texas about six months when he wrote to Secretary of State J. H. Starr: "I have asked $500 apiece—a price often paid in Texas for very inferior maps at times when money was doubled the value than now." Sandusky had asked $400 for the preparation of his maps of Austin.[4] Möllhausen also pointed out that Sandusky should not have received payment for his maps when he was already on the state payroll.

In 1841 Sandusky resigned his position in the Presi-

dent's office, giving the reason of ill health, and asking that he be given an appointment in the survey of the coast and harbors of Texas. After receiving the appointment he and his mother left Austin for Galveston. On their arrival they were guests of the Gail Bordens.[5] In 1842 Sandusky married Jane McKnight of Indiana County, Pennsylvania.[6] In 1844 he announced through the Galveston press that having established himself permanently he would "execute all kinds of maps, charts, landscapes, plans of cities and towns, also instruments of writing of every description in the neatest style and

[3] *City Gazette*, Austin, December 4, 1839; November 4, 1840; *Southwestern Historical Quarterly* 16 (1912–1913), 336; *Austin Statesman*, October 23, 1912; *Civilian and Gazette*, Galveston, May 17, 1839; Charles H. Gulick, Jr. (ed.), *The Papers of Mirabeau Buonaparte Lamar*, V, 491; Edwin Waller to Lamar, June 2, 1839, *ibid.*, III, 11; H. J. Jewett to Lamar, August, 1839, *ibid.*, V, 309.

[4] Letter, James H. Starr to Lamar, February 6, 1840, and February 8, 1840, Gulick (ed.), *Lamar Papers*, III, 330; Möllhausen to Lamar, V, 405.

[5] Letter, Sandusky to Lamar, May 8, 1841, and June 5, 1851, *ibid.*, V, 471, 476; Sandusky to Jewett, August, 1839, *ibid.*, III, 91.

[6] *The Civilian and Gazette*, Galveston, July 24, 1842.

81. Erhard Pentenrieder: *Main Plaza, San Antonio, Texas*

Engraving, c. 1856, 11″ x 8½″ (Courtesy of the Amon Carter Museum of Western Art,
Fort Worth, Texas)

on the most liberal terms." In 1845 he became import inspector.[7]

Of limited skill, his sketches of the city of Austin (preserved in reproduction) add important material to the early history and founding of the capital city. One print made in 1839 was "taken" on the "President's Hill" where St. Mary's Academy was afterwards built (Plate 80). The sketch shows the first capitol in Austin proudly flying the Lone Star, Bullock's Tavern, the Walsh blacksmith shop, George Hancock's Store, the Metz' Store and log cabin, Dutch John's Bakery—all facing Congress Avenue. The stockades appear in the engraving on the left. His original views of Austin appear to have been printed by Austin's early newspapers, as Secretary Jewett reported that the printing of Sandusky's sketches had been delayed because of trouble in the newspaper office. Reproductions of the Austin print, made years afterwards, have been preserved. Two important original Sandusky drawings, *Oak Point* and *Sketch of the Alamo*, are owned by the artist's descendants.[8]

Erhard Pentenrieder

Another print maker was Erhard Pentenrieder (1830–1875), who migrated from Aibling, Bavaria (c. 1852). He settled in San Antonio near the Guenther mill as a merchant and married a Miss Meyer.[9] He made a drawing for what was called in those days a "letter print" (Plate 81). This was engraved and printed in a shop owned by Pentenrieder and Blersch of San Antonio. Across the top of this fashionable stationery is a scene of San Antonio's Main Plaza. In the foreground is shown a group of the immigrant covered wagons drawn by oxen, busy citizens are on the Plaza, and in the background is the old San Fernando church. Tapering vignettes on the sides of the sheet (leaving space in the center for writing) are small pictures of buildings, including the missions Alamo, San José, San Juan, and Concepción, Indians, Mexicans, and animals of various kinds, while in the lower part is a cowboy in action— one of the earliest representations of this now familiar subject. A delicate outline decoration (sometimes colored) encircles the various drawings.

In 1856 the following advertisement of the Pentenrieder print appeared in the *Galveston News*:

First series of Texas views. Lithograph views of San Antonio beautifully executed by E. Pentenrieder, Esq., of San Antonio. Views of the Main Plaza, the Alamo Mission, San Juan, Concepción, and the costumes of Mexicans and Indians, Price ten cents each.
Price per dozen $1.00. N. M. Jones, No. 8 Strand.[10]

This unusual print bears the inscription "Drawn after Nature by Erhard Pentenrieder. Published by Pentenrieder & Blersch, San Antonio, Tex."

The ailing merchant, Pentenrieder, became an officer in the National Bank of San Antonio and served as a city alderman from 1867 to 1872. As did many Germans, he left Texas at the beginning of the Civil War. When he returned he opened his business on Commerce Street opposite the Masonic Hall, and dealt in wholesale and retail selling of fancy goods, stationery, and musical instruments.[11]

Daniel P. Whiting

Another early Texas print, in sharp contrast to the German reproduction, is a delicate rendering by Daniel Powers Whiting (1808–1892), a West Point graduate from Troy, New York. As an infantry captain he came to Texas with General Zachary Taylor in 1845. Whiting had had auxiliary training in topographical drawing, in which he showed considerable talent. Before coming to Texas he had served in the second Seminole War.[12] During the difficult winter of 1845 Whiting made a drawing, *Birds-eye View of the Camp of the Army of Occupation* (Plate 82), lithographed by Charles Parsons (1821–1910)[13] and circulated by G. & W. Endicott, in 1847. Parsons came to America from Roylands Castle, England, and entered a lithographic shop at the age of nine. He reached a high standard as a craftsman—as his prints of Whiting's drawing attest. The original lithographs show the minute work of both artists exemplified in the carefully drawn shadows of the horses—conveying a sense of perspective—as they cross the sandy beach. Whiting moved on to Mexico with his regiment and was breveted major for gallantry at the Battle of Cerro Gordo in 1847. In 1848 he published *The Army Portfolio*, a series of five lithographs illustrating his

[7] *Ibid.*, June 1, 1844.

[8] *City Gazette*, Austin, December 4, 1839; *Austin Statesman*, October 23, 1912.

[9] *The Daily Herald*, San Antonio, March 14, 1866.

[10] *Galveston News*, December 13, 1856.

[11] *San Antonio Express*, November 10, 11, 1875.

[12] George C. Groce and David H. Wallace, *New-York Historical Society's Dictionary of Artists in America, 1564–1860*, see Whiting, p. 682.

[13] *Ibid.*, see Charles Parsons, p. 489.

Birds-eye view of the
CAMP OF THE ARMY OF OCCUPATION,
COMMANDED BY GEN.ˡ TAYLOR.
Near Corpus Christi, Texas, (from the North) Oct. 1845.

82. Daniel P. Whiting: *Birds-eye View of the Camp of the Army of Occupation*
Engraving, 1845, 18¹⁵⁄₁₆″ x 24³⁄₁₆″ (Courtesy of the Amon Carter Museum of Western
Art, Fort Worth, Texas)

Mexican war experiences; four of these are in color (12″ x 19″) by the House of Endicott. The series includes a view of Corpus Christi, first of the series, three of activities near Monterrey, and one in the valley near Saltillo.[14]

Helmuth Holtz

Another artist-traveler made drawings of Matagorda and Indianola in the coastal area. This was Helmuth Holtz, a German sailor, who made note that these scenes were drawn from the royal yard on board the bark *Tex-*

ana (September, 1860). Perhaps it was from the same ship that he made the drawing *18 Miles from the Mississippi* at Atchafalaya River, Louisiana, "published by Helmuth Holtz, sole proprietor."[15]

The Matagorda print is designed in a rectangle (5″ x

[14] Daniel Powers Whiting, "1847 Corpus Christi," *Army Portfolio*; Library of Congress, *An Album of American Battle Art*, p. 128, Plate 51; *New Orleans Daily Delta*, August 28, 1847, D. P. Whiting prepared "exquisite sketches of Mexican Scenery."

[15] *18 Miles from the Mississippi*, National Archives Collection, No. 54, 1735.

83. Eigenthum d. Verleger: *View of Galveston*
Engraving (Courtesy of the Texas State Archives, Austin)

7″), showing in the center the hotel of the city, an eagle and United States Flag. Surrounding it are small engravings of the church, Masonic hall, courthouse, and other buildings. The drawings were sent to Germany where they were engraved by Lang.[16]

*Eigenthum d. Verleger, Gezeicht von C. O. Bahr
William C. A. Theillepape, and Louis Hoppe*

Other print makers, like Helmuth Holtz, stopped long enough in Texas to make a drawing or two. Eigenthum d. Verleger made a print of Galveston (Plate 83), one of New Braunfels, and one of San Antonio.[17] Gezeicht von C. O. Bahr made a sketch of Galveston (c. 1856) which was lithographed by Gedr von I. Williard of Dresden. "Taken from the bay side," the print represents Galveston only in a general way as far as accuracy of the scene is concerned, but the workmanship is of a high quality.[18]

William C. A. Theillepape came to Texas from Germany with his wife and daughters in the middle of the century. A versatile man, he was active in San Antonio affairs, a good musician, and a leader of the Beethoven Männerchor. He was appointed major of San Antonio

by General Joseph Reynolds in 1867. His small delicate drawing is evidence of his ability in this field. His letterhead, prepared and engraved in 1856, shows a scene on the Plaza—people, horses, a stage coach.[19]

In contrast to the work of Theillepape is another print, made by Louis Hoppe, who was probably a native of Fayette County, Texas. He pictures the Julius Meyenberg farm on Williams Creek near La Grange (Plate 84). This primitive print, produced wholly by the artist, both in the preparation and in the engraving, shows an unadorned view of the farm, with the Meyenberg family seated in the yard, surrounded by horses, dogs, and turkeys.[20]

[16] Congressional Library Exhibition (1845–1945), *Texas*, p. 22, No. 91.

[17] Stokes and Haskell, *American Historical Prints*, Plate L, 91, B.

[18] Collection of Engravings, Texas State Archives, Austin.

[19] Collection of Yale University Library, History Division, New Haven, Connecticut.

[20] Collection of the Witte Museum, San Antonio, Texas; Dutch descent, Hoppe, Frederick Barnhardt; E. Bénézit, *Dictionnaire— Critique et Documentaire des Peintres, Dessinateurs, Graveurs, et Sculpteurs*, see Hoppe.

Louis Hoppe fecit.

JULIUS MEYENBERG'S, FARM, Bluff William
Creek Settelment by *La Grange*, Fayette County, State of TEXAS

84. Louis Hoppe: *Julius Meyenberg's Farm*
Engraving, 7½" x 11¾" (Courtesy of the Witte Museum, San Antonio, Texas)

Agustus Koch, H. Brossius, and T. M. Fowler

A number of artists made what were termed bird's-eye views of cities. These are probably more akin to topography and map making than to landscape prints. Only a few of these will be mentioned; however, they do add in a small way to the work of the artist. They became especially popular just after the Civil War, when these men, as did the early portraitist, traveled from town to town making the sketches. When they reached a town a preliminary bird's-eye sketch was made and if there were sufficient numbers of subscribers the artist then lithographed his sketch of that particular place. By this method he might be assured, in advance, of a large enough sale to be financially safe.

On January of 1873, Agustus Koch, about whom only a few facts are known, came to Austin and, work-ing in the typical way, made a sketch of the city. The *Daily Democratic Statesman* stated that the sketch of Austin was made "with accuracy and beauty and that the artist's supposed elevation from which the view was taken was two thousand feet in height from which the beholder loses the view of the topographical inequalities and enables him to see and recognize every individual house in the city."[21] Mr. Koch was assisted at Austin by a Mr. Stoner, who took orders for him and who himself had made "admirable views of this type of print of Galveston and Houston."

Agustus Koch had lived at one time in La Grange, and this may have been his original home. Sometimes his views are horizontal—panoramic in nature—and at other times are designed in a rectangle, depending upon

[21] *Daily Democratic Statesman,* January 9, 1873.

154

the layout of the town. Traveling from place to place he was able to make views of Austin, Belton, Bastrop, La Grange, San Antonio, and Fredericksburg; his out-of-the-state prints include views of Atlanta, Georgia, and Leadville, Colorado.[22]

In the 1870's H. Brossius made small engravings of New Braunfels, as well as lithographic bird's-eye views of Waco, Jefferson, and Victoria, Texas.[23] A little later, T. M. Fowler, from Morrisville, Pennsylvania, apparently having success traveling in and out of towns, made lithographic bird's-eye views of Houston, Wolf City, Denison, Wichita Falls, Quanah, and Sunset (Montague County), and made a similar view of Oklahoma City, Indian Territory (1890).[24]

THE BARTLETT SURVEY

Another group of prints and drawings were made between the years 1845 and 1857 by artist-surveyors, artist-naturalists, and artist-scientists for various boundary, railroad, and wagon-road surveys. Published in reports of the United States or through private efforts, they were executed by men of keen observation, scientific mind, and talent. These illustrations are products of an era when American engravers were nearly perfect in the art. As documents of American expansion these surveys are important to Texas and the Southwest politically, intellectually, and esthetically. It is suggested that this field of graphic art deserves more study than is appropriate here.

John Russell Bartlett

It was necessary that the western boundary of Texas be laid out according to the treaty conference of Guadalupe Hidalgo of August, 1848. To make this boundary survey, President Zachary Taylor appointed John Russell Bartlett (1805–1886) of Rhode Island, a well-known antiquarian, ethnologist, and author. The report of the survey was published in 1854 in two volumes under the title *Personal Narrative of Explorations and Incidents in Texas, New Mexico, California, Sonora, and Chihuahua, Connected with the United States and Mexican Boundary Commission during the Years 1850, '51, '52, and '53.*[25] Bartlett was assisted by engineers, geologists, botanists, zoologists, physicians, topographers, and artists. The artists might be called upon by a member of the professional group to serve in any capacity, even as cook.

But it seems an evident fact that these reporter-artists had an impulse to picture the kind of place Texas was.

Their amazement of great distances, of deep canyons, and of the mesa of Llano Estacado is vividly depicted. Heinrich B. Möllhausen (1825-1905) in his *Journey to the Pacific* describes enthusiastically the Staked Plains or the Llano Estacado of western Texas:

. . . but we worked our way cheerfully from hill to hill and the eye continually rested on new objects in the landscape in which it could take pleasure. Antelopes were springing about on the dry hills, deer lurking behind the blue-green cedars, eagles and kites wheeling their flight through the air and lively little prairie-dogs peeping out and giving tongue from the opening of their dark abodes.[26]

And as they traveled further west on the Llano Estacado, he continues his description:

At sea the first thing you do is to look around the horizon for a sail, and to rejoice if you discover one; you feel less forlorn then, in the sublime solitude; but in the Llano you would seek in vain for such a consolation; no tree or shrub breaks the monotony of the plain; and while the ocean does not seem to sleep, and its heaving like the breathings of a leviathan show it to be still alive, the Llano Estacado is dead, and varied only by the deceitful mirage.[27]

The sketches of these pictorial reporters and their resulting prints are of special interest, for, in addition to furnishing us with pleasing views, they give us an accurate picture of the country just after the days of the Republic, before the period of dissipation of resources. In addition to sketches dealing strictly with scientific matters, the artists, following instructions, made drawings of pioneer life, activities of the Indians, and incidents and views as the troops traveled along the route to the Río Grande.

Henry Cleves Pratt

John Bartlett, leader of the survey, was an amateur artist himself, but he had with him on the commission a professional artist, Henry Cleves Pratt (1803–1880), "portrait, miniature, landscape and panorama painter" of Oxford, New Hampshire. Pratt as a youth was work-

[22] Daughters of the Republic of Texas Library, San Antonio, Texas.

[23] Barker Library, The University of Texas, Austin.

[24] *Ibid.*

[25] Robert Taft, *Artists and Illustrators of the Old West, 1850–1900*, p. 278; Dumas Malone, *Dictionary of American Biography*, II, 7.

[26] Heinrich B. Möllhausen, *Journey to the Pacific*, I, 238.

[27] *Ibid.*, I, 241.

85. Henry Cleves Pratt: *Portrait of John R. Bartlett*
Oil, 1852, 35″ x 28″ (Courtesy of Brig. Gen. W. C. Glasgow, El Paso, Texas)

6. Henry Cleves Pratt: *View of Smith's West Texas Ranch*
Oil, 1852, 32" x 50" (Courtesy of the Memorial Museum, The University of Texas at Austin)

ing on his father's farm when (c. 1817) Samuel F. B. Morse (1791–1872), on a visit to New Hampshire, discovered the boy's talent and took him to Charleston, South Carolina, and, in 1821, to Washington, D. C., teaching him the rudiments of painting. Pratt remained with him a number of years as an assistant in his studio. In 1845 he accompanied Thomas Cole (1801–1848) on a painting expedition to Maine, and in 1851 he joined the Bartlett group.[28] Pratt's excellent portrait of John R. Bartlett, made when he was stationed at El Paso (Plate 85), and one of James Wiley Magoffin reflect the best in his training by Morse and Cole. James Magoffin, who, it was said, "paved the way for General Kearny's bloodless conquest of New Mexico in 1845," was at Magoffinville in 1852 when Pratt was employed to paint his portrait.[29]

An example of Pratt's skill as a landscape painter is a panoramic view of Smith's West Texas ranch near El Paso (Plate 86), mistakenly called a view of Fort Bliss. Pratt pictures an artist on a high cliff, under an umbrella,

easel in hand, painting the broad distant view below, with the wagons and horses of the ranch corraled behind walls.[30] This oil landscape is owned by the Memorial Museum of The University of Texas. Another scene painted by Pratt at El Paso is shown in Plate 87.

When the survey was completed, Bartlett used some 130 of his own illustrations, but included only 30 of Pratt's. He explained that Pratt had made hundreds of sketches but that his work was chiefly of panoramic views too large to be used. To ease his conscience, Bartlett wrote in his report this about Pratt:

I should do injustice to our accomplished artist and draftsman Mr. Henry C. Pratt who accompanied me in my

[28] *New-York Historical Society Catalogue* (1941), p. 235; Groce and Wallace, *Dictionary*, p. 515.
[29] Interview, Brigadier General W. C. Glascow, El Paso, Texas, owner of the portrait of John R. Bartlett by Pratt.
[30] Rex W. Strickland, "Six Who Came to El Paso," *Southwestern Studies* (Fall, 1963), 12; Donald V. Brady, "The Theatre in Early El Paso," *Southwestern Studies*, IV, No. 1 (1966), 1.

Church at El Paso del Norte

87. Henry Cleves Pratt: *Church at El Paso del Norte*
Lithograph and water color, c. 1852, 17⅝" x 22¼" (Courtesy of the Amon Carter Museum
of Western Art, Fort Worth, Texas)

journeys to and from California, did I not speak of his valuable services. Besides the portraits of Indian tribes and illustrations of their manners and customs, Mr. Pratt has made a series of many hundred sketches representing the peculiar character of the country, extending from ocean to ocean, along the boundary line and in the states contiguous. Many of these sketches are panoramic views embracing wide districts of country and convey to the mind a better idea of it than the most elaborate description. I have therefore very reluctantly been compelled to omit the most important of them from the present work, as it would detract too much from their merits to reduce them to the size of an octavo page.[31]

Agustus Hoppin

Another artist who was important to the Bartlett report is Agustus Hoppin (1828–1896). His work throughout his career was chiefly in the field of illustration. Happenings on Bartlett's route between Fredericksburg and Horsehead Crossing on the Pecos in West Texas are the very essence of what might have

[31] John Russel Bartlett, *Personal Narrative of Explorations and Incidents in Texas, New Mexico, California, Sonora, and Chihuahua, Connected with the United States and Mexican Boundary Commission during the years 1850, '51, '52, and '53*, p. x; *National Intelligencer*, Washington, D.C., March 20, 1852.

158

appealed to the recorder of the local scene. Hoppin was a Rhode Islander, born in Providence, the son of Thomas Cole Hoppin and Harriet Jones Hoppin—the youngest of fourteen children. He attended Brown University and Harvard Law School, but at the beginning of law practice he turned to illustrating books and magazines, among which are Oliver Wendell Holmes' *Autocrat of the Breakfast Table*, Washington Irving's *Sketch Book*, Mark Twain's *Gilded Age*, and some of the illustrations for *Punchinello*. Such men as Hoppin finally developed a school of American illustration. Late in life (1872) he contributed some drawings to an experiment in Boston in which the artist's work was engraved by the Chemical Engraving Company in three hours. This rapid processing was said to be the step which initiated illustrated daily journalism in America.[32]

Hoppin joined Bartlett's survey group early in his career (1850). His work is always simple, light, and effective—with little or no shading. He sketched in a humorous vein, choosing subjects that appealed to his mood. In this report Bartlett describes a stampede of mustangs—"Kings of the Prairie"—whose disturbing presence was always dreaded by those who knew the wild horse. Hoppin saw the humor of their capers and in his characteristic way made a drawing on steel. This he signed "Hoppin, del." Hear what Bartlett had to say about the stampede:

Loma Blanca (White Hill)—As we approached, some low hills appeared whose sides showed banks of white sand. Herds of mustangs going full speed crossed and recrossed the broad prairie, presenting a beautiful spectacle as they [ran] for a mile or more with their long bushy tails streaming in the wind . . . Major Emory at this time was in advance of me about a half mile with his portion of the wagons. We saw the long line of mustangs approach him, and soon after pass before the whole herd following after and extending as far as the eye could reach across the prairie. The mules became restive and we could see the teamsters hurrying forward the wagons for protection behind each other. On went the great stream and the next moment one of the mule teams in advance sprang from the train and dashed off at full speed after and among the wild horses. The teamster in vain tried to restrain them. It was all to no purpose. Away they went, John Gilpin like, the wagon with six mules followed by all the loose animals that were driven with the train which had also partaken of the stampede. The herdsmen, in order to check the runaways, left the train and went in pursuit making altogether the most exciting spectacle we had yet witnessed. The chase continued for a mile; for the mules in the wagon

had become perfectly frantic with fear, surrounded as they were by equally frightened mustangs, and all bounded over the prairie at their utmost speed. Seeing the danger our men put on the lash and we hurried forward to render such aid as lay in our power. The men of our party fired at the herd which had the effect of breaking the line and turning it in another direction. The frightened herd made directly for us in the same long line, the termination of which we could not see, as it lost itself far in the distance. I now became alarmed fearing a general stampede among our mules; for nothing can restrain these timid creatures when frightened. If they cannot take their wagon with them, they become so frantic that they will tear themselves from their harness and flee away. Our first precaution was to close up the wagons, so that only those in the first one would see the mustangs. The mules of the second were placed alongside of the foremost wagon, the next by the side of the second and so on to the last, each wagon thus protecting the team that followed it. We now locked the wheels of all and men stood by the leaders to restrain and quiet them. As I had no inclination to be carried off against my will among a herd of frantic wild horses after the fashion of Mazeppa, I dismounted and hitched my mule to a wagon and with several others ran with my firearms to meet the advancing steeds which were nearly upon us, led off by a fearless stallion. We discharged our arms at them as they approached and fortunately with good effect. The leader was turned and the avalanche of wild animals swept by us like a tornado much to our relief.[33]

Another illustration of Hoppin's is included in the report—*Prairie-Dog Town* (Plate 88)—(which Goetzmann attributes to Pratt and Bartlett). At one point in his career he became interested in drawing animals, so no doubt it was another delight for him to reach "prairie-dog town." Bartlett describes the scene that Hoppin so happily made:

. . . On the plateau we entered a colony of the misnamed "prairie dogs" which extended in every direction as far as the eye could reach. The ground occupied by this fraternity was distinctly marked by the shortness of grass, which these little creatures feed upon, as well as by their hillocks some of which contain two or three cart-loads of earth, brought up by them from their excavated dwellings. We tried in

[32] Frank Weitenkampf, *American Grafic Art*, pp. 113–115, 147; Sinclair Hamilton, *Early American Book Illustrators and Wood Engravers, 1670–1870*, p. 152; Malone, *Dictionary of American Biography*, IX, 225 (Hibben and Jarvis); *Antiques Magazine* (July, 1944), 16.

[33] Bartlett, *Personal Narrative of Explorations and Incidents in Texas*, Agustus Hoppin, *Stampede of Train of Wild Horses*, II, 522–523.

88. Agustus Hoppin: *Prairie-Dog Town*
Engraving, c. 1850, 3½" x 5½" (Courtesy of the Texana Library, The University of Texas at Austin)

vain to get one of them as a specimen dead or alive. At least twenty shots were fired at them with pistols and rifles by several individuals of the party who considered themselves good marksmen, but they either dodged at the flash or if shot fell into their holes at the mouth of which they invariably sat. Not one was obtained. On examination drops of blood were seen near holes which showed that some of the shots had taken effect. In one instance I saw a rattlesnake enter one of the habitations but whether he belonged there or was an interloper it was impossible to tell. Small brown owls flitted about and lit on the hillocks in the midst of the prairie dogs with which they seemed to be upon good terms. For more than three hours our march continued through the vast domains of this community or "dog town" as they are usually called nor did they terminate when we stopped for the night.[34]

Hoppin's work which illustrates this description includes the details of the men shooting the little inhabitants of the prairie in various positions, their associates the snakes, and the long line of wagons winding its way on the tableland. The engraving follows Hoppin's customary simple line drawing—signed "[d]rawn, A. Hoppin." It is so similar to Hoppin's other humorous illustrations that we are inclined to think both these illustrations were more his work than Bartlett's or Pratt's.

Bartlett had been enmeshed in a bitter political con-

flict in Washington between the Whigs and Democrats upon the feasibility of the survey project—a discussion involving both United States senators from Texas, Thomas J. Rusk and Sam Houston. Conflict within the survey party itself arose between the army corps and the civilian group. There were many difficulties—hangings, murders, and Indian raids—over the period of three years.

THE EMORY SURVEY

The purchase of the Gadsden Tract resulted in the appointment of a new commission to redraw the boundary line. Consequently, another survey of the United States-Mexican border began in 1849 and was completed and published in 1857 as *Report on the United States and Mexican Boundary Survey Made under the Direction of the Secretary of the Interior, 1849–1857*, by William H. Emory, Major First Cavalry, and United States Commission. Probably the most comprehensive of any of the government reports, it contains prints as handsome as those in any similar publication. Emory, an experienced topographical engineer, has been described as a man of "picturesque language, flamboyant red whisk-

[34] *Ibid., Prairie-Dog Town*, I, 70.

89. Arthur Schott: *Military Plaza—San Antonio, Texas*
Engraving, c. 1849–1857, 6⅛″ x 8⁵⁄₁₆″ (Courtesy of the New-York Historical Society, New York City)

ers, and haughty grace, a perfect image of the romantic frontier-soldier." He was a man of commanding presence and scientific mind.[35]

Many individuals were assigned to do the writing, and in many instances we cannot exactly place the location where drawings were made; also, many of the place names have changed, and it is difficult to determine the east and west sides of the boundary. This survey, however, provides us with many factual prints of the west

border of Texas and of its people. Many of these were printed in larger size for public distribution.

The first volume of the report contains facts of general interest and has seventy-six steel engravings, twelve lithographs, and twenty wood cuts; some of each group have to do with the Texas scene. The second and third volumes contain the botany and zoology reports of the region and include a number of excellent colored plates of birds. The text of this part was prepared by Spencer F. Baird, the foremost zoologist of Pennsylvania.[36]

To consider the work of each artist represented in the survey is beyond the scope of the present study. The principal artists appearing in Volume One depicting Texas are Arthur Schott, A. de Vaudricourt, and John E. Weyss (or Weiss).

[35] Samuel Geiser, *Naturalists of the Frontier*, p. 281; Taft, *Artists and Illustrators*, pp. 276–277; Groce and Wallace, *Dictionary*, p. 585.
[36] William H. Emory, *Report on the United States and Mexican Boundary Survey Made under the Direction of the Secretary of the Interior, 1849–1857*, pp. 124, 832.

90. A. de Vaudricourt: *Río San Pedro—above Second Crossing*
Engraving, c. 1849–1857, 5⅜" x 8¼" (Courtesy of the Texana Library, The University
of Texas at Austin)

Arthur Schott

Arthur Schott (1813–1875), the first assistant surveyor under Major Emory, prepared 226 drawings, 25 of these in color. His section of the report is a delight to both naturalist and general reader. Birds depicted on the Río Grande at Ringgold Barracks are the sparrow hawk, the sharp-shinned hawk, and the chaparral cock (the road runner or *paisano*); at Eagle Pass, the scissor-tail; and elsewhere along the border, the barn owl and Texas screech owl. The thick-billed parrot was recorded at Río Grande, Texas (also recorded by John Woodhouse Audubon), and the prairie owl and the squirrel hawk at Fort Davis, Texas.[37] Schott's Indians, engraved on stone and reproduced in color, include portraits of the "Yumas," "Co-Co-Pas," "Riguenos," "Lipans," and "Papagos," all of the Río Grande region. These prints are remarkably successful, considering the experimentation in the use of color printing in progress at the time.[38]

Few incidents are known of Schott's life. That he was a man of talent—a naturalist, an engineer, a physician, and a well-known musician and linguist is certain. He made a scientific approach to problems in regional geography that even today are not wholly solved. Afterwards, Schott lived in Washington, D. C., where he contributed to the Smithsonian Reports (1856–1866) on geological subjects in the Río Grande country.

In addition to bird and Indian plates Schott made two excellent drawings of particular documentary value: the frontispiece in Volume 1, *Military Plaza—San Antonio, Texas* (Plate 89), and *The Military Colony opposite Fort Duncan*. Both were engraved on steel by James D. Smilie (1833–1909), of the noted Scotch family of engravers, who reached the United States by way of Canada.[39]

The artist's father, James Smilie, taught him to engrave bank notes on metal. The youthful Smilie engraved a series of illustrations for Cooper's novels. He was also an excellent etcher, and was the founder of the American Water Color Society. Upon returning in 1864 from a visit to Europe, he turned to painting and was elected to the American Academy in 1876.[40]

A. de Vaudricourt

Another artist of Emory's report was a Louisiana Frenchman, A. de Vaudricourt—topographical draftsman, musician, and drawing teacher—who made sketches and who, like Schott, profited through the engraving skill of Smilie. Little is known about Vaudricourt, who was head of the topographical party when working on the route from Indianola to El Paso. Vaudricourt had worked in New York previous to his joining the survey party. In February, 1844, he made a lithograph for Bouve and Sharp depicting the Mail Steamship *Bretannia* leaving her dock on a voyage to Liverpool. This print was dedicated to those who had undertaken and accomplished the task of cutting a canal through the ice one hundred feet wide and seven miles long.[41] He impressed the citizens of Indianola with his graces, for the press stated that "Mr. A. de Vaudricourt . . . an accomplished and gentlemanly draftsman and interpreter . . . has made a number of sketches of the most striking parts of our country."[42]

When the first volume of the report was published, it contained two illustrations by Vaudricourt, *Río San Pedro—above Second Crossing*, engraved by J. D. Smilie, son of James Smilie (Plate 90), and a colored lithograph, *The Plaza and Church of El Paso* (Plate 91); both were prepared by Sarony, Major, and Knapp of New York.[43] These are two examples of Vaudricourt's detail drawing: the *Río San Pedro* (a view similar to Pratt's oil painting *Smith's West Texas Ranch*) shows persons on a hill viewing the broad prairie below, with the survey tents and wagons arranged in a square. *The Plaza and Church of El Paso*, printed in several colors, shows the church in the background as worshippers enter the doorway. Swerving flocks of birds add interest, and citizens in the foreground complete the well-conceived scene.

John E. Weyss

John E. Weyss (c. 1820–1903) was another topographical artist who contributed many illustrations to the three-part report of Emory, in which capacity he served from 1849 to 1855. Little biographical information has been uncovered except that after working on the sur-

---

[37] *Ibid.*, "Birds," pp. 1–31, Plates I–XXV.

[38] *Ibid.*, "Indians," pp. 52, 78, 89.

[39] Groce and Wallace, *Dictionary*, see Arthur Schott, p. 585.

[40] William Dunlap, *History of the Rise and Progress of the Arts of Design in the United States*, pp. 269, 335; *Antiques Magazine* (June, 1948), 457.

[41] Stokes and Haskell, *American Historical Prints*, 5343b, 53G, 43h.

[42] *San Antonio Ledger*, October 10, 1850; *National Intelligencer*, Washington, D. C., November 2, 1850; September 24, 1851; July 22, 1851; Harry Peters, *America on Stone*, p. 392.

[43] Emory, *Report on the United States and Mexican Boundary Survey*, I, 42, 92.

91. A. de Vaudricourt: *The Plaza and Church of El Paso*
Lithograph, c. 1849–1857, 5⅜″ x 8¼″ (Courtesy of the Texana Library, The University of Texas at Austin)

vey Weyss served as major during the Civil War with a staff of engineers in the Army of the Potomac. After the war he served again with some of the Western surveys of the War Department. Several drawings in the Wheeler Report *United States Geographic Survey* are the work of John Weyss. *Brownsville, Texas*, drawn by John Weyss for the Emory report was engraved by James Smilie (Plate 92).[44] In this print Weyss shows the tents of the surveying party in the foreground, while across the Río Grande on the opposite bank is the city of Brownsville.[45]

Paulus Roetter

Paulus Roetter (1806–1844), a landscape and botanical painter from Nuremburg, Germany, and Thun, Switzerland, contributed illustrations to the "Cactaceæ of the

Boundary" prepared for the Emory report by George Englemann, of St. Louis. As a young man, Roetter had studied in Germany and Switzerland and had survived difficult times by teaching and painting miniature landscapes for tourists. His first plan on coming to America was to form a communistic colony, but when he located in St. Louis he began teaching drawing at Washington University and abandoned the idea of the colony. It was here he was associated with Englemann.[46] He was com-

[44] Emory, *Report on the United States and Mexican Boundary Survey*, "Brownsville, Texas," I, 60.
[45] *Evening Star*, Washington, D. C., June 24, 1903; Taft, *Artists and Illustrators*, p. 277.
[46] Groce and Wallace, *Dictionary*, see Roetter, p. 543; *Exhibition of Life and Landscape of the Father of Waters.*

92. John E. Weyss: *Brownsville, Texas*
    Engraving, c. 1849–1855, 5¾" x 8¼" (Courtesy of Still Pictures, United States Archives,
Washington, D. C.)

missioned to make drawings for sixty-one plates, and these exquisite illustrations are engraved with great precision by a number of artists. Taft in *Artists of the Old West* states that many of the original drawings have been preserved in the Missouri Botanical Gardens of St. Louis.[47] Roetter's sensitiveness to the subject and his fine work are shown in drawings of the palm-like Yucca, a cactus with a crimson-flowered spine, and an armed cereus, among a number of beautifully rendered types of cacti (Plate 93).[48]

John H. Richards and William H. Dougal

In the third volume of Emory's report (1857 ed.), in addition to the section on birds by Arthur Schott, there is a part devoted to mammals, reptiles, and fishes found on the western border of Texas. This section, outside our chief interest and purely scientific, was done almost completely by John H. Richards (1806–?) and William H. Dougal (1822–1875), with fine results in the engravings.

John H. Richards experimented with lithography, producing what was considered the first successful print of this type to reach national publication.[49] Richards was located in Philadelphia in 1843 and 1844, was employed

[47] Taft, *Artists and Illustrators*, p. 277.
[48] Emory, *Report on the United States and Mexican Boundary Survey*, "Cactaceae," p. 22.
[49] *Leslie's Magazine*, April, 1843.

93. Paulus Roetter: *Cactus*

    Engraving, c. 1849–1857, 9½ ″ x 6″ (Courtesy of the Barker Library, The University of Texas at Austin) at the Smithsonian Institution from 1855 to 1860, and in 1857 exhibited at the Washington Art Association. Plates accredited to Richards, some 130, in the Emory report are of mammals, birds, reptiles, and fish. William Dougal, the engraver, was responsible for the completion of Richards' work on steel and copper, with great credit to both artists. Dougal, of New Haven, Connecticut had worked at age fifteen as an apprentice with the New York engraving firm of Sherman and Smith. He engraved the plates for the Wilkes Expedition and those of Marcy's Expedition to the Red River of Louisiana. In the late 1850's he went to Washington to assist in the engraving of sketches for the Emory report. He remained in Washington, married there, and was engaged by the government on various publications until his death in 1875.[50]

It was the combined efforts of the personnel of the reconnaissance surveys which provided us with the beginning of geographical knowledge of the area, and an ethnological knowledge of the Indian tribes of the area. It is chiefly through their pictorial representations that this knowledge has been gained.

THE GRAY SURVEY

In 1848 the United States added a large area to its confines west of the Mississippi, and in this vast expanse there was not a mile of railroad. In 1853, when the United States Congress convened, the principal business was the development of a plan whereby a railroad could be constructed to connect the East with the West. The question at hand was what was the best route through the Rockies. Several suggested routes followed paths north of Texas. In 1849 the survey of the Pacific Railroad extended from the western border of Texas into the state as far as Preston, a village near present Denton. The first part of the survey was made and published by John Pope, and contained no work by artists, but a contemporary report was published in 1856 through the private efforts of A. B. Gray: *Survey of a Route for the Southern R. R. on the 32nd Parallel, by A. B. Gray for the Texas Western R. R. Company.*

Carl Schuchard

The Gray report contains thirty-two drawings by German emigrant Carl Schuchard (1827–1883), a topographical artist.[51] The instructions given to the group were "to note carefully the country through which they passed, the nature of the area as the climate, geology, plants and animals and the character and developments of its inhabitants."[52]

Carl Schuchard, artist of the survey, was the son of Johan and Wilhelmina Hartart Schuchard and was educated at Kassel and Hersfeld as a mining engineer. He came to California (1849) during the gold rush, but having no luck with gold, he left California and joined Gray's surveying group. This line of survey along the thirty-second parallel provided Schuchard with many opportunities for depicting scenes in both Texas and New Mexico.[53] Among a number of his fine sketches (later made into lithographs by Middleton Wallace and Company, Cincinnati) are *The Guadalupe Mountains, Pecos River*, and *American Antelope*, all drawn with a precise and delicate pencil.

On completion of the survey, Gray wrote of Schuchard's work, "Before closing this Report I beg to be permitted to refer to my assistants and men throughout the entire expedition . . . . Mr. Charles Schuchard was invaluable as an artist and assistant. The numerous accurate and well-executed views of Mr. Schuchard attest the talent and labor by him."[54]

Schuchard's work appears also in the *Journal* of Lieutenant Thomas W. Sweeney, who was at Fort Yuma in 1851 and 1853. In this scene the artist shows a steamboat, supposedly the *General Jessup*, near the shore. Fort Yuma is shown in the background.

[50] Groce and Wallace, *Dictionary*, see William Dougal, p. 185.
[51] Taft, *Artists and Illustrators*, p. 269.
[52] Andrew B. Gray, *Survey of a Route for the Southern R. R. on the 32nd Parallel, by A. B. Gray for the Texas Western R. R. Company.*
[53] Interview, Ernst Schuchard, San Antonio.
[54] Gray, *Survey*, p. 96.

CHAPTER 8

NATIVE ARTISTS AND
LATE-COMERS

Stephen Seymour Thomas

A NATIVE OF SAN AUGUSTINE, Texas, Stephen Seymour Thomas (1868–1956), was destined to break away from his early environment and become a world citizen. The paintings of his youth in his home environment, therefore, are those which properly come within the scope of this study and which have the greatest appeal to us. The unusual success of his youth, unschooled and unapprenticed, can be attributed only to a remarkable talent—a true creative instinct.

Seymour Thomas' parents, James Edward Thomas and Mary Landon Blount Thomas, were among the early settlers of San Augustine, the gateway on the eastern border of Texas for emigrant families from the Southern and Middle states. It was early a center of trade and a town where seeds of educational and cultural opportunities found rich soil; it was the sensitiveness of his parents and San Augustine neighbors that recognized in the boy's early efforts the promise of success.[1] His first attempt to draw was at the age of eight when he made a drawing of a daily companion, his dog. A prize from the local school for this drawing encouraged him,

and with eager boyish enthusiasm he wondered, "Why should I not make a picture of my father's friend Governor Oran Roberts?" The sketch was sent to Austin, and an encouraging reply was received from the Executive Office on December 23, 1880:

I thank you for the drawing of my likeness which your father sent me. It has been inspected by numerous persons of my acquaintance, all of whom pronounce it excellent. I carried Mr. Huddle [William H.] to see it, who is one of your best portrait painters that has been at Austin, and he pronounced it to be well done and being a Texan he was delighted to know that it had been drawn by a youth of Texas.

I trust that you may be able to cultivate your great talent in that all Texans shall be proud of your fame as a painter.

[Signed, Governor Oran Roberts][2]

[1] E. Cullen House Library, San Augustine, information on Father Garishe's encouragement to young Thomas; Mrs. Jean Haskell, daughter; information in files of the Witte Museum, San Antonio.

[2] Letter, Governor Oran Roberts to Stephen Seymour Thomas, San Augustine, Texas, December 23, 1880, Cullen House Library, San Augustine.

At fifteen, Seymour Thomas tried his hand at genre painting with good results. He painted a scene in the farm kitchen, *Weighing the Puppy* (Plate 94), and *The Well* (1885),[3] the latter showing the farm house and surrounding area. These childish paintings he did with equal youthful unconsciousness and freshness of expression.

But his *San José Mission* (San Antonio) was a remarkable accomplishment (Plate 95). He pictures the old Spanish mission with its magnificent time-worn carved stone entrance. Only one tower of the bisymmetrical design remains. The loneliness of the scene is broken by the presence in the compound of a man with a donkey, and beside him another very erect gentleman with an umbrella. The whole scene is presented with unusual perception. Some of Seymour's crayon portraits were being shown at this time, and one of them, *Mrs. Redwood*, received special mention by a New York critic.[4]

Years after *San José Mission* was painted, Thomas returned to America from abroad and received a letter from the owner of the mission picture. In answer to the letter the artist wrote:

Your letter recalls happy days of my youth when I spent hours laboring over the painting of "San José Mission" in the company of my twelve-year-old brother. The silent brooding melancholy ruins with the neglected graves of the Franciscan fathers who had toiled there among the Indians made a profound impression on the mind of a fourteen-year-old boy and I think has colored my whole life. The picture is a faithful portrait of the old building at that time.[5]

The success of the boy's efforts had been recognized by a local padre of San Augustine, who insisted that the boy be given an opportunity to receive training. In order to reach his goal the young artist had taken his *San José Mission* to San Antonio, where he raffled it off for a dollar per chance, and with so many interested customers (among them Colonel George Brackenridge) that he brought away two hundred dollars. This enabled him, then seventeen, to enter the Art Students' League in New York City.[6]

After a year's work in New York, Thomas was planning to study in Europe. He spent some time in Rome and in Paris, for travel was easy in those days and his parents were able to give him the needed funds. For further study he chose the popular Academie Julien in Paris, where many American students were studying.

Its popularity at this time caused its halls to be crowded and the criticisms from Professor Lefebvre (1838–1912) and others proved to be infrequent and hasty, but Seymour Thomas remained six years, working hard and absorbing the atmosphere of French aesthetic life and adjusting as far as possible to the techniques of his French teachers.

When he was twenty-four years old, he exhibited his *Innocent Victim* at the Champs Elysees Salon and afterwards at the World's Fair in Chicago (1893), where it won a prize. In this painting he portrayed a scene in which a Catholic Sister of Charity is being cared for after having been wounded during the Franco-German War. Both genre and landscape painting in France and America brought him medals and praise. *Bridge over the Seine River, Avenue of Trees, Studio in Paris*, and *Night on the Loire River* are among works he painted in France.[7]

In 1892, when in London, Thomas married Helen Haskell of San Francisco, California, and in 1894 he made a trip to America, stopping at Philadelphia. In December of that year he visited San Antonio. With the naïveté of a nineteenth-century moralist (as well as of William Faulkner and others who still hold this credo) he wrote from San Antonio to Mr. Morris of Philadelphia, whom he had just visited:

We have been in this delightful climate three days enjoying the balmy air and sunshine of mid-summer with every door and window in the house open to its widest capacity to let in the breath of flowers and the songs of mockingbirds . . . Of course this country here is like Sleepy Hollow, everything and everybody seems to enjoy the beautiful sunshine —no one has advanced or progressed, in fact, they seemed to have gone backwards to me. The spirit of rest prevails and I suppose would in time tell on the most energetic minds, for I find that many who came here from the north finally have joined the crowd of natives and "let things take care of themselves." What a pity man is only a success under adversity.[8]

[3] Collection of paintings, Dallas Museum of Art.

[4] "A New Yorker's Impression of a Texas Artist," signed "H. L. H." *San Antonio Express*, May 19, 1888.

[5] Letter of the original owner of *San José Mission*, and letter of artist to the original owner, *San Antonio Light*, November 23, 1944.

[6] Cullen House Library, San Augustine, information on Stephen Seymour Thomas.

[7] *Ibid.*, pp. 1–2.

[8] Letter, Seymour Thomas, San Antonio, to Mr. Morris, Philadelphia, Academy of Art, Philadelphia, December 7, 1894, Cullen House Library, San Augustine.

94. Stephen Seymour Thomas: *Weighing the Puppy*
Oil, 1884, 16" x 20" (Courtesy of the Dallas Museum of Fine Arts [Collection of Summerfield G. Roberts])

95. Stephen Seymour Thomas: *San José Mission*
Oil, 1884, 24" x 30" (Courtesy of the Dallas Museum of Fine Arts [Collection of Summerfield G. Roberts])

Thomas continues his letter to Mr. Morris with comments about some of the pictures he has turned over to him for exhibition, suggesting also that he might like to exhibit his *Little Girl with Apple Blossoms* (the girl was Abby Longyear).[9] In 1897, when Thomas was again in America, he undertook a large painting—an equestrian figure of General Houston which was displayed later at the Paris Salon in 1898. Although executed for citizens of the city of Houston, the painting was not accepted by them and remained with the artist until 1921, when he presented it on January 5 to the San Jacinto Museum.[10] The painting shows the General on a prancing charger, and, though skillfully executed, it was thought not to reveal the real spirit of General Sam Houston.

Between the years 1895 and 1905 Thomas received honorable mentions and prizes in Europe and America, including the Declaration of the Cross of Honor. Much of his work now was portraiture, which he painted in the modern French style. A large number of excellent portraits were of fashionable society figures of France and America in the early twentieth century. This work was his absorbing interest until his death in 1956.[11]

Ella Moss Duval

In the spring of 1877 eager visitors climbed to the third floor of New York's Domestic Building, Union Square, corner of Fourteenth and Broadway, to the studio of Ella Amelia Moss, who was to become a portraitist in Texas.[12] As the visitors approached the open door, they could see evidences of her thoroughness in study by the presence of a skeleton of a tall man and beside it a skull. As they entered, the artist was standing against a wall hanging of deep crimson Berlin flannel, brush in hand. She wore over her dress a small apron stiff with daubs of muted Düsseldorf colors, while in her hand was an easel, as Michelangelo once described his own, "with brush drops thick and thin." As the artist stood there with a shaft of north light from Union Square over her brown hair and fair complexion, she made an impressive picture. Once the visitors were inside the room they were told that an interruption was welcome.

In spite of the short time that Ella Moss had been in New York, on the walls were paintings in every state of progress: portraits of New York's fashionable citizens Dr. and Mrs. Grout playing chess, and a large canvas of Mrs. Charles Deems, wife of the pastor of the "Church of Strangers," exhibited at the last National

Academy (1877). On the adjoining wall was the portrait of the young musician Louis Gottschalk, who was then drawing crowds of New Yorkers to hear his rippling piano music, and not the least important was a portrait of the artist's mother, Mrs. Samuel Moss.

An unfinished painting of young Foster, the gifted choir boy of St. Ignatius Church, was leaning against the wall. This was to be shown at the next National Academy exhibition in March (1878). Next to it was the likeness of Mrs. Buckmaster, of Elizabeth, New Jersey. Genre paintings—some completed while in Europe—on the walls showed the diversity of her interests.[13]

Ella Moss was born in Pass Christian, Mississippi, August, 1843, the daughter of Samuel and Isabel Harris Moss, later of Philadelphia. When their daughter was still in her teens, her mother took her to Dresden to escape the perils of the approaching Civil War and to give her the advantage of an uninterrupted education. After her Dresden stay, she was sent to the fashionable Düsseldorf School for art instruction. Only one teacher seems to have held a prominent place in her art training, August Wilhelm Sohn (1829–1899). In her last year at Düsseldorf, Ella was awarded a prize of a year's study in Rome, but because her father's business in Philadelphia had taken a sudden turn of gloominess, she asked that she be given money instead. This request was granted, and soon after, mother and daughter were in New York with the idea of retrieving some of the father's fortune. It was in 1877 that Ella Moss established herself in the Domestic Building, New York City and began a very short but successful career.[14]

One of her commissions was a portrait of the second wife of Commodore Vanderbilt, which was to be a gift of the lady to the Reverend Dr. Deems. Ella Moss completed a bust portrait of the attractive New Yorker in a velvet bodice and lace scarf. To let her friends inspect her work, she invited them to her studio, a more convenient place than her home on Lafayette Square. The affair seemed to leave the impression generally that the

[9] *Ibid.*

[10] *Houston Post*, January 6, 1921; *Houston Chronicle*, April 19, 1951; *Austin American*, June 7, 1957.

[11] *Saturday Night*, Los Angeles, December 29, 1928.

[12] Letters, Mrs. Kate Duval Pitts, daughter, Providence, Rhode Island, to author, 1962–1963.

[13] "A Glimpse of a Lady's Studio," *New York Times*, signed "Clavering," May 22, 1877 (?).

[14] Family letters, 1878, 1883, in collection of Mrs. Kate Duval Pitts, Providence, Rhode Island.

96. Ella Moss Duval: *Dr. Ferdinand Herff*
　　Oil, 1888, 32″ x 26″ (Courtesy of Mrs. Ferdinand Herff, San Antonio, Texas)

Vanderbilt portrait (now unlocated) was a success, but the most unusual event came the next day when Mrs. Vanderbilt sent by a liveried footman the artist's pay in bags of small coin. The artist shrank from the task of counting the money; quick thinking solved her problem. She took the bags of money to the bank on the first floor of the building, where amid the merriment of the employees the unrevealed amount was counted.[15]

Before the year 1878 closed, a visitor to the studio, Burr G. Duval, asked that his portrait be painted as a gift to his mother. But he was told that the subject was not considered "an interesting type" to paint. It was not long after, however, that Ella Moss found him an interesting suitor, and in July of the following summer, 1879, they were married. Young Duval was just starting his law practice, and with scarcely enough money to pay their fare, they started to Texas (by way of Niagara) with some of her pictures. He was to take a position as secretary of the Southwestern Immigration Company at Austin.

Ella Duval now auspiciously started her career anew in Austin with a studio built in her home, "Where," as her husband said, "she could have paint up to her neck." She taught art classes in the capital city, and among her pupils in portraiture was Ida Weisselberg Hadra, whose short period of work will be discussed later in this study.

The Duvals in the early 1880's moved to San Antonio, where the artist taught first in the French Building and later in her home in Maverick Grove.[16] One of the first portraits which received praise from the press was of Mrs. J. T. Woodhull, "an ideal subject and an ideal type," Ella reported. Mrs. Woodhull was described as sitting in a cane chair, with an old East Indian shawl draped over her dress. She held a piece of knitting in her hands, while a spool of thread was about to fall to the floor.[17]

In addition to this romantic presentation of Mrs. Woodhull, there were other portraits: one of Dr. Fer-

dinand Herff, physician (Plate 96), which received special mention in the San Antonio paper of May, 1888; Miss Phillipa G. Stevenson, first head of St. Mary's Hall; and Duval West as a youth and as a judge. The last mentioned is now in the District Court Office in Austin.

While doing her painting Mrs. Duval constantly advocated the establishment of an academy of art in San Antonio. Until her death in 1911 in St. Louis, she made every effort to encourage San Antonio in its various art activities.

Edward Louis Grenet

Edward Louis Grenet (1856–1922), a native of San Antonio, won his art education by demonstrating that he had both the ability and the resolution required for a successful art career. When quite young, without his father's knowledge he persuaded a neighbor, Johann Conrad Beckmann (an artisan painter himself), to sit for a portrait, and it was not until the sitter and his father admitted that it was a good portrait that he confronted the elder Grenet with the idea of art training.[18]

Edward's father, Honoré Grenet, and his mother, Madeleine Grenet, before leaving their native town of Monthois, Ardennes, France, had inherited a small fortune. Their travels brought them, by way of New Orleans, to Texas. In San Antonio, Honoré Grenet recognized expanding business opportunities and decided to remain. Formerly established connections enabled him to import merchandise without difficulty from Rousseau, Olivier, and Co. of Paris. To his shop adjoining the Alamo he imported delicacies and the best French wines. Gradually a potpourri of merchandise, including glass, china, clocks, jewelry, and paintings, crowded his shop.[19] Above his place of business was a museum owned by the French naturalist Gustave Toudouze, whose collection consisted of birds, bird eggs, stuffed animals, flowers, and fossils. In this stimulating atmosphere young Edward, the eldest of the Grenet brood, spent his early years. When not in school, the young boy visited these rooms, running in and out of the aisles and around the tables, discovering innumerable curios and interesting objects.[20]

Business having outgrown his small quarters, Honoré Grenet bought the convent and the courtyard of the Alamo. The Alamo proper at that time was still being used by the United States Quartermaster Corps. In time, even more space for storage was needed and Grenet then added the Alamo proper to his shop, leasing it through

[15] "Artists Reception," *New York Times* (1877?); *San Antonio Express* (clipping, no date).

[16] *San Antonio Express*, May 10, 1888; May 13, 1888.

[17] *The Philadelphia Press*, January 29, 1877; "A San Antonio Picture," a San Antonio Paper (no date).

[18] Frederick C. Chabot, *With the Makers of San Antonio*, p. 263; *San Antonio Express*, November 20, 1875.

[19] *San Antonio Express*, February 21, 1882; February 28, 1882; Yanaguana Society, *Catalogue, Loan Exhibition of Old San Antonio Paintings*, p. 17.

[20] *The Daily Herald*, San Antonio, January 26, 1878.

97. Edward Louis Grenet: *The Mexican Candy Seller*

Oil, 1883, 29½″ x 22″ (Courtesy of Mrs. John Barhydt, Maitland, Florida)

98. Edward Grenet: *Lily Carolon*
 Oil, 1883, 29¾″ x 23¾″ (Courtesy of Mr. T. Griffith Jones, Austin, Texas)

Bishop Pellicer for ninety-nine years. It was not long before his business was valued in six figures and he was referred to locally as "the prince of merchants." But the success of his father's growing business did not attract young Grenet.[21]

Having convinced his father of his serious intentions and ability he set out to study in New York. Impressed with the importance of foreign study he left New York after only a short period for France to study with Tony Robert-Fleury (1837–1911) and Matisse's first instructor, Adolphe William Bouquereau (1825–1905). He reached his highest ambition when his work was recognized at the Grand Salon in Paris.[22]

In 1878 Edward returned to San Antonio, probably with the idea of beginning a career as an artist there. He established a studio in the Dauenhauer Building on North Commerce and a residence on the corner of El Paso and Pecos Streets. In December of 1879 Grenet married Eugénie Guilbeau, daughter of François Guilbeau, of Brittany, and María del Rosario Roman, citizens who were prominent in the Texas-Mexican frontier era.[23] Of Grenet's several genre paintings (which are not representative of his best work) are French Village, painted in Paris, and Mexican Hut and Child Peeping through the Fence, and Mexican Candy Seller (Plate 97), painted in San Antonio.[24]

As a portraitist Grenet found his greatest satisfaction and success, and these portraits are his greatest contribution to art. Among the San Antonians who sat for him were Constance Marucheau, Margarita Coll, William C. A. Theillepape, Margarita Castanola, and five-year-old George Carolon. In the latter part of his career, during a visit to France, he painted the portrait of General Pershing.

Grenet created a portrait of Mrs. Lily Carolon Butter-field, of San Antonio, in 1883 from a photograph, which has all the human expression and reality of a painting from life (Plate 98). The only design in the plain background is the inscription "Lily" in the upper left-hand corner[25]—reflecting the ancient provenience from the Renaissance period in the carefully designed letters. The soft flesh tones in his paintings of children show the influence of French teachers.

By inheritance and temperament Grenet was attracted to France, to which he returned to spend some twenty-odd years of his life among its congenial people. Between 1884 and 1894 he exhibited in many European cities: Munich, Berlin, Vienna, and Paris.

Ida Weisselberg Hadra

A pupil of Ella Moss Duval, Ida Weisselberg Hadra (1861–1885), who painted with individuality during her short life, deserves to be mentioned among the native Texas artists. She was born in Castroville, Texas, her parents, Gustav Frederick Weisselberg and Anna von Groos, having fled Germany during the revolution of 1848. Both were educated in Germany—Dr. Weisselberg at the Medical School at Jena. Anna von Groos' schooling was devoted to literary interests, an appreciation of which was passed on to the daughter growing up in Texas.[26]

At Castroville, Dr. Weisselberg obtained a license to practice and became a well-respected physician in his community. Governor E. J. Davis appointed Dr. Weisselberg (1872) to a position in the State Hospital for the Insane, which brought the Weisselbergs to Austin.[27] Ida then had the opportunity to study art with Mrs. Ella Moss Duval, under whose tutorage she painted a very successful portrait of her father (Plate 99); others were A Neighbor and Portrait of a Child. When Mrs. Duval left Austin, Ida attended classes at the Texas Female Institute, where Hermann Lungkwitz was teaching landscape. The influence of her teacher appears in her scenes around Austin, particularly in the quiet tones of her canvases, for Lungkwitz had not adopted entirely the brighter colors of his later work. Some of her landscapes include View of the Military Academy from East Austin (Plate 100), which Lungkwitz painted several times, Tenth Street, Austin, Looking West (Plate 101), The Old Ira Evans Home, and The Old Duval Home.[28]

In 1882 Ida married a young physician, Dr. Berthold Hadra,[29] and lived in San Antonio, where she continued

[21] Curt Bishop, "Texian Scrapbook, This Day in Texas" (assembled by David A. Keasler), San Antonio Express, September 16, 1962.

[22] Ibid., March 7, 1882; March 22, 1922; April 8, 1922.

[23] Chabot, With the Makers of San Antonio, p. 263.

[24] Information in files of the Daughters of the Republic of Texas Library, San Antonio.

[25] Interview, Mrs. Marian Jones, owner of portrait, Austin.

[26] Walter Prescott Webb (ed.), Handbook of Texas, see Dr. Berthold Hadra, I, 753.

[27] Interview, Mrs. Ida Hadra Vines, daughter, Dallas.

[28] Austin Statesman, November 6, 1885.

[29] Webb (ed.), Handbook of Texas, I, 753.

99. Ida Weisselberg Hadra: *Dr. Weisselberg*
    Oil, c. 1872 (Courtesy of Mrs. P. C. Vines, Dallas, Texas)

100. Ida Weisselberg Hadra: *View of the Military Academy from East Austin*
     Oil (Courtesy of Mrs. P. C. Vines, Dallas, Texas)

her studies with Mrs. Duval until her death in 1885. Some San Antonio views include *Bridge over the San Antonio River* (Plate 102), *San Antonio River Back of the Old Brewery,* and two still-life paintings, *The Hunter's Quest,* and *Products of the Garden.*[30]

Thomas Allen

Another artist who gravitated to Düsseldorf at this time was Thomas Allen (1849–1924), who graduated from the Royal Academy in 1876. He came to Texas for a short time to paint, and was able to leave some interesting scenes of San Antonio life. He was one of the

artists to whom John Baur calls attention in his *Unknown American Painters of the Nineteenth Century.* Probably the reason for Baur's lack of full knowledge of Allen's paintings is that Allen gave much of his time in service to many art organizations in the East and elsewhere. Furthermore, Thomas Allen had a definite interest in business in St. Louis and in Boston, which robbed him of some of his time for painting.[31]

[30] Collection of Mrs. P. C. Vines, Dallas, Texas.
[31] *New York Times,* August 27, 1924; Boston Museum of Fine Arts, Files (Charles H. Hawes); September 20, 1932; Robert Taft, *Artists and Illustrators of the Old West, 1850–1900,* pp. 346–347.

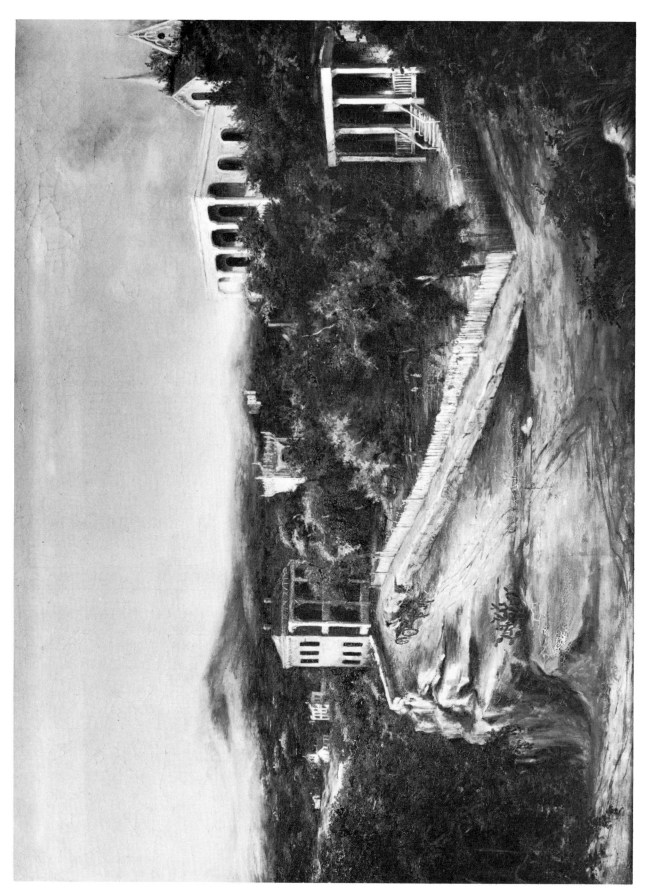

101. Ida Weisselberg Hadra: *Tenth Street, Austin, Looking West*
Oil (Courtesy of Mr. and Mrs. Dan Hopkinson, New York City)

102. Ida Weisselberg Hadra: *Bridge over the San Antonio River*
Oil, c. 1882–1885 (Courtesy of Mrs. P. C. Vines, Dallas, Texas)

103. Thomas Allen: *The Market Place, San Antonio*
Oil, 1878–1879, 25½" x 29¼" (Courtesy of the San Antonio Public Library).

104. Thomas Allen: *Mexican Women Washing at San Pedro Spring*
Oil, 1879, 18¼" x 26½" (Courtesy of the San Antonio Public Library)

105. Thomas Allen: *The Portal of San José Mission*
    Water color on paper, 1878–1879, 29¾″ x 24½″ (Courtesy of the Museum of Fine
    Arts, Boston)

Thomas Allen was born in St. Louis, a son of Thomas Allen and Annie G. Allen. His father was a congressman and a railroad builder, and young Thomas was following in his father's footsteps when he entered business as president of the MacAllen Company, of Boston, and was associated with the Wellesley (Mass.) Knitting Mills. It was this interest in business, as well as his art training, that prepared him, admirably, to perform various public services and to aid in the promotion of the arts.[32]

Allen attended Washington University in St. Louis, and it was in his second year that he was allowed to accompany Professor J. W. Pattison on a sketching expedition to the Rocky Mountains, west of Denver.[33] Young Allen made notes and sketches which encouraged him to go further into the technique of drawing. In 1871 he went to Paris, intending to remain for study, but art collections were scattered and some of the notable painters were absent. He proceeded to Düsseldorf and entered the Royal Academy in the spring of 1872. Allen was instructed by Professors Andreas and Carl Muller in the lower classes and by Eugene Ducker in more advanced work. During vacations he visited many art centers of the Continent, also of London. After having sojourned for a while in Texas, he returned to France in 1878 and went to Rouen, where he enjoyed the companionship of Edward Frère, Luigi Chialiv, Schenk, and others.

The first American showing of Thomas Allen's work was at the National Academy of Design in New York when he exhibited *The Bridge at Linnengen*. Later he had other exhibitions at the Academy. Upon establishing a studio in Boston, he was made a member of the American Society of Artists, and in 1884 he became an associate member of the National Academy.[34]

But in the intervening time Allen left his New England office and traveled to Texas (1878–1879), where he made three notable paintings in San Antonio: *The Market Place, San Antonio* (Plate 103), *Mexican Women Washing at San Pedro Spring* (Plate 104), and *The Portal of San José Mission* (Plate 105). Two others whose setting was probably in Texas are *The Covered Wagon* and *Toilers of the Plains*. *The Market Place* was exhibited at the Paris Salon in 1882.[35] Allen was represented in 1887 by his *On Guard*, now the property of the Berkshire Atheneum at Pittsfield, Massachusetts. He painted the street scenes in San Antonio with great sensitivity, showing an appreciation of the simple and the commonplace.

In 1893 Allen was a member of the International Board of Judges of Awards at the Columbian Exposition at Chicago, and he was chosen chairman of the Jury of Paintings at the World's Fair at St. Louis.

His leadership in the cause of art is shown by his election to the presidency of the Paint and Clay Club of Boston, and of the society of water color painters. He became vice-president of the Boston Art Club, chairman of the School of Drawing and Painting at the Boston Museum of Fine Arts, and chairman of the Art Commission of the City of Boston. In the year of his death, 1924, he had recently been made president of the Board of Trustees of the Boston Museum of Fine Arts.[36]

[32] Dumas Malone (ed.), *Dictionary of American Biography*, see Thomas Allen (father of artist), p. 206.

[33] Thomas J. Scharf, *History of St. Louis*, p. 1628.

[34] *American Art Annual*, Vol. 21, 1924, p. 282.

[35] *The Missouri Republican*, St. Louis, December 27, 1877; *San Antonio Express*, December 18, 1932; June 14, 1936; August 5, 1951.

[36] The Boston Museum of Fine Arts files.

CHAPTER 9

WITH NEW VISION—THE STATE
AS A PATRON OF THE ARTS

THE MIDDLE OF THE 1870's theoretically ended the Reconstruction period proper in Texas. But in 1873 Richard Coke, with a democratic legislature, took over the government from the carpetbagger Edmund J. Davis. Political conditions in the state were intractable, finances were muddled, the treasury stripped. State bonds could not be sold at any price and warrants with which all state operations were financed were being hawked in the streets of Austin at sixty cents on the dollar.

In the settled plantation regions east of the Brazos, Texans were still trying to make the adjustment from slave labor to hired hands who really did not want to work. Prices were low, production was low, and spirits were lower.

Law and order had completely broken down throughout the state. A resentment against the Yankee occupation troops and the state police under Governor Davis (whose failure was evident) created a sympathy toward the law breakers. Scalawags like Wesley Hardin, Sam Bass, and their gangs swaggered through the streets—

giving in later years the image of the two-gun Texan so glamorized in movies and on TV. Added to this situation, the Indians on the northern frontier were driving back the settlers, and the Mexican banditti to the south raided the ranches of that area. During the late 1870's and the 1880's the range wars were going on; the institution of ranching—which in its Southwestern environment brought the cowboy, the lariat, the six-shooter, and the horse into colorful perspective—provided in the last quarter of the century subject matter for Western paintings of artists like Frank Reaugh, Frederic Remington, and Charles Russell.

But what saved the artist at this time were the commissions which came from the state. They were eagerly sought because they provided adequate rations for the artist and the distinction which might be bestowed on them. The matter of American historical paintings had been looked upon with favor, and in the third quarter of the century the artists of Texas turned their attention to the pictorial treatment of subjects in Texas history. Notable contributions were made in the painting of his-

106. Louis Eyth: *Stephen F. Austin*
     Oil, 1873, 29¼″ x 25¼″ (The State Capitol, Austin, Texas)

torical scenes by Eyth and Huddle, and remarkable battle scenes by McArdle and Onderdonk.

Louis Eyth

As unreasonable as it may appear, one of the last acts of the legislature of Governor Davis' term was to pass a law providing for the painting of "Late President Burnet and other Texas Statesmen." A committee of five, Governor Davis, Colonel Ashbel Smith, Colonel A. M. Hobby, Judge John H. Reagan, and Governor James W. Henderson, was to select an artist.

Joint Resolution No. 86

Providing for painting certain portraits. First—Resolved by the Senate and House of Representatives of the State of Texas, that his Excellency Governor E. J. Davis, Ashbel Smith, A. M. Hobby, John H. Reagan and James W. Henderson be and are hereby appointed commissioners to have painted portraits of David G. Burnet, Mirabeau B. Lamar and Anson Jones, deceased, ex Presidents of the Republic of Texas; of Thomas J. Rusk, deceased, the first Chief Justice who presided over the Supreme Court of said Republic and of James Pinckney Henderson, the first governor of the State of Texas after its incorporation into the American Union and that when painted and properly framed said portraits under the direction of the Governor shall be placed in the Senate and House of Representative Halls. And, Resolved further that the Governor be authorized to have the portrait of General Stephen F. Austin now in the Representative Hall repaired and renovated by a competent artist.

Second—Resolved that the sum of three thousand five hundred dollars or so much thereof as may be necessary be and is hereby appropriated out of any money in the Treasury not otherwise appropriated to pay for painting and framing said portraits which shall be paid out of the State Treasury from time to time as may be necessary on the requisition of the Governor as Chairman of Said Board of Commissioners.

Third—Resolved that this joint Resolution shall be in force from and after its passage.

Engrossed Feb. 1st 1873, Kellian A. Wortham, Engrossive, Check[1].

Shortly afterward an amendment was added to the resolution that provided for the repairing and renovation of the portrait of Stephen F. Austin which was then in the House of Representatives Chamber. This opportunity was a godsend for the artists, who were always on the watch for patrons during hard times. Their mainstay had been the portrait, but now the new method of the daguerreotype was gaining public favor and lessening their opportunities.

Louis Eyth (1838–c. 1889), a portrait painter of Galveston seeking a commission, addressed two members of the state committee, Governor Davis and Ashbel Smith:

Portraiture being my branch of art I am more desirous to secure commissions, as the pictures in contemplation are, I presume to be such proportions as will admit of full size —thereby afford ample scope for the exercise of historical portraiture—[that] being the highest attainable degree of my art.[2]

Eyth had migrated to Galveston with some of his family at the age of fourteen and the only art training that he received which can be vouched for came in the years he spent with the well-known daguerreotypists and artists, Blessing and Company.[3] Eyth later applied for and received the commission of copying the early portrait of Stephen F. Austin, which he did faithfully with the lifelike sharpness of the original (Plate 106). This signed copy now is in the secretary of state's office in the State Capitol, Austin.

Eyth went to San Antonio, where he found another patron in the historian, James DeShields, of Farmersville and Dallas. James DeShields was a discriminating collector and dealer in art.[4] DeShields needed illustrations for some of his books, and for several years he commissioned Eyth and other Texas artists, including Henry McArdle and Robert Onderdonk, to make drawings and paintings. Eyth painted *The Speech of Travis to His Men at the Alamo* (Plate 107), made expressly for DeShields' *Tall Men with Long Rifles*, but for some reason not used by the author. Other paintings and sketches of Eyth's that passed through DeShields' hands and now remain only in photographic reproduction are *Surrender of Geronimo* (1885), *Death of Bowie: A Command from the Mexicans that He Be Killed* (Plate 108), and the *Battle of Plum Creek*.[5] Some of these appeared in

[1] *Journal of the House of Representatives, Thirteenth Legislature, Regular Session,* January 22, 1873, p. 80; January 31, 1873, p. 129; February 4, 1873, pp. 150, 166.

[2] Letters, Louis Eyth, Galveston, to Governor E. J. Davis, Austin, January 23, 1873; Eyth, Galveston, to Ashbel Smith, Hogg Island, January 23, 1873; *Index of Naturalization Papers,* Galveston, II, 15.

[3] *Galveston City Directory,* 1872–1873; 1874; 1882.

[4] *San Antonio City Directory,* 1887–1888.

[5] E. L. Callihan, "The Battles that Whipped Mexico," *Dallas News,* August 10, 1930. Illus. "Plum Creek Battle"; De Shields

c-9. Henry McArdle: *Battle of San Jacinto*

Oil, 8' x 14' (The State Capitol, Austin, Texas)

107. Louis Eyth: *The Speech of Travis to His Men at the Alamo*
6⅛″ x 9½″ (Courtesy of the Daughters of the Republic of Texas Library, San Antonio, Texas [Photograph; location of original unknown])

108. Louis Eyth: *Death of Bowie: A Command from the Mexicans that He Be Killed*
c. 1878 (Courtesy of the Daughters of the Republic of Texas Library, San Antonio, Texas [Photograph; location of original unknown])

newspaper stories and show a consistent level of good draftsmanship. Eyth had a knack of representing the historic scene with spirit and, at the same time, accuracy.

Henry McArdle

Swinging along a path in Ireland one might have seen Henry Arthur McArdle (1836–1907), still in his 'teens with pad and pencil hurrying along the Belfast coast to sketch sailing vessels. With him, though much older, was an obscure French teacher of Belfast, Professor Sauveur, equally enthusaistic for the jaunt. Quite early Henry's parents of French-Irish descent had discovered their son's aptitude for drawing. At fourteen, however, he was left an orphan and his care fell to a maiden aunt. We are uninformed as to the reason, but within the year the maiden aunt left with him for America and settled in Baltimore, Maryland.

Young McArdle painted enthusiastically, and as soon as age permitted he was enrolled at the Maryland Institute for the Promotion of the Mechanic Arts. Upon graduating he won the "Institute Medal of Honor" and a Peabody prize of $100 for outstanding work.[6]

One of McArdle's instructors at the Institute was David A. Woodward (1823–1909), who brought credit to himself by winning a commission to paint the portrait of Prince Edward VII of Wales. Later, when McArdle was working on his historical paintings in Texas, it was to Professor Woodward that he turned for criticism of his work.[7]

When the Civil War came, McArdle's career as an artist was interrupted by a period of service as a draftsman for the Confederate Navy, which was then building gunboats, and he later made topographical maps for General Robert E. Lee. It was his association in the

campaign of West Virginia with Lee, whose distinguished leadership McArdle admired, and the incident with Hood's Texas Brigade that caused him to envision the painting *Lee at the Wilderness*.

At the close of the war, McArdle married Jennie Smith, of Albermarle County, Virginia. Because of her ill health he was advised to take her to the West Indies or to Texas. McArdle decided on Texas, and in the winter of 1867–1868 they established themselves at Independence, Texas, McArdle remaining here some twenty-odd years as professor of art at Baylor Female College. His wife died in 1871, and he later married Miss Isophene L. Dunnington, of West Virginia.[8]

He now renewed his interest in his proposed painting, *Lee at the Wilderness*. He portrayed General Lee as he attempts to lead Hood's Brigade into the battle and is restrained by one of the Texans. One soldier seizes the bridle of Old Traveler to lead Lee out of danger, while others shout, "Lee to the rear!" When the painting was exhibited it received acceptance and appreciation by the public. When it was on exhibition at the State Fair in Houston, 1875, it was said that Jefferson Davis was greatly moved on viewing it. The picture was destroyed when the State Capitol in Austin was burned in 1881, and remains only in photographic form.[9]

McArdle was a man of intellectual curiosity and a tireless worker. His historical paintings, because of their large size and inclusion of implicit details, may be thought of as remarkable achievements rather than great art. His chief interest during his painting career was in history-making events, which he depicted as authentic as his study revealed and as monumental and dramatic as facts allowed.

Having read and studied Texas history he was impressed with its struggle for independence, and encouraged by James DeShields to depict some of the drama of the state's history he set about painting some war scenes. This led eventually to portraits of some of the state's early heroes, such as Moses Austin Bryan (Plate 109). As he was still teaching, the historic painting enabled him to add to his scant income.

With DeShields' encouragement to paint various battle scenes, McArdle started on a task with enlivened interest and painstaking preparation; it was in 1876 he began his large canvas, *Dawn at the Alamo* (Plate 110), which was completed only after seven years of labor. He sent photographs of this painting to his former teacher W. A. Woodward in Baltimore for criticism. Wood-

Papers, Daughters of the Republic of Texas Library, San Antonio, Texas; illustrations mentioned, *The Speech of Travis to His Men at the Alamo*; *Surrender of Geronimo*; *Death of Crockett*; and *Battle of Plum Creek*.

[6] C. W. Raines, *A Year Book for Texas, 1901–03*, I, 229, 409; Dorothy Renick, "Eyes of Texas," *San Antonio Express*, July 8–29, 1923.

[7] Lucy Salamanca, "Harry McArdle and his Noted Historical Paintings," *The Baltimore Sun* (supplement) June 14, 1931; Letter, William Cary Crane, Independence, to Committee of Legislature to paint portraits of President Burnet and others, January 27, 1873, Texas State Archives, Austin.

[8] Renick, *San Antonio Express*, July 8–29, 1923.

[9] Raines, *Year Book for Texas*, I, 249–250; pictures, letters, notes compiled by the artists, Texas State Archives, Austin.

109. Henry McArdle: *Moses Austin Bryan*
    Oil, 1890, 29¾″ x 24½″ (Courtesy of Mrs. Donald B. Hummel, Houston, Texas)

110. Henry McArdle: *Dawn at the Alamo*
Oil, 1876–1883, 7' x 12' (The State Capitol, Austin, Texas)

ward wrote in August, 1899, after examining the photograph:

The figures are well placed especially that of Crockett. . . . You have all the artistic and historical elements brought together in such an effective, truthful combination as to produce a grand composition. . . . I find no fault in the composition. Indeed, I must congratulate you on producing such a grand and truthful conception of that dreadful event. . . . It seems strange to me that so long a time should have passed by since this design was made without being placed on canvas.[10]

McArdle's interest in portraiture perhaps stood in his way when he was painting the battle scenes. The emphasis of verisimilitude draws attention to individuals to some extent, rather than the overall ideas involved in the scene. For this reason the viewer's attention is called to individuals in a way that might detract slightly from some of the violence and action in the battle which he knew must have been so furious. This emphasis on portraiture is particulary present in his next painting, *The Battle of San Jacinto* (Plate c-9).

McArdle uses conscientious interpretations of topography, uniforms, equipment, and personal likenesses. His practice of portraiture sharpened his eye, and to him the individual became an important part of his war scenes. He wrote:

In every part of my work I have arrived at natural action and historic truth which implies the necessity of models for every portion of my painting—from the movement and action of the horse and his rider to the details of arms, and uniforms, etc. . . . "The Battle of San Jacinto" portrays the moment when the Texas army commanded by General Houston, aided by General Edward Burleson, Sidney Sherman, and other officers, led the charge against the Mexicans, April 21, 1836.[11]

The painting shows Santa Anna in full retreat and the Mexican army completely routed.

McArdle was aided by General O. O. Howard of the United States Army when gathering photographs, daguerreotypes, and uniforms of both American and Mexican armies; arms such as old flintlock pistols, rifles, muskets, and sabres; and Mexican blankets and costumes which would assist him in making an authentic painting.[12] Meticulous care was shown by McArdle in the listing and description of these materials, which he considered valuable to future students of history.

After years of wrangling over the ownership, the leg-islature of Texas paid the McArdle heirs $25,000 for the two pictures, *Battle of San Jacinto* and *Dawn at the Alamo*.[13] McArdle had been a great admirer of Ernest Meissonier (1815–1891), the well-known French historical painter; he also received inspiration, no doubt, from the American artist James Walker (1819–1889) in his paintings *Battle of Gettysburg* and *Battle of Chapultepec*.

In 1873 the state legislature passed a bill to have portraits painted of some of its public men. McArdle applied through Dr. Cary Crane, president of Baylor College, to Governor E. J. Davis for a commission for some of the portraits, which resulted in his painting the portrait of Jefferson Davis.[14] The artist again sought Woodward's council, and some solid advice was given on the painting of a full-length figure: "Your canvas for Jeff Davis' picture of six feet—I would recommend that you paint him only to below the knees leaving a space over the head. In fact, full length portraits showing the feet are seldom unobjectable."[15] Accepting Woodward's advice, he painted a three-quarter side view, of the standing figure—the large portrait (71½" x 53½", 1890) which hangs in the Senate Chamber of the State Capitol. The Jefferson Davis portrait was accepted by the state in a ceremony March 7, 1891.

Messrs. Beauregard Bryan, C. C. Garett, B. Eldridge, C. C. Giddings, W. W. Searcy of Brenham and Mr. Thomas C. Clay and artist H. A. McArdle of Independence will present a magnificent portrait of Hon. Jefferson Davis in the Senate tonight.

The presentation will be made by Mr. Beauregard Bryan and will be responded to by Hon. F. R. Lubbock who will receive the elegant portrait on behalf of the State. The pres-

---

[10] Letter, D. A. Woodward, Baltimore, Maryland, to McArdle, Independence, August 29, 1889, Daughters of the Republic of Texas Library, San Antonio.

[11] Pictures, letters, notes compiled by McArdle, Texas State Archives, Austin.

[12] Raines, *Year Book for Texas*, II, 228–229, 409.

[13] *Journal of the Senate, Fortieth Legislature, Regular Session,* February 21, 1927, pp. 467–468.

[14] Letters, Corporal W. G. Wood, Galveston, to Ashbel Smith, Independence, January 27, 1873, on McArdle's ability as portraitist, Daughters of the Republic of Texas Library, San Antonio; Dr. Carl Crane, Baylor University, Independence, to E. J. Davis and committee, Austin, January 27, 1873; E. Van Hartan to Ashbel Smith, Austin, January 27, 1873, Texas State Archives, Austin.

[15] Letter, D. A. Woodward, Baltimore, Maryland, to McArdle, Independence, August 29, 1889.

111. Henry McArdle: *Settlement of Austin's Colony* or *The Log Cabin*
Oil, 1875, 83¼" x 60½" (The State Capitol, Austin, Texas)

entation will take place in the Senate Chamber promptly at 8 o'clock.[16]

It is a monumental work, but like other portraits of the artist lacks vibrancy, resulting chiefly from the use of a muted pallorlike skin tone and the absence of motion in the figure.

McArdle made other contributions in the realm of historical painting—*Ben Milam Calling for Volunteers* and *Deaf Smith Announcing the Destruction of Vince's Bridge*—both depicting incidents which occurred at the time of the Battle of San Jacinto. However, his best work as a historical document and a skillful portrayal of the subject is perhaps the *Settlement of Austin's Colony* or *The Log Cabin* (Plate 111); both titles are recorded in the artist's correspondence. Here McArdle has portrayed a convincing scene—the story of a morning in 1824. He makes the viewer feel the absence of comfort in the rough crowded cabin. There is the feeling of anxiety at the moment of the announcement that the "Carauchuas" are raiding. Austin appears calm and resolute as he reaches for a gun on the rafters.

An understanding of the events and a recognition of personalities may be more satisfactorily achieved by the reader if the artist's own explanation is given:

Horation Criesman, surveyor making on the puncheon floor lines of a piece of land for which Austin is about to issue title.

Baron de Bastrop, land commissioner with letter in hand [only partly shown on left of viewer].

Ran Foster, the hunter with pipe in hand and behind him Samuel M. Williams, Colonial Secty., all aroused to interest in the report of an Indian raid being made by a scout who is entering the door. The latter a new-comer indicated by his "store clothes." He had a struggle with some of the advance savages, is wounded in the head [head band] and takes with him a battle-ax and a bow. The latter tells Austin that the Carauchuas [Indians on the southern border of Texas] are doing the devilish work, indications of which are seen in the burning cabins in the background. Next is *Simon* the cook [head in window] who has left his fire to hear the prospect of losing his wooly scalp.

Austin is reading from a book [actually holding the book] marked "Laws of Mexico." He wears a sword illustrative of his authority as judge and commander of the Colonial troops. As the announcement is made he instinctively reaches for his rifle, all suggestive of the Empressario's many duties an[d] fearful trials of Colonization.[17]

This painting hung in the Capitol for many years before it was bought from the artist's family in 1927. Its purchase had been delayed because of a long controversy over the ownership—the contestants being the descendants of the artist and the DeShields family. The value was listed in 1904 by DeShields at $400, but in 1901 the legislature appropriated $1000 for the picture, which now hangs in the House of Representatives.[18]

In spite of his income from teaching, it was through the business acumen of DeShields that McArdle was able at any time to carry on his work through crises without great financial worry. A few years before his death (1906), he wrote DeShields from San Antonio, where he moved in 1889: "In reply to your favor of the 10th, as usual my financial condition is desperate—and if you will relieve me as you say you so often did in the past, I will make the two black and white drawings (for $100) but I want $50 right away. Trusting for a prompt response."[19] Among the McArdle portraits listed by Mr. DeShields were those of Sam Houston, Deaf Smith, Henry Karnes, William B. Travis, Baron de Bastrop, James A. Sylvester, Samuel M. Williams, Juan N. Seguin, Jack Hays, Rufus C. Burleson, Dr. Cary Crane, Goodwin B. Cotten, Ruben M. Potter (1886), and Mary Austin Holley. The last listed was a copy made from Matthew H. Jouett's portrait painted from life when Mary Austin was sixteen.[20]

It is probable that McArdle made bread and butter with the portraits that DeShields from time to time commissioned him to paint. His portraits seem often besmothered by dark and cheerless color; the viewer often experiences the feeling that he is looking at an old daguerreotype in the absence of sharp outline and clear colors. Even with these shortcomings of technique, his historic paintings are of value in the story they tell, perhaps more effectively than the written word. Great numbers of Texans have learned through his storytelling pictures the fortitude and sacrifice of the men who made Texas.

[16] *Austin Statesman*, March 7, 1891.

[17] Letter, McArdle, San Antonio to DeShields, Farmersville, March 13, 1906, Daughters of the Republic of Texas Library, San Antonio.

[18] James DeShields' list of McArdle's work, February 25, 1904, DeShields Papers.

[19] Letter, McArdle to DeShields, March 13, 1906.

[20] DeShields' list of McArdle's work.

William H. Huddle

Artist William Henry Huddle (1847–1892) spent most of his adventurous life in Texas. In spite of his deceptively strong physical appearance, his life was comparatively short. Yet he had an untiring working spirit and left many paintings of good solid character.

Sometimes appearing erratic, his adventures disclose a driving curiosity. On one occasion on Pecan Street in Austin he met an old slave, Mose, a type he had always wanted to paint. When he asked if he would pose for him with a violin, Mose replied, "No, suh, th' fiddl's the Devil's music box." But once Huddle had him in his studio and explained that angels played on such instruments as the lyre and harp, Mose studied the artist's kind but determined expression, and perhaps was imagining he could hear the jingle of silver in his pocket, then said, "Boss, gim'me dat fiddl'."[21] This portrait of the old slave (Plate 112), painted late in the artist's career, is one of his most interesting portrayals, despite the fact that Mose holds the violin stiffly, as if expecting the devil to jump out any moment. This was the year 1889, and Huddle had become an experienced and well-known painter in Texas. This three-quarter portrait represents the former slave in a wrinkled coat, with grey beard and hair, and kind quiet eyes. Here, as in other portraits of old people, Huddle shows a fine insight into character.

Early in 1885 Huddle experienced another interesting adventure in painting when he returned from his study in Munich. In a letter to a friend he speaks of wanting to experience a storm at sea that he might try his hand at painting a seascape: "I will sail from Bremen about the first of April and I guess I will have my curiosity gratified in the way of a storm-at-sea. I have always wanted to see a first class storm and April is the best month for them, so you see I will have lots to tell you when I come."[22]

21 Mrs. William Huddle, notes on artist's work (typescript); *Austin Statesman*, July 8, 1877; March 24, 1892.

22 Letter, William Huddle, Munich, to Miss Carver, Austin, February 9, 1885, collection of Mrs. Margarite Huddle Slaughter, Austin.

23 Mrs. Margarite Huddle Slaughter, notes and verbal information on father's life; *Austin Statesman*, March 24, 1892.

24 *Austin Statesman*, March 24, 1892; *Washington Post*, Flavius Fisher, May 9, 1905.

25 *Art Students' League Constitution and By-laws*, June 2, 1875 (Pamphlet).

An opportunity did occur, and he was able to witness a storm in all its fury. He asked that he be lashed to the deck, and there he made a sketchy painting in oil of the surging, churning ocean before him; it remains only as a symbol of the artist's versatility and his adventurous spirit.

Huddle's early life was much like any normal youth's of his time in Wytheville, Virginia, where he was born in 1847—the youngest son of Stephen Groce and Nancy Foster Huddle—and where he attended school. At a very youthful age he enlisted in the Southern cavalry, 1863, and served with General Nathan Forrest and General Joseph Wheeler. His father, a gunsmith, moved the family in the late 1860's to Paris, Texas (where Virginia relatives had moved earlier), and when William returned from his war service, he joined his father in the business of gunsmithing. Until young Huddle could escape his father's shop he spent many hours in drawing and sketching.[23] At eighteen, encouraged by his efforts as an amateur at portrait painting, he left Paris, Texas, to study with a cousin, Flavius Fisher (1832–1905), a portraitist whose early life was spent in Wytheville and who afterwards studied in France and Germany to prepare himself for the long and notable career he later enjoyed in Washington, D.C. He took Huddle under his wing, and it was during this period with Fisher that Huddle received his fundamental training in portraiture.[24] No doubt it was in Fisher's studio, too (and later through the influence of Elisabet Ney the sculpturist), that this young protégé was impressed with the importance of foreign study—a goal he set for himself and finally was able to reach. After three years of study with Fisher he returned to Texas, where he felt he would find professional opportunity. In 1874, however, he went to New York, where he entered the National Academy of Design, which through lack of funds was obliged in 1875 to close its doors temporarily. A group of students unhappy over the turn of events formed a cooperative class in drawing with L. E. Wilmarth as instructor. Huddle was one of the 123 students of the newly organized school, the Art Students' League.[25]

The next year Huddle came to Austin, registering his studio at the Cook Building and his residence at the Curtis House. In July of that year the local paper was discerning enough to call attention to the fact that Austin, then, had two good artists, William Huddle and

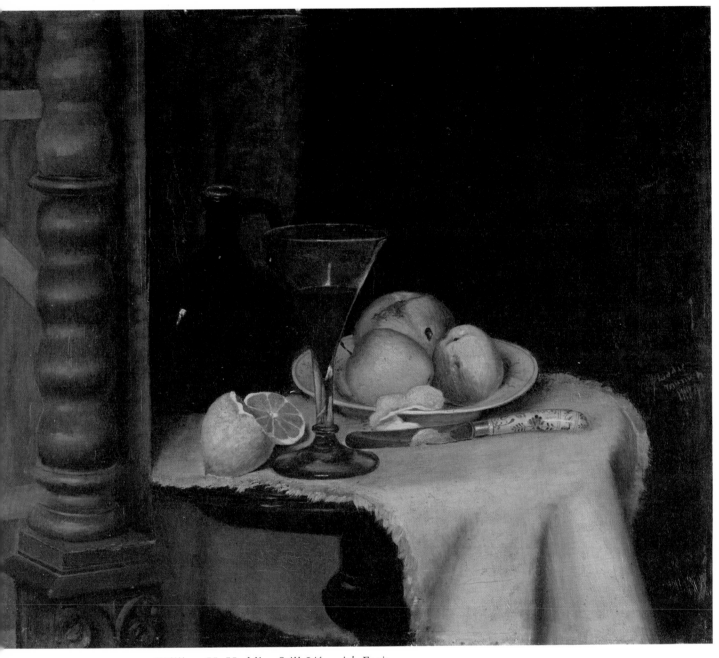

c-10. William H. Huddle: *Still Life with Fruit*
Oil, 1884, 16⅜″ x 19¾″ (Courtesy of the Dallas Museum of Fine Arts [Hoblitzelle Foundation])

112. William H. Huddle: *The Slave*
    Oil, 1889, 36″ x 28″ (Courtesy of the Dallas Museum of Fine Arts [Hoblitzelle Foundation Loan])

113. William H. Huddle: *Self-Portrait*
   Oil, c. 1874, 30" x 25" (Courtesy of Mr. Kelly Stevens, Austin, Texas)

Hermann Lungkwitz.[26] In November the news followed with the announcement that Mr. Huddle was exhibiting at the Travis County Fair," . . . this work taking up about three panels, filled with paintings and crayons." The news editor passed over other possible art items with the fact that "the new machine the telephone is being erected to connect the judges stand with the stables. This will afford a good opportunity to witness the working of that machine, it is worth going out to see!"[27]

When Huddle left Virginia he brought with him a self-portrait (Plate 113), which he had completed while a student of Fisher and which he always liked to display as an example of his work. The young artist is shown on a plain dark background, seated, holding his palette, and beside him is a companion—Fisher's dog. The flesh tones are good, and all in all it is a pleasing portrait. He displayed a skill in this painting which makes one wonder if he might not have reached greater heights in his work earlier had he continued under the spell of his American teacher rather than the influence of Munich, where he later studied.

In the spring of 1881 the artist made a trip to Leadville, Colorado, but it does not appear that the magnet was either the Indians, the mines, or the cowboys; it was referred to simply as a sketching tour.[28] Leadville, a mining town at that time, was at its peak boom and had been made important by Mrs. Frank Leslie and her illustrating artists. Another sketching tour was made to the Pedernales River in 1887. These trips may have been his own way of testing his ability in the field of landscape, but no doubt he was tempted to some extent by adventure and by his love of the out-of-doors. This intermittent interest in landscape may also have been due to the influence of his friend Hermann Lungkwitz and the realization that such experience was needed for the background of historical paintings which he had in mind to develop. Several scenes were painted on the Pedernales and others near Marble Falls and Austin. A half dozen of these unimpressive scenes represent his complete work as a landscapist. Whatever his purpose, it may be said he returned from these trips with seemingly renewed ardor for his portrait painting.

Huddle had completed a number of portraits of Texas governors when he launched on a project of a "gallery," which he planned would include all the presidents and governors of Texas. In the summer of 1884 he was made chairman of the committee to select paintings for the World's Fair, but he had other plans in mind: he hoped to be rescued in his undertaking of the gallery by a major commission from the Legislature to paint the remainder of the portraits and to have the state purchase the entire group. This was exactly what happened.[29] Encouraged by the thought of this increase in commissions, he renewed his interest in improving his technique, and interrupted his work on the gallery of portraits to prepare for further study. This time it was to be in Europe. He sailed in the fall of 1884. A letter written from Munich, October 24, gives us his first impression of a European art center:

My dear friend:
. . . It is now about one month since I left Austin and not one word have I heard from anyone and all together I feel as if I had "got left" . . . I don't know how to go about telling you about this town, and country—everything is so different from home—art, beer, and music is everywhere, picture galleries by the mile—statues of the great in war, statesmanship, art, and literature stand everywhere there is room for one. The King lives at this place—he is not in town now (I guess he will call on me when he returns) and Dukes and Princes and such cattle all thick as Colonels.[30]

Huddle noted that he would shorten his stay in Germany and would start home in February (1885), afterwards changing the date to April. The reason for his early return, he stated in a nostalgic mood to his friend (whom he married on his return to Austin), was that he was tired and "wanted to see the old Colorado sparkle—and your eyes." Less sentimental reasons were also given, such as the facts that expenses had been greater than anticipated and that cholera might pass from France to Germany in the spring, as was its habit, and he wished to avoid quarantine. In regard to his work he wrote:

I have studied hard and don't regret this trip but don't expect to see pictures when I come as all my time has been occupied by painting heads. Only one day on each head and often scraping it out and painting on the same canvas next day—I have finished a few things, though, one for you—a

[26] *Austin Statesman*, July 8, 1877.

[27] "Display at the Fair Grounds," *Austin Statesman*, November 13, 1877.

[28] *Austin Statesman*, March 27, 1881.

[29] H. P. N. Gammel, *General Laws of Texas, 1822–1897*, pp. 326–327, 387, 402.

[30] Letter, Huddle, Munich, to My Dear friend [Miss Carver], October 24, 1884, collection of Mrs. Margarite Huddle Slaughter, Austin.

114. William H. Huddle: *Sam Houston*
Oil, 1888, 5½′ x 4½′ (The State Capitol, Austin, Texas)

still life study—I know you will like it unless your imagination has painted it better than my pencil—however, we shall see.[31]

This still life (Plate c-10) is the only one of this type that he is known to have painted. It is a compact composition, a stereotyped arrangement grouped along a diagonal axis and painted after the Dutch and Flemish models—a wine bottle, napkin, and fruit painted with careful realism, with richness of tone and color, and with a successful effect of light. The artist recounted how difficult it was to keep the arrangement intact as fellow students robbed it daily. He then told how he drank the wine and ate the apple as a reward for a very interesting and skillfully painted still life, but left the lemon for his fellow students.[32]

As did many other artists studying abroad, Huddle brought home a portrait done in the Munich manner, a small bust portrait (c. 14″ x 16″) of a Bavarian peasant woman wearing the native headdress. It is painted on a dark background and reflects the severity of the peasant character.

Huddle's love of his profession and his inquisitive temperament made him a man of energy and vision. On his return to Austin, Huddle began his long and uninterrupted undertaking of completing the paintings of the presidents and governors. We hear of his activities from time to time through his friend Alexander Sweet, the editor and political satirist who achieved international recognition through his contributions at different times to Galveston, San Antonio, Austin, and New York newspapers. Through his column "Colonel Bill Short," Sweet (Austin, 1887) often tells of Huddle's fishing and hunting escapades and his sketching trips. In his Austin column he wrote: "He [Huddle] is busy now painting a large picture of Sam Houston. It represents the old man a few years before his death. The old lion seems feeble but he is a lion never-the-less, the fence cutters would never have pulled his tail twice in succession."[33] Sweet is referring to the action of Governor John Ireland in regard to the fence cutters of 1883, when there was strife between the lawless cattlemen who wanted to live under the old practice of the open range and others who were buying barbed wire to fence their land.

Again Sweet tells in his characteristic manner of Huddle's experience with a fire across the street from the Masonic building in Austin. In a building near his studio were the portraits he had painted of Texas' chief executives. Standing on the street when the fire started, Huddle mistook the reflection of the flames in the windows of his studio to mean that the fire had spread there. He called out to the crowd to help him get his portraits to safety with the promise, "I'll paint your portraits and place them on exhibition!" Sweet describes how each rescuer seized a portrait and with all possible speed carried it to a place of safety. "Poor Huddle's trouble began next day," wrote Sweet, "when his studio was thronged with the hardest looking mob that ever congregated in Austin since the legislature adjourned."[34]

But Huddle was to have another experience with a fire (1881) which destroyed a number of his paintings hanging in his studio in the old temporary Capitol. It was only because some of his work, including the *Surrender of Santa Anna*, was on exhibition in San Antonio at the time of the fire that it now remains.

As time passed, Huddle added to his gallery until he had the complete number of the governors and presidents of Texas. When the new Capitol was dedicated in 1888, he had ready about twenty portraits. The special session of the legislature in 1888 appropriated $10,000 for "statuary and portraits for the rotunda," and from this fund Huddle received $7,000 for his group of completed portraits. In addition, for the sum of $1,000 he was to paint in 1889 a portrait of Thomas J. Rusk, United States Senator (1846), who also served the state in many important capacities. These twenty portraits painted chiefly from engravings and daguerreotypes remain as historic records of many of our public men.[35]

In addition to the portrait of Sam Houston painted for the gallery of governors and presidents, Huddle was requested to paint another "large" portrait of Sam Houston. This second portrait (Plate 114) shows Houston in the picturesque costume said to have been one he chose to wear when entering the United States Senate (1846–1859)—a striped Cherokee blanket around his shoulders, a cane in his left hand, and a large beaver hat in his right hand. This likeness was made no doubt from

[31] Letter, Huddle, to Miss Carver, February 9, 1885.

[32] Mrs. Huddle, notes on the artist's life.

[33] Letters to J. Armory Knox, "My dear Knox," *Austin Statesman* (date missing).

[34] *Ibid.*, letter to J. Armory Knox, November 12, 1881.

[35] *Journal of the Senate, Twentieth Legislature, Called Session,* (1888), $10,000 appropriation for Presidents and Governors of Texas, p. 18.

the famous Frederick photograph taken in New York City and from Carl Iwonski's earlier life portrait in pencil. The heavily carved Senate chair in which he sits lends dignity to the portrait. It was among those commissioned by the Twentieth Legislature (1888), and now hangs in the House of Representatives in the State Capitol.

With his gallery of presidents and governors completed and sold to the state, Huddle was free from financial stress. Furthermore he was recognized as one of the leading portraitists of Texas. His work was no longer restricted to men (who dominated life in Texas) nor to political figures. He made portraits of his wife, of his mother-in-law, Mrs. Carver, and of Mrs. Sterling Fulmore—all of Austin—which show a charm and sensitivity surpassing in some respects his earlier work.[36] He also painted several self-portraits. With his portraits of political figures there is a certain monotony, for in these he used flat dark tones for the empty backgrounds, a habit adhered to in painting public figures.

In 1882 Huddle completed a portrait of John Salmon Ford, member of the Secession Convention, generally known as "Rip" Ford from the fact that during the Mexican War as adjutant he was compelled through pressures of war to shorten the comment "Rest in Peace" to "R.I.P." in the death notices he sent out. Ford was one of these remarkable characters in early Texas who seemed, as viewed from our present day, to serve with equal success as physician, ranger, soldier, editor, state senator, and politician. Lacking a more suitable place to display Ford's portrait, Huddle placed it in an Austin shop window belonging to Joseph A. Nagle. Its present location is unknown.[37]

Later Huddle completed a portrait of Colonel Jesse Lincoln Driskill, a Tennessean who came to Texas in 1849 and made a fortune in cattle. Huddle painted a full-length portrait of the rancher ". . . in a familiar pose . . . standing on the tesseleated floor of the hotel" which he had just completed.[38] This portrait also is one which has not been located.

Huddle had now attained a certain level of craftsmanship and a certain sensitivity which maturity had brought. From this time of 1889 until his death in 1892 Huddle painted some of the best portraits of his career.

A portrait of Madam Andrea Castanon de Villanueva Candelaria (March, 1891), an aged Mexican woman, is one of Huddle's best. While in San Antonio to discuss the possibility of painting portraits for the Brack-

enridge family, he learned that people were seeing the lady who for a small fee would tell of her experiences at the Battle of the Alamo. Despite the historical dispute on whether she was actually in the Alamo at the time of the siege, the legislature on February 12, 1891, gave her a pension to show their appreciation for her untiring work in administering to the stricken people of San Antonio during the yellow-fever epidemic and her service to the wounded and sick during the siege of 1836. This same Madam Candelaria is probably the one known in her younger days as the "patron of the fandango." Huddle made a trip to her home and was so impressed with the 106-year-old lady that he asked to paint her portrait. It is a portrait of no ordinary kind; it portrays with great sympathy the sadness and the tragedies of her life.[39]

When Oran M. Roberts was governor (1879–1883) he sat for his portrait, as did Mrs. Roberts. Retiring as governor he became a professor of law at The University of Texas. These are substantial portraits, and in spite of the Victorian primness of Mrs. Roberts' portrait they are particularly pleasing. Both paintings are the property of The University of Texas.

Attributed to Huddle is a portrait of Jacob Kuechler, whom governor J. J. Reynolds appointed commissioner of the General Land Office in 1870 and again in 1872. Kuechler had served as surveyor of Fredericksburg, Texas, and had married one of the sisters of the landscape painter Hermann Lungkwitz.[40]

At this point in his career Huddle became interested in painting historical events and began to envision a large picture of the surrender of Santa Anna to Sam Houston after the Battle of San Jacinto, April, 1836 (Plate c-11). It was now fifty years after the event, and while there were previously executed prints and there were eyewitnesses still alive, it was an enormous undertaking. The artist conceived the idea of representing not only the incident of Santa Anna and Houston's meeting itself, but also all the personalities who participated. This project required thorough research, including a trip to Mexico to study records and documents. He went to the San Jacinto battleground that he might make an authentic painting of the Treaty Oak and the surrounding area. When completed the historical scene contained some

[36] Mrs. Huddle, list of the artist's work.
[37] *Austin Statesman*, January 28, 1882.
[38] *Ibid.*, September 7, 1890.
[39] *San Antonio Express*, May 12, 1907; 22nd Legislature approved pension, April 13, 1891.
[40] Interview, Mrs. Walter Wupperman, Austin, owner of portrait.

thirty participants in position—each individual worked out carefully. Through the composition and the use of strong color, the artist has focused attention on the central figures of Houston and the Mexican captive. He succeeds to some extent in giving the mood of the tense moment—Houston lies wounded under a large oak talking to Santa Anna; Doctor Alexander W. Ewing, the surgeon general, is busy dressing Houston's wounded leg; and one of the soldiers is holding back those who would not deal with Santa Anna so kindly. Huddle was not proficient in figure drawing, but while the figures are stiff, on the whole they are well proportioned. Perhaps he shows other faults, considering the strict canons of draftsmanship of his time, yet he has envisioned a scene of great interest and historic value. In 1891 the Twenty-Second Legislature appropriated $4,000 for this picture and placed it in the rotunda of the State Capitol, where it still remains.[41]

Near the *Surrender of Santa Anna* is the full-length painting (1889), *David Crockett*. The artist shows Crockett in a buckskin suit, his coonskin cap in one hand and his gun, "Old Betsy," in the other. The huntsman is appropriately shown against a wooded background. This portrait, loaned to the state by the artist's family in 1893 following the artist's death (1892), was purchased in 1909 by the Thirty-First Legislature for $5,000.[42]

William Huddle, whose work is an example of talent and energy, painted many portraits of good quality during his life. The governors and presidents were necessarily painted from prints, photographs, and daguerreotypes. These paintings are a historical record with a quality consequent of the conditions under which they were produced; his paintings of the last years of his life are more emotionally satisfying because of the greater maturity of his work and the advantage of painting from life. The latter have vitality; they reflect the artist's sympathy and frank, shrewd observation.

Huddle lived and worked at a time when the older artists went to Europe to gain a greater skill by studying for a short period. But as time passed, artists sought art centers—Rome, Paris, Munich, Antwerp—for longer periods. They might return to America or they might choose to remain in a foreign atmosphere. They seemed to feel that this experience would insure them against failure. Following Huddle in point of time, we have Robert J. Onderdonk who did not go to Europe but worked solely in the climate of his own homeland. An account of his life contrasts strongly with that of Huddle,

both in temperament and in achievement, yet each made important contributions to art.

Robert Jenkins Onderdonk

Robert Jenkins Onderdonk's life (1852–1917) did not leave in the art world a meteoric path, transiently brilliant and quickly gone. Instead, as representative of a modest artist his work gathers greater distinction as time passes, and his place in the promotion of art in Texas is notable.

By the last quarter of the nineteenth century, when Onderdonk was most active, a stir had begun in the public consciousness of the larger cities of Texas to meet the need for organizations which would concern themselves with the advancement of art. Already such institutions were developing rapidly in New York, Chicago, Philadelphia, and St. Louis. From the days of the Republic there had been private teachers of art in the larger cities of Texas who had exhibited their work whenever and wherever it was possible, but Dallas was the first to put into action a group effort for the promotion of both a school of art and organized public exhibitions.

In subsequent years the same cultural pattern was initiated in Texas cities, as in the older regions of the United States, where this development had come about through the growth of the reading public (which paralleled a large increase in publications), the circulation of prints, and the opportunities given through private exhibitions. All these had a part in the advancement of art. The movement in Texas found its motivating force in 1889 when Robert Onderdonk was invited to exhibit his landscapes and portraits at the Dallas Fair; the exhibition resulted in an invitation to the artist to help organize and become director of the Dallas Art League.

A brief look at his early life and training will indicate the preparation which Robert Onderdonk had for this position. He was born in January, 1852, at St. Timothy Hall, Catonsville, Maryland, which was the old mystery-surrounded "Fountain Rock Manor," the former home of Major Samuel Ringgold, of Mexican War fame.[43]

---

[41] *Journal of the Senate, Twenty-Second Legislature, Regular Session* (1891), p. 520.

[42] Gammel, *Laws of Texas*, X, 128.

[43] Notes on life and work of Robert Onderdonk, Eleanor Onderdonk, San Antonio, Texas; "Where Ringgold Fell," *The Herald of Texas*, Brownsville, clipping (no date); Charles X. Harris, "Jacobus Gerritsen Strycker (c. 1619–1687): An Artist of New Amsterdam," *New-York Historical Society Quarterly*, X, No. 3 (October, 1926), 83–91.

Onderdonk's mother was the former Henrietta Stephenson of Somerset County, Maryland. The Onderdonks' earlier ancestor, Adriean Van der Donk, came to this country in 1642, settling finally on the Hudson River sixteen miles from New York City on the site of present-day Yonkers, an appellation often applied to Van der Donk himself in its meaning of "Dutch farmer." As well as recording the history of New Amsterdam, he was its first lawyer. In consequence of his importance, Van der Donk's portrait was painted (1654–1655) by Jacobus Gerritsen Strycker, "who drew it with his own hand" following the style of the best of the Dutch school; it is a fine example of very early painting in this country.

Robert Onderdonk's early education was received in Catonsville at the College of St. James, where, following the Civil War, his father, Henry Onderdonk, became headmaster. When Robert Onderdonk was twenty, he left Catonsville to study in New York City at the National Academy under L. E. Wilmarth (1855–1918). Only once, later in his life, did he exhibit at the Academy, and that was at the insistence of his son, Julian. He also worked at the Art Students' League, where his instructors were Walter Shirlaw (1838–1909) and James Carroll Beckwith (1852–1917). His last year at the Art Students' League was spent in study with William Merritt Chase (1849–1916), a year (1878) he always referred to with particular satisfaction. Chase and his contemporaries at the Art Students' League had not, as early as the seventies, abandoned the greys and browns of Munich, which they used so constantly and which are evident in Onderdonk's early work.[44]

While at the Academy, Onderdonk made short trips around New York City and its environs with sketchbook and pencil. These now priceless sketches, usually about 3½ by 6 inches, are sometimes of his companions, sometimes of rural scenes. Often the interest is heightened by the use of soft colored paper and a bit of Chinese white.[45] One sketch, a classroom exercise, shows a boy sitting on a high stool—a clever pen-and-ink sketch (c. 3" x 6") required by his instructor to be made in two minutes.

Once his New York study was completed, Onderdonk's thoughts turned to Europe, the goal of most students of the era. But a chance meeting with a friend, Walter Negley, also a Marylander and later of San Antonio, turned the events of his life when Negley persuaded him to consider going to Texas, a country where an artist, he argued, could make enough money to send himself to Europe whenever he desired.

Even with encouragement and the Onderdonk self-reliance, he did not succeed in his plan for foreign study. Following the probable ill-advice of his friend and after obtaining a few introductory letters, he set out for San Antonio in 1878 to take up his life work as artist and teacher. He lived there happily for three years, making frequent trips to the Nat Lewis ranch where he could wander with pad and pencil over the far reaches of the countryside.

In 1881 he met and married Emily Gould, whose family had migrated a year before from Newport, Rhode Island, and had settled in a section near San Antonio with the idea of becoming rich in ranching. Their one prize possession was a portrait of Emily, painted when she was quite young by the famous Charles Bird King (1785–1862), who started his career as a portraitist in Newport.[46]

But the Goulds had hard sledding in the face of droughts and cattle thieves. So, with the artist and his wife, they moved to Laurel Heights, San Antonio. This home, in which the artist spent his life, still remains (1963) in the Onderdonk family. The artist's announcement of his teaching in 1881 reads: "Studio, 402 East Houston Street, corner of Losoya Street—residence Nathan Gould on the hill east of Pedro Spring." This also was the announcement of the fact that the Goulds had given up ranching and had returned to live near the city. Here the artist-teacher could be seen each morning with his painting paraphernalia, walking toward Pedro Spring, where he took the newly installed mule car to the city studio. It was his habit throughout life to carry with him small thin panels of wood (often the top of a cigar box) on which he would paint small scenes on his walks. His love of nature is shown in his simple homelike motifs of a view of a garden, an old house, or a bridge. These very small paintings, a number in both oil and water color, were stored away in his home studio and forgotten. Recently these came to light, and they are treasured by many who enjoy Onderdonk's simple, soft-

[44] Dallas Museum of Fine Arts Collection, Dallas.
[45] Eleanor Onderdonk, notes on the work and life of Onderdonk; Lucy Runnels, "Dean of Texas Artists, Jeff Wright."
[46] The Texas Outlook, 9 (September, 1936); The Round Table (February 15, 1893).

c-11. William H. Huddle: *The Surrender of Santa Anna*

Oil, 1886, 71½" x 114" (The State Capitol, Austin, Texas)

115. Robert Jenkins Onderdonk: *The Twohig House*

Oil, 16½″ x 13½″ (Courtesy of the late Miss Eleanor Onderdonk, San Antonio, Texas)

116. Robert Jenkins Onderdonk: *View of the Old Ursuline Academy*
Oil, c. 1885, 10¾" x 14¾" (Courtesy of Mr. Henry Guerra, San Antonio, Texas)

tone scenes. On somewhat larger canvases and using richer colors he later painted such scenes as *The Old Bridge over the Trinity* (Dallas), *The Beet Garden, Field of Coreopsis, San Pedro Spring, The Cloud* (San José), and *Scene on St. Mary's Street*, all delightful reflections of his sketching and painting treks.

The income from his classes was meager; the charge per month per person was three dollars. When the invitation came from Dallas in 1889 to assist in the organization and directorship of the Art Students' League, he felt that circumstances demanded his acceptance. He was offered one hundred dollars per month for teaching, not a mean sum in those days, and with this came the privilege of maintaining a private studio. He accepted.

In February, 1893, his contract was renewed. It stipulated the length of term from October to June (summer months he was permitted to teach at the League on his own). Further, teaching hours during the term (which included almost all his waking hours), his salary, and other details were stated in an agreement signed by the president of the League, Mrs. Sidney Smith, and the artist. This contract was a milestone in the history of art in Texas.[47]

The next years were happy ones for the Onderdonks. Their weekends were full and pleasant. On Sundays, Onderdonk would take his small family of four on sketching and painting trips to the country. Late in 1896, on the death of his father-in-law, he returned to San Antonio and decided to remain. This required re-establishing himself once more in a long career of painting and teaching. With the responsibility of a family, he gave up all hope of European study. His home was now his kingdom, and in it he was almost a slave.

One venture away from San Antonio came in 1899, when he went to St. Louis on the invitation to try his hand at painting tile for the Straus Company, who wanted to experiment in painting directly on tile. But Onderdonk did not take to the craft idea; neither did he like city life.[48]

While in St. Louis he painted *View of the Mississippi at Quincy*, one of the more imposing of his works in size and subject. After painting this scene, he knew that he must return to his art.[49] Several canvases followed which remind one of the works of John Frederick Kensett (1816–1872) and Thomas Cole (1801–1848) in their quiet interpretation of nature: *On the Guadalupe, Gathering Storm*, and *Twilight on Elm Creek* (c. 18" x 24").

In their quiet, diffused glow of color they approach a poetic concept.

Some of Onderdonk's water colors show his interest in local scenes. Among these are *The Jacal, Fort San Antonio de Valero*, and *The Metate Girl*. His landscapes depicting scenes in and about San Antonio are best represented by *The Twohig House* (Plate 115), *The Grosbeck House with Terraced Garden, View of the Old Ursuline Academy* (Plate 116), *The Old Pumphouse*, and the missions: *Concepción, San José*, and the *Alamo*. In 1905 Onderdonk made a trip to New York, and no doubt he gained confidence and knowledge of the new trends in art when visiting other artists and seeing their work.

Onderdonk's interest in portraiture was not smothered by time or the interest in other types of painting, for when the opportunity came he painted portraits with substantial success. His study with Chase was now to pay off. Some of his best known portraits are those of the Honorable C. A. Culberson, Roger Q. Mills, Mrs. Floyd McGown (Plate 117), Mrs. Helen Marr Kirby, Mr. Floyd McGown, Dr. Ferdinand Herff, and Governor Joseph D. Sayers.

Onderdonk's interest in historical themes is expressed in his painting *Davy Crockett's Last Stand*. This painting (c. 36" x 48") appears to be a commission from James DeShields, who later listed its value at $400.00. The central figure of Crockett is in the act of striking down his foes, a dramatic moment at the Alamo on a morning in April, 1836. The painting expresses action and tenseness. In 1901 Onderdonk wrote to DeShields concerning a preliminary sketch:

. . . I finally decided to make a color sketch of it; though it is very roughly done and partly unfinished I send it to you as I think you can get a pretty good idea of the composition and the rush and action—"battle murder and sudden death" and etc. The grouping and lines are all made with reference to showing the overwhelming rush of the Mexicans and the determined stand of the few Americans who are rapidly being killed off by shots from the top of the building over the

47 Witte Museum, San Antonio, information on the life of Robert Onderdonk (typescript); Eleanor Onderdonk, notes on life and works of Onderdonk.

48 *Ibid.*, List of works in collection; *San Antonio Express*, January 29, 1928; *San Antonio Evening News*, February 16, 1950; *Dallas Morning News*, July 20, 1905.

49 James DeShields, Farmersville, Texas, list of paintings (holograph), February 25, 1904.

117. Robert Jenkins Onderdonk: *Mrs. Floyd McGown*
Oil, 42" x 36" (Courtesy of Mrs. Floyd McGown, Sr., San Antonio, Texas)

gateway and their charge through the entrance—I suppose you know that Crockett was not killed in the Alamo but defending the gateway of the building in the first assault.[50]

On completing the painting Onderdonk wrote (July 6, 1903) to DeShields concerning another artist's work, and commented on the historical basis of his own work:

I saw the picture of David Crockett in the *Journal*. It is an ordinary illustration, no great thought or action conveyed —also a popular version of the affair which I hope to eliminate and am striving with the daughters [Daughters of the Texas Revolution] to help me do—as I feel that without doubt I am correct in my conception, and have proof to back it up—no fairy tales or dramatic sentiment about it.[51]

During the late years of the nineteenth century there were serious recessions, which made it difficult for Onderdonk, as well as other artists, to make ends meet. Onderdonk no doubt found DeShields a friend indeed, but they did not always agree on prices. Onderdonk discovered that, after transportation costs to DeShields at Farmersville and the sales commission, little was left. In his late years straitened circumstances were particularly common.

In 1905 he complained about having to pay $25.00 on a $75.00 piece of work. However, he wrote in the same letter: "So if you will send me $52.00 and my drawing of Sam Houston (trusting you will not take the liberty of having it photographed as you did another sketch I sent you, as I consider that a breach of trust)—the only excuse is that you are probably not aware that artists consider their sketches sacred property."[52]

In this same letter he speaks rather despondently about his painting *Davy Crockett's Last Stand*: "Do this and I will send you the picture at once. If I could I would have sold the picture long ago but no one cares for historical pictures. Public buildings seem the only place for them and I hope you can dispose of it in that way to great advantage—if you do not wish to keep it."[53]

Finally in 1907 Onderdonk thanked DeShields for the last payment ($50) and said, "Now the picture is yours, lock, stock and barrel."[54] This large historical painting is now on loan by the descendants of the DeShields family to the Witte Museum, San Antonio.

Robert Onderdonk was never ambitious for public acclaim or public recognition. He was not a robust man, a fact which may account for his lack of assertiveness in putting his paintings in national exhibitions. His son Julian often chided him because of his carelessness in signing his work.

Onderdonk's paintings were never spectacular. In the last decade of his life they seem to bear a prophetic meaning for the period ahead. He did not have the difficulties in the use of light as some who went to Europe for their training. When his son was studying in New York he made a trip to see him and had glimpses of work of other artists, but actually he faced his problems in his own environment. A change toward a sort of incomplete representation was more noticeable in his later work. He gained an understanding of the poetry of color and light, of an atmospheric quality giving an effect of early morning or evening as in *Twilight on Elm Creek*, or of the weather as shown in his *Gathering Storm*, inspired perhaps by such qualities as he recognized in Inness or Corot; he had developed some of the characteristics presaging the era of the impressionists.

His work in the promotion and encouragement of the arts was an unselfish service to his community. In his pupils he was able to arouse genuine enthusiasm for painting. Though he worked from expediency, his work was always good in the craft of painting. His best work belongs chiefly to the last quarter of the nineteenth century when his quiet, unassertive personality was expressed in the rich freshness of his paintings that thus became in spirit a part of the period ahead.

[50] Letter, Robert J. Onderdonk, San Antonio, to James DeShields, Farmersville, December 17, 1901; Daughters of the Republic of Texas Library, San Antonio.

[51] *Ibid.*, July 6, 1903.

[52] *Ibid.*, June 19, 1905.

[53] *Ibid.*, June 19, 1905.

[54] *Ibid.*, June 18, 1907; Eleanor Onderdonk, notes on life and work.

APPENDIX: Little-Known Artists

Lawrence L. Cowen, Jr.

Lawrence L. Cowen, Jr., advertised in 1873: "That having removed my studio to the corner of Capitol and Milam Streets I am prepared to execute the most superior portraits in oil on canvas. Also qualified to make my own negatives for that purpose." The two leading daguerreotypists' galleries in Texas were Blessing and Co., Galveston, and H. B. Hillyer, Austin. (*Houston Daily Mercury*, November 6, 1873.)

Thurston J. Donnellan

Thurston J. Donnellan (1840–1908), a violinist as well as artist of French descent, was born in Houston, Texas, and started his art career at age eighteen. He studied in New Orleans and in Chicago. In 1875 he married Miss Jessamine Hawthorne. Donnellan's paintings, as far as is known, were never shown as a group and they have been scattered; however, some that have been mentioned from time to time are *The Fall of Babylon, The Feast of Belteshazzar, Lee's Surrender, Prayer before the Battle*, a portrait of Rubelle Nickholson, and several portraits of Sam Houston. (Information from files of Barker Library; *Houston Daily Mercury*, October 31, 1873; Walter Prescott Webb [ed.], *Handbook of Texas*, I, 513.)

Albert Fahrenberg, Sr.

The name of Albert Fahrenberg, Sr. (c. 1825–?) appears in the San Antonio City Directory of 1877–1878. *New-York Historical Society's Dictionary of Artists in America, 1564–1860*, by George C. Groce and David H. Wallace, gives the following information about Fahrenberg: "Portrait painter, native of Cologne, Germany, came to New York about 1850 and worked there as an artist and cigar maker until 1858, moved to Louisville then to New Orleans and to Texas." Only crayon portraits of this artist have been located. Crayon portraits were made of San Antonio citizens by this artist. A fine portrait of Mrs. Dorothea Kleine by Albert Fahrenberg may be seen at the Witte Museum. (Lousiana Census, 186, VII, 909.)

Mr. Ford

The following newspaper item indicates the presence of a Mr. Ford in early Washington-on-the-Brazos:

Our attention was called a few days since to some specimens of Mr. Ford's skill as an artist; and we were struck with astonishment and admiration at their accuracy and excellence. They were bust portraits of our fellow citizens, Dr. Heard, Major Scurry and their ladies. We profess to be somewhat of a judge of such things and in our opinion these are decidedly superior in accuracy of delineation, perfection of shades of color and faithfulness of expression to any effort of any artist that we have ever before seen in Texas; and we believe that we have seen specimens from all pencils of all of any note that have been here within the last seventeen years.

We do not know how long Mr. Ford designs remaining in our city but presume his stay will be measured by the extent of the patronage he may receive. Those who desire faithful and exquisitely finished portraits of themselves, families, or friends should not let the present rare opportunity slip, for they may rest assured that it will be many a day before such another will be offered to them.

(*Lone Star and Southern Watchtower*, Washington, Texas, June 26, 1852.)

William E. Henry

William E. Henry signed his portrait of Sam Houston "April 1848." If the 1850 Houston, Texas, census is correct he was a native Texan and his age was recorded as 19. The portrait, a primitive piece of work, was given by Sam Houston to his friend Matthew Cartwright, of San Augustine, Texas. The present owners are Matthew and James I. Cartwright of Terrell, Texas. (First Texas Census, 1850; information from Mrs. James Cartwright, Terrell, Texas.)

Walter Ingallis

"The undersigned respectfully announces to the citizens of San Antonio and vicinity that he has taken rooms at the Plaza House where lovers of art are invited to call and examine specimens. Persons wishing portraits, life size, of departed friends can have them painted accurately from daguerreotypes. Call and see."

Born in 1805, Walter Ingallis [Ingalls] painted portraits and still lifes, and was a scene painter. The younger brother of Gardner Ingallis, he died July 21, 1874. Walter Ingallis painted a portrait of Charles Sumner which was placed in the Senate Corridor of the United States Capitol. (Charles E. Fairman, *Art and Artists of the Capitol of the United States*; *San Antonio Daily Herald*, July 18, 1857.)

Charles Kneass

In February of 1835 Charles Kneass, of Philadelphia, advertised that he was offering "his professional services as a miniature and portrait painter." Later in the same year he announced that he had returned after an absence from Brazoria and would "wait on patrons at $12.00 and upwards—likenesses warranted." Like many of the artists of the pioneer country another business claimed part of his time, that of decorating houses, ". . . in the modern style with imitation doors and other ornamental work." Because of his early arrival in Texas he was awarded in 1839 a certificate for a half league of land in Polk and Hood Counties. Charles Kneass was thought to be the nephew of William Kneass, head of the United States Mint in Philadelphia. (*Texas Republican of Brazoria*, February 5, 1835; July 4, 1835; August 22, 1835; Land Office Files Certificates.)

Theodore Lehmann

The Houston *Morning Star* of 1839 announced the presence of German artist Theodore Lehmann. His studio was located in the building "recently occupied by the government—in the left hand passage upstairs." On June 16, 1842, William Bollaert in his *Texas* made entry that Lehmann was associated with Jefferson Wright, "who had acquired the title of Judge."

Further information in the paper states that the artist had enjoyed success in France and the United States—"an artist of reputation and standing, one sees. . . . the lips speaking, the eyes of beauty flashing and the form heaving with emotions from the canvas."

This is probably the same Theodore Lehmann who was painting in Philadelphia in 1830 and later in New Orleans. Artists of this surname reached some prominence in Europe. (*Morning Star*, Houston, December 17, 1839; January 3, 1840; January 7, 1840; William Dunlap, *History of the Rise and Progress of the Arts of Design in the United States*, III, 314; William Bollaert, *William Bollaert's Texas*, Entry, June 16, 1842.)

William Neuser

William Neuser is listed by Cline as a German immigrant artist (1837–1902), who came to New Orleans in 1855–56. A Mr. L. A. W. Neuser is listed as a portrait, landscape, and banner painter by Groce and Wallace with the same dates.

At Galveston a Mr. Neuser advertises:

Portrait and landscape painter [who] removed his studio to a convenient part of the city opens a class for drawing and painting in watercolors and oils for ladies and gentlemen. For particulars apply to his studio opposite the New Custom House between the Post Office and Church Streets. N. B. portraits of deceased or absent persons taken from ambrotypes and at the same prices as for life. Mrs. Neuser teacher of Piano Forte and Guitar.

(*Galveston News*, November 25, 1858; Isaac M. Cline, *Art and Artists of New Orleans during the Last Century*, p. 11.)

A. B. Peticolas

A. B. Peticolas came to Victoria, Texas, in 1858, joining Judge S. A. White's law firm. He served in the 4th Texas Cavalry, Company C during the Civil War. Some of the pencil sketches made during his early days in Victoria are *The Court House Square* (1862), *The Wheeler Home*, and *Victoria Hotel* (1862). (Victor M. Rose, *History of Victoria County*, p. 177.)

William Stevens

A crudely painted portrait of John S. Ford by William Stevens may be seen at the Texas State Archives. We read in the *Southern Intelligencer*, Austin, of June 1, 1859, the following announcement concerning Stevens' portrait painting:

Portraits in oil. By the assistance of a late mechanical invention the labor of portrait painting is so much diminished that the subscribers will now be able to execute for Twenty-five dollars [from] life, or from any picture you may wish copied. His work is warranted to give satisfaction and it will be his aim to act toward all "upon the plumb." Please call at his studio No. 21, Swenson's Building and examine specimens.

[signed] W. Stevens
. . . his advertisement in another column.

(*Southern Intelligencer*, June 1, 1859.)

Julius Stockfleth

Julius Stockfleth (1857–?), of Germany, came to Galveston late in the nineteenth century. A fact-finding search has resulted in the mention of his being an energetic painter of water colors and oils, and that when he was recognized as a marine painter of note he was living at 1203 Post Office Street. His *Charlotte M. Allen* in oil is now at the Samuel Williams House at Galveston. Other scenes attributed to him are *Galveston Wharf Scene, The Hurricane* (1900), *Completed Sea Wall*, and the *Judge and Mrs. William Jefferson Jones Home* at Virginia Point. Perhaps one of his most outstanding paintings (35″ x 50″) is of the sailing ship *Volun-*

C-12. Julius Stockfleth: *The Home Stretch of the* Volunteer *on the 27th of September 1887*
Oil, 1890, 35″ x 50″ (Courtesy of Mrs. K. C. ten Brink, Hopewell Junction, New York)

teer (Plate c-12). This ship was built for Charles Kellner, a cotton broker. Stockfleth has signed and dated his painting, "The Home Stretch of the 'Volunteer' on the 27th of September 1887—Julius Stockfleth, Galveston, 90." (Naturalization Papers, Galveston, Texas, III, 293; information from Mrs. Karl C. ten Brink, Hopewell Junction, New York, owner of the *Volunteer* painting.)

Mrs. S. A. Stuart

The following newspaper item tells of the presence of Mrs. S. A. Stuart in Galveston:

Mrs. S. A. Stuart from Savanah respectfully informs the ladies and gentlemen of Galveston that she has taken the house formerly occupied by the American Consul where she intends to follow her professional business of portrait painting having had considerable experience in the art. She hopes to be able to give entire satisfaction to those who may employ her. She will paint landscape, fruit, and flowers if required.

(The *Galvestonian*, April 4, 1840.)

John J. Tucker

John J. Tucker, a native Texan, held stubbornly to the idea of becoming a portraitist. When he was twenty he was apprenticed to a house painter, an experience which robbed him of much of his time. In the late 1820's young Tucker took off to Cincinnati and entered the newly organized Gallery of Fine Arts, organized by the Swedish artist Frederick Franks, a student of Dresden and Munich. While studying with Franks, Tucker received a legacy which enabled him to study in Italy. On his return he re-entered the Franks school, continuing his work in portraiture, and was mentioned as ranking with other successful members of the school, such as James and William Beard, William Powell, and Thomas B. Read. Some of Tucker's portraits were owned by Cincinnati citizens, G. N. Frankenstein, Dr. Shotwell, George Selves, and Mr. Whetstone.

In 1841 Tucker came to Texas and advertised from San Luis in Brazoria County, Texas, that his specimens of portraits might be seen at his rooms near Bennet's Hotel. When he exhibited in 1868 at Cincinnati he gave his address as Philadelphia. (*San Luis Advocate,* December 10, 1840; Edna Talbott Whitley, *Kentucky Ante-Bellum Portraiture*; Charles Cist, *Cincinnati in 1841—Its Early Annals and Future Prospects*; information from Cincinnati Art Museum, January 22, 1963; Groce and Wallace, *Dictionary of American Artists.*)

William A. Walker

William A. Walker (c. 1838–1921), an artist whose name appears in the Galveston Directory of 1876, "Corner Market and 21st r. same." He was a genre and portrait painter from Charleston, South Carolina, and Arden, North Carolina. He studied at Düsseldorf and returned to Charleston to paint. While still a young man he worked in Louisiana and Florida. Several small oil paintings, one of the Alamo (in bad condition), signed by the artist have been located. (*News and Courier*, Charleston, South Carolina, January 4, 1921; *Art News* [October, 1949]; *American Heritage* [Autumn, 1950], 55.)

SOURCES CONSULTED

Books and Articles

American Art Annual, XXI (1924–1925), 282.

Arrington, Joseph E. "Skirving's Moving Panorama: Colonel Fremont's Western Expeditions, Pictorialized," *Historical Society Quarterly* (June, 1964), 48–62.

———. "Story of Stockwell's Panorama," *Minnesota History*, XXXIII, No. 7 (Autumn, 1953), 21.

Art Digest (March 1, 1947).

Arthur, Standley Clisby. *Audubon: An Intimate Life of the Woodsman.* New Orleans: Harmanson, 1937.

Audubon, John James. *Audubon and His Journals.* Edited by Maria R. Audubon with zoological and other notes by Elliott Coues. 2 vols. New York: Charles Scribner's Sons, 1960.

———. *Bird Biographies.* Edited by Alice Ford. New York: Macmillan Co., 1957.

———. *Birds of America.* Introduction by William Vogt. New York: Macmillan Co., 1937.

———. *The Birds of America from Drawings Made in the United States and Territories.* 8 vols. New York: G. R. Lockwood and Son, c. 1870.

———. *Ornithological Biography.* 4 vols. Edinburgh: A. Black, 1831–1849.

Audubon, John Woodhouse. *Audubon's Western Journals: 1849–1850.* Cleveland: H. Clark Co., 1906.

Audubon, Lucy. *Life of John James Audubon, the Naturalist.* Introduction by James Grant Wilson. New York: G. P. Putnam Sons; London: Knickerbocker Press, 1901.

Austin, Mattie Alice. "The Municipal Government of San Fernando de Béxar, 1730, 1800," *Quarterly of the Texas Historical Association*, VIII, No. 4 (1904–1905), 293–294, 301.

Baker, William M. *Life and Labours of Reverend Daniel Baker, D.D.* Philadelphia, 1809.

Barker, Eugene C. (ed.). *The Austin Papers.* Annual Report of the American Historical Association, 1919. 3 vols. Washington, D.C.: Government Printing Office, 1924.

———. *Life of Stephen F. Austin, Founder of Texas 1793–1836.* Austin: Texas State Historical Association, 1949.

Barker, Virgil, *American Painting, History and Interpretation.* New York: Macmillan Co., 1950.

Bartlett, John R. *Personal Narrative of Explorations and Incidents in Texas, New Mexico, California, Sonora, and Chihuahua, Connected with the United States and Mexican Boundary Commission during the Years 1850, '51, '52, '53.* 2 vols. New York: D. Appleton & Co., 1854.

Barvard, John. *Geographical Panorama of the Mississippi River with the Story of Mike Fink the Last of the Boatmen, A Tale of River Life.* Boston: John Putnam, 1847.

Baudelaire, Charles. *The Mirror of Art: Critical Studies.* Translated and edited with notes and illustrations by Jonathan Mayne. London: Phaidon Press, 1955.

Baur, John I. H. *American Painting in the Nineteenth Century.* New York: Frederick A. Praeger, 1953.

———. *Unknown American Painters of the Nineteenth Century.* New York: Praeger, 1953.

Bénézit, E. *Dictionnaire—Critique et Documentaire des Peintres, Dessinateurs, Graveurs et Sculpteurs.* 37 vol. Paris: Ernest Grund Editeur, 1907–1950.

Bergstrom, Ingvar. *Dutch Still-Life Painting in the Seventeenth Century.* Translated by Christina Hedstrom and Gerald Taylor. London: Faber and Faber Limited, 1956.

Berlandier, Luis, and Rafael Chovel. *México Comisión de límites, Diario de Viage de la Comisión de límites que pusó El gobierno de la república bajo la dirección del Exmo Sr. general de división d Manuel Mier y Terán. Lo escribieron por su órden Los individuos de la misma Comisión de Luis Berlandier y d Rafael Chovel.* México: Tip. de J. R. Navarro, 1850.

Biddle, Edward, and Mantle Fielding. *Life and Works of Thomas Sully.* Philadelphia: Wickersham Press, 1921.

Biesele, Rudolph Leopold. *History of the German Settlements in Texas, 1831–1861.* Austin: Von Boeckmann-Jones, 1930.

Biographical Dictionary of the American Congress, 1774–1961. Washington, D. C.: Government Printing Office, 1961.

Bollaert, William. *William Bollaert's Texas.* Edited by W. Eugene Hollon and Ruth L. Butler. Chicago: The Newberry Library; and Norman: University of Oklahoma Press, 1956.

Bostick, Sion R. "Reminiscences of Sion R. Bostick," *Quarterly of the Texas Historical Association*, V, No. 2 (1901–1902), 85–96.

Brady, Donald V. "The Theatre in Early El Paso," *Southwestern Studies,* IV, No. 1 (1966), 1.

Brooks, Charles Mattoon, Jr. *Texas Missions—Their Romance and Architecture.* Dallas: Dealy and Lowe, 1936.

Brown, John H. *Life and Times of Henry Smith.* Dallas: A. D. Aldridge & Co., 1887.

Bryan, James P., and Walter K. Hanak. *Texas in Maps.* Austin: The University of Texas, 1961.

Bryan, M. *Bryan's Dictionary of Artists and Engravers, 1785–1824.* Edited by Geo. C. Williamson Bell. 5 vols. London: G. Bell & Sons, 1902–1905.

Bugbee, L. G. "The Old Three Hundred," *Quarterly of the Texas Historical Association,* I (1897–1898), 109.

Burkhalter, Lois. "My Real Friend Jo," *American Heritage,* XVI, No. 3 (April, 1965), 44–45.

Burroughs, Alan. *Limners and Likenesses: Three Centuries of American Painting.* Cambridge, Mass.: Harvard University Press, 1936.

Bushnell, David. *Seth Eastman, Master Painter of the North American Indian.* Smithsonian Miscellaneous Collections, Vol. 87, No. 3. Washington, D. C.: Smithsonian Institution, 1932.

Butler, Ruth Lapham. *Check List of Manuscripts in the Edward E. Ayer Collection.* Chicago: Newberry Library, 1937.

Carson, William G. B. *Managers in Distress: The St. Louis Stage (1840–1844).* St. Louis: Historical Documents Foundation, 1949.

Catlin, George. *Catlin's North American Indian Portfolio: Hunting Scenes and Amusements, Rocky Mountains and Prairies of America from Drawings and Notes of the Author George Catlin.* London: Egyptian Hall, 1841.

———. *Letters and Notes on the Manners, Customs, and Condition of the North American Indian.* 2 vols. London, 1841.

Chabot, Frederick C. *San Antonio and Its Beginning.* Comprising four members of the San Antonio Series with appendix by Fred C. Chabot. San Antonio: Artes Graficas Printing Co., 1936.

———. *San Antonio of the 17th, 18th and 19th Centuries.* San Antonio: Naylor Printing Co., 1929.

———. *With the Makers of San Antonio.* San Antonio: Artes Graficas, 1937.

Cheney, Sheldon, *A New York History of Art.* New York: The Viking Press, 1962.

Cist, Charles. *Cincinnati in 1841—Its Early Annals and Future Prospects.* Cincinnati: Charles Cist, 1841.

Cleland, Robert Glass. *This Reckless Breed of Men, the Trappers and Fur Traders of the Southwest.* New York: Alfred A. Knopf, 1950.

Clements, Clara, and Lawrence Hulton. *Artists of the Nineteenth Century.* Boston: Houghton, Osgood & Co., 1879.

Cline, Isaac M. *Art and Artists of New Orleans during the Last Century.* New Orleans, 1922.

Clopper, J. C. "Journal and Book of Memoranda for 1828, Province of Texas," *Quarterly of the Texas Historical Association,* XIII (1909–1910), 62.

Coke, Desmond. *Confessions of an Incurable Collector.* London: Chapman & Hall, 1928.

Cowdrey, Mary Bartlett. *American Academy of Fine Arts and American Art Union.* New York: New-York Historical Society, 1953.

———. *American Art Union Transactions, 1844–1849.* New York: New-York Historical Society, 1941–1943.

———. *National Academy of Design, 1849.* Vol. 1. New York: New-York Historical Society, 1941–1943.

Cullums. George W. *Biographical Register of the Officers and Graduates of United States Military Academy of West Point, N. Y.* Boston: Houghton Mifflin, 1891.

Cumberland, Charles C. "The Confederate Loss and Recapture of Galveston, 1862–1863," *Southwestern Historical Quarterly,* LI, No. 2 (October, 1947), 109–130.

Dabbs, Jack (Trans. and Ed.). "Additional Notes on Champ D'Asile," *Southwestern Historical Quarterly,* LIV (April–July, 1951), 347–358.

D'Amico, Fondata Da Silvio. *Encyclopedia Dello Spettacolo.* 5 vols. Roma: Casa editrice le Maschere, 1962.

De Voto, Bernard A. *Across the Wide Missouri.* Boston: Houghton Mifflin Co.; Cambridge: The Riverside Press, 1947.

Donaldson, Thomas. *The George Catlin Indian Gallery in the U. S. National Museum, the Smithsonian Institution, with Memoir and Statistics.* Annual Report Smithsonian Institution. Washington, D. C.: Smithsonian Institution, 1885.

Dunlap, William. *History of the Rise and Progress of the Arts of Design in the United States.* Edited by Frank W. Bagley and Charles Goodspeed. 3 vols. Boston: Goodspeed and Co., 1918.

Dwight, Edward H. "Audubon, the Artist," *Audubon Magazine* (January–February, 1963).

Eastman, Seth. *A Seth Eastman Sketchbook, 1848–1849.* Introduction by Lois Burkhalter. Austin: University of Texas Press, 1961.

Elder, Robert A., Jr. "Seth Eastman," *Art Journal,* XXI, No. 4 (Summer, 1962).

Emmit, Chris. *Texas Camel Tales.* San Antonio: Naylor Printing Co., 1932.

Emory, William H. *Report on the United States and Mexican Boundary Survey Made under the Direction of the Secretary of the Interior.* Washington, D. C. A. O. P. Nickolson, Ex. Doc. 135, 1857 U. S. 832.

Ewers, John C. *George Catlin, Painter of Indians and the West.* Smithsonian Report No. 4251. Washington, D. C.: Smithsonian Institution, 1955.

———. *Hair Pipes in Plains Indian Adornment: A Study in Indian and White Ingenuity.* Smithsonian Institution, Bureau of American Ethnology, also Anthropological Papers No. 50 from Ethnological Bulletin 164, pp. 29–85.

Exhibition of Life and Landscape of the Father of Waters. St. Louis: The Von Hoffman Press.

Fairman, Charles E. *Art and Artists of the Capitol of the United States.* Senate Document No. 169. Washington, D. C.: Government Printing Office, 1913.

Fielding, Mantle. *Dictionary of American Painters, Sculptors and Engravers.* New York: Paul A. Struck, 1906.

Flanagan, Sue. *Sam Houston's Texas.* Austin: University of Texas Press, 1964.

Flexner, James T. *America's Old Masters, First Artists of the New World.* New York: Viking Press, 1939.

————. *First Flowers of Our Wilderness, American Painting.* Boston: Houghton Mifflin, 1947.

————. *The Light in Distant Skies, 1760–1835.* New York: Harcourt, Brace Co., 1954.

————. *That Wilder Image.* Boston and Toronto: Little, Brown & Co., 1963.

Fornell, Earl Wesley. *The Galveston Era: The Texas Crescent on the Eve of Secession.* Austin: University of Texas Press, 1961.

Fowler, Harlan D. *Camels to California: A Chapter in Western Transportation.* Stanford: Stanford University Press, c. 1950.

Friend, Llerena. *Sam Houston, the Great Designer.* Austin: University of Texas Press, 1954.

Frost, J. *The Mexican War and Its Warriors.* New Haven and Philadelphia: H. Mansfield, 1850.

Galveston City Directory. 1872–1873; 1874; 1882.

Gammel, H. P. N. *Laws of Texas, 1822–1897.* 10 vols. Austin: Austin Book Co., 1898.

Gardner, Albert Ten Eyck. *Vanderlyn's Panorama of Versailles.* New York: Metropolitan Museum of Art, 1956.

Gasser, John, and Thomas Sidney (eds.). *The Nature of Art.* New York: Crown Publishers, Inc., 1964.

Geiser, Samuel W. "Audubon's Visit to Texas," *Southwest Review,* XVI (Autumn, 1930), 111.

————. *Naturalists of the Frontier.* Dallas: Southern Methodist University Press, 1937.

General Land Office. *Abstract of Valid Land Claims, Compiled from the Records of the General Land Office and Court of Claims of the State of Texas, Austin, Texas.* Austin: John Marshall & Co., *State Gazette* Office, 1859.

Gilson, Etienne. *Painting and Reality.* National Gallery of Art, Bollinger Series XXXIV, 4. New York: Pantheon, 1957.

Girard, Just. *Adventures of a French Captain.* Translated by Lady Blanche Murphy. New York: Benziger Bros., c. 1878.

Goetzmann, William H. *Army Exploration in the American West, 1803–1863.* New Haven: Yale University Press, 1959.

————. *Exploration and Empire.* New York: Knopf, 1966.

Gómara, Francisco López de. *La Historia General de las Indians.* Antwerp: En Casa de Juan Steelsio, 1554.

Gombrich, E. H. *Art and Illusion.* 2d ed. New York: Pantheon, 1961.

Gray, Andrew B. *Survey of a Route for the Southern R. R. on the 32nd Parallel, by A. B. Gray for the Texas Western R. R. Company.* Cincinnati: Wrightson and Co's. (Railroad Record), 1856.

Green, Thomas J. *Journal of the Texian Expedition against Mier. Subsequent Imprisonment of the Author, His Suffering and Final Escape from the Castle of Perote. Reflections upon the Present Political and Probable Future Relations of Texas, Mexico and the United States by General Thomas J. Green, Illustrated by Drawings Taken from Life by Charles McLaughlin a Fellow Prisoner.* New York: Harper Bros., 1845.

Groce, George C., and David H. Wallace. *New-York Historical Society's Dictionary of Artists in America, 1564–1860.* New Haven: Yale University Press; London: Oxford Press, 1957.

Gruber, Francis S. *William T. Ranney, Painter of the Early West.* Washington, D.C.: Corcoran Gallery of Art, 1962.

Gulick, Charles A., Jr., and others (eds.). *The Papers of Mirabeau Buonaparte Lamar.* 6 vols. Austin: Von Boeckmann-Jones, 1921–1927.

Gunn, Jack W. "Ben McCulloch: A Big Captain," *Southwestern Historical Quarterly,* LVIII, No. 58 (July, 1954), 17–18.

Guterman, Norbert. *Art and the Spirit of Man.* Translated from the French by Rene Huyghe. New York: Abrams, 1942.

Haberly, Loyd. *Pursuit of the Horizon: A Life of George Catlin, Painter and Recorder of the American Indian.* New York: Macmillan Co., 1948.

Hamilton, Sinclair. *Early American Book Illustrators and Wood Engravers, 1670–1870.* Princeton: Princeton University Press, 1858.

Harper's Weekly (June 15, 1860), 375, 381; (March 23, 1861), 182, 184.

Harris, Charles X. "Jacobus Gerritsen Strycker (c. 1619–1687): An Artist of New Amsterdam," *New York Historical Society. Quarterly,* X, No. 3 (October, 1926), 83–91.

Hart, Charles H. (ed.). *Register of Portraits Painted by Thomas Sully, 1801–1811.* Philadelphia, 1909.

Hasse, Adelaide R. *Reports of Explorations Printed in the Documents of the United States (1801–1871).* Washington, D.C.: Government Printing Office, 1899.

Hecke, J. V. *Reife durch die Vereinigten Staatten von Nord-Amerika, in den jahren 1820 und 1819.* 2 vol. Berlin: Von J. Val Hecke, 1820–1821.

Heilbron, Bertha L. "Documentary Panorama: John Stevens and His Sioux War Pictures," *Minnesota History,* XXX (March, 1949), 20.

Herrick, Francis Hobart. *Audubon the Naturalist: A History of His Life and Time.* 2 vols. New York and London: D. Appleton and Company, 1917.

Hogan, William Ransom. "Rampart Individualism in the Republic of Texas," *Southwestern Historical Quarterly,* XLIV (1940–1941), 459.

————. *The Texas Republic.* Norman: University of Oklahoma Press, 1946.

Horgan, Paul. *Great River: The Rio Grande in North American History.* 2 vols. New York: Holt, Rinehart & Winston; Toronto: Clarke, Irwin & Co., 1954.

Houston, Sam. *Autobiography.* Edited by Donald Day and Harry H. Ullam. Norman: University of Oklahoma Press, 1954.

————. *Writings of Sam Houston, 1813–1865.* Edited by Amelia W. Williams and Eugene C. Barker. 8 vols. Austin: University of Texas Press, 1938–1943.

Howell, Edgar M. *Herman Stieffel, Soldier Artist of the West.* United States National Museum, Bulletin No. 225. Washington, D.C.: Smithsonian Institution, 1960.

Huxley, Aldous. *On Art and Artists.* Edited and introduced by Morris Philipson. New York: Harper & Bros., Publishers, 1960.

Index of Naturalization Papers. Galveston, Texas.

Isham, Samuel. *History of American Painting.* New York: Macmillan Co., 1927.

James, Henry. *The Painters Eye—Notes and Essays on the Pictorial Arts.* Selected and edited with an introduction by John L. Sweeney. Cambridge, Mass.: Harvard University Press, 1956.

James, Marquis. *The Raven: A Biography of Sam Houston.* New York and Indianapolis: Bobbs-Merrill Co., 1929.

Joseph, Donald (trans.). *A Story of Champ d'Asile as Told by the Colonist.* Edited with an introduction by Fannie E. Ratchford. Dallas: The Book Club of Texas, c. 1937.

Journal of the House of Representatives, Fourth Legislature (1851).

Journal of the House of Representatives, Thirteenth Legislature, Regular Session (1873).

Journal of the Senate, Twentieth Legislature, Called Session (1888).

Journal of the Senate, Twenty-Second Legislature, Regular Session (1891).

Journal of the Senate, Twenty-Seventh Legislature, Regular Session (1901).

Journal of the Senate, Fortieth Legislature, Regular Session (1927).

Karolik, M. and M. *Collection of American Paintings 1815–1865.* Cambridge, Mass.: Harvard University Press, 1949.

————. *Collection of American Watercolors and Drawings, 1800–1875.* 2 vols. Boston: Museum of Fine Arts, 1962.

Kennedy, John F. "The Arts in America," *Creative America.* New York: The Ridge Press, 1962.

Lanman, Charles. *A Summer in the Wilderness.* Philadelphia: D. Appleton and Co., 1847.

Larkin, Oliver W. *Art and Life in America.* New York: Rinehart & Company, Inc., 1949.

Lee, Rebecca Smith. *Mary Austin Holley: A Biography.* Austin: University of Texas Press, 1962.

Leymarie, Jean. *The Spirit of the Letter in Painting.* Translated by James Emmons. New York: Hallmark Card, Inc., 1961. Distributed by World Publishing Co., Cleveland.

Library of Congress. *An Album of American Battle Art.* Washington, D.C.: Government Printing Office, 1947.

"The Lone Star Flies over Texas Republic," *Antiques Magazine* (June, 1948).

Mallett, Daniel Trowbridge. *Index of Artists. International-Biographical.* 2 vols. New York: R. R. Bowker Company, 1935 (Supplement 1940).

Malone, Dumas (ed.). *Dictionary of American Biography.* New York: Charles Scribner's Sons, 1932.

Malraux, Andre. *The Voices of Silence.* Translated by Stuart Gilbert. Garden City: Doubleday, 1953.

Martin, Thomas W. *French Military Adventures in Alabama, 1818–1828.* Birmingham: Birmingham Publishing Co., 1949.

McCracken, Harold. *George Catlin and the Old Frontier.* New York: The Dial Press, 1959.

————. *Portrait of the Old West.* New York: McGraw-Hill, c. 1952.

McDermott, John Francis. *The Art of Seth Eastman.* A Traveling Exhibition of Paintings and Drawings. Washington, D.C.: Smithsonian Institution, 1959–1960.

————. "Barvard's Mississippi Pamphlets," *The Papers of the Biographical Society of America,* XLIII (1949), 48–62.

————. *The Lost Panoramas of the Mississippi.* Chicago: University of Chicago Press, 1958.

————. *Seth Eastman, Pictorial Historian of the Indian.* Norman: University of Oklahoma Press, 1961.

McGann, Thomas T. "The Ordeal of Cabeza de Vaca," *American Heritage,* XII (1960), 32–35.

McGinsey, B. B., "Seth Eastman," *Southwestern Historical Quarterly,* LI (1947–1948), 32–37.

McIntire, Robert. *Martin Johnson Heade.* New York: Pantheon Press, 1948.

Mobley, James M., "The Academy Movement in Louisiana," *Louisiana Historical Quarterly* (1947), 880.

Moelling, Peter. *Reise-Skizzen in Poesie und Prosa,* Galveston: Gedruckt in der Office des *Apologeten,* c. 1857.

Möllhausen, Heinrich B. *Diary of a Journey from the Mississippi to the Coasts of the Pacific with a U.S. Government Expedition.* 2 vol. London: Longman, Brown, Green and Roberts, 1858.

Montgomery, Morton L. (comp. by). *Biographical Annals of Berks County, Pennsylvania.* 2 vols. Lancaster, Pennsylvania: Everts & Peck & Richards, 1886.

Morris, Leopold. *Pictorial History of Victoria, and Victoria County.* San Antonio: Clements Printing Company, c. 1953.

Morton, Ohland. "Life of General Don Manuel de Mier y Terán as It Affected Texas-Mexican Relations," *Southwestern Historical Quarterly,* XLVII (1943–1944), 37–38.

Mueller, Esther. "Hermann Lungkwitz and Richard Petri, Artists of Fredericksburg," Newspaper Clipping.

Muir, Andrew F. "Intellectual Climate of Houston," *Southwestern Historical Quarterly,* LXII (January, 1959), 312–321.

———— (ed.). *Texas in 1837.* Austin: University of Texas Press, 1958.

Mullins, Marian Day. *The First Census of Texas, 1829–1836.* Special Publication of the National Geneological Society No. 22 and *Texas Citizenship Lists 1821–1845* and other Records of the Republic of Texas. Washington, D.C., 1959.

Norton, A. B. *The Journal of the Texas State Convention, February 7, 1866–April 2, 1866.*

O'Brien, Esse F. *Art and Artists in Texas.* Dallas: Tardy Publishing Co., 1935.

Odell, George C. D. *Annals of the New York Stage.* 15 vols. New York: Columbia University Press, 1927–1949.

Olmsted, Frederick Law. *A Journey through Texas or a Saddle-trip on the Southwestern Frontier.* New York: Dix Edwards & Co., 1857.

Panofsky, Erwin. *Studies in Iconology: Humanistic Themes in the Art of the Renaissance.* New York: Oxford University Press, 1939.

The Panorama with Memoirs of Its Inventor, Robert Barker and His Son, the Late Henry Aston Barker. London: J. & W. Robins, 1857.

Peters, Harry. *America on Stone.* New York: Doubleday, Doran & Co., 1931.

Philadelphia City Directory. 1861.

Proctor, Ben H. *Not Without Honor: The Life of John H. Reagan.* Austin: University of Texas Press, 1962.

Raines, C. W. *A Year Book for Texas, 1901–03.* 2 vols. Austin: Gammel Publishing Co., 1902–1903.

Ramsdell, Charles. *San Antonio: A Historical and Pictorial Guide.* Austin: University of Texas Press, 1959.

Ray, Worth S. *Austin Colony Pioneers.* Austin: Privately Printed, 1949.

Reeves, Jesse Siddall. *The Napoleonic Exiles in America: A Study in American Diplomatic History, 1815–1819.* Johns Hopkins University Study Series, Vol. XXIII. Baltimore: Johns Hopkins University Press, 1905.

Reinders, Robert. *A Social History of New Orleans, 1850–1880.* New Orleans: Pelican Publishing Co., 1964.

Richardson, Edgar P. *Painting in America, the Story of 450 Years.* New York: Thomas Y. Crowell Co., 1956.

Richardson, Rupert N. *Texas, the Lone Star State.* 2d ed. Englewood Cliffs, New Jersey: Prentice Hall, 1958.

Roemer, Ferdinand. *Texas, with Particular Reference to German Immigration and Physical Appearance of the Country.* Translated by Oswald Mueller. San Antonio: Standard Printing Co., 1935.

Rose, Victor M. *History of Victoria County.* Laredo: Laredo *Daily Times* Printers, 1883.

Round Table (February, 1893).

Ruthven, A. S. *Proceedings of the Grand Lodge, 1837–1856.* Galveston: Richardson & Co., 1857.

San Antonio City Directory. 1877–1878; 1881–1882; 1887–1888.

Sánchez, José María. "A Trip to Texas in 1828" (Translated by Carlos E. Castaneda), *Southwestern Historical Quarterly,* XXIX (April, 1926), 249–250.

Sanderson, Ivan T. "A-h-h B-l-o-o-w-s," *American Heritage,* XII, No. 1 (1960), 48–49.

Santa Anna, Antonio López de. *The Mexican Side of the Texas Revolution by the Chief Mexican Participants.* Translated by Carlos E. Castañeda. Dallas: P. L. Turner Company, c. 1928.

Santleben, August. *A Texas Pioneer: Early Staging and Overland Freighting Days on the Frontier of Texas and Mexico.* Edited by I. D. Affeck. New York and Washington: The Neale Publ. Co., c. 1910.

Scharf, Thomas J. *History of St. Louis.* L. H. Everts & Co., 1883.

Schoolcraft, Henry Rowe. *Historical and Statistical Information Respecting the History, Condition and Prospects of the Indian Tribes of the United States.* 6 vols. Philadelphia: J. B. Lippincott & Co., 1851–1857.

Setton, Kenneth M. "The Norman Conquest," *The National Geographic,* CXXX, No. 2 (August, 1966), 206–251.

Sheridan, Francis C. *Galveston Island; or a Few Months off the Coast of Texas: Journal of Francis C. Sheridan 1839–1840.* Edited by Willis W. Pratt. Austin: University of Texas Press, 1954.

Smith, Henry Nash. *Virgin Land, the American West as Symbol and Myth.* Cambridge, Mass.: Harvard University Press, 1950.

Soulie, Maurice. *Autour de L'aigle Enchaine le Complot du Champ D'Asile.* Paris: Marpon & Cie, c. 1830.

Stokes, I. N., and Daniel C. Haskell. *American Historical Prints: Early Views of American Cities from the Phelps Stokes and Other Collections.* New York: Public Library, 1932.

Strange, Alexander. *The Strange Family, 1911.*

Strickland, Rex. W. "Six Who Came to El Paso," *Southwestern Studies,* VI, No. 3 (Fall, 1963), 12–15.

Strobel, Abner J. *History of Brazoria County, the Old Plantations and Their Owners of Brazoria County, Texas.* Houston: Union National Bank, 1926.

Sweet, Frederick A. *The Hudson River School, and the Early American Landscape Tradition.* Chicago: The Art Institute of Chicago; New York: Whitney Museum of American Art, 1945.

Taft, Robert. *Artists and Illustrators of the Old West, 1850–1900.* New York and London: Charles Scribner's Sons, 1953.

"Texas in Pictures," *Antiques Magazine* (June, 1948), 453–459.

Texas Outlook, IX (September, 1936).

Thieme, Ulrich, and Felix Becker. *Allgemeines Lexikon der bildenden Künstler.* 37 vol. Leipzig: E. A. Seemann, 1920.

Tiling, Moritz Philipp G. *History of the German Element in Texas from 1820–1850.* Houston: M. Tiling, 1913.

Tuckerman, Henry T. *Books of Artists: American Artist's Life.* New York: G. P. Putnam & Son; London: Sampson Low & Co., 1867 and 1870.

Turner, Frederick J. *The Frontier in American History.* New York: Holt and Company, 1920.

Underberg, Dr. Elfriede. "Herausgegeben Deutsche Literatur in Entwicklungsreihen, Reihen Politische Dichtung," *Die Dichtung der ersten deutschen, Revolution 1848–1849.* Die Universität, Ludwig A. Frankl.

Vestal, Stanley. *Joe Meek, the Merry Mountain Man.* Caldwell, Idaho: The Caxton Printers Ltd., 1952.

Victor, Mrs. Frances Fuller. *River of the West.* Columbus, Ohio: Long's College Book Co., 1950.

Von Hagen, Victor W. "Artist of the Buried World," *American Heritage,* XII, No. 4 (June, 1961), 8–19.

Warren, Harris G. *The Sword Was Their Passport: A History of American Filibustering in the Mexican Revolution.* Baton Rouge: Louisiana State University Press, 1943.

Warren, Robert Penn. *How Texas Won Her Freedom.* San Jacinto Monument, Texas: San Jacinto Museum of History, 1959.

Waugh, Julia. *Castro-Ville and Henry Castro, Empresario.* Included, "Adventures of a Castrovillian" translated from original manuscript penciled by Auguste Fretelliere. San Antonio: Standard Printing Co., 1934.

Webb, Walter Prescott. *The Great Plains.* Boston: Ginn and Company, 1931.

———— and others (eds.). *The Handbook of Texas.* 2 vols. Austin: State Historical Association, 1952.

Weitenkampf, Frank. *American Grafic Art.* New York: Henry Holt & Company, 1912.

Wheelock, Thomas B. *Journal of the Campaign of the Regiment of Dragoons.* U.S. Senate Document 2nd Sec., 23 Congress, Vol. I. Washington, D.C.: Government Printing Office, 1834.

Whiting, Daniel Powers. *Army Portfolio.* Baltimore: Lithographs by E. Weber and Co., 1847.

Whiting, William A. C. *Reports of the Secretary of War, 31st Congress.* 1st Session Document, No. 64. Washington, D.C.: Union Office, 1850.

Whitley, Edna Talbott. *Kentucky Ante-Bellum Portraiture.* National Society of Colonial Dames of the American Commonwealth of Kentucky, 1956.

Williamson, George C. (ed.). *Cyclopedia of Painters and Engravers.* London: George Bell and Sons, 1904.

Winfrey, Dorman (ed.), assisted by James Day and others. *Texas Indian Papers, 1825–1843.* Austin: Texas State Library, 1959–1961.

Yanaguana Society. *Catalogue, Loan Exhibition of Old San Antonio Paintings.* San Antonio, 1933.

Zieglschmid, A. J. F. "Pioneer Artists of Texas," *American-German Review* (October, 1942), 4–6.

————. "Richter's Sketches in the United States," *American-German Review* (February, 1943), 18–21.

Newspapers

Austin American, March 7, 1915; June 7, 1957.

Austin Statesman, July 8, 1877; November 13, 1877; March 27, 1881; November 12, 1881; January 28, 1882; November 6, 1885; September 4, 1887; May 3, 1890; September 7, 1890; March 7, 1891; March 24, 1892; October 23, 1912.

Baltimore Sun (Supplement), June 14, 1931.

City Gazette, Austin, December 4, 1839; November 4, 1840.

Civilian and Gazette, Galveston, May 17, 1839; July 24, 1842; June 1, 1844; July 8, 1865.

Colorado Tribune, Matagorda, Texas, May 29, 1852; September 4, 1853.

Daily Democratic Statesman, Austin, January 9, 1873.

Daily Herald, San Antonio, March 14, 1866; January 26, 1878.

Daily Mercury, Houston, October 21, 1873.

Daily Union, St. Louis, September 23, 1850.

Dallas Morning News, July 20, 1905; August 10, 1930; August 21, 1932.

Evening Star, Washington, D. C., June 24, 1903.

Galveston News, June 3, 1851; August 16, 1856; December 13, 1856; April 6, 1861.

Herald of Texas, Brownsville, clipping, no date.

Houston Chronicle, April 19, 1951.

Houston Post, January 6, 1921.

Lone Star and Southern Watchtower, Washington, Texas. May 10, 1851; May 24, 1851; June 7, 1851; November 15, 1851; November 17, 1851; November 22, 1851.

Long Island Star, Brooklyn, New York, August 24, 1809.

Missouri Republican, St. Louis, December 27, 1877.

Morning Star, Houston, April 29, 1841; November 8, 1842; November 10, 1842.

National Intelligencer, Washington, D. C., November 2, 1850; July 22, 1851; September 24, 1851; March 20, 1852.

Neu Braunfelser Zeitung, October 7, 1857; August 18, 1938.

New Orleans Bee, June 5, 1857; August 24, 1858.

New Orleans Bulletin, May 29, 1945.

New Orleans Crescent, June 5, 1857.

New Orleans Daily Delta, August 28, 1847.

New Orleans Daily Picayune, June 24, 1841; August 17, 1841; August 12, 1842; November 3, 1842; December 25, 1842; November 24, 1849; November 27, 1849; November 28, 1849; March 3, 1852; March 6, 1852; March 7, 1852; March 10, 1852; April 30, 1852; May 1, 1852 (Saturday Evening Edition).

New York Sun, April 2, 1846.

New York Times, November 21, 1857; May 22, 1877; August 27, 1924.

Philadelphia Press, January 29, 1877.

The Republic, St. Louis, February 28, 1897.

Republican, New York City, September 20, 1840.

Richmond Reporter, Richmond, Texas, July 12, 1856.

Richmond Standard, Richmond, Virginia, March 27, 1880.

San Antonio Campaign News, September 22, 1888.

San Antonio Evening Light, March 3, 1882.

San Antonio Evening News, February 16, 1950.

San Antonio Express, February 20, 1849; May 24, 1866; November 10, 1875; November 11, 1875; November 20, 1875; February 21, 1882; February 28, 1882; March 3, 1882; March 7, 1882; May 10, 1888; May 13, 1888; May

19, 1888; November 8, 1902; May 12, 1907; March 22, 1922; April 8, 1922; July 8–29, 1923; January 29, 1928; December 18, 1932; April 15, 1934; June 14, 1936; April 20, 1948; August 5, 1951; September 16, 1962.

San Antonio Herald, January 1, 1857; September 12, 1857; October 16, 1857; July, 1858 (date incomplete), May 8, 1860; January 26, 1878; February 16, 1950.

San Antonio Ledger, October 10, 1850.

San Antonio Light, November 23, 1944; February 22, 1946.

Saturday Night, Los Angeles, December 29, 1928.

Semi-Weekly Creole, New Orleans, February 1, 1860.

Southern Intelligencer, Austin, October 21, 1857.

Telegraph and Texas Register, Columbia, August 2, 1836.

Telegraph and Texas Register, Houston, April 28, 1837; April 29, 1837; May 2, 1837; May 9, 1837; May 25, 1837; June 3, 1837; October 7, 1837; October 11, 1837; October 18, 1837; November 25, 1837; December 16, 1837; February 17, 1838; March 3, 1838; March 17, 1838; March 31, 1838; April 14, 1838; June 11, 1838; June 16, 1838; August 4, 1838; November 18, 1840; November 20, 1840; February 24, 1841; April 8, 1841; April 28, 1841; June 2, 1841; March 9, 1842; June 15, 1842; October 19, 1842; June 21, 1843; April 6, 1845; May 21, 1845; June 4, 1845; June 18, 1845.

Texas Banner, Huntsville, October 20, 1849.

Texas Republican, Marshall, October 11, 1849; January 3, 1850; March 7, 1850; May 17, 1851; January 24, 1852; June 6, 1852.

Texas State Gazette, Austin, August 30, 1851; October 29, 1851; December 6, 1851; February 14, 1852; March 6, 1852; May 17, 1856; January 8, 1859.

Tri-Weekly State Gazette, Austin, August 30, 1851; October 29, 1851; November 1, 1851; December 6, 1851; February 14, 1852; March 6, 1852; July 30, 1853; May 17, 1856; January 8, 1859.

Tri-Weekly Telegraph, Houston, May 20, 1863; June 26, 1863; July 13, 1863; July 24, 1863.

Washington Post, Washington, D. C., April 17, 1892; May 9, 1905.

The Weekly Journal, Galveston, Texas, May 25, 1851; June 16, 1851.

Manuscripts and Letters

[*Note: All letters to the author (starred items) will be deposited with the Amon Carter Museum of Western Art, Fort Worth, Texas, after the publication of this volume.*]

Andrews, Ambrose, Great Barrington, Massachusetts, to Philip Schuyler. April 8, 1825. New York Historical Society, New York City.

Art Student's League. "Constitution and By-Laws," June 2, 1875.

Asbury, Samuel E., Bryan, Texas, to E. Winkler, Austin. Texas State Archives, Austin.

Asbury Papers. Texas State Archives, Austin.

Augustus Stern House Library, San Augustine, Texas. List of work of Stephen Seymour Thomas (typescript).

Ayer Collection, Chicago Historical Society, Chicago, Illinois.

Baker, Dr. L. W., to S. M. Swenson, Austin, March 9, 1852. The University of Texas Archives, Austin.

*Baldwin, Mrs. F. T., Houston, Texas. February 28, 1962; July 23, 1962. Enclosed copy of Behné's letter (copy) to Governor A. J. Hamilton, March 31, 1886.

Behné, Gustavus Augustus, Galveston, Texas, to A. J. Hamilton, Austin. March 31, 1866. Collection of Mrs. F. T. Baldwin, Houston, Texas.

*Benedict, Mother M., Corpus Christi, Texas. January 6, 1965. Concerning Eugenie Aubanel Lavender.

Bingham, Charles, American Antiquarian Society, Boston, to Taylor, Metropolitan Museum, New York City. September 22, 1932. New York Public Library, New York City.

[Borremeo, Sister]. "Biographical notes on Eugenie Aubanel Lavender." Barker Library, The University of Texas, Austin.

Bounty Warrants, Military Service Records. General Land Office, Austin, Texas.

Bryan, Guy M., Quintana, Texas, to Mrs. S. M. W. Compton, San Antonio, Texas. August 20, 1891. The University of Texas Archives, Austin.

Castro, Henri, Castroville, Texas, to Anson Jones. September 1, 1844. Castro Papers. Texas State Archives, Austin.

Catlin, George, Paris, France, to Sir Thomas Phillips. Original Letters, 1840–1860. Thomas Gilcrease Institute of American History and Art, Tulsa, Oklahoma.

*Catterall, Mrs. Ralph, Valentine Museum, Richmond, Virginia. October 4, 1962.

Century of Progress International Exposition (catalogue). Chicago, Illinois, 1933.

Chadwick Family Letters. Collection of Austin D. Kilham, Charlottesville, Virginia.

*Clarke, Mrs. Gay Thompson, New Orleans, Louisiana. May 8, 1959; May 15, 1959; May 27, 1959; August 20, 1959. Concerning Thomas Jefferson Wright.

*Clift, G. Glenn, Kentucky Historical Society, Louisville, Kentucky. June 4, 1963.

Crane, William Cary, Independence, Texas, to Governor E. J. Davis, Austin. January 27, 1873. Governor's Letters. Texas State Archives, Austin.

Cupples, George. "Henry Castro Papers, 1836–1846." Texas State Archives, Austin.

*Daiker, Virginia, Art Division, Library of Congress, Washington, D. C. August 17, 1964. Concerning Texas Prints.

Dallas Museum of Fine Arts. Dallas Texas.

Daughters of the Republic of Texas Library. San Antonio, Texas.

Deas, George, San Antonio, Texas, to Governor Hansborough Bell, Austin. January 14, 1850. Governor's Letters. Texas State Archives, Austin.

DeShields, James, Farmersville, Texas. List of paintings in his possession (holograph).

Donaldson, Andrew J., to Miller. July 27, 1845. Miller Papers. Texas State Archives, Austin.

Eastman, Seth. Diary, August 1846–August, 1849 (original copy). Paul Adams, San Antonio, Texas.

*Edsall, Mrs. Katherine B., Peabody Museum, Harvard University, Cambridge, Massachusetts. October 3, 17, 27, 1960. Enclosed list of Seth Eastman's drawings.

Elmendorf, Mary S. "Our Ancestors." Genealogical notes on Wueste Family. In possession of author.

*Ewers, John C., Washington, D. C. August 13 and 20, 1963. Concerning Catlin in Texas.

"Exhibition of 18th and 19th Century American Paintings from Lynchburg Homes." Randolph-Macon Women's College, Lynchburg, Virginia. 1954.

Eyth, Louis, Galveston, Texas, to Ashbel Smith, Hogg Island. January 23, 1873. Governor's Letters. Texas State Archives, Austin.

———, Galveston, Texas, to Governor's Committee. January 23, 1873. Governor's Letters. Texas State Archives, Austin.

———, Galveston, Texas, to Governor E. J. Davis, Austin. January 23, 1873. Governor's Letters. Texas State Archives, Austin.

*Field, Mrs. Ruth F., Missouri Historical Society, St. Louis. March 5, 1964.

*Freely, John A., Victoria Public Library, Melbourne, Australia. February 16, 1959.

General Land Office Records (Texas). General Land Office, Austin.

Gentilz, Theodore. Business Card in possession of author.

———. List of His Paintings, 1888 (Holograph). Daughters of the Republic of Texas Library, San Antonio, Texas.

———. Map of Mexico, revised and corrected by Lorenzo Castro. Texas State Archives, Austin.

———. "A Method of Perspective for Artists" (Holograph). Under litigation, San Antonio, Texas.

*Haas, Oscar, New Braunfels, Texas. Enclosed copy of letter to F. C. Humphrey from Controller's Office Records, Austin, concerning Iwonski.

Hamilton, A. J., Austin, to Mrs. Sam Houston, Huntsville, Texas. March 31, 1866. Hamilton to Mrs. Sam Houston, Independence, Texas. April 16, 1866. Governor's Letters. Texas State Archives, Austin.

*Hogg, Miss Ima, Houston. April 6, 1961. Enclosed information from Mrs. Katherine Evans, Galveston.

Holley, Mary Austin, to Mrs. Brand. December 30, 1837. Mary Austin Holley Papers. The University of Texas Archives, Austin.

Houston, Sam. May 7, 1849. Enclosed article from *Texas Republican*, Marshall, Texas, January 24, 1852. Houston's Letters. The University of Texas Archives, Austin.

Houston, Mrs. Sam, Huntsville, Texas, to Sam Houston, Washington, D. C. January 28, 1850. Houston's Letters. The University of Texas Archives, Austin.

*Howell, Mrs. Henry W., Frick Reference Library, New York City. October 17, 1957; October 27, 1959; March 11, 1960.

Huddle, William H., Munich, Germany, to Miss Carver, Austin. October 24, 1884; February 9, 1885. Collection of Mrs. Margarite Huddle Slaughter, Austin.

Huddle, Mrs. William H. List of paintings, artist's work, and biographical notes (typescript). Collection of Mrs. Margarite Huddle Slaughter, Austin.

Indian Papers, 1838. Texas State Archives, Austin.

Iwonski, Carlos, El Paso, Texas, to Daughters of the Republic of Texas Library, San Antonio. October 12, 1940.

James Jerome Hill Reference Library, St. Paul, Minnesota. List of drawings by Seth Eastman.

Jouett, Matthew, Fayette County, Kentucky, to Thomas Sully. November 12, 1822. Philadelphia Academy of Art, Philadelphia, Pennsylvania.

*Kilham, Austin D., Charlottesville, Virginia. June 29, 1966; August 11, 1966.

*Kuehne, Richard E., West Point, New York. January 27, 1966.

"List of Paintings of Mrs. Eugenie Aubanel Lavender." LaRetama Library, Corpus Christi. No date.

Lungkwitz, Hermann, Wheeling, West Virginia, to Adolph Lungkwitz, New York City. March 8, 1951. Collection of Ernest von Rosenberg, Austin.

*Lungren, Mrs. Charles, Lancaster County Historical Society, Lancaster, Pennsylvania. February 16, 1962.

McArdle, Henry, Independence, Texas, to D. A. Woodward. August 29, 1889. Governor's Letters. Texas State Archives, Austin.

———, Independence, Texas, to D. A. Woodward, Baltimore. Daughters of the Republic of Texas Library. San Antonio, Texas.

———, San Antonio, Texas, to James DeShields, Farmersville, Texas. March 13, 1906. Daughters of the Republic of Texas Library. San Antonio, Texas.

———. "List of Paintings." 1904. Daughters of the Republic of Texas Library. San Antonio, Texas.

———. Notes on Sam Houston. Author's Collection.

———. Scrapbook of Notes and Biographical Information (Holograph). Texas State Archives, Austin.

Meyers, Mae Estelle. "Lives and Works of Hermann Lungkwitz and Richard Petri," M.A. Thesis, The University of Texas, 1936.

*Moore, Mrs. Vivian, Harrodsburg, Kentucky. November 20, 1959; February 22, 1960.

Morfi, Father Juan Agustín. "Memorias para la Historia de Texas." Library of Congress, Washington, D. C.

Muster Rolls. General Land Office Records. General Land Office, Austin.

Naturalization Papers. District Court. New Braunfels, Texas. 1854.

Nimitz Hotel Register. Fredericksburg, Texas. 1853.

*Norton, R. W., Norton Museum of Art, Shreveport, Louisiana. May 5, 1962; March 13, 1963; June 17, 1963. Concerning Guillaume.

Onderdonk, Eleanor. Notes on life and work of Robert Onderdonk. In possession of author.

Onderdonk, Robert, San Antonio, Texas, to James DeShields,
Farmersville, Texas. June 18, 1907; December 17, 1901;
July 6, 1903; January 17, 1905; June 19, 1905. Daughters
of the Republic of Texas Library. San Antonio, Texas.

Onderdonk, Mrs. Robert, San Antonio, Texas, to James De-
Shields, Farmersville, Texas. December 17, 1901; July 6,
1903; January 17, 1905; June 19, 1905; June 18, 1907.
Daughters of the Republic of Texas Library. San Antonio,
Texas.

*Pitts, Mrs. Kate Duval, Providence, Rhode Island. May 16,
1962; July 20, 1962; August 25, 1962; September 21,
1963.

*Ranney, Claude J. M., Malvern, Pennsylvania. April 21,
1960; September 22, 1960; July 29, 1961.

Ranney, William. Business Card. Collection of Claude J. M.
Ranney, Malvern, Pennsylvania.

Reily, J., Nacogdoches, Texas, to Colonel Raquet, Nacogdoches. November 20, 1838. The University of Texas
Archives, Austin.

Richter, Ludwig, Germany, to Hermann Lungkwitz, Austin.
c. 1857. Collection of Ernest von Rosenberg, Austin.

Roberts, Governor Oran, Austin, to Stephen Seymour
Thomas, San Augustine, Texas. December 23, 1880. E.
Cullen House Library. San Augustine, Texas.

Sánchez y Tapia, José María and others. Sketchbook of a
trip to Texas, 1827–1828. Thomas Gilcrease Institute of
American History and Art, Tulsa, Oklahoma.

*Sias, Mrs. Paul, Bucks County Historical Society, Doyles-
town, Pennsylvania. January 8, 1964.

Smith, Ashbel, Brenham, Texas, to J. B. Robertson, Houston.
January 3, 1873. Governor's Letters. Texas State Archives,
Austin.

*Smith, Dr. Hubbard W., Greely, Colorado. March 6, 1960.

*Smith, J. Lyle, Waurika, Oklahoma. November 30, 1955.

Smith, Lucy C., Huntsville, Texas, notes on Thomas Jefferson Wright in possession of Mr. Robert Hanman, Austin.

Sophienburg Museum, New Braunfels, Texas.

*Stephenson, B. Collinwood, Laing Art Museum, New-
castle-upon-Tyne, England. June 17, 1960.

*Stout, Mrs. Bruce, Fort Wayne, Indiana. May 18, 1960;
Franklin, Indiana, April 10, 1963.

Swenson, S. M., Austin, to William S. Pierson, New York.
March 13, 1854. The University of Texas Archives, Austin.

Thomas, Stephen Seymour, San Antonio, Texas, to Mr. Morris, Philadelphia, Pennsylvania. December 7, 1894. Fine
Arts Academy, Philadelphia.

————. Notes on, by Mrs. Jean Haskell (daughter). E. Cullen House Library, San Augustine, Texas.

*Todd, Frederick, West Point, New York. March 4, 1965.

"Two Pioneer Texas Artists." University of Texas Exhibition
List and Biographical Notes. Austin, April 13–15, 1934.
Author's Collection.

*Tylor, Mrs. Stella, San Antonio, Texas. January 14, 1962.

Van Harten, E., Galveston Texas, to Ashbel Smith, Austin.
January 27, 1873. Governor's Letters, Texas State Archives, Austin.

*Watlington, H. Stirling, New York City. June 21, 1964.

Webb, J. Watson, Petrópolis, Brazil, to Emperor Don Pedro
II, of Brazil. February 20, 1884. Collection of Mrs. Howard Houseley, Lumberville, Pennsylvania.

Wharton, Thomas. Diary (Micro-film). Barker Library. The
University of Texas, Austin. Original in New York City
Public Library.

Witte Museum. San Antonio, Texas.

Wood, W. G., Galveston, Texas, to Ashbel Smith, Independence, Texas. January 27, 1873. Daughters of the Republic
of Texas Library, San Antonio, Texas.

Woodward, D. A., Baltimore, Maryland, to McArdle, Inde-
pendence, Texas. August 29, 1889; October 20, 1890;
February 19, 1896. Daughters of the Republic of Texas
Library. San Antonio, Texas.

Interviews

Baldwin, Mrs. F. T. (Houston, Texas), concerning the Sam
Houston portraits.

Bell, Mrs. Paul (Houston, Texas), concerning the McArdle
portraits.

Bryan, J. P. (Jackson Park, Texas), concerning the Austin
portrait.

Butterfield, J. C. (San Antonio, Texas), concerning the
Lily Carolon portrait by Iwonski.

Cook, Mrs. Raymond (Houston, Texas), owner of the
George Catlin portrait of Austin.

Fretelliere, Olin (San Antonio, Texas), concerning Gentilz'
work.

Groves, W. E. (New Orleans, Louisiana), concerning Pomarède (by telephone).

Hanman, Mrs. Robert (Austin, Texas), concerning Thomas
Jefferson Wright.

Head, Mrs. W. P. (Terrell, Texas), custodian of the Henry
portrait of Houston.

Hogg, Miss Ima (Houston, Texas), concerning the Flintoff
portrait of the Jones children.

Jones, Mrs. Marian (Austin, Texas), concerning Grenet's
work.

Murray, Mrs. Emily G. (San Antonio, Texas), concerning
the portraits of Mrs. Lavender.

Onderdonk, Miss Eleanor (San Antonio, Texas), concerning her father's work.

Pitts, Mrs. Kate Duval (Providence, Rhode Island), concerning her mother's life.

Ramella, Mrs. Louis (Austin, Texas), concerning the Iwonski portrait of the Schenk sisters.

Schenk, Mrs. B. W. (Austin, Texas), concerning the work
of Petri and Lungkwitz.

Schuchard, Ernst (San Antonio, Texas), concerning the work
of Carl Schuchard.

Slaughter, Mrs. Margaret (Austin, Texas), concerning the Huddle portraits.

ten Brink, Mrs. Karl C. (Hopewell Junction, New York), owner of the Stockfleth ship painting.

Vines, Mrs. Ida H. (Dallas, Texas), concerning the work of Ida W. Hadra.

Von Rosenberg, Ernest (Austin, Texas), concerning the work of Petri and Lungkwitz.

Walker, Ganahl (San Antonio, Texas), owner of the Iwonski still life.

Westervelt, Mrs. V. O. (San Antonio, Texas), concerning the Indian portraits of Iwonski.

Wupperman, Mrs. Walter (Austin, Texas), concerning the work of Petri and Lungkwitz.

INDEX

Italicized page numbers indicate illustrations

Abbie Chambers, by Flintoff: 57, *61*
Academie Julien (Paris): 169
Academy of Design (New York City): 29
Adams, Hardin B.: 129
Adelina Staffel, by Wueste: 121
Adelina Wueste Staffel, by Wueste: 118, *119*
Adkins, Judge George, Building: 69
Adolph Lungkwitz, by Petri: 79
Adoration of the Kings and Shepherds, by
  Petri: 77
Advice on the Prairie, by Ranney: 43
Agua Dulce, Texas: 122
Aguayo, Marquis de: 31
"Aigleville": 12
Akademie de Bildenden Künste (Dresden):
  75, 87
Alamán, Lucas: 6
Alameda, San Antonio, The, by Lungkwitz:
  89, *92*
Alamo, the: battle of, 39, 69, 108, 188, 189,
  190, 192–193, 202, 207–209; appear-
  ance of, 103; paintings of, 108, 151,
  188, 189, 190, 192–193, 207, 213; as
  warehouse, 174–175; mention of, 105
Alamo, The, by Gentilz: 108
Alamo, by Onderdonk: 207
Allen, Annie G.: 185
Allen, George R.: 23–27, 74
Allen, Thomas, Jr.: 179–185
Allen, Thomas, Sr.: 185
Almonte, Juan N.: 9, 10
American Academy of Art (New York
  City): 34, 163
American Antelope, by Schuchard: 167
American Art Union (New York City): 29,
  39, 50
American Art Union (Texas): 56, 97
American Institute (New York City): 29
American Panorama of the Nile: 71
American Society of Artists: 185
American Water Color Society: 163
Andreas, Professor: 185
Andrews, Ambrose: 17, 27–29, 74
Andrews, Mrs. Ambrose: 28
Andrews, Elijah: 27
Andrews, Mary Ann Stone: 27
Annals of the New York Stage: 72
Army of the Potomac: 164
Army Portfolio, The: 151
*Art and Artists of the Capitol of the United
  States:* 55
Artists of the Old West: 165
Art Students' League (Dallas): 207
Art Students' League (New York City):
  169, 196, 204
Ashe, Mr. ———: 18
Aubanel, General ———: 97
Aubanel, Etienne: 97
Aubanel, Julienne Antoinette Fortin: 97
Audion, Captain ———: 99
Audubon, John James: 43–49
Audubon, John Woodhouse: 44, 48–49, 163
Audubon, Lucy Bakewell: 44

Audubon, Maria: 49
Audubon, Victor: 49
Audubon College: 98
Austin, Stephen F.: 4–6, 7–9, 32, 33, 63, 64,
  68, 187, 188, 195
Austin, Texas: painters in, 63, 88, 91, 142,
  148, 154, 177, 196, 201, 202; pictures
  of, *149, 151, 155, 177, 179, 180, 199;*
  mention of, 48, 65, 72, 136, 168, 174,
  188, 190, 211
Austin College: 63
Austin colony: 6, 9, 10, 194, 195
Autocrat of the Breakfast Table: 159
Avenue of Trees, by Thomas: 169

Bachman, John: 44
Bagby, Thomas M.: 21
Bahr, Gezeicht von C. O.: 153
Baird, Spencer F.: 48, 161
Baker, the Reverend Daniel: 63
Baker, Dr. L. W.: 72
Baker, William M.: 63
Balzac, Jean Louis: 11
Banvard, John: 50, 70–71
Barbier, Jules: 98
Barilleros, San Felipe, by Gentilz: 110, *111*
Barker, Henry Aston: 70
Barker, Robert: 69–70
Barnum, P. T.: 72
Bartlett, John Russell: 155, 156, 157, 159,
  160
Barton's Creek, by Lungkwitz: 91
Bass, Sam: 186
Bastrop, Baron de: 195
Bastrop, Texas: 155
Batterson, Isaac: 46
Battle of Chapultepec, by Walker: 193
Battle of Galveston, The, by Moelling: 68,
  73
Battle of Genappe: 72
Battle of Gettysburg, by Walker: 193
Battle of Gettysburg, The, by Philippoteaux:
  72
Battle of Lake Erie, The, by Garneray: 12
Battle of Plum Creek, by Eyth: 188
Battle of San Jacinto, The, by Guillaume:
  144, *146*
Battle of San Jacinto, by McArdle: opp. 188,
  193
Battle of Trafalgar, by Barker: 70
Battle of Waterloo, The: 72
Battles of the Crimea: 72
Baudelaire, Charles: 97
Baur, John: 179
Bayeux Tapestry: 69
Baylor College: 193
Baylor Female College: 190
Bean, Ellis Peter: 9
Beard, James: 213
Beard, William: 213
Beckmann, Johann Conrad: 174
Beckwith, James Carroll: 204

Bee children: 121
Beet Garden, The, by Onderdonk: 207
Beethoven Männerchor: 153
Beggar Boy, by Wueste: 121
Behné, (Gustavus) Augustus: 141–145
Behné, Julia Meyer Keim: 142
Behr, Dr. Norman: 79
Behr, Ottomar von: 79
Bell, Samuel: 136
Bell Silversmith Shop (San Antonio): 89
Belton, Texas: 155
Ben Milam Calling for Volunteers, by Mc-
  Ardle: 195
Bennett, ———: 56
Benton, James G.: 68, 69
Beowulf Slaying the Dragon, by Petri: 75
Berlandier, Jean Louis: 6, 7
Bexar County Courthouse: 30–31
Bierstadt, Albert: 43, 86
Big Bend country: 105
Big Thicket, the: 65
Big Tree, by Gentilz: 117
Bingham, George Caleb: 43
*Birds-eye View of the Camp of the Army of
  Occupation,* by Whiting: *151,* 152
Birds of America, The: 49
*Bivouac of Confederate Troops on the Las
  Moras, Texas,* by Iwonski: *133,* 136
Blanco River: 53
Blessing and Company: 188, 211
Bodmer, Karl: 86
Bollaert, William: 21, 212
Bonaparte, Joseph: 11
Bonheur, Marie Rosalie: 97
Bonnell, George: 18, 91
Bononi, Joseph: 71
Book of Artists: 40
Boone, Daniel: 6
Borden, Gail: 149
Boston Art Club: 185
Boston Museum of Fine Arts: 185
Bouquereau, Adolphe William: 177
Bouve and Sharp: 163
Bowie, James: 188, 189
Bowles, Chief: 21, 63
Brackenridge, George: 169
Bracket, Texas: 105
Brady, Matthew: 23
Brazoria, Texas: 212
Brazoria County, Texas: 213
Brazos County, Texas: 10
Brazos River: 4, 7, 10, 38, 68, 186
Brenham, Texas: 193
Brentano, Lorenz: 75
Bretannia (ship): 163
Bridge at Linnengen, The, by T. Allen: 185
Bridge over the Seine River, by Thomas: 169
Bridge over the San Antonio River, by
  Gentilz: 105
Bridge over the San Antonio River, by
  Hadra: 179, *181*
Brooks, W. T. H.: 54
Brossius, H.: 155

225

Brown, William Mason: 40
Brownsville, Texas: 98, 164
Brownsville, Texas, by Weyss: 164, *165*
Bryan, Beauregard: 193
Bryan, Guy Morrison: 4, 6, 62, 63, 138
Bryan, Mary Angelica: 57, 59
Bryan, Moses Austin: 190, 191
Bryan, Pryor M.: 57, 58
Buckmaster, Mrs. ———: 172
Buffalo Bayou: 46, 47, 48
Buffalo Camp Yard (San Antonio): 103
Bufford, J. H.: 6
Bullock's Tavern (Austin): 151
Bunyan Tableau, The: 72
Bureau of Indian Affairs: 50
Burleson, Edward: 63, 65, 68, 89, 193
Burleson, Rufus C.: 68, 195
Burnet, David G.: 141, 188
Burt, Charles K.: 4, 5
Business Card, of Gentilz: 117
Bustamante, Anastasio: 6
Butterfield, Lily Carolon: 177

Cabeza de Vaca, Álvar Núñez: 3
"Cactaceæ of the Boundary": 164
Cactus, by Roetter: 165, *166*
Caddo Indians: 9, 52, 79
Calles, Plutarco Elías: 105
Camel Ride, The, by Gentilz: *104,* 105
Camino Real: 6
Campbell (schooner): 44
Camp of the Lipans, by Gentilz: 117
Camp Verde, Texas: 105
Canary Islanders: 31
Candelaria, Andrea Castanon de Villanueva: 103, 202
Candle Seller, The, by Gentilz: 105
Capture of the Harriet Lane, *The,* by Moelling: 73
Carauchua Indians: 195
Carbould, ———: 71
Carlshafen (Indianola), Texas: 122
Caro, Ramos: 10
Carolon, George: 177
Carolon, Lily: 129, 131, 176, 177
Carousel, The, by Behné: 142
Carré, Michel: 98
Cartwright, James I.: 211
Cartwright, Matthew (San Augustine, Texas): 211
Cartwright, Matthew (Terrell, Texas): 211
Carrying Water from a Stream, by Petri: 86
Carver, Mrs. ———: 202
Cass, Louis: 34
Castanola, Margarita: 177
Castro, Henri: 99, 100, 101
Castroville, Texas: 99, 100, 101–102, 108, 116, 177
Catherwood, Frederick: 70
Catlin, Clara Bartlett Gregory: 32, 34
Catlin, George: 31–39, 41, 43, 49
Catlin, Polly Sutton: 32
Catlin, Putman: 32
Cavit, Mrs. Alexander: 6
"Cedar Point" (Houston's home): 136
Cerro Gordo, Battle of: 151
Chadwick, Edward: 36
Chadwick, Joe: 35–36, 37
Chalkley, Dr. Thomas: 21

Chambers, Abbie Chubb: 57, 61
Chambers, Thomas Jefferson: 57, 60, 63
Chambonde de la Rouviere, Count: 97
Champ d'Asile: 11, 12–13
Champs Elysees Salon (Paris): 169
Chapel Hill, Texas: 73
Charlotte M. Allen, by Stockfleth: 212
Chase, William Merritt: 204, 207
Chemical Engraving Company: 159
Cheraquis, by L. and J. M. Sánchez y Tapia: *8, 9*
Cherokee Indians: 8, 9, 21, 63
Chialiv, Luigi: 185
Chihuahua, Army of: 30
Child Peeping through the Fence, by Grenet: 177
Chovell, Ralph: 7
Christ Entering Jerusalem, by Petri: 77
Christian Apologist: 73
Church at El Paso del Norte, by Pratt: *158*
Churchill, J. E.: 56–57
Cíbola, Seven Cities of: 3
Cincinnati, Texas: 15
City Art Museum (St. Louis): 72
Civil War: painters during, 30, 118, 122, 125, 145, 151, 164, 190, 212; paintings of, 72, 136; period before, 88–89, 141, 172; mention of, 142, 147, 154, 204
Civil War, by Philippoteaux: 72
Clark, William: 34
Clarke, Sir William J.: 68
Clay, Henry: 29
Clay, Thomas C.: 193
Clift and Road, by Lungkwitz: 88
Clinton, DeWitt: 34
Clinton, Texas: 46
Cloud, The, by Onderdonk: 207
Coast Scene with Figures, by Ranney: 39
"Co-Co-Pas" Indians: 163
Coke, Richard: 186
Cole, Thomas: 89, 97, 157, 207
Coll, Margarita: 177
Colorado Tribune: 56
Columbia, Texas: 10, 39
Columbian Exposition: 185
Columbus, Texas: 65
Comanche Chief, by Gentilz: *114,* 116
Comanche Indians: descriptions of, 9, 47, 53; raids by, 15, 89, 98; pictures of, 32, 35, 36, 54, 83, 114, 116, 117; travels among, 34–36, 54, 79; mention of, 18, 44, 105
Comanches on the March, by Gentilz: *116,* 117
Comanche War Party on the March Fully Equipped for War, Texas, by Catlin: 32, *opp. 36*
Completed Sea Wall, by Stockfleth: 212
Compton, Mrs. S. M. W.: 4, 6
Concepción, by Gentilz: 108
Concepción, by Onderdonk: 207
Concepción Mission: 69, 108, 151, 207
Convention Hall (Austin): 136
Cooper, James Fenimore: 163
Cordova, Battle of: 10
Coronado, Francisco Vásquez de: 3
Corot, Jean: 209
Corpus Christi, Texas: 48, 65, 68, 69, 98, 99, 152

Correggio, Antonio: 98
Cos, Martín: 10
Cotten, Goodwin B.: 195
Council House Fight: 54
Course of Instruction in Ordnance and Gunnery for Use of Cadets of the United States Military Academy, A: 68
Courtenay, T. E.: 71, 72
Courting Scene, A, by Ranney: 39
Covered Wagon, The, by T. Allen: 185
Cowen, Lawrence L., Jr.: 211
Crane, Dr. Cary: 193, 195
Creation, by C. L. Smith: 69
Creation and Deluge, The: 72
Criesman, Horation: 195
Crockett, David: 193, 203, 207, 209
Crockett Street, by Lungkwitz: 91
Crossing the Nueces River, Texas, by Eastman: 54
Crucifixion, The, by Lavender: 99
Crucifixion, The, by Petri: 77
Crusader (cutter): 44
Culberson, C. A.: 207

Dabney, Robert Louis: 145
Daguerre, Louis Mandé: 70
Daily Democratic Statesman: 154
Dallas, Texas: 188, 203, 207
Dallas Art League: 203
Damon and Pythias: 69
Dance of the Braves, A, by Eastman: 50
David, Jacques Louis: 43
David Crockett, by Huddle: 203
Davis, Edmund J.: 177, 186, 188, 193
Davis, Jefferson: 105, 190, 193
Davis Mountains: 105
Davy Crockett's Last Stand, by Onderdonk: 207, 209
Dawn at the Alamo, by McArdle: 190, *192,* 193
Deas, Charles: 32, 39
Deas, George: 32
Deaf Smith Announcing the Destruction of Vince's Bridge, by McArdle: 195
Death of Bowie: A Command from the Mexicans that He Be Killed, by Eyth: 188, *189*
De Candolle, Augustin Pyrame: 7
Deems, Dr. and Mrs. Charles: 172
Deer in the Pedernales, by Lungkwitz: 91, *95*
Delaroche, Paul: 97, 98, 145
Delaware Indians: 53
Denison, Texas: 155
Denton, Texas: 167
DeShields, James: 188, 190, 195, 207, 209
Develle, ———: 71
D'Hanis, Texas: 102
Dickeson, Dr. M. W.: 72
Dickinson, Anson: 32
Dr. Daniel Heuser, by Wueste: 118
Dr. Ferdinand Herff, by Duval, *173, 174*
Dr. Weisselberg, by Hadra: 177, *178*
Dodge, Henry: 35
Donnellan, Jessamine Hawthorne: 211
Donnellan, Thurston J.: 211
Dosch, Ernst: 125
Dougal, William H.: 165–167

Doughty, Thomas: 89
Drawing of the Black Beans, by Gentilz: *opp. iii,* 108
Drayman, The, by Gentilz: 105
Driskill, Jesse Lincoln: 202
Drunkards, The, by Gentilz: 110
Ducker, Eugene: 185
Dunlap, William: 28, 43
Düsseldorf School of Art: 118, 142, 172
Dutch John's Bakery (Austin): 151
Duval, Ella Amelia Moss: 172–174, 177, 179
Duval, Burr G.: 174
Duval Home (Austin): 177
Dwarfs of the Nibelungen, by Petri: 75

Eager, Robert: 118
Eager, Sarah Riddle: 118, 120
Eagle Pass, Texas: 121, 163
Earle, Ralph E. W.: 6
Early Views of American Cities: 12
Eastman, Mary Henderson: 50
Eastman, Robert: 49
Eastman, Sarah Lee: 49
Eastman, Seth: 39, 49–55, 68, 79, 89, 105, 117
East Side Plaza at San Antonio, by Samuel: 30, *31*
École des Beaux-Arts (Paris): 97
Edward VII, Prince: 190
Edward Steves, by Iwonski: *127*
Egan, John J.: 72
18 Miles from the Mississippi, by Holtz: 152
Eldridge, B.: 193
Elise Lungkwitz, by Petri: *77, 78,* 129
Elijah Being Fed by the Raven, by Petri: 77
Elijah's Ascension into Heaven, by Petri: 77
Elks and Buffalo Making Acquaintance on the Texas Prairie on the Brazos, by Catlin: *38*
Elliott, Charles Loring: 40
El Paso, Texas: 157, 158, 163, 164
Embarkation of the Pilgrims, by Weir: 50
Emigrants Attacked by Comanches, by Eastman: 54
Emma, Mary, Bertha, by Wueste: 118, *121*
Emory, William H.: 160–161, 163
Emory Survey, The: 160–167
Encampment of Covered Wagons, by Ranney: 43
Enchanted Rock, by Lungkwitz: 89
Endicott, G. & W.: 151, 152
England (ship): 98
Englemann, George: 164
Espíritu Santo de Zuñiga Mission (La Bahía): 3
Everett, Stephen M.: 48
Ewing, Alexander W.: 203
Eyth, Louis: 187, 188–190

Fahey, Mr. ———: 71
Fahrenberg, Albert, Sr.: 211
Fairman, Charles E.: 55
Fall of Babylon, The, by Donnellan: 211
Fall of the Alamo, The, by Gentilz: 108
False Wichita River: 35
Fandango, The, by Gentilz: *101, 103, 111*
Fannin, James: 36

Farmersville, Texas: 188, 209
Father Frank, by Lavender: *96, 99*
Faulkner, William, 169
Faust: 98
Fayette County, Texas: 153
Feast of Belteshazzar, The, by Donnellan: 211
Field of Coreopis, by Onderdonk: 207
First News of the Battle of Lexington, by Ranney: 39
Fisher, C. Rhodes: 44
Fisher, Flavius: 196
Fishing in the Lower Adirondacks, by Andrews: 29
Fishing with Bow and Arrow, by Gentilz: *115, 117*
Flatrock Creek, by Lungkwitz: 88
Flintoff, Thomas: 57–68, 74, 138
Ford, Mr. ———: 211
Ford, J.: 138
Ford, John Salmon (Rip): 202, 212
Forest and River Halle, by Lungkwitz: 88
Forrest, Nathan: 196
Fort Bliss: 157
Fort Brown, Texas, by Eastman: 54
Fort Chadborne: 54
Fort Clark: 136
Fort Crawford, Wisconsin: 50
Fort Davis: 163
Fort Duncan: 54, 163
Fort Gibson: 34, 35
Fort Inge: 53
Fort Martin Scott: 53, 79, 85, 86
Fort Martin Scott, by Petri: *85, 86*
Fort Ringgold: 49
Fort San Antonio de Valero, by Onderdonk: 207
Fort Snelling, Minnesota: 50, 53
Fort Yuma: 167
Foster, ———: *172*
Foster, Ran: 195
Four Indians on a Rock, by Petri: 83
Fowler, T. M.: 155
Fox Field, Chief: 18
Fox Indians: 34
Frame House on Shoal Creek, by Lungkwitz, 91
Franco-German War: 169
Franco-Prussian War: 125
Frankenstein, G. N.: 213
Franks, Frederick: 213
Fredericksburg, Texas: 52, 53, 79, 86, 88, 89, 90, 129, 155, 202
Frederick Wilhelm II: 118
Fremont, Colonel John: 72
French Academy (Paris): 97, 115
French Revolution, The, by Philippoteaux: 72
French Village, by Grenet: 177
Frère, Edward: 185
Fretelliere, Auguste: 99–101, *102–103,* 116
Fretelliere, Henrietta Gentilz: 103
Fretelliere, Louisa: 117
Fretelliere, Marie: 117
Fulmore, Mrs. Sterling: 202
Funeral of an Angel, The, by Gentilz: *102,* 105

Gadsden Tract: 160

Gaines Crossing (Sabine River): 14
Gallagher, Peter: 129
Galveston, Texas: artists in, 57, 99, 141, 142, 188, 212, 213; pictures of, 153, 154; mention of, 27, 28, 44, 65, 145, 149, 201, 211
Galveston, Battle of: 68
Galveston Bay: 47
Galveston Island: 11, 44–46
Galveston News: 57, 139, 141, 151
Galveston Wharf Scene, by Stockfleth: 212
Garett, C. C.: 193
Garneray, Ambrose Louis: 11–13
Garneray, Jean François: 11
Gathering Juice from the Maguey Plant for Pulque, by Gentilz: 111, *112*
Gathering Storm, by Onderdonk: 207, 209
Gazette (Austin): 63
General Jessup (steamboat): 167
Geneva Academy: 7
Genoveva, by Petri: 75
Gentilz, (Jean Louis) Theodore: 74, 99–118
Gentilz, Jean Pierre: 117
Gentilz, Marie Fargeix: 103, 117
Gentleman, A, by Heade: 141
George W. Smyth, by Flintoff: *65, 66*
Germania Gesangverein, by Iwonski: 125
Geronimo, Chief: 188
Giddings, C. C.: 193
Gilbrede, Thomas: 50
Gilcrease, Thomas, Institute of American History and Art (Tulsa): 72
Gilded Age: 159
Going to the City, by Gentilz: 105
Going Visiting, by Petri ["Austin, Texas" and "1849" were added by an unknown person]: 83, *opp. 84,* 86
Goliad, Texas: 36
Gómara, Francisco López de: 3
Goras, Juan: 31
Gottschalk, Louis: 172
Gounod, Charles François: 98
Graebner, Rowel: 121
Granado-Bethencourt home (San Antonio): 31
Grand Cosmorama of a Picturesque Voyage around the World: 72
Grand Salon (Paris): 177
Gray, A. B.: 167
Grayson, Tabetha Childress: 129
Grayson, Thomas W.: 129
Gray Survey, The: 167
Greek, The, by Lavender: 97, 98
Green, Thomas J.: 68, 108
Grenet, Edward Louis: 174–177
Grenet, Eugénie Guilbeau: 177
Grenet, Honoré: 174
Grenet, Madeleine: 174
Groce, George C.: 211, 212
Grosbeck House with Terraced Garden, The, by Onderdonk: 207
Grout, Dr. and Mrs. ———: *172*
Guadalupe Hidalgo, conference of: 155
Guadalupe Mountains, The, by Schuchard: 167
Guadalupe River: 53, 122, 207
Guenther, Carl H.: 83, 129, 151
Guenther, Mrs. Carl H.: 129

Guenther's Mill on Liveoak Creek, by Lungkwitz: 88
Guilbeau, François: 177
Guilbeau, María del Rosario Roman: 177
Guillaume, Louis Mathieu Didier: 144, 145–146
Guizot, François Pierre: 98, 99
Gulf of Mexico: 15, 53, 65
Gutiérrez, Sancho: 3
Guy Morrison Bryan, by Flintoff: 62, 63

Haberly, Loyd: 34
Hadra, Dr. Berthold: 177
Hadra, Ida Weisselberg, 174, 177–179, 180, 181
Hamilton, Andrew J.: 63, 142
Hamilton's Pool, by Lungkwitz: 91
Hancock's Store (Austin): 151
Handy, Robert: 138
Hardin, Wesley: 186
Harding, Chester: 6
Harper's Weekly: 136
Harp of the Winds, The, by Martin: 91
Harris, Edward: 44
Harrisburg, Texas: 9
Harris County, Texas: 10, 46
Hartley, Jerry: 65
Haskell, ———: 12
Hastings, Battle of: 69
Hay Making, by Behné: 142
Hays, John Coffee: 44, 49, 89, 100–101, 195
Hays' Rangers: 103
Heade, Martin Johnson: 138, 139-141
Heard, Dr. ———: 211
Hecker, Friedrich: 75
Heed, Joseph Crowell: 139
Heed, Sarah John: 139
Heinrich (ship): 99
Hempstead, Texas: 73
Henderson, Ana Marie Truxton: 50
Henderson, James Pinckney: 188
Henderson, James W.: 188
Henderson, Dr. Thomas: 50
Henderson Yoakum, by Allen: 23, 24
Henry, Joseph: 36
Henry, William E.: 211
Herff, Ferdinand: 173, 174, 207
Hermann Lungkwitz, by Petri: 77
Heuser, Daniel: 118
Heuser, Louisa Joegel: 118
Heyland, Jean Christophe: 7
Hicks, Edward: 141
Hicks, Thomas: 141
Hill Country, by Lungkwitz: 88, *opp.* 92
Hill of Cedars near Austin, by Lungkwitz: 91
Hillyer, H. B.: 211
Historia General de las Indias, La: 3
Historical and Statistical Information Respecting the History, Condition and Prospects of the Indian Tribes of the United States: 54
Hobby, A. M.: 188
Holley, Mary Austin: 17, 28, 195
Holmes, Oliver Wendell: 159
Holtz, Helmuth: 152–153
Holycon (packet): 28
Holy Family, by Behné: 142
Holy Family, The, by Petri: 77

Home Stretch of the Volunteer *on the 27th of September 1887,* by Stockfleth: *opp.* 212
Hood County, Texas: 212
Hood's Texas Brigade: 190
Hoppe, Louis: 153, 154
Hoppin, Agustus: 158–160
Hoppin, Harriet Jones: 159
Hoppin, Thomas Cole: 159
Horsehead Crossing (Pecos River): 158
Horton, Albert C.: 123
Horton Town, Texas: 122, 123, 137
Hour of Prayer, The, by Gentilz: 115
Houston, Sam: and artists, 15, 18, 21, 49; portraits of, 17, 23, 27, 28–29, 31, 57, 136–137, 138, 139, 140, 141–142, 143, 145, 172, 193, 195, 200, 201, 202, 211; in politics, 27, 47–48, 160; character of, 138–139; death of, 142–145; mention of, 36
Houston, Mrs. Sam: 27, 142, 145
Houston, Texas: 15, 17, 23, 27, 44, 47, 73, 97, 98, 154, 155, 172, 190, 211
Howard, George Thomas: 86
Howard, O. O.: 193
Hubbel, Captain ———: 39
Hübner, Julius: 75
Huddle, Nancy Foster: 196
Huddle, Stephen Groce: 196
Huddle, William Henry: 23, 91, 168, 188, 196–203
Hudson River: 72
Hudson River School: 50, 97
Humboldt, Alexander von: 34
Humfray, John Basson: 68
Hunter's Quest, The, by Hadra: 179
Hunting Wild Horses, by Ranney: 41
Huntsville, Texas: 15, 21, 23, 63, 73, 136–137
Hurricane, The, by Stockfleth: 212
Huxley, Aldous: 88
Hydes Tavern (Nacogdoches): 18

illustrirte Mississippi, Das: 53
Incarnate Word Convent (Corpus Christi): 98
Independence, Texas: 73, 190, 193
"Independence Hall," *Washington-on-the-Brazos Panorama,* by Benton and Smith: *opp. 68,* 68–69
Indian Hunters, by Eastman: 50
Indian Maid, by Petri: 82, 83
Indian Mother and Child on a Donkey, by Petri: 83
Indianola, Texas: 53, 74, 77, 105, 122, 152, 163
Indian on a Horse, by Petri: 83
Indian Point, Texas: 53
Indians. *See* individual persons or tribes
Indians on Horses at a Stream, by Petri: 83
Indians Spearing Fish, by Eastman: 50
Indian Territory: 155
Indian Women at Work, by Eastman: 50
Indian Women Washing Clothes, by Gentilz: 117
Ingallis, Gardner: 212
Ingallis, Walter: 211–212
Inness, George: 209
Innocent Victim, by Thomas: 169

Institute of Mechanical Arts (Brooklyn): 39
Iowa Indians: 34
Ireland, John: 201
Irion, Dr. Robert: 18 n.
Irving, Washington: 44, 159
Iwonski, Adolph von: 122
Iwonski, Carl G. von: 74, 89, 121, 122–137, 147, 202
Iwonski, Leopold von: 122–123
Iwonski, Marie Kalinowsky-Tschirski von: 122

J. Lyle Smith, by Wright: 15, 16
Jacal, The, by Onderdonk: 207
Jackson, Andrew: 6, 44
Jaeger, Adelina Heuser: 118
Jarvis, John W.: 21
Jasper, Texas: 65
Jefferson, Texas: 69, 155
Jerusalem, by Catherwood: 70
Jerusalem Delivered, by Tasso: 75
Jewett, J. H.: 148, 151
Johanna Steves, by Iwonski: 126
Jones, Anson: 15, 100, 188
Jones, Elizabeth Giberson: 65
Jones, Ella: 65
Jones, Lewellyn: 65
Jones, Walter C.: 65
Jones, Warrick: 65
Jones, William Jefferson: 65, 66, 68, 212
Jones Children, The, by Flintoff: 65, 67, 68
Joseph Chadwick, by Catlin: 36, 37
Jouett, Matthew H.: 17–18, 195
Journal of the Texian Expedition against Mier: 108
Journey to the Pacific: 155
Juan N. Seguin, by Wright: 18, 19
Judge and Mrs. William Jefferson Jones Home, by Stockfleth: 212
Julia, by Petri: 79
Julius Meyenberg's Farm, by Hoppe: 153, 154

Kapp, Dr. Ernest: 129
Kapp, Julia: 129
Karnes, Henry: 195
Kearny, Stephen W.: 157
Keenan's Hotel (Huntsville): 23
Kellner, Charles: 213
Kenedy, Mifflin: 97, 98
Kensett, John Frederick: 207
Keslers (store): 97
Kickapoo Indians: 9
King, Charles Bird: 204
Kiowa Indians: 116, 117
Kirby, Mrs. Helen Marr: 207
Kleberg daughters: 98
Kleine, Mrs. Dorothea: 211
Kneass, Charles: 212
Kneass, William: 212
Koch, Agustus: 154–155
Kuechler, Jacob: 75, 91, 202
Kuechler, Marie Lungkwitz: 75, 83, 91

La Bahía, Texas: 3, 36
Lacour, Pierre: 145
Lafitte, Jean: 11

La Grange, Texas: 153, 154, 155
Lallemand, Charles François Antoine: 11
Lamar, Mirabeau B.: 148, 188
Lang, ———: 153
Lanman, ———: 53
Laredo, Texas: 6, 21
Las Moras Creek: 133, 136
Lasso, The, by Ranney: *42, 43*
"Laureles" (Kenedy's ranch): 97
Lavender, Charles: 97–98
Lavender, Eugenie Etienne Aubanel: 96, 97–99
"Lavender Hall" (Audubon College): 98
Lea, Mrs. Nancy: 26, 27
Lea, Temple: 25, 27
Least Tern, by Audubon: *45,* 47
Leavenworth, Henry: 34
Lee, Robert E.: 145, 190
Lee at the Wilderness, by McArdle: 190
Lee's Surrender, by Donnellan: 211
Lefebvre, ———: 169
Lehmann, Theodore: 212
Leona River: 53
Leslie, Mrs. Frank: 199
Leslie, Robert: 50
Lessing, Conrad: 118
Letters and Notes on the Manners, Customs, and Conditions of the North American Indian: 34
Lewis, Henry: 53, 72
Lewis, Nat: 204
Lewis and Clark Expedition: 34
Liberty, Texas: 57
Lily Carolon, by Grenet: 176, 177
Lily Carolon, by Iwonski: 129, *131*
Lipan Apaches: 53, 79, 81, 83, 116, 117, 134, 135, 137, 163
Lipan Indian, by Iwonski: *134, 135,* 137
Lipan Indian, by Petri: *81,* 83
List of Paintings, by Gentilz: *110*
Little Girl with Apple Blossoms, by Thomas: 172
Liveoak Creek: 83
Live Oaks Two Miles from Fredericksburg, Texas—Encampment of Caddo Indians, by Eastman: *52,* 53
Live Oaks with Two Small Figures, by Eastman: 53
Llano Estacado: 155
Loan of a Lover: 69
Log Cabin, The, by McArdle: *194,* 195
Lone Star and Southern Watchtower: 56, 68
Long, Mrs. Jane: 6
Longfellow, Henry Wadsworth: 73
Longyear, Abby: 172
Louis XVII: 11
Louise, Queen: 118
Louis Philippe, King: 97
Lubbock, F. R.: 193
Ludlow, Noah M.: 69
Lungkwitz, Adolph: 75, 79, 83
Lungkwitz, Alice: 89
Lungkwitz (Carl) Hermann (Frederick): 53, 74–75, 77, 79, 83, 86–97, 123, 147, 177, 199
Lungkwitz, Elsie Petri: 75, 77, 78, 79, 88, 129
Lungkwitz, Freideriche Heckt: 75
Lungkwitz, Helene: 89

Lungkwitz, Johann Gottried: 75
Lungkwitz, Martha: 83, 89, 91
Lungkwitz, Max: 83, 89
Lungkwitz, Teresa: 75, 77, 79, 83
Lydia Ann Mason, by Wright: 21, 22, 23

MacAllen Company: 185
McArdle, Henry Arthur: 188, 190–195
McArdle, Isophene L. Dunnington: 190
McArdle, Jennie Smith: 190
McCulloch, Ben: 136
MacGillivary, William: 47
McGown, Floyd: 207
McGown, Mrs. Floyd: 207, 208
McIntire, Robert G.: 139
McLaughlin, Charles: 68, 108
McManus, Gaston: 98
McManus, Mrs. ———: 98
McNeil, Charles: 145
Madison, Dolly: 34
Madonna and Child, by Lavender: 98
Madonna of the Cup, by Petri: 77
Madonna of the Roses, by Petri: 77
Magoffin, James Wiley: 157
Magruder, J. Bankhead: 73
Main Plaza, San Antonio, Texas, by Pentenrieder: *150, 151*
Mainzer Adelsverein: 77
Mansion House (Matagorda): 68
Marble Falls, Texas: 199
Marcy Expedition: 167
Marie Amélie, Queen: 97
Marie Oekers, by Iwonski: *129, 130*
Marine View, by Ranney: 39
Market, The, by Gentilz: 105
Market Place, San Antonio, The, by Allen: *182,* 185
Marshall, Texas: 18 n., 69
Martin, Mr. ———: 71
Martin Johnson Heade: 139
Marucheau, Constance: 177
Mary (schooner): 10
Mary Angelica Bryan, by Flintoff: 57, *59*
Mary Anoints the Feet of Jesus, by Petri: 77
Maryland Institute for the Promotion of the Mechanic Arts (Baltimore): 190
Mason, James: 21
Mason, Lydia Ann Smith, 21–23
Matagorda, Texas: 56, 57, 65, 68, 152
Matagorda Bay: 53
Matisse, Henri: 177
Matthew 17:27, by Petri: 77
Maverick, Sam: 129, 132
May, George: 142
May, Julia Meyer Keim: 142
Mechanics Institute Fair (New York City): 39
Medina County, Texas: 30
Medina River: 54, 99, 100, 117
Meek, Joe: 43
Meggison, Judge ———: 56
Meissonier, Ernest: 193
Melbourne Museum (Vermont): 12
Melville, Herman: 12
"Memorias para la historia de Texas": 3
Menchaca, José Antonio: 31
Men Seated around a Table, by Petri: 86
Metate Girl, The, by Onderdonk: 207

Metate Girl Grinding Corn, by Gentilz: 110
Metropolitan Museum (New York City): 72
Metz' Store (Austin): 151
Mexican Bread Makers, by Gentilz: 110
Mexican Candy Seller, The, by Grenet: 175, 177
Mexican Girl, by Wueste: 121
Mexican Hut, by Grenet: 177
Mexican Jacal on the Rio Grande above Brownsville, by Eastman: 54
Mexican Oxcart and Jacal, by Gentilz: 105, 106
Mexican War: 30, 39, 43, 72, 202, 203
Mexican War: 72
Mexican War Drummer, by Ranney: 43
Mexican Women Washing at San Pedro Spring, by Allen: *183,* 185
Mexico: 6, 7, 49, 86, 108, 110, 111, 115, 151, 152, 193
Meyenberg, Julius: 153, 154
Micheaud, F. F.: 99–100
Mier Expedition: 21, 68, 108
Mier y Terán, Manuel: 6, 7, 9
Milam, Ben: 195
Milam Guards: 21
Military Colony opposite Fort Duncan, The, by Schott: 163
Military Institute, Austin, by Lungkwitz: 91, 94
Military Plaza—San Antonio, Texas, by Schott: *161,* 163
Miller, Alfred Jacob: 39, 41
Mills, Roger Q.: 207
Minnesota Historical Society (St. Paul): 72
Mississippi River and Indian Life, The, by Pomarède: 71
Missouri Botanical Gardens (St. Louis): 165
Mrs. Floyd McGown, by Onderdonk: 207, 208
Mrs. Nancy Lea, by Allen: 26, 27
Mrs. Redwood, by Thomas: 169
Modelli, ———: 71
Moelling, Peter A.: 68, 73
Möllhausen, H. B.: 149
Möllhausen, Heinrich: 149, 155
Montague County, Texas: 155
Monvoisin, Ramon Quesada: 115
Moonlight, by Andrews: 29
Moore, Dr. Francis: 139
Morehouse, Edwin: 21
Morfi, Father Juan Agustín: 3
Morgan, James: 48
Morning Star (Houston): 28, 212
Morris, Mr. ———: 169, 172
Morse, Samuel F. B.: 157
Moses Austin Bryan, by McArdle: 190, *191*
Moss, Isabel Harris: 172
Moss, Samuel: 172
Mount, William Sidney: 39–40, 43
Mt. Bonnell, by Lungkwitz: 91
Mt. Vesuvius: 72
Mourning for the Dead, by Eastman: 50
Muller, Carl: 185
Munich Galleries: 142
Murillo, Bartolomé: 98
Music Festival Poster, by Petri: 76, 77

Myth of the Dragon's Teeth, The, by Petri: 75

Nacogdoches, Texas: 9, 15, 18
Nadaco Indians: 9
Nagle, Joseph A.: 202
Napoleon I: 12, 75, 86, 97, 98
Napoleon at St. Helena, by Delaroche: 98
National Academy of Design (New York City): 27, 28, 39, 43, 50, 141, 145, 172, 185, 196, 204
National Bank of San Antonio: 151
National School of Mathematics and Drawing (Paris): 103
Neagle, John: 32
Negley, Walter: 204
Neighbor, A, by Hadra: 177
Neuser, William [L. A. W. Neuser]: 212
Neuser, Mrs. William: 212
New Bedford Whaling Museum: 72
New Braunfels, Texas: 77, 79, 83, 86, 88, 89, 122, 125, 129, 136, 153, 155
New Orleans, Louisiana: pictures of, 12; artists in, 29, 39, 68, 70, 71, 138, 211; mention of, 32, 44, 49, 53, 69, 72, 98, 110, 174
New Washington, Texas: 48
New York City: pictures of, 12; artists in, 27, 34, 39, 40, 141, 177, 196, 204, 207, 211; artists exhibit in, 28, 29, 43, 50, 69, 70, 72, 169, 185; mention of, 49, 73, 139, 167, 201, 202, 203
New-York Historical Society: 27
New-York Historical Society's Dictionary of Artists in America, 1564–1860: 211
New York Sun: 139
Ney, Elisabet: 196
Nickholson, Rubelle: 211
Night on the Loire River, by Thomas: 169
Norton, Representative ———: 142
Nott, William: 39
Nueces River: 54

Oak Point, by Sandusky: 151
Odell, George: 72
Old Bridge over the Trinity, The, by Onderdonk: 207
Old Duval Home, The, by Hadra: 177
Old Gentleman Leaning on a Cane, by Wueste: 118
Old Ira Evans Home, The, by Hadra: 177
Old Mill, by Lungkwitz: 91
Old Mill Bridge, by Lungkwitz: 91, 93
Old Pumphouse, The, by Onderdonk: 207
Omaha Indians: 34
On Art and Artists: 88
Onderdonk, Emily Gould: 204
Onderdonk, Henrietta Stephenson: 204
Onderdonk, Henry: 204
Onderdonk, Julian: 204, 209
Onderdonk, Robert Jenkins: 105, 188, 203–209
On Guard, by Allen: 185
On the Guadalupe, by Onderdonk: 207
On the Pedernales, by Lungkwitz: 88
On the Wing, by Ranney: 41
"Orange Grove" (Morgan's home): 48
"Orozimbo" (Phelps' home): 10

Orr, ———: 73
Osceola, Chief: 34
Otter Belt, Quahadi, by Gentilz: 117
Otto, Captain ———: 122
Oxcart, The, by Gentilz: 100, 103

Padron-Chaves home (San Antonio): 31
Paint and Clay Club (Boston): 185
Palo Alto Crossing, by Lungkwitz: 88
"Papago" Indians: 163
Paris, Texas: 196
Paris, University of: 98
Paris Salon, the: 145, 172, 185
Parrita, Texas: 7
Pattison, J. W.: 185
Pawnee Pict Indians: 34, 35, 36
Payday in the Market, by Gentilz: 110
Peaceable Kingdom, by Hicks: 141
Peale, Charles Wilson: 14, 32
Peale, Rembrandt: 32
Pecos River: 158, 167
Pecos River, by Schuchard: 167
Pedernales River: 53, 79, 86, 88, 91, 95, 199
Pedro II, Don: 141
Pellicer, Bishop: 177
Pennsylvania Academy of Fine Arts: 29, 32, 141
Pentenrieder, Erhard: 151
Pentenrieder, Mrs. (nee Meyer): 151
Perrine, Mr. ———: 68
Perry's Expedition to Japan, by C. L. Smith: 69, 72
Personal Narrative of Explorations and Incidents in Texas, New Mexico, California, Sonora, and Chihuahua, connected with the United States and Mexican Boundary Commission during the Years 1850, '51, '52, and '53: 155
Persons, Charles: 151
Peticolas, A. B.: 212
Petri, (Frederick) Richard: 53, 74–86, 87–88, 121, 129, 137
Petri, Geb Weis: 74
Petri, Heinrich: 74
Phelps, Dr. James A. E.: 10
Philippoteaux, Paul: 72
Phillips, Sir Thomas: 34
Pilgrim's Progress: 72
Pioneer Cowpen, The, by Petri ["Austin, Texas" and "1849" were added by an unknown person]: 83, *84,* 86
Plaza and Church of El Paso, The, by Vaudricourt: 163, *164*
Plaza at San Antonio, Texas, by Eastman: *51,* 53
Plowing in the Nivernaise, by Rosa Bonheur: 97
Plumbe, John: 138, 139
Polk County, Texas: 212
Pomarède, Leon de la: 71
Pope, John, 167
Portal of the San José Mission, by Allen: *184,* 185
Porter, D. D.: 105
Portrait of a Child, by Hadra: 177
Portrait of a Gentleman, by Heade: 141
Portrait of a Young Lady, by Heade: 141
Portrait of John R. Bartlett, by Pratt: *156, 157*

Potter, Ruben M.: 195
Potts, Cornelia Ringgold: 146
Powell, William: 213
Prairie-Dog Town, by Hoppin: 159, *160*
Pratt, Henry Cleves: 155–158, 159, 160, 163
Prayer before the Battle, by Donnellan: 211
Preliminary Sketch for Hunting Wild Horses by Ranney: 40, 41
1ère Vue d'Aigleville Colonie du Texas ou Champ d'Asile, by Garneray: 12, *13*
Preston, Texas: 167
Procession with the Holy Ark, by Petri: 77
Products of the Garden, by Hadra: 179
Profile of a Man with Glasses, by Petri: 79, 80
Profile of an Early Settler, by Petri: 79
Pryor M. Bryan, by Flintoff: 57, *58*
Punchinello: 159

Quadrupeds of North America: 48, 49
Quanah, Texas: 155
Queisser, Robert: 79
Quicha Indians: 9
Quihi, Texas: 54, 102
Quintana, Texas: 10

Raguet, Anna: 18
Raguet, Henry: 18
Ranney, Clarissa Gaylord: 39
Ranney, Margaret O'Sullivan: 39
Ranney, William: 39
Ranney, William Tylee: 39–43
"Raven Hill" (Houston's home): 27
Read, Thomas B.: 213
Reagan, John H.: 188
Reaugh, Frank: 186
Reconstruction period: 186
Red Fish Bar: 17, 47, 48
Red Jacket, by Catlin: 34
Red River: 35, 167
Redwood, Mrs. ———: 169
Reily, J.: 18
Reise-Skizzen in Poesie und Prosa: 73
Remington, Frederic: 186
Renegale, Mr. ———: 28
Report on the United States and Mexican Boundary Survey Made under the Direction of the Secretary of the Interior, 1849–1857: 160
Retreat, The, by Ranney: 43
Returning from the City, by Gentilz: 105
Reynolds, Joseph J.: 153, 202
Richards, John H.: 165, 167
Richardson, Willard: 139
Richmond, Texas: 23, 27, 73, 141
Richter, (Adrian) Ludwig: 75, 88
Richter, Carl: 75
Rigaud, Antoine: 11
"Riguenos" Indians: 163
Ringgold, Samuel: 203
Ringgold Barracks: 163
Río Bravo del Norte: 6
Río Frío: 53
Río Grande: 21, 49, 50, 53, 54, 99, 105, 108, 121, 155, 163, 164
Río Grande, Texas: 163
Río San Pedro—above Second Crossing, by Vaudricourt: *162,* 163

River of the West: 43
Rives, William Cabel: 145
Robert-Fleury, Tony: 177
Robert Queisser, by Petri: 79
Roberts, Oran M.: 168, 202
Roberts, Mrs. Oran M.: 202
Robson, Robert: 141, 145
Roemer, Dr. Ferdinand von: 125
Roetter, Paulus: 164–165
Rooster Race, The, by Gentilz: 105
Rosenberg Library (Galveston): 145
Ross, Mrs. Charles Worthington: 146
Rousseau, Olivier, and Co.: 174
Rowel Graebner, by Wueste: 121
Royal Academy (Düsseldorf): 179, 185
Royal Academy (London): 29
Ruins of the Monastery, by Lungkwitz: 88
Ruíz, Francisco Antonio: 108
Rusk, Thomas J.: 160, 188, 201
Russell, Benjamin: 72
Russell, Charles: 186

Sabinas Creek: 53
Sabine River: 6, 14, 65
St. Helena and Funeral of Napoleon: 72
St. Mary's Academy (Austin): 151
St. Mary's College (San Antonio): 117
St. Mary's Hall (San Antonio): 174
St. Michael and Satan, by Petri: 75
St. Patrick Preaching, by Lavender: 99
Sala, Mr. and Mrs. ———: 68, 69
Sam Houston, by Behné: 142, *143*, 145
Sam Houston, by Heade: 138, *140*, 141
Sam Houston, by Huddle: 200, 201
Sam Maverick and the Terry Rangers, by Iwonski: 129, *132*
Samuel, William M. G.: 30–31
San Antonio, Texas: pictures of, 3, 31, 51, 53, 69, 77, 87, 89, 92, 105, 110, 111, 147, 148, 150, 153, 155, 161, 163, 169; descriptions of, 7, 54, 179, 182, 185; artists in, 27, 30, 68, 88, 99, 102, 103, 105, 117, 118, 123, 129, 174, 177, 188, 202, 204, 207, 211; mention of, 11, 18, 21, 101, 116, 121, 125, 136, 151, 195, 201
San Antonio, by unknown artist: 147, *148*
San Antonio de Béxar, by Lungkwitz: 77, 87, *89*
San Antonio River: 91, 105, 179, 181
San Antonio River Back of the Old Brewery, by Hadra: 179
San Augustine, Texas: 14–15, 168, 211
Sánchez y Tapia, José María: 6, *7*–9
Sánchez y Tapia, Lino: 6, 7, 8
Sandusky, Elizabeth Clarno: 148
Sandusky, Jane McKnight: 149
Sandusky, John: 148
Sandusky, William H.: 148–149, 151
San Felipe de Austin, Texas: 7, 63, 68
San Fernando de Béxar, Texas: 18, 31
San Francisco de la Espada, by Gentilz: 108
San Jacinto, Battle of: 10, 11, 39, 47, 63, 129, 144, 146, 193, 195, 202
San Jacinto District: 9, 10
San Jacinto Museum: 172
San José, by Onderdonk: 207
San José de Aguayo, by Lungkwitz: 91

San José Mission: 3, 54, 69, 151, 169, 184, 185
San José Mission, by Gentilz: *107*, 108
San José Mission, by Thomas: 169, *171*
San José Mission Window, by Gentilz: *108*
San Juan Capistrano, by Gentilz: 108
San Juan Capistrano Mission: 3, 54, 91, 151
San Luis, Texas: 213
San Miguel River: 54
San Pedro Spring: 54, 105, 183, 185, 204, 207
San Pedro Spring, by Gentilz: 105
San Pedro Spring, by Onderdonk: 207
Santa Anna, Antonio López de: 9–10, 36, 103, 129, 193, 201, 202, 203
Sarah Riddle, by Wueste: 118, *120*
Sarony, Major, and Knapp: 163
Sauveur, Professor ———: 190
Sayers, Joseph D.: 207
Scene in the Austrian Alps, by Lungkwitz: 88
Scene in Tyrolean Alps, by Lungkwitz: 88
Scene on St. Mary's Street, by Onderdonk: 207
Scene Southwest of Austin, by Lungkwitz: 91
Scheffer, Ary: 97, 98
Schenck, Caroline: 124, 129
Schenck, Frederick: 129
Schenck, Johanna: 124, 129
Schenck Sisters, The, by Iwonski: *124*, 129
Schiff, Johann Dethard: 122
Schoolcraft, Henry Rowe: 54
Schott, Arthur: 161, 163, 165
Schroedter, Adolph: 118
Schroedter, Alvina Heuser: 118
Schuchard, Carl: 167
Schuchard, Johan: 167
Schuchard, Wilhelmina Hartart: 167
Schuyler, Philip: 27–28
Scott, Martin: 86
Scott, Winfield: 34
Scouting Party, by Ranney: 43
Scurry, Major ———: 211
Searcy, W. W.: 193
Seco River: 54
Seguin, Erasmo: 18
Seguin, Juan Nepomucena: 18, 19, 195
Seguin, Texas: 53
Self-Portrait, by Huddle: *198*, 199
Self-Portrait, by Petri: 79
Self-Portrait, by Wright: 20
Selling of Cardinals on the Plaza, by Gentilz: 111, *113*
Selves, George: 213
Seminole Indians: 50, 151
Seneca Indians: 34
Settlement of Austin's Colony, by McArdle: *194*, 195
Seven Cities of Cíbola: 3
Shad Fishing on the Hudson, by Ranney: 39
Shaw, James B.: 97
Shawnee Indians: 53
Shepherd's Valley, Texas: 23
Sherman, Sidney: 193
Sherman, Texas: 63
Sherman and Smith: 167
Shirlaw, Walter: 204
Shoal Creek, by Lungkwitz: 91

Shooting of the Seventeen Decimated Texians, by Gentilz: *opp. iii*, 108
Shotwell, Dr. ———: 213
Shylock, by Petri: 77
Sibley, Henry S.: 53
Sigel, Franz: 75
Simon, Marie Oekers: 129, 130
Sioux Indians: 34, 50, 72
Sioux Indians Breaking Up Camp, by Eastman: 50
Sisterdale, Texas: 79, 129
Sketch Book: 159
Sketch of the Alamo, by Sandusky: 151
Skirving's Moving Panorama: Colonel Fremont's Western Expeditions: 72
Slave, The, by Huddle: 196, 197
Smilie, James: 97
Smilie, James D.: 163, 164
Smith, Ashbel: 18, 188
Smith, Charles L.: 68, 69
Smith, Deaf: 17, 21, 28, 31, 195
Smith, Harriet Wright: 15
Smith, Henry: 17, 27, 29
Smith, J. Lyle: 15, 16
Smith, John Rowson: 50
Smith, Robert Thompson: 15
Smith, Mrs. Sidney: 207
Smith, Sol: 69
Smithsonian Institution: 36, 167
Smith's Ranch: 157, 163
Smyth, George Washington: 65, 66
Sohn, August Wilhelm: 118, 172
Solms-Braunfels, Prince Carl of: 122
Somervell, Alexander: 21
Soullard, D. V.: 28
Southern Plains: 34–35
Southwestern Immigration Company: 174
Speech of Travis to His Men at the Alamo, The, by Eyth: 188, *189*
Spotted Sandpiper, Buffalo Bayou, Texas, by Audubon: 46, *47*
Squaw, by Gentilz: 117
Staffel, Adelina Wueste: 118, *119*, 121
Staked Plains, the: 54, 155
Staked Plains, by Eastman: 54
Stampede, by Ranney: 43
Starr, J. H.: 149
Stephen F. Austin, by unknown artist: 4, *5*
Stephen F. Austin, by unknown artist: 63, 68
Stephen F. Austin, by Catlin: 32, *33*
Stephen F. Austin, by Eyth: *187*, 188
Stephen F. Austin, by Flintoff: 63, *64*
Stevens, John: 72
Stevens, William: 212
Stevenson, Phillipa G.: 174
Steves, Edward: 127, 129
Steves, Johanna: 126, 129
Still Life: Bottle, Gun, Powderhorn, Pipe, by Iwonski: *128*, 129
Still Life with Fruit, by Huddle: *opp. 196*, 201
Stockfleth, Julius: 212–213
Stokes, ———: 12
Stoner, Mr. ———: 154
Strange, James: 9–11
Straus Company: 207
Strycker, Jacobus Gerritsen: 204
Stuart, Gilbert: 14, 17
Stuart, Mrs. S. A.: 213

Studio, The, by Gentilz: 115
Studio in Paris, by Thomas: 169
Study of Oak Trees, by Ranney: 43
Sully, Thomas: 14, 17, 32, 43, 142
Sumner, Charles: 212
Sunlight, by Andrews: 29
Sunset, Texas: 155
Sunset in the Salzburg Alps, by Lungkwitz: 88
Supply (ship): 105
Surrender of Geronimo, by Eyth: 188
Surrender of Santa Anna, by Huddle: 201, 202–203, *opp*. 204
Surveying in Texas before Annexation to U.S., by Gentilz: *opp*. 100, 102
Survey of a Route for the Southern R.R. on the 32nd Parallel, by A. B. Gray for the Texas Western R.R. Company: 167
Sweeney, Thomas W.: 167
Sweet, Alexander: 201
Swenson, S. W.: 72
Sylvester, James A.: 195

Taft, Robert: 165
Tall Men with Long Rifles: 188
Tamale Seller, The, by Gentilz: 105
Tasso, Torquato: 75
"Taucahue" Indians: 9
Taylor, Zachary: 151, 155
Tejas Indians: 9
Telegraph and Texas Register (Houston): 21, 44, 139
Temperance Hall (Washington-on-the-Brazos): 56
Temple Lea, by Allen: 25, 27
Tenth Street, Austin, Looking West, by Hadra: 177, *180*
Teresa, by Petri: 79
Teresa Lungkwitz by Petri: 77
Terrell, Texas: 211
Terry Rangers: 129, 132
Texana (bark): 152
Texas, The University of: 6, 63, 145, 146, 157, 202
Texas Banner (Huntsville): 23
Texas Bear Hunt, A, by Petri: 86
Texas Female Institute: 177
Texas Militia: 21
Texas Panhandle: 116
Texas Republic: 30, 155
Texas Republican (Marshall): 69
Texas Revolution: 10, 30, 69
Texas River, by Lungkwitz: 91
Texas State Archives: 212
Texas State Gazette (Austin): 4, 65
Theatre at the Old Casino Club, San Antonio, Texas, by Iwonski: *123*, 125
Theillepape, William C. A.: 153, 177
Thomas, Helen Haskell: 169
Thomas, James Edward: 168
Thomas, Mary Landon Blount: 168
Thomas, Stephen Seymour: 168–172
Thomas Jefferson Chambers, by Flintoff: 57, 60, 63
Toilers of the Plains, by Allen: 185
Tomson, G. A.: 68
Toudouze, Gustave: 174
Townes, Robert: 141
Trail, The, by Gentilz: 110

Trapper's Last Shot, The, by Ranney: 43
Travis, William B.: 188, 189
Treatise on Topographical Drawing: 50
Treaty Oak: 202
Trinity River: 11, 15, 17, 44, 47, 48, 103, 207
Trumbull, John: 14
Trumbull, Colonel John: 28
Tucker, John J.: 213
Tuckerman, Henry T.: 17, 40
Twain, Mark: 159
Twiggs, David E.: 53, 136
Twilight on Elm Creek, by Onderdonk: 207, 209
Twohig House, The, by Onderdonk: 205, 207

United States Geographic Survey: 164
Unknown American Painters of the Nineteenth Century: 179
Ursuline Academy (San Antonio): 206, 207

Vanderbilt, Mrs. Cornelius: 172
Van der Donk, Adriean: 204
Vanderlyn, John: 72
Vaudricourt, A. de: 161, 162, 163
Vera Cruz, Mexico: 6
Verleger, Eigenthum d.: 153
Vernet, Horace: 97, 98
Versohnung und Essau darstellend—Eigene Erfindung, Die, by Petri: 75, 77
Veterans of 1776 Returning from War, by Ranney: 39
Victor, Frances F.: 43
Victoria, Texas: 99, 155, 212
View of Austin, by Sandusky: *149*
View of Fredericksburg, Texas, by Lungkwitz: 89, 90
View of Galveston, by Verleger: *153*
View of Smith's West Texas Ranch, by Pratt: *157*, 163
View of the Highlands from West Point, by Eastman: 50
View of the Military Academy from East Austin, by Hadra: 177, *179*
View of the Mississippi at Quincy, by Onderdonk: 207
View of the Old Ursuline Academy, by Onderdonk: 206, 207
Views of Berlin, by Barker: 70
"Virginia Point" (W. J. Jones' home): 65, 212
Volunteer (sailing ship): 212
von Jendern, Miss ———: 118
von Rosenberg, William: 91
Voyage to California: 72

Waco, Texas: 98, 155
Waco Indians: 53
Wagner, Wilhelm Richard: 75
Walker, James: 193
Walker, William A.: 213
Walker County, Texas: 15, 23
Wallace, Big Foot: 30, 155
Wallace, David H.: 211, 212
Walsh blacksmith shop (Austin): 151
Warren, Mr. ———: 71
Washington, George: 17, 39, 98
Washington Art Association: 167
Washington-on-the-Brazos, Texas: 15, 23, 27, 56, 68, 69, 73, 211

Washington's Mission to the Indians, by Ranney: 39
Washington University (St. Louis): 164, 185
Watermelon Race, The, by Gentilz: 108, *109*
Water Seller, The, by Gentilz: 105
Wayne, Henry C.: 105
Webb, J. Watson: 141
Webster, Daniel: 44
Wedding at the Cathedral, The, by Gentilz: 105
Wedge, Mr. ———: 141
Weigal, ———: 71
Weighing the Puppy, by Thomas: 169, 170
Weir, Robert W.: 40, 50, 68, 69
Weisselberg, Anna von Groos: 177
Weisselberg, Gustav Frederick: 177, 178
Well, The, by Thomas: 169
Werner, Anton von: 118
West, Duval: 174
Western Art Union (Cincinnati): 50
Weston, Thomas: 15
West Side Main Plaza, by Samuel: *opp. 28*, 30, 31
Weyss (Weiss), John E.: 161, 163–164
Whaling Voyage, A, by B. Russell: 72
Wharton, Thomas K.: 72
Wheeler, Joseph: 196
Wheeler Report, the: 164
Whetstone, Mr. ———: 213
White, Edwin: 39
White, S. A.: 212
Whiting, Daniel Powers: 151–152
Whiting, William A. C.: 32, 86
Wichita Falls, Texas: 155
Wichita Indians: 35, 117
Wilkes Expedition: 167
Williams, Samuel May: 4, 9, 195, 212
Williams Creek: 153
Williard, Gedr von I.: 153
Wilmarth, L. E.: 196, 204
Wimar, Karl F.: 86
Witte Museum (San Antonio): 89, 121, 209, 211
Wolcott, Oliver: 34
Wolf City, Texas: 155
Woodbury, Levi: 44
Woodhull, Mrs. J. T.: 174
Woodward, David A.: 190, 193
Wool, John E.: 30
Wortham, Kellian A.: 188
Wright, Benjamin: 15
Wright, (Thomas) Jefferson: 15–23, 27, 28, 74, 212
Wueste, Daniel: 118, 121
Wueste, Emma: 118
Wueste, Louisa Heuser: 118–121
Wueste, Dr. Peter William Leopold: 118

Yale School of Fine Arts: 141
Yaqui Indians: 105
Yellow Stone (steamboat): 129
Yguanés, by L. and J. M. Sánchez y Tapia: 9, *opp. 12*
Yoakum, Henderson K.: 23, 24
Yuma Indians: 163

Zeitung (New Braunfels): 136